Mirabilis · facta · est · scientia ·
tua · ex · me ·

Psalm. 138

INSTITUTO DE ESTUDIOS ILERDENSES
DE LA EXCMA. DIPUTACION PROVINCIAL DE LLEIDA
CONSEJO SUPERIOR DE INVESTIGACIONES CIENTIFICAS

# Gaspar de Portolá

# EXPLORER AND FOUNDER
# OF CALIFORNIA

by
**F. BONEU COMPANYS**

Translated and revised by
**ALAN K. BROWN**

LERIDA, 1983

© F. Boneu Companys
Publisher: Instituto de Estudios Ilerdenses
Virgili i Pagès, S. A. Bobalà, 3. Lleida
D. L.: L-701-1983
I.S.B.N.: 84-00-05531-4
Printed in Spain

Supposed portrait of Don Gaspar de Portolá, nowadays in the «Parador Nacional de Turismo» of Arties, in the Aran Valley (Lérida) in which touristic complex one can find the ancestors house of the California founder's family.

To María Dolores, Xavier, Fernando and Joaquín, with all my love.

# Foreword

*Like everyone born within the maze of damp cob-
blestoned alleys of the city of Balaguer, I have heard the
voice of bygone generations speaking from out of the
familiar smalltown quiet that seeps into all its old corners, where small squares and porticoed streets hold the
secret footprints of centuries of history, the very heart-
beat of human life; the voice of those who have left each
of the present dwellers with the impress of their great-
ness and independence, self-respect and courage, toil and
devotion.   Many a time, while seeking out the cries that
convey the grief and pain of the dwellers within, I have
glanced over the façades of its old buildings, missing the
carven coats of arms which signify a town's ancient aristocracy. To find them, I have searched the records of the
city's life of yesteryear, and have been pleased with the
times that went before me and with the men who signed
us with the mystic seal of strong character, our predecessors and forefathers who doubtless still mark the psychology of their successors with the unmistakable traits
of men of Balaguer: active, and inveterate dreamers; rest-
less, yet dutiful and enthusiastic; generous to a fault and
tolerant; punctilious, sombre and proud.   I have wished*

*I could express my feeling for those who carved the finest
hours of our history upon the city's old walls, for those
who suffered in their flesh the slings and arrows of
countless wars and endured both the humiliation of felt
defeat and the pride of acknowledged victory, who toiled year upon year in deepest anonymity to earn us our
municipal appellation of Worthy and Honorable.   And
I have retained a particularly deep regard and feeling
for our forgotten nobility: those whose names are still
alive and hardy, their deeds gone with the wind.*

*To know that one is clothed with a splendid past is
like the feeling of being sheltered by the warm family
hearth, like being a child with a secret to keep, like holding the hand of a friend.   In lovingly plumbing the life
and death of the noble clan of the Portolás of Balaguer,
I have forged a new bond of friendship; I have suffered
over what must have made them suffer and grieved with
their grief, and with them too I have flung out their banners of glory and honor as if they were my own.*

*I learned from my father to value the unimportant
joys of little things, the beauty of the blue sky, the
smoothness of a book's pages, the quiet of vesper-time,
the pleasure of sweating through long summer hikes, the
sadness of something unachieved, the boundlessness of
hopes and dreams.   Through him I learned also of the
glories of my town, which were read on cold winter eve-
nings out of Father Pou's* Historia de Balaguer, *a volume kept upon the shelves of his scant library as if it
were our own family history; and though there was nothing in it about us, I felt as though I were represented by
those who had played the leading roles of centuries in
the same streets where I was living then.*

So it is not surprising that I enthusiastically accepted the task of tracing the genealogy of the Portolá Family of Balaguer, firstly because it was imperfectly known, and also on account of one figure among its members, a figure who was familiar and unknown at the same time. I ask the pardon of my readers, as they turn the pages of this book, for any glaring errors which I may have been unable to catch and emend as any historian would be able to.    There are frequent breaks in the historical narrative which may possibly have affected the continuity of the whole.    In trying for an agreeable style, I have failed to please my own self, and I have certainly fallen short as a man of letters and a linguist...    What I do hope is both to have achieved a more complete understanding of history, while spending many months in company with sympathetic persons from whom I have received undeserved kindnesses; and that I may now be able to feel myself surrounded by well-disposed readers who will doubtless judge my work by the standards of friendship.    My "twenty-fifth hour", the time left over after a full dedication to my profession as physician, has already borne very pleasant fruits.    Reader, I hope that I may count on your own sympathy among them.

I shall begin this publication with the study of the genealogy of the Portolá family, from the moment they first appear as residents of Balaguer city after leaving their ancestral lands in the Valle de Arán, in the year 1658.    By employing all the sources within my reach, I have managed to trace the family history in parish records and in the notarial archives and civil registers of Balaguer, Lérida, Borrasá and Figueras.    I have gathered material relating to the direct line, without attempting a study of collateral branches, which are now scattered throughout Lérida province, Andalucía and even Germany. *During the research, some unknown documents have turned up which I have copied in full, and at other times I have relied upon notes drawn from the historian Father Sanahuja, from whom I have taken standards of exposition and documentary references which I have personally checked. Most of the time it has proved necessary to undertake personal research in national archives and museums, where I have obtained some surprising items and previously unknown documents. I have thereby constructed the Portolá genealogy down to the year 1944, when the last holder of the name died. Among the surprises turned up are the existence of two field marshals, a Knight of the Order of Ronda, two Knights of the Royal and Distinguished Order of Charles III, one Knight of the Habit of St. James, a mayor of La Bisbal, and one industrious pharmacist.*

*After I had become versed in Don Gaspar de Portolá y de Rovira's career, I was distressed to realize how he has been almost totally neglected in the fullest accounts of Spanish and Spanish-American history. This caused me to broaden my research in national and foreign archives, where I have obtained a great deal of help and material. Thus while I began my work intending to make only a genealogical study of the Portolá family, I have completed it with a biography of the conqueror and colonizer of California—the only biography of him, I may say, from the point of view both of length and of the documentation provided. What I wish is to detail our Gaspar de Portolá's importance in the winning of California by the expedition which he commanded, and to develop the figure of this man of Balaguer. For me, there is not the slightest doubt that without him, the fate of the California expeditions would have been entirely different—as indeed happened once he had departed from the newly discovered Pacific Coast. The works and deeds of Don Gaspar have been overshadowed and obscured by the figure of the Franciscan, fray Junípero Serra, and his imposing work of colonization. It is my wish that this biography may lead to a more complete study which will fill in the gaps in our knowledge concerning the many years which Gaspar de Portolá devoted to the service of king and country.*

*And I do not feel it enough merely to broadcast Portolá's historical importance to the four winds; I wish to have his other sides recognized, the plain man, the honest soldier, the earnest Christian, the Leridan who loved his native soil; I want his professional travels known, which for years carried him to and fro over Europe and later drove him to new seas, to unknown horizons in the lands of California, there to open, with the clean sword of a Catalonian nobleman, furrows watered with the blood of Spanish men. There may exist, there do exist, more heroic pages, more resounding conquests; but I doubt that anyone can point to a military occupation carried out with more integrity and better missionary results than the one achieved by Captain of Dragoons Portolá and the missionary friar Father Serra. From this stems the deep respect which Californians feel for Spain's work of colonization, and their living affection for Serra and Portolá, two names honorably enrolled upon the first pages of their land's history.*

*The year 1770, in the reign of Charles the Third, provides an oasis of peace and calm, a pause in the already ongoing dismemberment of the Spanish Empire, on whose compass the sun never set. Here the notion of a conquest has been joined to that of missionary effort in a common task with spiritual and social ends. The men who strive to realize these seek only the service of the "two Majesties," God and the King, and claim no further honor nor better fame than the faithful fulfillment of their callings. Captains and pioneers with no pretensions to being heroes, they opened the gates of a new world, left their footprints as they passed, forged new bonds of friendship, filled the air with church-bells, wrote their names in the sands of the shores—and went quietly away, without once suspecting how shore, air and friends had been molded by the faith and kindness which they preached.*

*His Californian venture alone would give Don Gaspar de Portolá the right to be honored as one of Spain's heroes, even without the later and enduring chapter of his love for his own province of Lérida. In the loneliness of old age, bachelorhood and illness, on viewing once more the streets of his impoverished and decayed city of Lérida and knowing human suffering as few others do, he opened the last chapter of his fame by providing for the founding, after his own death, of the "Casa de Misericordia y Expósitos," the charity and foundling hospital of Lérida. And today, as California enters her third century, the cities of Balaguer, Lérida and Artíes proclaim their own gratitude to Don Gaspar de Portolá with deep respect and affection.*

*Those readers who are acquainted with previous works of research upon Captain Portolá, particularly those of the Franciscan Pedro Sanahuja, will recognize how many new original documents are presented here, some of them real discoveries never before mentioned in works of California history. Here I should like to begin my long list of personal thanks to all those who have made it possible for a tyro in historical research to have the satisfaction of seeing his work in print: To the Archivo de Simancas, whose resources were made available to me through its director, Don Amando Represa, with whose advice I hope to be able some day to complete my acquaintance with the vast documentary material in his keeping; to Corvette Captain Don Roberto Barreiro of the Museo Naval of Madrid; to Señorita Rosario Parra, director of the Archivo General de Indias of Sevilla; to Don José Antonio Martínez Bara, Director of the Archivo Histórico Nacional, who has shown a true tolerance for my frequent inquiries and has been guide and counselor during my visits to Madrid; to Señorita Julia Méndez Aparició, director of the Public Library of Toledo, who made possible my research in person and the discovery of one of the most interesting documents published here; to Don Felipe Mateu y Llopis, director of the Central Library of Barcelona, and to D. Pedro Bohigas, who made the manuscripts of that library available to me; to the assistant director of the Archivo de la Corona de Aragón, Don Antonio María Aragó; to the Servicio Histórico Militar; to the Gabinete de Documentación y Publicaciones of the Ministery of Justice; to the Archivo General Militar of Segovia and to Don Eduardo Rodeja de las Heras, a relation of the last Portolá around Figueras, from whom I received invaluable information and material.*

*Special mention, for closeness and personal participation in this work, is due to the Rev. D. Pedro Codern, Archpriest of Balaguer, who opened to me the study of the parish archives of my native city; to Don Luis Pijuán Vila, Archivist-Notary of Balaguer; to the Members of the Instituto de Estudios Ilerdenses, Patronato "José*

*María Quadrado" of the CSIC, the señores Alonso García,
Díez-Coronel Montull, Hernández Palmés A., Lladonosa
Pujol, Pita Mercé, Sarrate Forga, Tarragó Pleyán, Reve-
rendo Jesús Tarragona, Tortosa Durán—all friends to
whom I have applied many times for aid and advice; to
my artist friend Víctor P. Pallarés for the excellent
sketches with which the book is illustrated, to the brothers Sarrate for the drawing of the genealogical tree and
of Portolá's routes in America; to José María Monill
Oriola for some of the photographs, drawn from their
private collection; to Professor Alan K. Brown of the
Ohio State University; to the California Historical Society, to the San Mateo County Historical Association,
to the Bancroft Library of the University of California,
to the Instituto de Estudios Ilerdenses of the Chamber
of Deputies, wich bore the expenses of the Spanish edition
and to all those who have helped and encouraged me, my
most sincere thanks.*

F. Boneu Companys

*Lérida, June 1970*

*Between the time of this work's first publication by the Instituto de Estudios Ilerdenses in 1970, on the occasion of the bicentennial of the founding of California, and the present appearance of an English edition, some twelve fruitful and productive years have been spent in increasing the public knowledge and awareness of Gaspar de Portolá y de Rovira of Lérida.*

*As impressive and moving as was the tribute which, on that occasion, the Lérida Provincial Chamber of Deputies, through its own cultural Institute, paid to the memory of the American career of one of its favorite sons through academic and social functions that brought together official representatives from the State of California, from towns of the Province of Lérida, from the Catalonian nobility, the military estate, diplomatic bodies and cultural organizations, today we are especially pleased to be able to offer our English-language readers a translation and updating of that literary work. We are aware of the great esteem California has for Portolá as the founder of the State and the head of the military expedition that opened the Camino Real. Therefore, we do not want to discuss those historical events which are well-known by the Californians. We only intend to offer in English the work which was edited in Spain and, at that moment so kindly accepted by the official representation of the State of California, as well as by cultural institutions.*

*Fundamental to the mission of the Instituto is the forwarding and investigation of the traditional cultural manifestations of our land in their numerous facets—history, art, customs, archaeology, sociology, poetry, and so forth—that fall within the purview of the state Consejo Superior de Investigaciones Científicas, of which we have been an active branch since our first founding. Therefore it can come as no surprise that we are exercising a renewed effort, through establishing the reporting function of the "Ponencia permanente Gaspar de Portolá", to keep the study of this distinguished citizen of Lérida alive— both because of his origin and his personal connection with our lands and because of his role in the last of Spain's acts of colonization in America; and, along with his own outstanding part in the expedition he commanded in search of the "harbor of Monterrey", the part played by other Leridans and Catalans who first opened paths for the settlement and christianizing of the Pacific Coast of the United States. Over the years, Portolá has often been passed over by historical writers, cast into the shade, surely, by the stature of the Franciscan missionary Junípero Serra during the subsequent development of the numerous California missions. As was remarked by José María Razquin in this book's original Spanish edition, "the figure of Portolá was left in the shade because he lacked a panegyrist of the sort that Junípero Serra, who accompanied him on his path, had shoals of. Portolá left no descendants. Serra had a legion of brothers of his religious order who have concerned themselves with exalting his sayings and deeds. All the same, there is no separating the two of them, for one was a soldier, the captain of the conquest, while the other was the friar who supplied the religious dimension..."*

*Through these years of fruitful work, we have had the pleasure of seeing our friendly relations growing closer with so many towns and institutions in California, years in which we have rejoiced at welcoming distinguished persons, cultural groups, civic delegations who have chosen to make the journey to our land—years we now proclaim as splendid ones, made so by the ever spreading awareness of our countryman's historical figure in all circles.*

*The success has been absolute, because from that date the popularity of Gaspar de Portolá has increased due to many publications, cultural and civic acts, from which I wish to emphazise the founding of the association «Amics de Gaspar de Portolá», an entity which, supported by the Generalitat de Catalunya, has begun a wide interrelation with California in order to establish a closer scientific colaboration between both communities.*

*We wish to register here the cities of Pacifica, San Diego, San Francisco, Los Angeles, Palo Alto, El Cerrito, Stanford, Sacramento, Monterey, Santa Monica, San Mateo, Santa Barbara, and many other municipalities with which we are continuing in contact; the University of California at Berkeley, Western California University, University of Arizona, Ohio State University, Stanford University, and the historical associations of San Mateo County and Oakland, the Santa Barbara Museum, the Bancroft Library-archive; the city of Monterey, which with such deep appreciation accepted the gift made them by King Juan Carlos I of a bronze statue, the replica of one set up at Balaguer in Spain; the California state government, which through the then Governor, Mr. Ronald Reagan, sent a noteworthy delegation to the province of Lérida to open a permanent interchange that we are still maintaining.*

*Once the book had gone out of stock, the Institute availed itself of the fortunate circumstance of a long-standing friendship between the author and Professor Alan K. Brown of the Ohio State University in order to produce an edition of the book in English as a counter-piece to the version first published in Spanish. Professor Brown, a specialist in the English language with a deep knowledge of California history, a researcher and author of numerous studies in that field, has achieved a meticulous translation of the original text, revising, comparing and updating it with the latest findings of original research. Out of this collaboration has come a definitive text, doubtless the fullest available for understanding the California accomplishment and the men who brought it to its successful close. We feel certain this version will be received in America with the same interest it won here in Spain.*

*From Catalonia to California, and in homage to all those who untiringly toil for lasting understanding between our peoples, we do feel proud to publish this book.*

F. B. C.

*Lérida, October 1983*

# Translator's introduction

With the original publication of this book in Spanish, a topic and a personality that had been neglected by historical writers in recent years received a new treatment. The exploration and settlement of the harbors of San Diego and Monterey on the American west coast was accomplished by Spanish forces in the later eighteenth century in a single operation, a not unheroic struggle against disappointment, hunger and fatigue, and disease that took over a hundred lives. By virtue of his position of command, the man who is the subject of this book is usually placed first among the founders of California. At the same time, there has been a certain amount of unclarity about who he was and exactly what his rôle was, particularly for Californians, who as recently as their state and national bicentennial celebrations —the period when this book first appeared and when the present revision was undertaken—were used to seing their earliest settlers depicted as rough *adelantado* types wearing conquistadors' morions.

Fernando Boneu Companys, a physician from Gaspar de Portolá's home province and originally from his native town, gives us a great deal of new documentary information and informed discussion that adds up to a portrait of a regular army officer in a three cornered hat, unselfconsciously dedicated to his assigned task in the wilderness and apparently expecting very little reward or glory for completing it.   This was a man who professed what he called "blind obedience" to his instructions even if it killed him, and the remark, as it occurs in one of his letters while on the expedition, does not seem in any way theatrical or foolish.   A formal and literarily oriented biography of this figure is still not possible.   The long unfulfilled need that the present publication answers is for a full documentary treatment, and it is natural that the two poles of interest that are reflected in the organization are Portolá's homeland and family history on the one hand, and the California adventure on the other.

Dr. F. Boneu, the author, and his colleagues of Balaguer, Lérida, and the Instituto de Estudios Ilerdenses, have a perspective slightly different from that of most New World readers, especially those of us coming from the much-altered part of the world that Gaspar de Portolá was the first to explore, and from a society with somewhat less settled ways.   Portolá's countrymen see a figure who stepped out of a still partly familiar background, performed important deeds overseas in "the Indies", and came home at the end to leave his property and his name connected with the hospitals, charities and public buildings in their provincial capital.   Nearly forty years ago now, it was a Leridan scholar and Franciscan priest who, in the journal *Ilerda* (named from the antique Latin term for the city), first argued that California's Portolá must be identical with the Gaspar de Portolá y de Rovira whom he found mentioned in the local records.   This investigation, which went all but unnoticed in America,[1] has now been carried through to completion by Boneu.

The author's own personal preface explains how his researches grew from a sense of concealed significances in the past of the society he saw surrounding him, how he turned to an elaborate investigation of the connections of ancient Balaguer families (much of which is presented here—including, as he amusingly remarks at one point, with a true genealogist's wryness, a distant namesake of his own who just missed marrying into the Portolá clan), and how finally he found himself trying to understand and explain a complex of historical events whose value and

---

1.  Pedro Sanahuja, O.F.M., "Don Gaspar de Portolá, Gobernador y explorador de la Alta California," *Ilerda*, V (1945), 59-117.   The article was, to be sure, conspicuously catalogued in the card file of a major public research collection, the Bancroft Library, University of California, Berkeley.

meaning were debatable in their own time, and which two centuries of cultural and political changes in our civilization have
done a good deal to obscure.  The tone of the book that resulted
from all this is modest and concerned with the directly documented facts.  No panegyric is indulged in for its own sake,
despite Boneu's wish to proclaim Gaspar de Portolá's accomplish-
ments "to the four winds," as the Visigothic kings of ancient
Spain were once proclaimed.  The present translator, in fact,
would like to stress that he finds the author's historical judg-
ments, however modestly he expresses them and however much
he avoids the rôle of a universal historian who would assess the
importance of the whole series of events, strikingly good.  A number of documents and sources, some of them familiar to American
scholars for some time, were not accessible for the compilation
of the original edition, yet they often verify Boneu's conjectures
and conclusions.  And on the other hand, both in the present
volume and in a later important monograph that shows a greatly
deepened special acquaintance with the California expeditions,
Boneu has been the first to make a careful use of a surprising
number of previously neglected or unknown materials.

The formal genealogy that opens this book may be skipped
by many readers, so that a few words might be said about its
content.  Through registers of births, baptisms, wills and property transactions, all freighted with half-feudal claims and le-
galisms, the author traces a family history from that early
seventeenth century Portolá who established an entail—a legal
requirement of direct male succession to the family titles and
property, in other words a device to perpetuate his own financial
and social success in his own name.  It may seem, to a modern
reader, an act of pride that turned into something like a real
family curse (though the autor, attuned to the social necessities
of earlier centuries, regards it more impartially than this).  Over
two centuries' time, the entail certainly produced some hurriedly
arranged marriages, legal and financial crises and lawsuits, and
at the end an opportunity for near swindling of some family
members, so that the two brothers who simply walked away from
the whole aristocratic pretence, leaving town to establish elsewere
a new Portolá line of, as the author puts it, hard-working drug-
gists, are easy to sympathize with.

With the book's first narrative chapter, we see how in the
middle of this public record of family fortunes (which despite
the fascinating way in which it mirrors and epitomizes European

social history, would probably not have in itself drawn a historian's attention) the life and career of Gaspar de Portolá comes as a rising line in the generally declining curve. What the public history's implications are for private life in this family environment is perhaps harder for any reader to assess. On the one hand, the history of financially arranged marriages could encourage reading between the lines for certain hints that family affection tended to be restricted to mother-and-daughter relationships; on the other hand, the author calls our attention to family groupings holding together well under the stress of the European wars that periodically and destructively swept through the province, situated dangerously near the national border. The one thing that is clear about Gaspar de Portolá's family situation and nurture is that, like every other younger son of a family with aristocratic pretensions who showed no evident vocation for the church or a limited sort of legal career, he was practically bound to become an army officer. The situation was not found only in Spain. It is an amusing individual touch, however, that even fairly late in his career the conqueror of California was burdened with having to look after the business affairs of an aged aunt who supported a series of what may have been religious charlatans.

The army career which Portolá entered at the earliest possible age and lowest possible commissioned rank involved what we would feel to be extremely primitive conditions—low pay, supplies few and of poor quality, and almost incredibly slow promotion, even for a subaltern with one or two high-ranking relations. After nearly nine years, we find him made a lieutenant in order to fight as part of the Bourbon forces in Italy in the War of the Austrian Succession. There he took part in numerous sieges and skirmishes, was wounded in one of the battles about Modena (if that is what his curt and scant service record means by "Madona"), and, after the failed attack on Piacenza, participated in the Spanish army's successful breakthrough to Tortona. A lieutenant he remained after the war for twenty years—mostly of garrison life, we have to assume, except for the abortive Portuguese campaign of the Seven Years' War in 1762—until close on his fiftieth year. (Much later, in his will, he was to leave his younger brother a pension to be enjoyed until reaching the rank of captain.)

Gaspar de Portolá's promotion to the rank with which he appears in the history of the American west coast came as a sweetener for what any unambitious officer in his position may well have regarded as a disaster, an assignment—not one for which Portolá had volunteered, as he admits later—to permanent duty overseas. The cadre for the "Army of America"—part of the military buildup being carried on in the expectation of a future clash between Spain and England in "the Indies", as the world beyond Europe was still commonly called—landed at Vera Cruz on the Gulf of Mexico late in 1764. On November 17th there, a local unit was re-formed into the Dragones de España, the «Spain Regiment» of dragoons, with half the company officers being newly arrived Spaniards (the Dragoons of America were a sister regiment, partly staffed by Flemings and Italians). The uniform, as officially described, was a standard dragoon blue with red facings, white accouterments, and a double row of metallic buttons; the regimental commander was Colonel Domingo Elizondo; and the eighth and last company was under the new Captain Portolá.[2] The elements of the new army marched through Mexico City on Ash Wednesday, February 20, 1765, on their way to pay their vows at the shrine of the Virgin of Guadalupe; a young Mexican wrote to his father of the popular excitement over the files of men moving in such perfect unison, the bands and drummers, the mustached soldiers in blue coats, yellow waistcoats, fur caps, burlap leggins and knapsacks, and the officers carrying short pikes and wearing ceremonial boat-shaped hats with gilt—some of them no more than boys.[3] Later, there were riots in some of the cities of the colony when these military units resorted to forcible recruitments to fill their ranks. Exactly what Captain Portolá's duties were for the next two years is not yet known; by 1770, he was listed as second in line in his regiment for promotion (following a major who had fought the British in Florida and Georgia), but this was well after the beginning of the events that were to propel him into the light of history.[4]

---

2. Archivo General de la Nación, México (hereafter referred to as AGM), ramo Correspondencia de los Virreyes, Croix, t. 17, nos. 65 and 95; cf. Lyle N. McAlister, "The Reorganization of the Army of New Spain, 1763-1766," *Hispanic American Historical Review*, XXXIII (1953), 2-3, 17, 19-20; *Artes de México*, XV, no. 102, "Crónica del traje militar en México, del siglo XVI al XX»; María del Carmen Velázquez, *El estado de guerra en Nueva España 1760-1808* (México, 1950), p. 69.

3. Sutro Library, San Francisco, F. de Zúñiga y Ontiveros, Notes of notable happenings, both truthful and exquisite (and annotated almanac, Mexico, 1764-72), a letter from his son, tipped in opposite the date.

4. AGM, Correspondencia de los Virreyes, Croix, t. 17 no. 196. The "second squadron" of the Dragoons of Spain was stationed at the Gulf port of Vera Cruz during most of the mid-1760's—ibid., t. 11, fol. 37; etc.

Enormous powers for the fiscal reform of the colony had been bestowed on José de Gálvez, a royal official sent to Mexico in 1765. This is not the place in which to discuss in detail how he began planning to add what he and his supporters spoke of as a new empire to the Spanish possessions in the far northwest. The centerpiece of the enterprise was to be a military expedition of over a thousand men, to be transported in ships built upon the Gulf of California. By means of this force and fleet, the Indian troubles in the province of Sonora were to be suppressed, after which the savage Apaches of the Gila River in present Arizona were to be conquered, and trade was to be developed across the Gulf with what was then called California, the long barren peninsula occupied only by some Jesuit mission stations and a mining camp or two. Early in 1767, new military units were formed up at Mexico City, cannons were cast for the expedition, and Portolá's own colonel, Elizondo, was put in command of it. Toward the end of April the regiment, preceded and followed by other infantry and cavalry, departed the capital for the Pacific coast, where their transport vessels were nearing completion on the malarial tropical coast below Tepic. Near this town they encamped in June.

Secret orders had now come from Spain demanding the simultaneous arrest and deportation of all members of the Jesuit religious order, including all of the missionaries in Sonora and Lower California. This astonishing exercise of political power, a major operation of state that convulsed the whole colony, was put into the hands of José de Gálvez and of the military command structure. Among manuscripts belonging to the Huntington Library (San Marino, California) there is the draft of instructions requiring Colonel Elizondo to embark with officers and troops, giving out his destination publicly as Guaymas in Sonora, but making sure to take Captain Portolá and his company, and in fact setting sail directly for California, off whose shore a set of sealed orders are to be opened. These are present, and require Captain Portolá to be secretly sworn, upon his honor and his sword, as interim governor of the peninsula; after which a final sealed order, obviously dealing with the arrest of the Jesuits, is to be put into effect, and Portolá is to be left with a hundred troops to rule the territory.[5] As Boneu suggests in

5. Huntington Library, San Marino, Calif., Huntington Manuscript 22487 (dated June 3, 1767). The genuineness of the contents is supported by Viceroy Croix' mention, in another document, of Elizondo and his regiment sailing to California—see M. del Carmen Velázquez, *El estado de guerra...*, p. 106.

this book, the exact reasons for this appointment may never be known.   The Jesuits, however, who controlled the small military force on the peninsula, were officially suspected of all sorts of sedition, and it is possible that the captain's good family connections seemed to mark him out as likely to be reliable in a politically sensitive situation.

The seizure of Lower California was not carried out exactly as planned in these instructions, mainly because of a lack of transport; but by the time the vessels would have been needed, at the middle of July, 1767, it had become clear to everyone that the fears and rumors about Jesuit resistance were groundless. The boats that the government shipyard on the coast had ready at that time were two sloops, each just thirty three feet in length, and poorly constructed.[6]   In a rather gossipy letter also preserved in the Huntington Library, a local official describes Portolá's attempt to embark fifty soldiers—half dragoons and half "mountain fusileers" enlisted in Mexico—with their commissioned and non-commissioned officers.   The ships proved to be overloaded as well as leaky, so that the only other craft available, a small boat used by the owner of a mining camp on the other side of the Gulf, was added to the flotilla.   Colonel Elizondo, whose intervention proved necessary in order to settle the arrangements, came down to the coast with his dragoons, calling down a plague on the shipyard manager and criticizing both sides in the dispute for falling to get together.   The letter writer mentions that despite Portolá's being such a friend of Elizondo, the captain had kept his orders for California secret from his colonel (as he was required to do, under pain of capital punishment, it may be added) all along the way from Mexico City, and until he had received secret official confirmation of them.   Now he first asserted his independent command by overriding one of the colonel's orders and taking the owner of the small boat along with him as he sailed.[7]

The terrific summer storms of the lower Gulf obeyed no orders but nature's, and after three days the boats were driven

---

6. The *Sonora* and the *Sinaloa*. The *Sinaloa* is described according to the commander, Estorgo, who sailed it across the Pacific to the Philippines immediately afterward. Nicholas P. Cushner, S. J., ed., *Philippine Jesuits in Exile, The Journals of Francisco Puig, S. J., 1768-1770*, Bibliotheca Institutionis Historicae Societatis Iesu, 24 (Rome, 1964), pp. 179-80. The vessel's deck width was eleven feet (English).

7. Huntington Library, Brannan Collection, HM 4041, Diego Peiran to Miguel Porzel y Manrique (undated).

back to port.[8]  A second attempt to cross to the Californian peninsula was made the last week in August, when only one vessel of the three made it across—creating a strange and rather embarrassing situation, since the few dragoons who came ashore were forbidden, in the Governor's absence, to explain what they were doing there.   Driven back to the harbor again, Portolá with the rest of his forces decided to wait out the season, until after the autumnal equinox, which eighteenth-century seamen regarded as marking a turn in the weather.  On October 19-20 the boats set out to begin beating about in the Gulf again, and this time, after nearly a month and a half, the Governor's own boat was the one to make a successful landing, though far south of the intended spot.[9]

Our author Boneu provides a good description of the situation, partly drawing on Portolá's first letter-report to the Viceroy of New Spain, the highest authority in the colony, to whom he was now directly responsible.  In the same letter in which he speaks of his overland, cactus-infested ride to take command of the small missionary and military capital of Loreto, he adds frankly, "The fact is, Sir, that in order to serve in this country, one has to be more cowboy than soldier."[10]  Over on the mainland his old colonel, Elizondo, was having a similar experience, and, like Portolá, after his initial sally into the country he changed his troops' uniform for the leather buffcoats worn by the soldiers of the frontier garrisons (still worn by some Lower California cowboys in our own time), to avoid, as he put it, having a dragoon charge against the Indians end with soldiers dangling by their bandoleers from the nearest cactus tree, like Absalom by his hair.[11]  The small force of buffcoated troops that formed the Jesuit-controlled garrison of the California mission settlements proved to be in a very good state of discipline, and much of Portolá's correspondence with Mexico City—from which it

8.  Donald W. Rowland, *The Elizondo Expedition against the Indian Rebels of Sonora*, unpublished dissertation, University of California (Berkeley), 1930, p. 102.  This never published study is the best that has been done on the Sonora expedition and the early years of the San Blas settlement.

9.  Mary Margaret Downey, R. S. C. J., *The Expulsion of the Jesuits from Baja California*, unpublished dissertation, University of California (Berkeley), 1940, p. 133, figures the date of arrival as December 2, from various sources. The Jesuit narrators, and Francisco Palou in his "News from New California," all give some details about the voyages, disagreeing on dates.

10.  AGM, ramo Californias, t. 76, fol. 17v. "Lo cierto, Señor, es que para hacer el servicio en este País, más ha de tener de Vaquero que de Soldado..."

11.  *Documentos para la historia de México*, cuarta serie, t. II (México, 1856), pp. 148-49 (Guaymas, June 6, 1768); etc.

took some two months to get a reply—is concerned with getting supplies and pay for them. On his first arrival he had encountered their commanding officer, Fernando de Rivera y Moncada, a captain with a long record of frontier service in the peninsula and, until that moment, its titular governor. The new Governor, after a series of intense private conferences, elected to let Rivera continue in his position, despite the potential embarrassment of their both holding the military rank of captain.[12] There may have been a moment or two later on when Portolá had to regret this decision. While still on the way north to Loreto, at the mining camps Portolá likewise arranged to meet with an ex-soldier of the same "Californias Company," José Francisco de Ortega, and persuaded him to re-enlist as his sergeant, an act that would also affect the future considerably in a land neither of them had ever seen and perhaps had never thought much about.[13]

The arrest of the Jesuit missionaries was, as Boneu indicates, an anticlimax. On arrival at Loreto, the Governor was presented with the keys of the mission headquarters, but promptly turned them all back to the Jesuit administrators save for one key to an office where there was a small amount of silver that had to be inventoried in the presence of the Father Superior, who was then away on a journey. The missionaries were collected from the outlying stations, and sailed from the country forever; the worst problem from the Governor's point of view was the need to appoint unqualified common soldiers to administer the individual missions, for lack of any other non-Indian personnel. In narratives written in several languages, published and unpublished, the exiled Jesuits have little but good to say of Captain Portolá's gentlemanly execution of his unwelcome instructions with respect to themselves. For obvious reasons, they tend to stress his disillusionment with earlier rumors of their territory's riches, and the tedious exile that he and other European gentry would face in the isolation of Loreto, where the only entertainment would be the sound of a guitar.[14] They were, however, wrong about this.

---

12. Miguel del Barco, S. J., *Historia natural y crónica de la Antigua California*, ed. Miguel León-Portilla (México, 1973), pp. 270 and 362.
· 13. This rest upon authority of Junípero Serra's representation to the Viceroy, March 13, 1773, paragraph 7. *Writings of ... Serra*, ed. Antonine Tibesar, O. F. M., vol. I (Washington, D. C., 1955), p. 300.
14. Johann Jakob Baegert, S. J., *Observations in Lower California*, translated and ed. M. M. Brandenburg and Carl L. Baumann (Berkeley and Los Angeles, 1952—a translation of the German edition of 1772), pp. 118, 169-70; Miguel del Barco as cited above, and the "Sterkianowski" account as cited below. Portolá to the Viceroy, AGM, Californias, t. 76, fol. 20.

At first most of the excitement did seem to be local. The Governor decided that the troops which had arrived with him were useless in that country, and progressively returned them to the mainland.[15]  In April of 1768 a government transport ship carrying soldiers and missionaries to Guaymas on the Sonora side was blown to shore near Loreto, and had to be revictualled from the scanty supplies on hand.  Toward the middle of the following June, a similar unplanned arrival faced the Governor with a much more serious decision.  This was a crowded shipload of Jesuit missionaries being brought under military guard from Guaymas; bound for Mexico and return to Europe afterward, they had been driven to and fro in the Gulf for nearly a month, suffering from putrid water and food, and incipient scurvy, in the blazing heat.  The leader of the Franciscan missionaries that had now replaced the California Jesuits, Junípero Serra, was allowed to visit the anchored ship, followed by a number of local citizens.[16]  At the end of nine days, however, the Governor felt constrained to send a launch with orders to tow the vessel out to sea, and only relented when two of the three ship's officers expressed their opinion in writing that it was impossible for them to sail,[17] and after he had visited on board himself.  In the upshot, he allowed the passengers to land to recuperate, and supplied them with whatever fresh meat and porridge he had on hand; unexpectedly, however, it was the desert fruits collected by Indians that seemed more delicious and valuable to their health.  After two weeks of this, a soldier riding in from the desert announced that the Jesuits' archenemy, the Visitor-General José de Gálvez himself, had landed to the southward.  Some of his entourage had preceded him, so that the news was not a total surprise, but Portolá the next morning renewed his orders for the ship to leave.  Two days later, when everything was

---

15. AGM, Correspondencia de los Virreyes, Croix, t. 12, fol. 173; ramo Californias, t. 76 (Portolá to Viceroy Croix, Aug. 24, 1768).

16. This episode is narrated in an account attributed to the Jesuit father Sterkianowski, printed (as far as the portion that concerns us) by Alberto Francisco Pradeau, M. D., *La expulsión de los jesuítas de las provincias de Sonora, Ostimuri y Sinaloa en 1767*, Biblioteca histórica mexicana de obras inéditas, 24 (México, 1959), pp. 88-91. According to the footnote on p. 64, the actual author was Jaime Matheu, S. J. (a native of Lérida); the source of the actual information was the missionary Francisco Ita, S. J.

17. These details are not from the Jesuit account, but from the original correspondence between the Governor and the ship's officers, Bancroft Library, Bolton Papers 190 (photostat from Biblioteca Nacional, México). Portolá's sixteenth letter-report to the Viceroy, July 9, 1768 (AGM, Californias, t. 76) explains the necessity of his having let the Jesuits ashore, and also mentions still another boat blown to the peninsula.

ready for the sail, he visited the prisoners in friendly fashion and invited their senior members to dinner with him, where he impressed on them the threat of capital punishment hanging over himself as well as them and the necessity of leaving quickly. Next morning before dawn, he boarded and personally saw the ship out into the open Gulf before returning to land in his harbor launch.

Portolá's treatment of the Jesuit missionaries is to be compared with what they found waiting for them upon the other side of the Gulf, where Visitor-General Gálvez' agents forced them on a fast ride through the swamps. Twenty of them died of fever and exhaustion, and are carried as martyrs on the rolls of their religious order.[18]

The Governor had in fact known for some three months that Gálvez was planning to visit the Californian peninsula. It is unlikely that he had been advised of the full extent of the Visitor-General's plans, whose detailed development is controversial to this day.[19] The desirability of a naval expedition to occupy the "harbor of Monte-Rey" on the coast north of California is mentioned in a project drawn up by Gálvez (to which the Viceroy also lent his name) in January, 1768.[20] Recently it has been emphasized that the document also indicates that one of Galvez' associates had previously returned to Spain with the intention of persuading the government to issue instructions that would favor the idea.[21] The royal order that actually caught up with Gálvez as he was on his way to Lower California may have been less favorable than he had hoped; his nominal superior, the Viceroy of New Spain, through whose hands it had passed on the

18. The details are in the Matheu account, and more briefly in Baegert's book. See Gerard Decorme, S. J., *La obra de los jesuítas mexicanos durante la época colonial, 1572-1767*, t. I (México, 1941), pp. 408-10.

19. Of four relatively recent one-volume histories of California that I take at random from the shelf, two assert that the founding expeditions were sent by royal order, two tend to give the credit to Gálvez.

20. The copy in Houghton Library, Harvard, MS Sparks 98, portfolio 3, first item, has the Viceroy's autograph referral to the bishop of Puebla and the Archbishop of Mexico, Francisco Lorenzana, and their opinions; Lorenzana refers to the document as the plan of the señor Visitador general.

21. Theodore E. Treutlein, *SanFrancisco Bay: Discovery and Colonization, 1769-1776* (San Francisco, 1968), pp. 1-2, and note 3. It can be added that the agent, Field Marshall Ricardos, himself paid the very large amount of 1.000 pesos for his passage back to Spain, so that his mission was evidently felt to be highly important—AGM, Correspondencia de los Virreyes, Croix, t. 11 y 10., fol. 183 and 351 (where the date of sailing from Vera Cruz is given as June 8, 1767).

way, had added to it a covering letter that makes it clear the
Visitor-General's firm intention on setting out from Mexico City
had already been not to stop short of reaching Monterey. The
Viceroy, in the letter, forbade Gálvez to undertake the expedition
in person.[22] It seems clear that without this prohibition, Portolá's function would have been very different. He might still
have been in charge of the overland elements of the Expedition,
but the overall command, as the ships undertook their nearly
disastrous sail into northern latitudes, would have lain with Visitor-General Gálvez, who already on his arrival in Lower California was showing signs of instability, and who within a period
of months was to suffer a complete mental collapse, in Sonora,
as his far-reaching plans ran into serious difficulties.

While still in Lower California, in September, 1768, Gálvez
writes that in accord with the Governor and the *Ministro Presidente* of the missions (Junípero Serra) he is taking all possible
measures for founding new settlements as far north as Monterey.[23]
Portolá's instructions for the march, dated February 20, 1769,
and included later in the text of this book, style him as "Governor
and Commander in Chief of this Peninsula of Californias," and
leave a certain number of choices to his judgment—including
the possible use of firearms against the Indians—but are somewhat hazy as to his exact relations with the other officers, particularly the sea commanders and Captain Rivera, all of whom
had their own detailed instructions, rather as though Gálvez were
still trying to run the Expedition by remote control. Of course,
both Portolá and Gálvez had been impressed by the special skills
of Rivera and his frontiersmen, who were to form an advance
section or exploring party, so that consultation between the two

---

22. Huntington Library, Galvez Papers GA293: "V. S. ha salido a essa expedición con el ardor que me consta, de no parar hasta llegar a Monterey ... No
por esso me empeñare á obligar a V. I. a que emprehenda por si esta Expedición,
por la necesidad que tienen de su presencia, los demás graves asumptos de
Californias, y Sonora..." The rest of the context also makes the situation clear,
and the contents of the document are verified by the Viceroy's communication
to Madrid, May 19, 1768, mentioning his previous conferences with Gálvez on
the subject in exactly the same terms as the letter does, and adding that
"conseqüente a las mismas havía salido de esta Capital el proprio Ministro con
el fin de asegurar el Puerto de Monte Rey, y reconocer aquellos parages,"
even before the arrival of the royal order (a type of document which, despite
its name, did not usually require immediate action and was often indefinitely
disregarded). AGM, Correspondencia de los Virreyes, Croix, libro 16 y 6.º,
no. 15 (to Grimaldi), fol. 115.
23. Archivo General de Indias, Seville, Audiencia de Guadalajara 512 (consulted on Bancroft Library microfilm, roll 1, reel M.493, frames 3-20); Santa
Ana, September 8, 1768, original, to Minister of the Indies Arriaga.

captains was envisaged only in cases of necessity, and the Governor's actually directing Captain Rivera when and where to scout is mentioned only in connection with their final arrival at "Monte Rey."[24]

These arrangements—and whatever other injunctions may have been given by word of mouth—worked well enough until necessity first stepped in and then became severe. From San Diego northward, the scurvy among the ship crews and frightening inroads of disease even among the soldiers forced a general agreement, assented to by Portolá, that a single movement was the only thing possible, with European troops and officers mingled in one body with the American buffcoats, all proceeding mounted overland. After this the goal proved to be much farther away in terms of travel, and also harder to find, than their instructions anticipated. Some of the disagreements that arose during the six-month exploration are clear from a close reading of the Expedition records. The Americans kept looking for signs (such as pine trees, with which they identified the redwoods) and Indian reports of "Monte Rey" long after the others, led by the opinion of the brilliant young engineer Costansó, were sure that Rivera and his scouts had mistakenly passed it by.[25] Relations were presumably not made any easier by the fact that the Europeans—Costansó, Lieutenant Fages and his infantry detachment, and Portolá himself—all came from the same corner of the Iberian peninsula. Elsewhere I have compared this situation to the way in which any late eighteenth century British expedition was likely to be dominated by a Scottish element.[26] Behind everything else, no doubt, was the rankling irregularity of the command relationship between the two army captains.

The journals kept during the Expedition occasionally describe Portolá—always referred to as "the Commander" or "the Governor"—making decisions such as when to halt for the night,[27] though Rivera's scouts, usually led by Sergeant Ortega, naturally

---

24. See note 37 below.
25. Frank M. Stanger and A. K. Brown, *Who Discovered the Golden Gate?* (San Mateo, 1969), passim; Stanger and Brown, "Discovery of the Redwoods," *Forest History*, XIII (October, 1969), 8-10.
26. "The Men of the 'First Expedition'," *La Peninsula* (San Mateo, Calif.), XV (February, 1969), 5.
27. Journal of Juan Crespí, O. F. M., August 29, 1769. On this document, see Raymund F. Wood, "Juan Crespí: The Man Who Named Los Angeles," *Southern California Quaterly*, LVIII (1976), note 9, pp. 230-31, and my own earlier publication referred to there.

enough determined most of the camping sites for the days ahead. When the Americans still insisted that "Monte Rey" must lie just beyond, the sources agree that it was Portolá's decisions to allow them a certain number of days and a strictly limited amount of provisions in order to scout ahead to prove their proposition—though in his own journal, he himself carefully notes that Ortega's last northward sally was at Captain Rivera's direct order. The most serious decisions—whether to go ahead, to stop, to turn back—were entrusted to command councils, of the sort sometimes practiced in naval expeditions. On four occasions the Commander set forth the Expedition's current situation in writing and solicited written opinions from his three officers (sometimes including the two missionary friars in the invitation, partly as a matter of courtesy); he would then add his own view, and after that each participant would contribute a brief recommendation or "vote". The procedure worked surprisingly well in producing unanimous decisions. Dr. Boneu, the author of this book, is inclined to give Portolá the credit for the idea; whoever originally suggested it (it does not seem to be hinted at in Gálvez' instructions), Portolá was responsible for its successful management, even as the disagreements increased and the tone of individuals' opinions gradually became acrimonious.

When the present book was originally published, it was not yet widely known that the original documents of these councils had survived and had been acquired by a North American research collection. In a later and excellent monograph covering many aspects of the Expedition, Boneu has been privileged to publish the material, an English edition of which is unfortunately not yet possible.[28] These fascinating records, in the participants' own handwritings, show Portolá finally asserting vigorous command when, back at San Diego from their exploration, with supplies running out, with Indians all around who have already attacked and slain, with Captain Rivera and the young Catalan Lieutenant Fages wrangling with each other over which one of them is more willing to stay on in the threatened settlement eating the meat of slaughtered pack mules, he renders a final decision, using the language of a judge, as to who shall go and who shall stay (it was Rivera who lost).[29] The long historical

28. F. Boneu Companys, *Documentos secretos de la Expedición de Portolá a California: Juntas de Guerra* (Instituto de Estudios Ilerdenses, Lérida, 1973), 165 pp. Cf. Stanger and Brown, *Who Discovered the Golden Gate?* pp. 13-15; Brown, "The Men of the First Expedition," pp. 9-11.

29. Boneu, *Documentos secretos*, p. 98: "Hallo por conveniente para el Servicio de ambas Majestades lo que expongo en mi parecer..."

debate over whether it was Father Serra or Portolá that was responsible for not abandoning San Diego in 1770 perhaps has been oversimplified, since these documents show that each step of the Expedition's successive withdrawals southward was discussed as a temporary or tactical retreat. The obscure and unhelpful role played by Vicente Vila, the dying sea captain who in theory commanded the expedition by sea, is now more thoroughly documented, if no easier to understand.

Portolá's command was climaxed, after the opportune arrival of a relief ship, by a second march overland to claim what it had been decided must be Monterey Harbor in the name of the King (the blank legal format for taking possession of the land and some other instructions are found in the new Portolá papers subsequently published by Boneu) and the beginnings of the new settlement there. The Governor then, no doubt by pre-arrangement with the Visitor-General when the Expedition was planned, effectively resigned his office by taking ship for Mexico to report directly to the government. This may have seemed like a sufficient reward at the time, all the more since Gálvez had suffered his breakdown, the Sonora expedition had apparently become bogged down, and public opinion toward all of the Visitor-General's projects had soured completely.

The present book scrupulously traces the captain's career from the moment, not long afterward, when it began to appear that the Spanish empire would not, after all, be completely ungrateful for extraordinary service. After presenting the usual sort of petitions—which no doubt he was encouraged to do—he received first a brevet promotion and then the hardly to be hoped for boon of a return to the homeland, with a permanent increase in rank. The story thereafter is uneventful for American readers.[30]

A further item that needs to be mentioned, however, is a political pamphlet (unprinted, of course; in Spain and its pos-

---

30. A legal account of the picturesque but routine ceremony of his taking possession of the governorship of the city of Puebla in Mexico on his return to the New World has long been known; while in that office, he was slightly involved in pursuing an investigation of a minor scandal involving some local convents. A document in Catalan included as an appendix to the original edition of this book contained an inventory of the Portolá mansion some twenty years after Colonel Gaspar de Portolá's death; the only possible trace mentioned of his career in the Indies is a Spanish translation of Robinson's *History of America* among the library books.

sessions such works circulated only in manuscript) directed against José de Gálvez in 1773, just before his political fortunes began to rise again and while Lieutenant Colonel Portolá was on his extended visit home. The document, composed by one of Gálvez' former assistants who had good reason to hate him, has an appendix purporting to be a letter written from Madrid by Portolá to a "friend" (obviously the author of the pamphlet himself), describing the writer's personal experience in the California expeditions, and emphasizing the suffering involved and the new country's uselessness to Spain. A number of vivid details—including the often quoted statements that the explorers returned to San Diego, after failing to find Monterey, "stinking of mules" from their unwelcome diet, and that Serra then told Portolá he had been to Rome without seeing the Pope—these have the ring of firsthand experience.[31] On the other hand, the sequence of events is described so wrongly—supposedly with several months spent at San Diego, and with the exploration of the "maze of inlets and lakes" toward San Francisco placed after the occupation of Monterey—that Portolá cannot possibly have written the account as it stands; in fact, supposing that he had contributed any of the information in the pamphlet, it is unlikely that he had been allowed to review it. Of course it is natural to suppose that he did agree to let his name be used, but the document is not very reliable as evidence for the depth of his supposed disillusionment;[32] there is no sign that he ever had any illusions about the usefulness of the new settlements, and in fact the "letter's" warnings that they could never be adequately supplied or defended from Mexico might well express Portolá's original and unvarying serious opinion as a military man. Given the part that he had played in founding San Diego and Monterey, it would have been, or was, a remarkably impartial judgment, and one which of course in the long run was proved correct.

What should be said, in summary, about the leader of the California expeditions that we now call by his name? If the

31. The document was first discovered by Charles E. Chapman, who translated it in his *History of California: The Spanish Period* (New York, 1921), pp. 225-28, and used it heavily in *The Founding of Spanish California* (N. Y., 1916), pp. 96-98.
32. Donald A. Nuttall, "Gaspar de Portolá: Disenchanted Conquistador of Spanish Upper California," *Southern California Quarterly*, LIII (1971), 185-98, Chapman, *A History of California*, had already noted that in "some of the minor details... it varied a little from the facts." Boneu, *Documentos secretos*, pp. 160-64, prints the original text, and in a note deals with a number of the problems, expressing some doubt of its authenticity.

strict role of a translator-introducer may be laid aside for a moment, I wish to reject the view of a certain California historian
who referred to Gaspar de Portolá as "only a mediocre man."
In a publication of my own I also did not set Portolá's originality,
and perhaps by implication his iniciative as well, very high, but
in a passage of the present book, Dr. Boneu in answer points
out that for Portolá, in the military context in which he lived and
by which he expected to be judged, initiative was an aspect of
carefully defined duty.  What we can say is that, when he had
thrust upon him limited autority and unlimited responsibility
for two of the most "original" missions of his time, the government's mindless expulsion of the Jesuit order and the quixotic
project of José de Gálvez, Captain Portolá acted humanely and
successfully.  His considerate treatment of the Jesuits, especially
the shipload of prisoners blown out of their course, was dange-
rous for him (Gálvez had hanged or imprisoned scores of Me-
xicans for expressing sympathy with the expelled fathers by riot-
ing).  The one expression of personal pride in the letters he
wrote during the exploration and settlement of Upper California
is over the fact that not one life was lost during the six months'
march of the detachment under his command in search of Monterey.  He held the entire expedition together despite its command and personality problems, getting effective collaboration
between those directly under his orders and others such as the
independently-minded Serra and the sailing master Juan Pérez.
Afterward, he is the only one to admit—in his petition for promotion—having felt the grueling fear of Indian attack that they
had undoubtedly all suffered the whole time, and it was probably
his own decision to suppress the documents that could have been
used to discredit the behavior of the self-destructive Rivera and
the envious or worse Vila.[33]    Undoubtedly his overall success
changed history.

In the revision involved in producing the English edition of
this book, the strong documentary basis of the work has required
reviewing the records of Portolá career in America, and locating
further copies in New World archives that were not originally

---

33.  The newly discovered records of the command councils were apparently
preserved in the vicinity of Lérida after his death; only a copy of the first council, when things were still reasonably harmonious, was known previously, and
that was attached to the copy of his journal of the Expedition. (For my
earlier remarks, see "Some Leaders of the 'First Expedition,' 1769," *La Peninsula*, XV, October, 1969, pp. 3-6; some of the factual material on Portolá's
family was superseded by the publication of Boneu's book about that time).

accessible to the author, in order to present the material as reliably as possible. An example is the table of organization, equipment and supplies for the California expeditions, published by Boneu for the first time.[34] Miguel Costansó's journal of the First Expedition (as it was afterward referred to in Spanish California) fills an entire chapter of the book. An excellent edition and translation of this document (based on one copy of it, collated with another text signed by Costansó himself), by F. J. Teggart and Manuel Carpio, appeared in 1911, but in such a limited publication that the author of this book assumed that the version which he uncovered in the Naval Museum at Madrid was an entirely new discovery. Since the two texts do have some striking differences,[35] advantage has been taken of the situation to add the variants from still other versions, in order to show what Costansó thought it worthwhile to add and delete as he worked up his entries.[36] Similar procedures have been followed for as many of the documents as possible, though in the case of the Captain's own journal, given as an appendix, the translated text is based only on the previously printed texts of two rather poor copies. The original is lost.

It has not been unknown for published translations of texts in this particular historical area—American West Coast and Southwest Hispanic-period studies—to miss niceties of syntax (the *For all that*'s and *Had it but*'s) or to be over-"literal" in rendering eighteenth-century Spanish diction by English words that only happen to look similar, so that an interested reader may just possibly have become accustomed, in the past, to a flat style in translated documents that makes highly educated writers seem childish, and observant frontiersmen sound almost mentally deficient. For this reason, alone, it seems desirable to state here that the styles in these translations are strictly a rendering of the sense, and that every effort has been made to avoid sounding specialist.

The original Spanish edition contained, as appendices, a number of documents relating to Portolá family titles and pos-

---

34. There are also, in the archives, individual and more detailed tables for the separate elements of the expeditions.

35. See Stanger and Brown, *Who Discovered the Golden Gate?*, p. 70 and pp. 71-109.

36. The terms "early draft," "revised draft," and "final version" are used without prejudice to the question of when and by whom the existing manuscripts were actually copied, a matter which is still under investigation; the terms refer only to the state of the text represented by the various copies.

sessions.  Since it was felt that these were interesting mostly
for Iberian readers, they have been replaced with some of the
Captain's correspondence while on the Expedition—narrative
letters written in his own hand, and translated before only in a
newspaper publication seventy-five years ago.  Within the book's
text, a few documents of relatively minor interest have been
removed from the present translation because of more or less
recent English-language publication by others.  Where there are
overlaps with other published translations, any discrepancies
that the reader might discover by comparing them should be
regarded as deliberate—this is the case, for example, with the
paragraph in Gálvez' instructions to Portolá dealing with how
to respond to an Indian attack.[37]

Finally, as affects the main text of the book, some passages
or statements have been modified, qualified or curtailed if they
seemed to be of doubtful value in the light of fuller information.
While no particular attempt has been made to add all the references to North American studies and publications that were not
originally available to the author, some footnotes have been supplied for quotations that could be found in such a standard
source as *The Writings of Junípero Serra*, edited by Tibesar,
especially in cases where the source originally cited was less
trustworthy.  Dr. Boneu has provided an extremely generous
blanket permission for such changes, and I am correspondingly
grateful.  I should also like to express the great pleasure that the
work on these texts has provided, and to take full responsibility
for the changes from the original edition, as my part in a personally valuable cooperation.

Alan K. Brown

---

37. "Pero si ... se opongan obstinadamente a su tránsito, se usará entonces
de la fuerza, tomando de modo las disposiciones que a la primera demostración
se les haga conocer la superioridad de nuestras Armas sin ensangrentar no
obstante la acción, una vez que cedan, o se rindan los que se manifestaren
enemigos...": the phrase *sin ensangrentar no obstante la acción* plainly goes
with the following words (which would be ungrammatical without it as an
introduction to the clause).

## II. *Don Gaspar de Portolá y Pont, nobleman, and his consort Doña Isabel Ana Bellver.*

*Issue: Don Ignacio, Don Nicolás, Don José, Don Ramón, Don Francisco, Don Juan, Doña Francisca.*

The eldest of the Portolás of Artíes, Don Gaspar de Portolá y Pont, is established both at Balaguer and at Ager, as appears in the instruments which he executes frequently at both places. We know his birthplace from his will, dated the 10th of March 1687, in which he is also described as "Doctor of Law, domiciled in the City of Balaguer and the Town of Ager, legitimate and natural son of Bartolomé Portolá, esquire, at the Town of Artíes in the Valle de Arán."[1] There is some question as to the place of the signing of this will, which is first mentioned by the historian Father Pou, since some sources give it as the Town of Ager and others as Balaguer. The uncertainty may have arisen from the name of the notary, Don Juan de Revert, who though belonging to Balaguer in 1690 had previously worked at Ager, and contin-

---

1. Pou, Father, *Historia de Balaguer* (1913).

ued to be the Portolá family notary, a fact which leads some to connect him with Ager and others with Balaguer. For my own part, I have come across no public records earlier than 1696, but possibly some material belonging to that notary's early years in Balaguer may exist mixed up with the Ager registers.

The Balaguer branch of the Portolás commences with Don Gaspar, who moved there officially in the year 1656 at which time he was married to Doña Isabel Ana Bellver and had fathered the first three male offspring, Ignacio, Nicolás and José.

The Magnífico Señor Don Gaspar de Portolá y Pont was the first of his family to reach the heights of the nobility. King Philip IV by a writ signed at Madrid on the 11th. of September 1664 commissioned the Governor of the Principality of Catalonia, Don Gabriel de Llupiá, to knight Doctor Don Gaspar de Portolá, a ceremony carried out according to the laws of chivalry. I present the document here in the full form in which it has come to me.[2] Names are given in their original spelling in all of the material transcribed here.

"IN DEI NOMINE, AMEN. Be it known unto all men that in the presence of myself, Balthasar Oriol y Mercer, Notary by commission of His Majesty in the Realms of the Crown of Aragón, practicing in this Lieutenancy-General of Catalonia, in the City of Barcelona, and in the presence of the witnesses named below, did appear Doctor Gaspar de Portolá, within the precincts of the dwelling of the Very Honourable and Respectable Señor Don Gabriel de Lupián, Knight of the Order of St. James, of His Majesty's Council of War and his Governor-General in this Principality of Catalonia and County of Cerdeña, which dwellings are situate in the Palacio de la Condesa so known and called here in this City of Barcelona; and did in the presence of that gentleman in a hall of that dwelling, together with other parties present, offer and exhibit in due form to the said Señor Don Gabriel de Lupián a commission of His Majesty to the following effect:

"PHILIP, by the Grace of God king of Castille, of Aragon, of León, of both Sicilies, of Jerusalem, of Portugal, of Hungary, of Dalmatia, Croatia, Navarre, Granada, Toledo, Valencia, Galicia, Majorca, Sevilla, Sardinia, Cordova, Corsica, Murcia, Jaén, Algarbe, Algeciras, Gibraltar, of the Canary Islands, of the East and West Indies, of the Islands and Mainland of the Ocean Sea, Archduke of Austria, Duke of Burgundy, of Brabant, Milan, Athens, Cyprus, Count

---

2. Archivo de la Corona de Aragón, Barcelona, legajo 521.

*of Hapsburg, Flanders and Tyrol, of Barcelona, of Sardinia, Marquess of Oristan, Count of Gocean:*

"To our honoured, noble and well-loved councillor Don Gabriel de Lupián, Knight of the Order and Soldierhood of St. James of Spain, belonging to our Council of War and now acting as Governor-General in our Principality of Catalonia and County of Cerdeña, greeting and esteem. Having found that our faithful and well-loved Doctor Gaspar de Portolá is sprung from honorable and respected parentage and possesses sufficient wealth and therefore is desirous of being declared a belted knight and has so besought us in writing; that, the services which he has rendered having been stated, we should be pleased to grant it him; we, indeed, desiring to add a brilliant fulfillment to our favors conferred upon the said Gaspar de Portolá and upon his descendants, and to respond to his wishes, do give and grant you permission and full empowerment in this affair. Wherefore in accord with these presents, expressly considered by our sure knowledge and royal authority, we do direct, charge and order you Don Gabriel de Lupián to invest the said Don Gaspar de Portolá by our authority with the belt of knighthood and other proper effects of the knightly calling, conferring upon him all such insignia of knighthood as it is customary to do in such cases, and upon completion of this ceremony, to inform us thereof, so that we may in answer to his petition forward to him a timely testimonial of our favor and conferral; the which, if not obtained within six months from the day preceding the date of these present letters, shall by our will cause our present grant and favor to be void and of no effect. By these presents we do grant you full place, authority and our royal voice to act in all of the preceding matters.

"Given at our City of Madrid the eleventh of September in the Year of the birth of Our Lord, one thousand six hundred and sixty four.—I THE KING.—[Witnessed by] Dr. Cristóbal Crespo, Vice-chancellor, Count of Albatierra, and by the Treasurer-General, Don Pedro de Villacampa. Don Jorge de Castellvi, Marquis de Ariza. *Exeas. Real.* Don Miguel de Galva. Vilarosa R. S, Don Antonio Ferrer.

"Miscellaneous, book XVIIII, folio 114, commission to Don Gabriel de Lupián of Catalonia, to knight Dr. Gaspar Portolá, a native of that principality. By nomination. Ten *sueldos* to be paid for stamp duty. Villanueva, Office of the Protonotary. Directed from the King's hand to me Don Diego de Saba. Place for the stamp."

I the aforesaid Baltasar Oriol y Mercer having read this aloud in a clear voice, the said Don Gabriel de Lupián accepted it with due reverence and placed it over his head and proclaimed himself ready to carry out His Royal Majesty's order, in accordance with which the said Doctor Gaspar Portolá requested and petitioned the said Don Gabriel de Lupián to arm and knight him with the form and ceremony customary upon such an occasion; and the said Don Gabriel de Lupián asked him, Will you receive the order of knighthood? and he replied, I will, and the said Don Gabriel de Lupián said further to him, Will you know how to maintain it properly, and will you defend His Majesty as you are required to whatever befall? to which the said Doctor Gaspar Portolá answered Yes; and with him kneeling before the said Don Gabriel de Lupián, the sword which he bore sheathed at his side was drawn out and bared and with it he gave him three blows, to wit one upon the head and two upon the shoulders, saying at each, God and the Blessed Virgin Mary and the Apostle St. James make thee a good kinght; and then it was put into the hand of the said Don Gaspar Portolá and he sheathed it again, promising to keep the Code of Knighthood; and the said Don Gabriel de Lupián said, In virtue of His Majesty's commission and the power granted to me, I do raise thee to the dignity of a knight; and the said Gaspar de Portolá accepted the dignity and asked that a record be drawn up in witness of it, and Señor Don Gabriel de Lupián required me, the said commissioned notary above named, to do so and to provide one and several faithful transcripts for the issuance of the customary patent testimonial to him.

"At which were present as witnesses Don Agustin de Goyri, Don Pedro de Pons, and Francisco de Padellás, knights dwelling at Barcelona, and many others.

"Done in the said City of Barcelona, the fourteenth of November in the Year of the Birth of Our Lord Christ one thousand six hundred sixty four." [Sealed.]

The king sent the corresponding patent on the 26th of March, 1665, granting Portolá a coat of arms consisting of two mountains with three stars upon one side, earth and sky upon the other, and a bridge and river.[3] This description, from a document preserved in the Archivo de la Corona de Aragón and described by Fray Pedro Sanahuja, fails to agree with those found in the García Garrafa *Enciclopedia Heráldica y Genealógica*, vol. 74, pp. 55-56. The description there given is:

"PORTOLÁ. Arms: Quartered, first and fourth quarter gules, with an eagle or, second and third azure, with a wing lowered argent. Above the whole an escutcheon azure, with a *portalada* [a portal] or, with a gate gules. This coat of arms is the same as what other Catalonian heraldry writers attribute to the Portalá line, hence we deduce that Portolá and Portalá are the same family name. We will add

---

3. Archivo de la Corona de Aragón, Reg. 75, fols. 245-47.

Coat of arms of the House of Portolá, reproduced by García Garrafa and «Adarga Catalana».

that a handwritten note found in our copy of *La Adarga Catalana*, enlarging on what Garma y Durán has to say in that work, claims that the coat of arms described actually belonged to the Barons of Balaguer, and that it is only the bearings contained in the crest which are those of the Portolá or Portalá name, the quartered arms pertaining strictly to the Valls lineage of Olot, which was the line of the holders of the baronage of that illustrious barony in the second half of the eighteenth century. Another description which we have come across of the Portolá arms is: First and fourth quarters or, with an eagle sable, and second and third azure, with a wing lowered or. In this blazon the hues of the first and fourth quarters and of the figure in the second and third quarters are different, and the crest is left out." [4]

We include here a photographic reproduction of the coat of arms found in the church at Castellnou de Monsech on the altarpiece preserved there, which agrees with Father Sanahuja's description, and is the same which is kept at the chapel of the town of Artíes in the Valle de Aran.

At a later date, a patent granted by His Majesty Charles II under the date of November 4th., 1682, conferred on Portolá a title of nobility; he figures in this document as a native of Val de Aran and resident of Balaguer.[5, 6]

"WE, CHARLES, *by the Grace of God king of Castille, of Aragon, of Leon, of both Sicilies, of Jerusalem, etc.*

"There being no greater reward which can be given to virtue than that of the name and honor of its possessor being held present to mind, it is fitting and proper that kings and sovereigns must reward their subjects for the very things by which their name and fame are celebrated among posterity. Wherefore, we, not unmindful of the faithfulnes and zeal toward our royal crown shown by our well-beloved Gaspar de Portolá, a resident of our City of Balaguer and native of the Val de Arán in our Principality of Catalonia and considering also the welcome services which he has performed toward ourself, following in the footsteps of his predecessors, at several times and occasions, both political and military; in view of all this, and of his deserts and contributions, wish to make you the said Gaspar de Portolá a worthy return out of our munificence, you being already vested with the girdle of knighthood, by bestowing a patent of nobility, humbly requested of us by you, in the form and fashion

4. Archivo Cat. L. T. 82 AG., fol. 279 recto.
5. Archivo Histórico Nacional, Madrid, *Carlos III*, expediente 1546.
6. Archivo de la Corona de Aragón, Reg. 88, pp. 193 and following.

which we have since determined to grant.   Therefore, in compliance
with the present letter, with steadfast validity for all future times, by
our sure knowledge and royal authority, we do deliberately and expressly distinguish you the said Gaspar de Portolá, your descendants
in the male line and all your issue and theirs and their posterity, born
or to be born, with the title of nobility; and we do decorate, make
and determine you nobles; according to the ranks of the human condition, we repeat, we name you and them as nobles.   And so for the
rest, each and every one according to recognized standing of rank and
eminence existing as such, we will and command you and your children in the male line, all your issue and theirs and your posterity
descended through the male line, to be held and named, besides being
treated, reputed and written, as such, both in justice and without, in
both temporal and spiritual matters, in sacred and profane, even
though they should be affairs in which particular mention should be
made of the present patent; that you may enjoy, use and discharge
all the employments, acts, honors, dignities, offices, rights, liberties,
insignias, privileges, favors, prerogatives, and exemptions, which other
nobles and those of noble descent in the abovementioned Principality
and counties enjoy, use and discharge at will, both by right and by
custom; and we will, enjoin and command, both in our name and
in that of our successors, that you and all your offspring and posterity descending from you in the various degrees of the direct male line
shall enjoy, use and discharge the aforesaid title of nobility, both by
the raising of banners and family insignia, and by disposing of all
and each of the privileges arising from the title of nobility, from our
grants and those obtaining from our ancestors and those belonging by
right, use or custom in any sort, and according to the sort and fashion
that has been generally granted to other nobility of our aforesaid
Principality of Catalonia and the Counties of Rosellón and Cerdeña,
notwithstanding expressions to the contrary or any other impediments
whatsoever.

"Wherefore, we do say and send to our honourable, glorious and
respectworthy nobles, magnificoes and well-loved councilors and
faithfull servants, to all lieutenants, captains-general, and presiding
councilors whatsoever, those in charge of the Chancellery, Doctors of
our royal Audiencias, Regent charged with our General Governance,
those acting for our General Governance, the Chief Justice of Aragon
and his lieutenants, Masters, Baillies-General, Royal Attorneys, Vicars,
Baillies, Subvicars, Subbaillies, sworn Counselors-at-law, Consuls, and
in fine all other attorneys and each of our officials and subjects of
whatever dignity, rank, and degree or condition present or future out
of the said officials, lieutenants or regents of entrusted, and more
especially to honourable Dukes, Marquises, Counts, Viscounts, Barons,
noble Knights and other our subjects, present and future, of our
realms and domains of the crown of Aragon, that if they should fail
to observe what is ordered herein they will incur our royal displeasure

and wrath, and the penalty of two thousand gold florins of Aragon to be carried to the royal treasury and exacted irremissibly from the goods of any who act in this manner. Therefore they are to cause to be fulfilled, maintained, and inviolably observed this our patent given to you the said Gaspar de Portolá and to your children and all your issue and theirs and the posterity born and to be born from you in the direct male line; to hold, maintain, respect, honor and treat you as Noble and as Noblemen, to allow you to use and dispose of all privileges, favors, liberties, immunities and all the things previously mentioned. They are in no wise to attempt anything to the contrary for any reason or cause, inasmuch as our officials and subjects hold and wish to hold our favor, and desire not to fall into our displeasure and the penalty aforesaid. But we will and do expressly command, that before making use of this patent, you are obliged to present it at the office of the Secretary of our *Registro de Gracia* for the recording of the aforesaid matters, as will be shown by our Secretary's note written upon the same, and should you fail to perform this within the quarter-year from the present date, we command the person or persons to whose execution these matters belong not to receive the present favor, and we declare it to be without force or effect. In witness whereof we have commanded these presents to be drawn up and sealed with the impress of our royal and common seal. Given at our City of Madrid, the fourth of November in the Year of the Birth of the Lord one thousand six hundred eighty two, the eighteenth of our reign. I the King.

"Sent by the King to me Dr. Francisco Thgdo. de Berbegal, seen by Dr. Pedro de Aragón, Chairman Villacampa, and by the Treasurer-General. Extracted in the Secretaría de Mercedes as his Majesty commands. Madrid, fifth of November, one thousand six hundred eighty two.—Luis Antonio Daza.

Miscellaneous, book VII, folio C. F. xxxxiii. Title of Nobleman in favor of Gaspar Portolá, native of Principality of Catalonia. By nomination. Stamp duty one thousand one hundred *sueldos*. Bernardo Pujol, lieutenant of Protonotary's Office."

On January 8 in the year 1658 the first fruit of the wedding between Don Gaspar de Portolá y Pont and Doña Isabel-Ana de Portolá y Bellver of which I have any documentary notice was baptized in the parish church at Balaguer. It was a boy, to whom was given the name of Ramón Buenaventura Francisco Gaspar José Ignacio, his godparents being the youth José Fontana, "a poor student," and the servant-maid Francisca Llinassa.[7]

7. Balaguer Parish Archive, Baptisms (1644-1672), fol. 139.

The following year, February 20th., 1659, sees the baptism of
FRANCISCO Gaspar Antonio, "son of Doctor Gaspar Portolá, domi-
ciled at Balaguer, and of Señora Isabelana Portolá y Bellver."
Acting as godparents are IGNACIO Portolá, *germá del batejat*,
that is to say brother of the baptized child, and mistress Teresa
Sabater.[8]

On September 11, 1661, the baptismal waters are administered to JUAN Francisco Nicolás José, a son of the same couple,
"all of the present City," with sponsors Juan Bautista Arrufach
and Señora Elena Trilla.[9]   And finally, on December 24th, 1662,
the sole female child of the marriage is christened FRANCISCA
Isabelana Antonia Teresa.   Her godparents are Licentiate Don
Luis de Portolá, son of the brother of Don Gaspar, and Francisca
Carví.[10]   Let it be noted that this Doña Francisca de Portolá is
referred to later in her father's will as Doña Teresa de Portolá
y Bellver, wife of the nobleman Don José de Subirá, with which
marriage begins the line of the baronage of Abella.

All the children of the original marriage have now made their
appearance save for Nicolás and José, who will shortly arrive on
the scene.

Don Gaspar de Portolá, then, lived at Ager and at Balaguer,
where he made his will on the 10th of March, 1687, before Notary José de Revert,[11] at which time he was "Baron and Lord of
Castellnou de Monsech, Lord of Beniure, Estorm, San Esteban de
la Sarga, Subveguer de Gotlar, Castellan of the castellanies of
Claramunt and Montlleó of the Valley of Ager, Lord of the
marches of Pradell and the third part of that of Margalef in the
Veguería of Lérida." [12]

"The Honorable Don Gaspar de Portolá, Doctor, *doncel*,"
says Father Sanahuja, "purchased the seigniory of La Torre and
the march of Pradell, with jurisdiction civil and criminal, high
and low, simple and mixed domain, from Most Excellent Fernando Manuel de Cardona y Cardona, Count of Birabén, of
which seigniory the aforesaid Portolá took possession on May

8.  Ibid., fol. 152.
9.  Ibid., fol. 177.
10. Ibid., fol. 189.
11. Balaguer Notarial Archive, notary Larrosa, vol. 219, fol. 49.
12. SANAHUJA, fray Pedro, *Don Gaspar de Portolá...*, «Ilerda», III, n.º 5, p. 63.

7th of the same year." [13]  The purchase took place on January 7th.

In September 1660, the 19th, "the baillie, *paheres* and councilors of the Town of Ager" sold by means of a letter of privilege for the price two hundred gold *doblas* paid by "the Magnifico Don Gaspar de Portolá, Doctor of Law, domiciled in the City of Balaguer," the castellany of Abella and part of the district or plain called *de Dos Querons y Aspros* at Ager; Don Gaspar transferred the plain back to the Town of Ager on September 14th, 1670, on condition of their paying him a sum of 60 pounds annually. [14]

He had also acquired, from Doña Inés de Pinós y de Agulló, Dowager Countess of Vallfugona, a third part of the Castle and Seigniory of Margalef, by a purchase effected before the notary Don Ramón Vilaná Perlas in the city of Barcelona on March 5th, 1667.  The property could not be purchased free and clear because the seignory of Margalef was subject to the crown, and a long lawsuit over it arose which was inherited by the next generation and only settled, as we shall see, in the time of Doña María Francisca de Portolá y Valls.

As appears from his will, Don Gaspar de Portolá died in his Balaguer residence, located upon the market square, on October 22, 1688.  Also in accordance with his will, he was to be buried in the church of the castle of Monsech, but as the tomb and chapel there were still under construction, as the following will show, the interment took place in the Dominican convent at Balaguer, in the chapel named Santo Domingo Soriano.

In a document dated November 16th, 1696, Don NICOLÁS de Portolá y Bellver, "domiciled at the Town of Ager," renders an account to his cousin Don Francisco de Portolá, grandson and heir of Don Gaspar de Portolá y Pont by his son Don Ignacio de Portolá y Bellver, listing a payment of 68 pounds due to the Ager mason Juan Millach for construction done upon the chapel and tomb at the castle of Castellnou de Monsech; 87 pounds to the sculptor Jacinto Bacona of the town of Figuerola de Orcau for the altarpiece for the said chapel; "Item, expenses for the transfer

---

13.  Ibid., p. 63.
14.  Ibid., p. 64.

of the body of Don Gaspar de Portolá, to be brought from the burial-place at the Chapel of Santo Domingo Soriano, where it now lies, to the said chapel of the aforesaid church of Castellnou, to which it is to be transferred and buried, according to the testamentary disposition of the deceased, my late father and your grandfather." [15]   In addition to this valuable information, this document puts us in touch with another son of Don Gaspar, Don Nicolás de Portolá y Bellver, who lived at Ager and married Doña Teresa Ferrer.    The last son, of whom we have no documentary knowledge, is Don José de Portolá, surely appearing as identical with Reverend José Portolá, Doctor in Both Laws, priest and Abbot of San Esteban de la Sarga, named as attorney by the Baron of Castellnou de Monsech, Don Francisco de Portolá.[16] And possibly he is the one referred to in a document preserved in the Lérida Cathedral archives witnessing to the fact that Don Nicolás de Portolá and his spouse Doña Teresa de Portolá y Ferrer together with José de Subirá are realizing a quit-rent upon their lands, cellarage and buildings at Ager, "property formerly belonging to José de Portolá." [17]   Don Nicolás, on April 15, 1707, stands as godfather to the child María, daughter of Don Francisco de Portolá and Doña María de Portolá y Bardaxí, who was first baptized *in extremis* at the Portolá house by the same sponsor who is now present at the baptismal font in the Balaguer parish church.[18]

When the work upon the chapel and tomb of the Castellnou Castle church had been completed, the body of the first of the Portolás of Balaguer was transferred thither from its resting place in the Dominican Convent on March 24th, 1669, by the prior and his community of friars, the remains being accepted by Don Francisco de Portolá y de Subirá, grandson and heir of the deceased, whose son and natural heir Don Ignacio had predeceased him.[19]

---

15.  Balaguer Not. Archive, notary José de Revert, vol. 40, fol. 414 (A.D. 1696).
16.  Ibid., vol. 41, fol. 201 (1697).
17.  Balaguer Parish Archive, Baptisms, 1707.
18.  Balaguer Notarial Archive, notary José de Revert, vol. 42 (1699).
19.  Ibid., vol. 40, fol. 407 (1696).

III.   *Don Ignacio de Portolá y Bellver and his consort Doña María de Subirá.*

*Issue: Don Francisco, Don Gaspar Cayetano, Doña Teresa and Doña María.*

Don Ignacio was, or was to have been, the natural heir to the family title, but died before inheriting it from his father Don Gaspar de Portolá.    All of the documents which we cite here declare the brothers Don Ignacio and Don Nicolás to be residents of the town of Ager unlike the double residences maintained by the grandfather Don Gaspar and the grandson Don Francisco. At Don Ignacio's death, which left his children Francisco, Gaspar Cayetano, Teresa and María all of minor age, their own grandfather Don Gaspar de Portolá y Pont became their guardian, and in accordance with the normal laws of succession in the Principality gave orders in making his will that the family title should devolve upon his grandson Don Francisco, while Don Nicolás de Portolá, being the second son, was named as guardian of the children of his deceased brother.

I shall give here a document which clearly states this line of descent together with the details of the skipped succession. "Don Francisco de Portolá y Subirá, Baron and Lord of the barony of

Castellnou de Monsech and of Pradell, Castellan of Claramunt
and Montlleó in the Valley of Ager, Resident of the Town of Ager,
son of the Noble Don Ignacio de Portolá y Bellver, deceased,
domiciled in this town and in the City of Balaguer, grandson
and universal heir of the Noble señor Don Gaspar de Portolá
y Pont, deceased, resident of the City of Balaguer and the Town
of Ager," does acknowledge and declare that his uncle Don Nicolás de Portolá y Bellver has exercised the guardianship both
of himself and of "his brother Gaspar de Portolá y Subirá and
his sister Doña Teresa de Portolá y Subirá" between the first of
October, 1688, and the day of granting of this document, November 18th, 1696,[20] the date of his majority and of his assuming
charge of the Portolá heritage.  Don FRANCISCO must have been
born in the town of Ager[21] and therefore in the year 1677, according to my calculation, in order to leave sufficient time in Don
Ignacio's generative cycle for the birth of another brother in
between the heir and Doña Teresa, a child baptized with the
grandfather's name Gaspar, and with Cayetano for a second given
name.   Note that there is no mention in the preceding document of the sister Doña María, who must have died earlier.

Don Ignacio de Portolá's second son was, as has been said,
baptized Gaspar Cayetano, and must have been born in 1678.
On January 17th, 1699, this Don Gaspar Cayetano de Portolá y de
Subirá stands godfather to the first child of his brother Francisco and the Señora Doña María de Portolá y Bardaxí, the child's
godmother being "the Very Noble Lady Doña Gertrudis Bardaxí
y Lausán."

The first daughter, third fruit of the marriage between Don
Ignacio de Portolá and Doña María de Subirá, was named TERESA
de Portolá y Subirá, and came into the world at the town of Ager
in the year 1679. This Doña Teresa is one of the most remarkable
personages of the Portolá family, and clearly led a stormy life.
It would be interesting just to list the long series of traces left
by her in the local archives during her many years of life at
Balaguer, and the long list of her familial and business quarrels
carried on until her death.  She was a conspicous example of
the noblewoman who during a long existence always carries
with her a special halo of awe and dignity.

---

20.  Archivo Histórico Nacional, *Carlos III*, exped. 2.143, p. 1.
21.  Balaguer Parish Archive, Baptisms (1697-1715), fol. 25.

She contracted matrimony twice. The first time was with a nobleman, Don Tomás de Bullfarines y Fontova, of a family with deep roots, wealthy inheritance and much political power, decided partisans—like the Portolá family—of the Archduke Charles of Austria.   Teresa's marriage must have been celebrated in 1700, when she was twenty years of age, inasmuch as on August 31, 1700, Doña Teresa de Bullfarines y de Portolá stood sponsor along with Jacinto de Bullfarines to a daughter of José and Gertrudis de Bullfarines.[22] The Bullfarines de Balaguer were very well known for the part they played in the wars, particularly in the taking of the city in 1652, when they were the first to enter the castle being held by the French and receive the surrender of the city.   José Roger, with his uncles Isidro and José Almenara and other valiant citizens, opened Balaguer to the troops of Philip IV.   José de Bullfarines was named knight on August 27th, 1693.[23]

Several children were born of this marriage, none of whom survived: a daughter named Josefa, born April 29th, 1791, whose godparents were Francisco de Portolá and Jerónima de Bullfarines;[24] a boy named Francisco born January 20, 1704;[25] another called Antonio in the year 1707;[26] a girl named María, born 1710;[27] and in 1711 a boy named Ignacio.[28]

The second marriage, which took place on September 10th, 1713, was between "Doña Teresa de Bullfarines y de Portolá, relict of Don Tomás de Bullfarines of Balaguer, and Don Juan de Montaner, fadrí [bachelor], son of José de Montaner and of Isabel de Montaner y Llarissa."[29]   This is in all probability the José de Montaner who took over the governorship of Balaguer in 1644 in the face of the popular opposition to the pretentions of Barcelona in favor of Louis XIII of France.   In the next year of this marriage to Don Juan de Montaner, who was a Lieutenant-Colonel of the Palencia infantry regiment quartered at Balaguer, the first child is born, and baptized on 3rd of July,

22. Ibid., 1707, fol. 51.
23. Archivo Histórico Nacional, Consejos, leg. 18.669, n.º 63.
24. Balaguer Parish Archive, Baptisms (1697-1715), fol. 7 verso.
25. Ibid., unnumbered folio.
26. Ibid., fol. 181.
27. Ibid., unnumbered folio.
28. Ibid.
29. Balaguer Parish Archive, Marriages (1713), fol. 75.

1714, with the names of Francisco, Antonio, Federico, the god-parents being His Excellency Fadrique de Soto, colonel of the Palencia Regiment, and Doña Lucía de Nogués.[30]    But this sole child of the second marriage did not survive either.

Don Juan de Montaner appears to have died on September 28, 1713, having arranged his will at Balaguer before Notary Sales y Novell on September 25th of the same year.  By this will, Don Juan de Montaner, "Lieutenant-Colonel of the Palencia Regiment quartered at Balaguer, son of the nobleman Don José de Montaner and of Doña Isabel de Montaner y Llarissa, husband and wife deceased of the city of Barcelona," orders his wife Doña Teresa de Montaner y de Portolá named as usufructuary of all of his goods, and designates his cousin Don Fermín de Montaner his universal heir.[31]    While married to Bullfarines, Doña Teresa became godparent to Antonia, Manuela, Mariana, daugther of Francisco de Portolá and María de Portolá y Bardaxí, on December 26, 1703.[32]    In 1720, now wife of Montaner, she stood sponsor to the confirmation of Margarita Portolá, daughter of Francisco and Teresa.[33]    (I have no other record of this Margarita, and I doubt that she was the daughter of Francisco de Portolá and Teresa de Rovira.    Or else it may be that in the baptismal register she bears a different name from that which is given in the register of confirmations.)    June 14, 1736, she is sponsor of Francisca, a daughter of Antonio de Portolá and Francisca de Portolá y Valls,[34] and on June 8, 1738, sponsors the confirmation of Gertrudis, daughter of the same pair.[35]

Here I wish to include, in abbreviated form, the will of Doña Teresa de Montaner y de Portolá, which like many another document provides some acquaintance with this lady's strong personality, and contains data of obvious importance for other personages as well.    After the will I shall place some related documents which serve to explain and connect its contents.

Before the Balaguer Notary José Larrosa, on June 12th., 1754, "Doña Teresa de Montaner y de Portolá, relict of Don Juan de Montaner, sometime Lieutenant-Colonel of His Majesty's Troops, stationed at Balaguer upon the day of his death," names

30. Ibid., Baptisms (1697-1715), unnumbered folio.
31. Balaguer Notarial Archive, notary Sales y Novell, vol. 46, fol. 25 verso.
32. Balaguer Parish Archive, Baptisms (1697-1715), unnumbered leaf.
33. Ibid., Book of Confirmations, fol. 22.
34. Ibid., Baptisms (1734-1760), fol. 26.
35. Ibid., Confirmations, fol. 76.

as her testamentary executors the Prior of the Discalced Friars
of Balaguer, the Reverend Andrés Aranés, a beneficiary of the
town of Ager, *al pressent domiciliat a ma Casa*, "presently
dwelling in my house," and José Larrosa, Royal Notary.   She
asks that her body be entombed "in the Church of the Discalced
Fathers" (the present parochial church of St. Joseph) "before the
altar of *San Albert* and at the side of my late husband Don Joan
de Montaner."   Immediately upon her death, she orders that
her money be used to say Masses for the eternal repose of her
soul, seven hundred and fifty low Masses to be distributed as
follows among the churches of the locality: a hundred in each,
beginning with the Dominicans, the Escuelas Pías, the Franciscans, the Discalced Friars, the Trinitarians and the Church of
Santo Cristo; the number remaining, up to seven hundred and
fifty, to be divided among the "novice chaplains of Balaguer."
The will continues with some gifts to her maids, in its Catalan
dialect, and adds: "I leave and bequeath to my nephew Don
Josep de Portolá, at present employed in the King's service, one
hundred Barcelona pounds paid one time only."   Elsewhere she
states that on December 9, 1753, in order to pay the beneficiary
Reverend Andrés Aranés "thirteen years' salary," she had given
him a piece of land in the place known as *Horta d'Amunt*.   And
should there be anything left over it is to be distributed as alms
among the needy.   She signs the will in her house on the "above
named Carrer de Avall." [36]

Two years after the drawing of the will, on April 12, 1756, she
executes a document in which "as usufructuary of the goods of
her spouse Don Juan de Montaner, by a will executed before
Royal Notary Don José de Sales y Novell," "in order to collect
the sums due her for the service of her late husband to His Royal
Majesty (God keep him), by right owing to her," she grants
power of attorney to "Don Gaspar de Portolá, Lieutenant of
Grenadiers in the Numancia Regiment of Dragoons, her nephew." [37]   On June 11, 1756, claiming that she has "no more money
to support myself upon," she sells her house in the Calle de Aba-
jo (Land Road) "facing the River Segre upon the east, the house
and garden of Don Pere Bellí, Royal Notary, upon the south, the
said Lower Road upon the west, and the house of Joseph Sales
and the Rev. Jaume Planas upon the north" to the beneficiary

36.  Balaguer Notarial Archive, notary Larosa, 1754, fol. 62.
37.  Ibid., vol. 218, fol. 174.

Andrés Aranés, «to whom I owe money." [38]    Again, upon the same
date, she orders that the large dowry given to her upon her
marriage be returned to her brother Francisco, since she is
dying without succession.[39]    In September of 1757, she adds a
first codicil to her will, whereby the balances due to Don Juan de
Montaner are to be equally distributed between her nephews
Don Gaspar and Don José de Portolá, "officers in the armies of
Spain," whom she also names as executors of her will.[40] The
second and final codicil is added on January 6th, 1758, ordering
an inscription for her tomb which is to read plainly, *Sepultura
de Don Juan y Doña Teresa de Montaner y Portolá y dels seus:*
Tomb of Don Juan and Doña Teresa de Montaner y Portolá and
their children.    Apparently Don Gaspar de Portolá had already
been able to collect the balances due, but, "my nephew Don Joseph de Portolá having died," they are to be distributed among
the needy.[41]    Doña Teresa died at 79 years of age, "a little more
or less," at Balaguer, "an inhabitant there for many years," on
May 20th, 1758.[42]

Following her death, the sum of 742 pounds, 4 *sueldos*,
4 *dineros* is delivered to Doña Francisca de Portolá y Valls,
widow of Don Antonio de Portolá, and her daughter Doña María
Francisca de Portolá y Rubalcava on August 19, 1759, by the
Balaguer notary Don José Larrosa, from the executors of the will
the provisions of the marriage contract of said Doña Teresa and
her first husband Don Tomás de Bullfarines on Fabruary 1st,
1700, and by the agreement made between Don Juan de Montaner
and Doña Teresa de Montaner, husband and wife, and Don Francisco de Portolá.[43]    The same ladies receive 318 pounds from the
peasant Pedro Arqués for the sale of a piece of land and from
the final disposition of Doña Teresa "for the restitution of the
dowry and dues which she received in her day." [44]

The second child of Don Ignacio Portolá, the heir, was named
MARÍA, Teresa, Isabelana, Antonia, and was baptized April 25,
1680, in the Balaguer parish church, the godparents being her

38.  Ibid., fol. 76.
39.  Ibid., fol. 78.
40.  Ibid., fol. 95.
41.  Ibid., fol. 97.
42.  Balaguer Parish Archive, Book of Deaths (1734-1772), fol. 252.
43.  Balaguer Notarial Archive, notary Sales y Novell, vol. 68.
44.  Ibid., fol. 3.

grandfather and grandmother Don Gaspar and Doña Isabel Ana Bellver.[45]   This daughter must have died before the drawing up of her grandfather's will, since she is not named in it.

Don Ignacio himself must have died before the date of that will, that is, before March 10th, 1687.

---

45.  Balaguer Parish Archive, Baptisms (1672-1699), fol. 84.

IV.  *Don Francisco de Portolá y Subirá with his first wife, Doña María de Bardaxí y Lussán. Issue: Don Antonio, Doña Antonia, Doña Teresa.*

*Second marriage with Doña Teresa de Rovira y Sanispleda.*

*Issue: Don Antonio, Doña Francisca, Don Antonio, Don Gaspar, Don Francisco, Doña Benita, Doña Josefa, Don Benito, Doña Ramona and Don José.*

The death of Don Ignacio, the Portolá heir, at an early age but with a goodly number of descendants forced the grandfather Don Gaspar in his will to name as heir his son's eldest child, Don Francisco de Portolá, who succeeded to the inheritance on the grandfather's death October 22d, 1688.[46]  All of Ignacio's sons remained under the guardianship of Don Nicolás until 1696, at which date the heir, on reaching his majority, entered into the

---

46.  Balaguer Notarial Archive, notary Sales y Novell, vol. 52, fol. 3.

Portolá inheritance, thereafter titling himself "Baron and Lord of the Barony of Castellnou de Monsech, Beniure, Estorm, San Esteban de la Sarga, Pradell and of the march of La Fuliola, Castellan of the towns of Gerp, Claramunt and Montlleó in the Valley of Ager, and of the third part of Margalef." Thus he appears in manifold documents in the notarial registers of that period, almost all of them drawn up by the notary José de Sales y Novell of Balaguer.

Specifically, on June 13th, 1735, Don Francisco de Portolá y Subirá, accompanied by his son Don Antonio de Portolá y de Rovira, proclaims the two of them by the above-listed titles, and in so doing declares himself heir of his grandfather Don Gaspar, while the son Don Antonio is declared heir of Don Francisco.[47] Notice that the son is Don Antonio de Portolá y de *Rovira*, and so evidently a child of the second wife, which pre-supposes that the eldest child of the first marriage, named Don Antonio de Portolá y *Bardaxí*, must already have died. We shall return to this later. Don Francisco's coming into his inheritance in 1696 must mean that he was some twenty years of age and about to marry, since his first offspring is born in 1699.

The first marriage is contracted with Doña María de Bardaxí y Lussan, possibly in 1698; the bride is the daughter of the well-known "Noblewoman Doña Gertrudis de Bardaxí." Three sons are the fruit of this marriage, whom we have in the Bala-guer parish records, all clearly identified. The eldest is baptized on January 17th, 1699, in Balaguer parish church, sponsored by his father's brother, Don Gaspar Cayetano de Portolá y Subirá, and the grandmother of the newborn Doña Gertrudis. He is given the names ANTONIO, Benito, Diego, José, Pablo, and Gaspar.[48] On December 26th, 1703, the girl child ANTONIA, Manuela, Teresa, Mariana is baptized, daughter of the Portolá-Bardaxí match, with Doña Teresa de Bullfarines y de Portolá and her husband Don Tomás de Bullfarines as godparents.[49] The child MARÍA, Teresa, Jerónima is baptized on April 15, 1707, daughter of the same parents and sponsored by Jerónima de Bullfarines and Nicolás de Portolá, the latter of whom had had to baptize her earlier *in extremis* in the Portolá home, as we have seen.[50]

---

47. Ibid., fol. 104.
48. Balaguer Parish Archive, Baptisms, fol. 25.
49. Ibid., unnumbered leaf.
50. Ibid., fol. 18.

Wooden coat of arms, from the family chapel which existed in the town of Castellnou de Montsec and which was a part of the funerary altar-piece of the family.

de Montaner y Subirá receiving the child as godparents at the font.[60]

(Of these two godparents, the first was a brother of the child's guardian with whom we shall shortly become acquainted; the other, though named Doña Teresa and a Subirá married to a Montaner, should not be confused with the Doña Teresa de Montaner y de Portolá of whom we have already seen so much and who was the sister of the child's father Don Francisco de Portolá y Subirá, the man whose family we are now studying.)

A second BENITA, further named Josefa, Petronila, María Antonia, daughter of the same couple, and sponsored by José de Nogués and Petronila de Nogués, is baptized on January 10, 1722, in the Balaguer parish church.[61]    The re-use of the name would seem to show the premature death of the first Benita; we shall return to the surviving child when we come to speak of the lady named Josefa de la Cruz, alias Josefa de Arteaga.

A boy named BENITO, José, Ramón, and Melchor, child of the same parents, is baptized in the same church on February 14, 1723, godparents Don José Eva (a minor) and Doña Josefa Camats, of Sanahuja;[62] and likewise a girl, RAMONA, Teresa, Benita, María Antonia, with godparents Don Ramón Eva and Doña Eva of the town of Castelló de Farfañ, May 22nd, 1725.[63]

We now come to the last son of Don Francisco de Portolá and Doña Teresa de Rovira, the one named Don JOSÉ de Portolá; touching the date of his birth, we again lack any precise documents, but in some affidavits executed at Balaguer on May 14, 1743, before Notary Fortuny by Doña Josefa de Arteaga y de Portolá and others, the young gentleman is declared to be *caballer estudiant de diset anys de edad poc més o menos*, a student sixteen years of age more or less, a statement which puts Don José de Portolá's birthdate back into the year 1726.[64]    He was confirmed on July 6, 1734, by Bishop Ramón de Nogués, and sponsored by his own brother Don Gaspar de Portolá y de Rovira, in a ceremony held in the Palace Chapel in the present Casa del Santo Cristo.[65]    When on October 28, 1746, Don José de Portolá

---

60. Ibid., Baptisms (1716-1733), fol. 96.
61. Ibid., fol. 120.
62. Ibid., fol. 140.
63. Ibid., fol. 173.
64. Balaguer Notarial Archive, notary José Plá, vol. 79, fol. 35.
65. Balaguer Parish Archive, Confirmations (1715-1779), fol. 56.

was named attorney by Don Pedro García de Arteaga, husband of
Doña Josefa de Portolá and guardian of María Francisca de
Portolá y de Valls, the minor daughter and heir of Don Antonio
and Don Francisco de Portolá, he must already have attained his
majority, a fact which again places his birthdate in 1726 or
earlier.   On September 19, 1737, he is godfather to Gertrudis,
the daughter of his brother Antonio.[66]

Acting as attorney of Don Pedro de Arteaga, on October 28,
1746, he seems to have sold to Don José Terré de Subirá upon
reversion the civil and criminal jurisdiction of the manor of
Beniure, for 600 Barcelona pounds.   Later on, Doña Francisca
and her daughter Doña María Francisca de Portolá repudiate the
sale as illegitimate and by an agreement with them Don José
Terré y de Subirá renounces it, receiving in return a number of
privileges, among them that of naming the mayor of Beniure.[67]

We meet Don José de Portolá again as a professional soldier after he has joined the Batavia Regiment of dragoons on the
island of Majorca in the service of His Majesty Ferdinand VI, the
document concerns his claim against the guardian Don José Terré de Subirá for certain sums due him.[68]   Once more, and in a
similar context, we find him in 1757 an Ensign of Grenadiers in
the Savoy infantry regiment of the King's forces, receiving the
sum of 300 pounds at the hands of the above-mentioned Doña
Francisca de Portolá y de Valls and Doña María Francisca de
Portolá y Rubalcava; the documents state in Catalan that they
are "pressingly required to make prompt payment to the aforesaid Don Josep de Portolá y de Rovira of the amount of 300
pounds by him demanded and requested to be paid, as part of
his legitimate dues paternal and maternal." [69, 70]

He is mentioned, but as already dead, by Doña Teresa de
Montaner y de Portolá in a second codicil to her testament, the
exact wording being *trobantse difunt Don Joseph de Portolà, mon
nebot*, "my nephew, Don José de Portolá, being deceased"; the
date of this codicil is 1758.   Yet this must be wrong; he must
actually have been alive then and much later, when his brother

---

66.  Ibid., Baptisms (1734-1760), fol. 40 verso.
67.  Balaguer Notarial Archive, notary Sociats, vol. 156, fol. 7.
68.  Ibid., notary Sales y Novell, vol. 61, fol. 33.
69.  Ibid., vol. 67, fol. 94.
70.  Ibid., fol. 93.

Don Gaspar de Portolá in his own will drawn up before the Notary Madriguera at Lérida on May 29th, 1786, states that Don José de Portolá y de Rovira, First Lieutenenant of the Guadalajara Infantry Regiment, is to be left an annual pension of 60 pounds until reaching the rank of captain.[71]

Last of all, we shall consider the daughter who appears in the documents under the name of JOSEFA, and whose birth Father Sanahuja dates after that of José, i.e. in 1727-1728.    I do not think this can be correct, given the known facts, and for the following reasons.    Her lady mother Doña Teresa was already dead at the time the second daughter was about to enter religion as Sister Rosa, on October 13, 1730; the birthdate therefore was earlier.    José was born in 1726, Ramona in 1725, Benito in 1723, Benita (the second) in 1722; Benita (first) was born in 1720 and before her Francisco, Gaspar, Antonio, Francisca (Sister Rosa), and Antonio, leaving as the only possible years 1727, 1728, 1729. Apparently she was confirmed in the year 1734 together with her brother José de Portolá and her niece María Francisca de Portolá.[72]    But on the other hand, Doña Josefa de Portolá y de Rovira married on the 5th of October, 1738, "the Honble. Don Pedro García de Arteaga, native of Burgos city, Colonel and Brigadier of the Frisia Regiment, domiciled at Balaguer..."; the witnesses of this wedding are Captain Juan de Riga, Count Riga, Manuel Valenciano, Lieutenant-Colonel of the said Regiment, and many others.[73] Obviously, if "Doña Josefa de Portolá y de Rovira, daughter of Don Francisco de Portolá y Subirá and Doña Teresa de Portolá y de Rovira, deceased" entered into matrimony in 1738, she could not have been born between 1727 and 1729.    All that I can suppose is that she was born long before that date, not as Josefa, but as that Benita, JOSEFA, Petronila whom we have seen baptized on January 10, 1722; and later, know as Josefa, married Don Pedro García de Arteaga.    Someday it may be possible to find proof for this supposition, which is only a theory now, but in my belief is in agreement with the known and normal dates of the child's life and social development, and with the fact that second names are often the ones used among adults.

On March 27th, 1739, the Honble. Don Pedro García de Arteaga and his spouse Doña Josefa García de Portolá sponsor the

---

71. SANAHUJA, fray Pedro, Don Gaspar..., p. 106 (see note 12 above).
72. Balaguer Parish Archive, Confirmations (1715-1779), fol. 56.
73. Ibid., Marriages, fol. 195.

child Francisco, Pedro, José, Bonifacio, son of Don Antonio de Portolá y de Rovira and Doña Francisca de Portolá y de Valls.[74]

Don Pedro García de Arteaga is a Lieutenant General of the King's Armies when, in 1746, he is mentioned as guardian of María Francisca de Portolá y de Valls, by reason of the deaths from old age of her father Don Antonio de Portolá y Rovira (July 21, 1740)[75] and her grandfather Don Francisco de Portolá y Subirá (on July 23, 1743).[76]   Meanwhile, on April 22nd, 1742, Don Pedro García de Arteaga had been named *Corregidor* and Governor of Lérida, one of the many appointments made in Catalonia after the drastic measures taken by Philip V against the traditional Catalan - Aragonese privileges and liberties.[77]   Among various documents issued by him as Governor, an interrogatory addressed to the City Council on March 14, 1747, relating to various questions of city government and containing sixteen questions and answers, has been quoted by Tarragó Pleyán.[78]

Of the marriage between Don Pedro and Doña Josefa, only a single child was born, a son who came into the world at Balaguer and was confirmed at the same city on April 10th, 1744, with Don José de Nogués as godfather.[79]   Here, in this confirmation entry for the child José García de Portolá, as well as in the marriage pact, we find authentic evidence as to the true family name of the father, Don Pedro García de Arteaga, and as will be seen, this information is supported by the documentation of his knighthood in the Order of Saint James.   It thus appears that this Don Pedro García de Arteaga is the same man as Don Pedro de la Cruz Mayor, Lieutenant General of the Royal Armies, Military and Civil Governor of the City of Lérida, husband of the Honble. Señora Doña Josefa de la Cruz y de Portolá, spoken of in the matrimonial contract dated February 4, 1752, between Doña María Francisca de Portolá y de Valls and Don Antonio Domingo de Rubalcava y Magarola, in which also figure her other guardians and uncles, Don Gaspar de Portolá y de Rovira and Don José de Portolá, as well as Don José Terré y de Subirá.[80]

74.   Ibid., Baptisms, fol. 62.
75.   Ibid., Deaths, fol. 40
77.   Archivo Histórico Nacional, *Consejos*, leg. 17,958, *Lista de los Corregimientos que van anexos a los Gobernadores Militares de los Reinos de la Corona de Aragón.*
76.   Ibid., fol. 64.
78.   *Ilerda*, n.º XXIX, pp. 288 and following.
79.   Balaguer Parish Archive, Confirmations, fol. 85.
80.   Balaguer Not. Archive, notary Sales y Novell, vol. 64, fols. 60, 61, 62, 72.

Altar-piece of the Portolás' chapel in Arties. The family
coat of arms is in both sides.

Under his other name, Don Pedro de la Cruz Mayor, Doña Josefa's husband, entered the Order of Knighthood of St. James; the following curious information extracted from the docket in the National Históric Archive:

"By a decree of January 16th, 1743, His Majesty bestowed the Charge of Provision of Castile in the Order of St. James upon Field Marshal Don Pedro García de Arteaga, presently Lieutenant General of his armies, and by another decree of July 20th, of the same year, determined to bestow the future possession of the same Charge upon his son Don José Arteaga y Portolá; whereupon, the aforesaid Lieutenant General, being obliged to present his Genealogy to the Council to undergo the proofs necessary for him to assume the Habit of St. James, has represented to me that his present family names are mistaken, his true name being Don Pedro de la Cruz Mayor..." [81]

The son of this marriage, Don José de la Cruz y de Portolá of Balaguer, contracted marriage on June 13, 1790, at Bujalance, with Doña María Carlota de Linares y Lazarino, a native of Oran and daughter of Don Juan de Linares y Camacho, of Bujalance, and Doña Juana María Lazarino y Fernández, native of Alburquerque; like his father, he belonged to the Order of St. James.[82] His son in turn was named Don Carlos de la Cruz Mayor de Linares y de Portolá; he was born in Madrid, served as secretary of the legation in London, and by a decree of 1 December, 1829, entered the Royal and Distinguished Order of Charles III.[83]

Now let us return to Don Francisco de Portolá y de Subirá. His sons have become well known to us; let us repeat that his natural heir was his son Don Antonio de Portolá y de Rovira, since the children of his first marriage with Doña María de Bardaxí had died.    However, Don Antonio also predeceased his father, so that the Portolá inheritance passed to the eldest child of Don Antonio, a female named María Francisca, who at the age of nineteen entered into the titles and estate of her grandfather. His wives Doña María de Portolá y de Bardaxí had died between 1707 and 1710, Doña Teresa de Portolá y de Rovira between 1726 and 1730.   Properties acquired by Don Francisco included (on October 6, 1700) to the Royal Monastery of Poblet, with the estates and civil and criminal jurisdictions of La Fulioleta and Las

81. Archivo Histórico Nacional, *Ordenes Militares, Santiago*, legajo 76:7549.
82. Ibid., pp. 80-85.
83. Archivo Histórico Nacional, *Carlos III*, expediente 2.143.

Franquesas, in return for the sum of 14,000 pounds, as appears from notarial entries [84] made before the Tarragona notaries Don José Aleix and Don Francisco Ardébol.[85]  In 1702 he had been recognized as noble by the Cortes, as appears from Don Francisco Xavier de Garma y Durán's work, *Próceres y Ciudadanos de honor del Principado de Cataluña.*

On August 25, 1741, Don Francisco de Portolá sold the rights possessed by him upon the third part of the Castle and Lordship of Margalef to Señora Doña Francisca de Rubí, widow, of Fivaller, and to her son Don Juan de Fivaller y de Rubí, before the Barcelona notary Juan Bautista Plana.[86]  This sale was to give rise to much long-drawn-out litigation, since the property proved to be subject to the Crown, and in the end, as will be seen, the heirs were forced to pay a heavy restitution.  Don Francisco, during the last years of his life, was subjected to a wardship, as he was held to have become demented.

"Don Pedro Terré y de Subirá, Abbot of San Esteve de Monsech, and Don José Terré y de Subirá of the town of Santa María de Meiá, together with the nobleman Don Gaspar de Portolá (absent), being named in a document drawn up at the behest of Doña Francisca de Portolá y de Valls upon July 12th, 1742, by the magnifica and Doctor in both Laws Don Antonio de Rubies, and executed before de Notary Francisco Fortuny on August 30th, 1742, as wards and guardians of the person and goods of the nobleman Don Francisco de Portolá y de Subirá, insane of mind and mad..." [87]

Don Francisco de Portolá made his will before notary Francisco Fortuny on August 1st, 1740, and died at Balaguer on July 23, 1743.[88]

84.  Balaguer Notarial Archive, notary Raurer, vol. 404, fol. 77.
85.  Ibid., notary Armengol y Sala (1815), fol. 163.
86.  Ibid., notary Sociats, vol. 162, fol. 13.
87.  Ibid., notary Rosinyach (1743), fol. 32.
88.  Balaguer Parish Archive, Book of Deaths (1734-1772), fol. 64.

## V. *Don Antonio de Portolá y de Rovira and his consort Doña Francisca de Valls y de Torres. Doña María Francisca, Don Mariano, Doña Francisca, Doña Gertrudis, Don Francisco and Don Antonio.*

From the marriage between Don Francisco de Portolá and Doña María de Bardaxí sprang a son baptized Antonio [89] who must have died young, since in later documents Don Francisco himself and his similarly-named son of the second marriage, Don Antonio de Portolá y de Rovira, are declared to be the heirs in entail of the original Don Gaspar and of Don Francisco respectively,[90] and Don Francisco himself speaks of Don Antonio de Portolá y de Rovira in no uncertain terms as *"filius et hereder Universalis meus," "my son and universal heir."* [91]

As we have learned from the documents, a son born to Don Francisco and Doña Teresa de Rovira at the Monastery of San

89. Ibid., Baptisms, fol. 25.
90. Balaguer Notarial Archive, notary Sales y Novell, vol. 52.
91. Ibid., notary M. Fortuny (1739), fol. 340.

Cugat del Vallés or one of its dependencies was baptized Francisco, Antonio, and was the heir, but he also must have died,
since a second Antonio de Portolá y de Rovira was baptized at
Balaguer in 1716, and is named by his father as son and universal heir.

On November 6th, 1732, at the town of Cubells, Don Antonio
de Portolá y de Rovira married—by proxy, represented by Don
Francisco de Vall y Freixa, in the residence of Don Antonio de
Gay y de Valls—Señora Doña Francisca de Valls y de Torres,
daughter of Don Bruno de Valls y Freixa and Doña María de
Torres, both of them residents of Cervera. The wedding was
recorded in the records of the Church of San Pedro in the town
of Cubells.[92]   The marriage agreement was drawn up before the
notary Fortuny on November 2nd, 1734, Doña Francisca bringing to the matrimony 7,300 pounds, a sum made over *in toto* on
August 28 th, 1740.[93]

The first fruit of this marriage was a girl who was named
MARÍA, Lucrecia, Francisca at her baptism in Balaguer on November 8th, 1733, her godparents being Francisco de Valls of the
city of Cervera and Josefa de Portolá of the city of Balaguer.[94]
Her confirmation also took place in Balaguer, on July 6th, 1734,
in the Palace Chapel with the Bishop of Jaca, Don Ramón de
Nogués, officiating, and Doña Josefa de Portolá acting as sponsor.[95]   Father Pedro Sanahuja seems to confuse this child with
another girl of the same name whom he dates in 1735 and whom
I have been unable to find mentioned in the records which he
cites.

The first male child was born on December 11th, 1734, and
named MARIANO, Gaspar, Francisco, and José, son of Don Antonio
de Portolá and Doña Francisca de Portolá y Valls, man and wife,
with Don Gaspar de Portolá y de Rovira and Doña Mariagna Sulla
acting as godparents.[96]   But this offspring must have died pre-
maturely, since no other record mentions his name.

On June 14th., 1736, a girl-child of the same pair was baptized and christened FRANCISCA, Antonia, Teresa, Benita, her spon-

92. Archivo Histórico Nacional, *Carlos III*, expediente 1.546.
93. Balaguer Notarial Archive, notary Sales y Novell, vol. 51 (1737), fol. 145.
94. Balaguer Parish Archive, Baptisms (1716-1733), fol. 290.
95. Ibid., Confirmations (1734), fol. 56.
96. Ibid., Baptisms (1734-1760), fol. 10.

Panoramic view of the family house of the Portolás in the town of Arties in the Arán Valley in Lérida and which today is a part of the «Parador Nacional de Turismo, Gaspar de Portolá».

The same agreement witnesses that Doña Francisca reserves the amount of 3,000 pounds "to be expended in favor of milady Doña Antonia de Portolá y de Valls, her second daughter, in case of her reaching majority, with the express condition that if she becomes a nun she shall not be entitled to the whole three thousand pounds but only that portion that shall be required for her entering into religion, and the rest shall be included in the universal bestowal made upon Doña María Francisca her daughter, and if she shall be given in carnal marriage, it shall be at the pleasure of the said Doña Francisca... and in case the said Doña María die before being bestowed in matrimony, the said three thousand pounds shall remain included in the bestowal." This mention of Doña María, without anything being said of the other sister Doña Gertrudis, indicates that the latter must have died earlier.

The marriage thus agreed to between Doña María Francisca and Don Antonio Domingo de Rubalcava y Magarola, son of Don Antonio de Rubalcava y Cots, an officer of the General Accounting Office of the Principate of Catalonia and Perpetual Alderman of Barcelona, and of Doña Francisca de Rubalcava de Magarola y Sentmenat, took place on February 21st, 1752, in the Church of Santa María at Balaguer, and was again ratified in the Portolá family residence on the 19th of April, 1752.[109]   At the time, Don Antonio was twenty two years of age, and Doña María Francisca nineteen.   Don Antonio's baptismal entry tells us that he had been christened in the Church of Saints Justo and Pastor in the City of Barcelona on February 14th, 1730, with as godparents the Noble Señor Don Antonio de Cots y Piñana and Doña Antonia de Magarola y de Sentmenat.[110]   The status and titles of nobility belonging to Don Antonio de Rubalcava y Cots were royal conferrals descending in his family line from his great-grandfather, Don Francisco González de Rubalcava, a Knight of the Order of St. James.[111]

The offspring of this marriage was a single daughter, baptized at Balaguer on February 4th, 1753, and named MARÍA, Josefa, Francisca, her godparents being Don Francisco de Valls y Torres and Doña Francisca de Portolá y de Valls.[112] The fact that María

---

109.  Balaguer Parish Archive, Marriages, fol. 260.
110.  Archivo Histórico Nacional, *Carlos III*, expediente 1.564.
111.  Ibid.
112.  Balaguer Parish Archive, Baptisms (1734-1760), fol. 192.

Josefa, as she was generally known, was the only daughter is also proved by the Letter of Conferral of the title of Baron of Castellnou de Monsech in favor of Don Antonio (de Portolá) de Vilallonga y Manresa in 1801 by King Charles IV, in which it is stated that she is "only daughter of Don Antonio Domingo de Portolá, now deceased." [113]

On Doña María Francisca's wedding in 1752, we find her giving power of attorney to her husband Don Antonio Domingo de Portolá to take possession in her name of all the Portolá family possessions which she had inherited under the will of her father Don Antonio de Portolá y de Rovira dated May 20th, 1740, and that of ther grandfather Don Francisco dated August 1st, 1740, both drawn up before the Balaguer notary Don Francisco Fortuny. By this power of attorney she provides for her husband to take actual and physical possession in her name of the Barony of Castellnou de Montsech, of its bounds, of the places of Beniure, Estorm, San Esteban, La Fulioleta, Las Franquesas, and of the whole inheritance of her forebears.[114] Don Antonio Domingo, who has already assumed the Portolá family name, fulfills the provisions of his wife's power of attorney; a document found in the Balaguer notarial registry, dated May 16th, 1752,[115] contains the following record of his taking possessions of Las Franquesas:

Don Antonio Domingo de Portolá y Rubalcava ... took possession of the quarters called Priory of Las Franquesas, ... land belonging to the House of Portolá, ... district of La Fulioleta ...

"Standing in person before the orchard gate lying in front of and contiguous to the Church and large building of the former Convent of Nuns, all belonging to the aforesaid Priory, Señor José Terrer took Don Antonio Domingo by the hand and both entered the said orchard, in the presence of myself and the witnesses below named, and in token of possession of this orchand and its decayed building, pulled up a handful of grass from the same orchard and scattered it in the air, and also picked fruit from some trees and cast it upon the ground; likewise he walked all about the orchard and then through the decayed building attached to the said orchard, and ordered part of a wall there to be torn down, and required myself and the undersigned to bear witness to all of the above."

---

113. Archivo Histórico Nacional, *Carlos III*, expediente 1.564.
114. Balaguer Notarial Archive, notary Sales y Novell, vol. 64, fols. 72-74.
115. Ibid., fols. 75-76.

This procedure of taking possession, so normal at that period, is found used later by other members of the Portolá family. Indeed the Conquistador of California used the same ceremony in order to take possession in the name of the King of Spain of the lands discovered and won in the year 1770.

The marriage between María Francisca and Antonio Domingo proved to be not as happy as could have been hoped, and soon there began a series of disagreements between husband and wife and more or less prolonged separations. In notarial documents, Don Antonio de Portolá is fairly often mentioned as absent from Balaguer, but by February 28th, 1760, i.e. eight years after the wedding, we find a formal separation in effect: "Doña Francisca de Portolá, relict of Don Antonio de Portolá, and Doña María Francisca de Portolá y de Rubalcava, wife of the nobleman Don Antonio de Rubalcava y Magarola, dwelling in the City of Barcelona, separated from conjugal matrimony." [116] He was still absent and separated from his wife when on June 8th, 1763, Doña Francisca and Doña María Francisca, in the presence of witnesses Don Francisco and Don Luis de Valls, promise to liquidate the accounts pending with Don José Terré y de Subirá over the guardianship of the children of Don Francisco de Portolá.[117]

The separation must have lasted till the death of Don Antonio Domingo de Portolá y de Rubalcava, giving rise to a long legal suit which was setled by the sentence of the Royal Audiencia of the Principality of Catalonia on June 15th, 1767, ordering the above-named Don Antonio, administrator of the House of Portolá, to pay six hundred pounds annually "for support" to Doña María Francisca de Portolá, which she began receiving quarterly after September 1767, as appears in a great many records in the Balaguer registry. That it was a final separation is established by Doña María Francisca's later statement that she is the widow of Don Antonio de Portolá, "domiciled on the City of Barcelona upon the day of his death." [118]

Among a great many documents signed by the mother and daughter both jointly and individually, I shall mention some that seem to me especially interesting. We have learned already that Don Francisco de Portolá y Subirá spent the last days of his

---

116. Ibid., vol. 69 (1760-1761), fols. 19-20.
117. Ibid., notary Antonio Abril, vol. 197, fols. 108-110.
118. Ibid., notary Francisco Giró, vol. 225, fol. 190.

life in wardship, a victim of mental alienation; it will be recalled that the declaration of his incapacity was made at the instance of Doña Francisca de Portolá y de Valls.[119]

Don Francisco de Portolá had sold the third part of the Castle and Lordship of Margalef to Doña Francisca de Rubí, a widow of Fivaller, and to her son Don Juan. This sale was opposed by the Crown on the grounds that the said Lordship as subject to the Royal House. In consequence of a sentence passed down on January 10th and April 22nd, 1743, Doña María Francisca de Portolá y Valls y de Rubalcava was to pay to Don Juan de Fivaller y Rubí the sum of two thousand three hundred Barcelona pounds, the amount amerced of Don Francisco de Portolá for the sale. He left as his guarantor Doña Gertrudis de Rubies y de Gay, widow of Don Ignacio de Rubies in the town of Cubells, Don Antonio de Rubies y de Gay signing as her empowered attorney.[120]

Another document which I shall mention is the annulment of a marriage agreement and bans between Doña María Francisca de Portolá y de Valls and Don José Boneu de la Villa de Calaf, the witnesses to which, the prior of the Dominican Convent and the Reverend Castells, declare and swear upon the Gospels that "they know and are able to state that, a marriage contract having been signed and the bans published, the said betrothal was dissolved by agreement upon both sides. And they say they know this because they are fully notified that said José Boneu sent a letter to said Doña Francisca, mother of the aforesaid Doña María Francisca, which this witness held in his hands, and in which he asked for the ring back which he had given the abovementioned Doña María Francisca at the time of contracting the said betrothal..." What the cause may have been for breaking off such an advanced relationship we do not know. All that is certain is that the annulment of a betrothal with a Boneu who might have become a Portolá took place on February 15th, 1752, six days before the wedding with Don Antonio Domingo de Rubalcava.[121]

Don Antonio Domingo de Portolá y Rubalcava must have died at Barcelona before April 22nd, 1775, the date upon which

---

119. Ibid., notary Rosinyats, fol. 32 (1743).
120. Ibid., notary Sociats, vol. 162, fol. 30.
121. Ibid., notary José Plá, vol. 85, fol. 24.

Doña María Francisca de Rubalcava y de Valls, his widow, redeems quit-rents from Don Gaspar de Portolá y de Rovira to the amount of 3,700 pounds which she had received from her uncle, who was then a lieutenant colonel attached to the army staff of Barcelona. Not having the money with which to pay him, she gives him six pieces of land in the sections of Vilanova and Huerta de Amunt, upon a contract of redemption.[122] On the same date in 1775 she has ceased to receive the amount adjudged to be paid by her husband by the decision of the Royal Audiencia of the Principality of Catalonia referred to above.[123]

Again, on February 11th, 1783, Doña María Francisca and her daughter Doña María Josefa together with her husband Don Antonio de Vilallonga sell the so-called Rubalcava Tower at San Vicente de Sarriá in Barcelona for the amount of 7,668 pounds.[124]

Doña María Francisca died at Balaguer on November 7th, 1807, and was interred in the Convent of Santo Domingo in the Portolá family chapel. Her burial entry in the register calls her Baroness of Castellnou de Monsech, widow of Don Antonio de Portolá y Rubalcava, and daughter of Don Antonio de Portolá and Doña Francisca de Portolá y de Valls.[125] She was seventy-five years of age and had made her will on February 16th, 1807, before the notary Armengol Sala y Doménech. The will ordered two thousand Masses to be celebrated for her, divided between the Dominican and Franciscan convents and the parish church, and for the purchase in perpetuity of three indulgences for herself and her husband. She further elects to be buried in the family chapel, orders three hundred pounds bestowed in a single payment upon each of her grandchildren and great-grandchildren, and names her grandson Antonio heir and her dearest daughter as usufructuary. The will, left sealed in the possession of the above-named notary, was opened and read at the request of the Baron of Castellnou de Monsech, Don Antonio (de Portolá) y de Vilallonga, husband of deceased's daughter Doña María Josefa, on November 7th, 1807, in the precincts of the Portolá house at Balaguer.[126]

---

122. Ibid., notary Sociats, vol. 171, fols. 37-39.
123. Ibid., vol. 184, fol. 7.
124. Ibid., vol. 180, fol. 22.
125. Balaguer Parish Archive, Deaths, fol. 30.
126. Balaguer Notarial Archive, notary Armengol y Sala (1807), fol. 136.

VII. *Doña María Josefa de Portolá y Rubalcava, married to Don Antonio (de Portolá) de Vilallonga y Manresa.*

*Issue: Doña María, Don Antonio, Don Buenaventura, Doña Francisca.*

Doña Francisca de Portolá y de Valls, widow of Don Antonio de Portolá, had been left the sole beneficiary of the possessions of the House of Portolá, while her daughter Doña María Francisca was the universal heiress to the estate. Doña María Francisca's and Don Antonio de Rubalcava's daughter became heiress in her turn to the Portolá inheritance, in the same circumstances as had her mother, the only difference between the two situations being that Doña María Josefa de Portolá y de Rubalcava was not under the guardianship of anyone other than her own mother and grandmother.

Doña María Josefa was thirteen years old when her grandmother Doña Francisca died and left as heiress her own daughter Doña María Francisca, who in turn left as her own heir—as has been said—her grandson Don Antonio, but as usufructuary her daughter Doña María Josefa.

For this reason—the momentary heir to the titles of the House of Portolá, Doña María Josefa, being a female—the entailment created by Don Gaspar de Portolá y de Pont was once again automatically invoked.  On March 13, 1779, the heiress, Doña María Josefa de Portolá y de Rubalcava, twenty-six years of age, daughter of Doña María Francisca de Portolá y de Valls, widow of Don Antonio Domingo de Portolá, de Rubalcava y Magarola, was wed in the Portolá residence upon the Plaza del Mercadal at Balaguer to the nobleman Don Antonio de Vilallonga y Manresa.  The groom had been baptized on January 24 th, 1754, in the Church of San Juan y San Pedro de las Abadesas, with the names Antonio, Narciso and José, and was therefore twenty-five years old; his parents were Don José de Vilallonga y de Sala, deceased, and Doña Josefa de Vilallonga de Manresa y de Alberti, now married to her second husband Don Cristóbal de Farnés, a captain of dragoons attached to the Gerona garrison.[127]  The bridegroom, who once again had to assume the name Portolá, was a lawyer admitted to the bar, and attorney-general and senior alderman of Balaguer.[128]

Earlier, on March 14th of that year, the marriage agreement had been drawn up before the notary Don Jaime Sanjuán of Barcelona, by the contracting parties; the terms themselves had been agreed upon at Balaguer on the 9th of that same month,[129] and are almost the same as those that had been agreed to between the bride's mother and father: Doña María Francisca names her daughter as her heir, and Don Antonio de Vilallonga brings to the marriage the sum of one thousand six hundred pounds, received by the mother and daughter on March 22nd of that year.[130]

From this marriage is born, on July 7th, 1781, a girl-child named MARÍA, Rosa, Antonia and Isabel, sponsored at the font by Don Antonio de Rubies y de Gay and Doña Francisca de Portolá y de Valls, in a baptismal ceremony on the 20th of that month in the church of Santa María at Balaguer, the infant being registered as the daughter of Don Antonio de Portolá y de Vilallonga and of Doña María Josefa de Portolá y de Vilallonga de Rubalcava y de Valls [sic].[131]

---

127.  Balaguer Parish Archive, Marriages (1779), fol. 169.
128.  Archivo Histórico Nacional, *Carlos III*, expediente 1.564.
129.  Balaguer Notarial Archive, notary Jacinto Rincón, vol. 298, fols. 74-75.
130.  Archivo Histórico Nacional, *Carlos III*, expediente 1.546.
131.  Balaguer Parish Archive, Baptisms (1760-1799), fol. 49.

The second child and first male offspring of this marriage was born and baptized on April 17th, 1784, son of Don Antonio de Portolá y de Vilallonga y Manresa and of Doña María Josefa de Portolá y Rubalcava, the godmother being Doña María Francisca de Portolá y de Rubalcava. The infant was christened Antonio, José, Francisco.[132]

Another male child was born and baptized on May 16th, 1788, and named Buenaventura, Antonio, and José, son of the nobleman Don Antonio de Portolá y Vilallonga and the noblewoman Doña María Josefa de Portolá y Rubalcava [sic]; "godfather was Brother Salvador Martorell y Subirana, belonging to the Order of St. Francis." [133]

Finally, on February 15, 1790, a daughter was born and once again sponsored by the grandmother Doña María Francisca de Portolá y Valls; named as child of Don Antonio de Vilallonga and Doña María Josefa de Portolá y Rubalcava [sic], she was christened Francisca, Antonia, and Gertrudis.[134]

Apparently none of these daughters survived. No documentary references to any of them are found after the baptisms, and no record of any of the four being confirmed.

Don Antonio de Portolá de Vilallonga y Manresa lived always at Balaguer woth his wife Doña María Josefa. The Portolá family fortunes and prestige, seriously damaged by wars, politics, and the negligence of some members of the family, had been going steadily downhill; bit by bit the family holdings shrank and debts mounted up. Eventually the male members were forced to seek, by means of careers in the army or the law, support both for themselves and for the family titles. At his death, Don Antonio de Portolá y de Vilallonga left an acknowledged indebtedness of thirteen thousand pounds, when he had brought only the sum of one thousand six hundred to his marriage.

King Charles IV bestowed on him the of Baron of Castellnou de Monsech, by a privilege signed at San Lorenzo del

132. Ibid., fol. 140.
133. Ibid. (1784-1800), fol. 75.
134. Ibid., fol. 116.

Escorial on November 13th, 1801.[135]   It was granted in response
to a proof of the nobility of the Portolás and Vilallongas and
of the existence of the title since time immemorial:

"...their predecessors have been in quiet and peaceful possession
of the title of Barons of Castellnou de Monsech, and have been held
and respected as such in the Principality without any denial or
opposition by any one whatsoever, they having meanwhile styled
themselves as proprietors with jurisdiction over other attached settlements, with a perpetual entail to the said Barony... Since you are
unable to present any receipt of baronage or several ancient documents to witness of the immemorial possession of the aforesaid
Barony, therefore you have petitioned Me to be pleased to grant
you by renewed favor the said title of Baron with the aforesaid
denomination of Castellnou de Monsech...; I have determined to
grant to you, your heirs and successors the title of Baron with the
denomination of Castellnou de Monsech, ...but with the understanding that by this grace conferred by these presents upon you and
your successors, neither you nor they are empowered to claim
or to acquire any manner of jurisdiction in the place, property or
estate held by you with the aforesaid title of Baron of Castellnou
de Monsech, other than that which you at present hold in dominion
over it." [136]

In his will, Don Antonio names has heir his own son Antonio, and in his stead if necessary Buenaventura, with his wife
Doña María Josefa remaining as usufructuary of the entire inheritance:

"...I desire the heir to pay for Buenaventura's studies toward
graduation if the latter should wish to take a degree, or in the opposite case to settle ten thousand pounds upon him; should he
become a soldier, he is to be endowed with three hundred pounds
annually until reaching the rank of captain; the same pension is to
be given if he enters the ecclesiastical state, until he shall obtain a
benefice or prebend."

Don Antonio de Portolá de Vilallonga y Manresa died at fifty-
three years of age, on the 10th of January, 1807, in the city of
Balaguer, and was buried in the Cementery of Santa María.  By
the death register it appears that he was the son of Antonio de

135. Archivo de la Corona de Aragón, R. A. *Privilegiorum*, fol. 15.
136. Archivo Histórico Nacional, *Carlos III*, expediente 1.546.

Vilallonga and Josefa de Vilallonga y Manresa, that he was married to Josefa de Portolá y Rubalcava y de Valls, and that he had made his will on September 28th, 1799, before notary Sala of Balaguer.[137] Don Antonio de Vilallonga y Manresa's noble descent is proved both by his family names—Vilallonga, Manresa— and by the documents cited here,[138] among them notably a Brief of Nobility granted by King Ferdinand II of Aragón to Don Antonio de Manresa in the year 1484,[139] in a certified copy prepared by the archivist of the Crown of Aragon Don Francisco Xavier de Garma y Durán on August 29th, 1763.

Doña Josefa de Portolá, de Vilallonga y de Rubalcava's own entry in the register of deaths tells us she passed on on March 28th, 1825, as widow of Don Antonio de Vilallonga, aged 72 years, that she was Baroness of Castellnou, and that she had made her will before the notary Armengol Sala of Balaguer [140] on September 8th, 1815. This will names as her executors her sons and her daughter-in-law Doña Maria Luisa de Portolá y de Requena, appoints the place of burial, and orders a distribution of alms among the poor. As sole heir she names her eldest son, Don Antonio de Portolá y Vilallonga, and commands him to make an endowment upon her second son Don Buenaventura, leaving to the former's judgment the amount in money or property which can be given, which in any case will be less than the testatrix would have wished, "in view of the losses and damages suffered by my house and inheritance during the late destructive war with the French," *haguda consideració de les disminucions y desgracias que han patit ma Casa y Patrimoni durant la última destructora guerra amb los francesos.* She signs the document upon her sick bed, "in the second-storey room with a window facing the alley called *del Portalet del Segre,* in the residence which I own about the Plaza Mayor in the said City, today being the eighth of September and in the year from the Birth of Our Lord Jesus Christ one thousand eight hundred and fifteen." [141]

---

137. Balaguer Parish Archive, Deaths (1807), fol. 24.

138. Archivo de la Corona de Aragón, *Fernando II de Aragón.*

139. Archivo Histórico Nacional, *Carlos III,* expediente 1.546, pp. 129 and following.

140. Balaguer Parish Archive, Deaths, fol. 2.

141. Balaguer Notarial Archive, notary Armengol Sala y Domínguez, vol. 321, fols. 179 verso-180.

We shall be concerned with Don Antonio, the heir, in the next chapter, while here we shall review the career of the second son, named Don Buenaventura de Portolá y Vilallonga. Born in Balaguer, he studied for a baccalaureate and licentiate in law at the University of Cervera, and as a lewyer was named Constitutional Mayor of the city of Balaguer, March 20th, 1820. Later he rose to become Lord Mayor of the town of Curiel in Old Castile, Judge of Aínsa in Aragon, and finally Mayor of the town of Bisbal in Gerona, on February 20, 1828. [142, 143, 144] While in that last position, he became godfather of his nephew Don Antonio's second daughter.[145] He died at the age of 70 in Balaguer, a bachelor and intestate, and was buried in the Santa Maria Cemetery there, December 14, 1848.[146]

142. Balaguer Parish Archive, Deaths, fol. 362.
143. Balaguer Notarial Archive, ibid., (1821, 1827-1828), fol. 43 verso, 15-72.
144. Archivo Histórico Nacional, *Carlos III*, expediente 1.546.
145. Borrasá Parish records.
146. Balaguer Parish Archive, Deaths, fol. 362.

VIII.  *Don Antonio de Portolá y de Vilallonga,*
*married to Doña María Luisa de Requena y*
*Santisteban.*

*Issue: Don Antonio, Don Francisco, Doña*
*María Luisa, Don Buenaventura and Doña*
*María de la Encarnación.*

Don Antonio de Portolá y de Vilallonga succeeded to the
headship of the Portolá family as the first in the male line after
two generations of female heirs whose husbands had taken the
family name, in accordance with the entail established in a preceding century.  Don Antonio gave proof of his noble descent
upon his admission to the Royal *Maestranza* of Knighthood of
Ronda on May 20th, 1801, at the age of seventeen years.

"...I, Don Félix de Atienza, Salvatierra y Tavares, a Knight of the
Very Honorable Royal *Maestranza* of this City of Ronda, the Senior
Brother of which is His Serene Highness the *Infante* Don Pedro, as
Secretary *ad int.* by the decease of the proper holder of the office,

do hereby certify, that Don Antonio de Portolá y Vilallonga has been received as a member of this honorable royal Corps of Knighthood, with the approval of His Serene Highness the Senior Brother, and as such has had entered upon the master register the corresponding entry, upon the twelfth page, with this note: *Don Antonio de Portolá y de Vilallonga, a resident of the City of Balaguer in Catalonia, received May 20th. eighteen hundred and one.* In witness whereof and by order of Brigadier Don José Moctezuma y Roxas, Lieutenant of His Royal Highness, I do give these presents, signed by my own hand and sealed with the great seal of this Royal Corps, at Ronda, June twenty fifth eighteen hundred and one." [147]

Only eight days after the death of his father, his lady mother, Doña María Josefa, widow of Don Antonio de Portolá y de Vilallonga, "grants her whole power to the Nobleman Don Antonio de Portolá y de Vilallonga, Knight Member of the Very Honorable *Maestranza* of the City of Ronda and Baron of Castellnou de Monsech, her son and only heir..." [148] His title as Baron of Castellnou de Monsech was confirmed on May 21st, 1807, by a Royal Brief of Succession signed by King Charles IV in the Palace of Aranjuez.

"...THE KING. Don Antonio de Portolá y de Vilallonga, Baron of Castellnou de Monsech: By your letter of February twenty-fourth of this year, addressed by you to my Council of the Chamber, in compliance with my determination expressed in a Royal Order of October the nineteenth, one thousand seven hundred ninety seven, in which I saw fit to command that every one holding a baronage should upon a vacancy therein resort to the Secretaries of the Chamber to obtain a Brief of Succession, I have learned of the decease of your father Don Antonio de Portolá y Vilallonga, former Baron of Castellnou de Monsech, and that you have succeeded to him in the said baronage and his universal inheritance. I doubt not that you shall serve me with the same loyalty and love as your aforesaid late father, and I thank you for your good will in offering to continue it, and shall hold the offer in mind for the purpose of favoring and rewarding you. And a record of this my Brief is to be taken in the General Accountancy Offices of Income and Expenditure of my Royal Exchequer within two months from this date, with the record of Income expressing the amount paid, without which measure I order that this shall be of no force and be not received nor complied with in any tribunal within or without the Court. Signed at Aranjuez, May twenty first, eighteen hundred seven.—I THE KING.—By

147. Archivo Histórico Nacional, *Carlos III*, expediente 1.546.
148. Balaguer Notarial Archive, notary Armengol Sala y Dominguez, vol. 318.

command of Our Lord King.    Royal duties, one hundred thirty one
*reales*, forteen *maravedís*, eight *tomines*.    Recorded in the account-
ancies general of income and expenditure of the royal exchequer:
in the former at folio 11, Aragon account of this year, it appears
that this party has satisfied the half-annate duty, eighteen thousand
seven hundred fifty maravedís for the reason expressed in this
Brief.    Madrid, June twenty fifth, eighteen hundred and seven." [149]

Later he initiated an application for the Royal and Distinguished Order of Charles III, which was granted after a presentation of the necessary proof, on April 26th, 1816: [150] after
which the Baron of Castellnou de Monsech, Beniure, Estorm,
San Esteban de la Sarga, Pradell and of the mark of La Fuliola,
Castellan of the towns of Claramunt and Montlleó in the Valley
of Ager and of Gerp, Member of the Maestranza of Knighthood
of Ronda, could also style himself a Knight of the Royal and
Distinguished Order of Charles III.

Following this generation, however, the heirs of the House
of Portolá cease to employ the title of Baron of Castellnou or
to observe the entail created in the will of the family's first
nobleman.

After the signing of a marriage agreement on July 8th, 1800,
before Don Tomás de Sancha y Prado at the capital city of
Madrid, Don Antonio contracted matrimony by proxies at Madrid and Balaguer, the bride being a native of the capital.    She
was named Doña María Luisa de Requena y Santisteban, was
six years older than the groom, and was the daughter of the
nobleman Don Francisco de Requena, Brigadier and Councillor
of the Council of the Indies, and of Doña María Luisa de Requena y Santisteban, a native of "the Province of Guayaquil in the
Americas."

To this pair, on July 12th, 1801, was born and baptized at
Balaguer the first child, named Antonio, Francisco de Paula,
and José, his godparents being Don Antonio de Portolá y de
Valls.[151]

The second male child was born December 21st, 1802, and
christened Francisco de Asís, Tomás, Buenaventura; godparents

149.  Archivo Corona de Aragón, *Privilegiorum*, fol. 404.
150.  Archivo Histórico Nacional, *Carlos III*, expediente 1.546.
151.  Balaguer Parish Archive, Baptisms (1801), fol. 77.

Don Buenaventura de Portolá y Vilallonga, the father's brother, and Doña Josefa de Portolá y Rubalcava, the grandmother.[152]

The first daughter of the Portolá—Requena marriage whom we know of was born on August 7th, 1804, and baptized on the 8th, with the names MARÍA, Luisa, Buenaventura, her sole godparent being Don Francisco de Requena, who was represented by Don Buenaventura de Portolá y de Vilallonga.[153]

Another male child was born and named BUENAVENTURA, Cristóbal, José, his godfather being Don Buenaventura de Portolá y de Vilallonga; from this baptismal entry, it appears that the maternal grandfather, Don Francisco de Requena, had become a Field Marshal. The child was baptized in the Church of Santa María on June 10th, 1806, and had been born in the Portolá House on the Plaza del Mercadal at Balaguer on the day before.[154]

There was one more daughter, named MARÍA de la Encarnación, the date of whose birth I have not learned.

Don Antonio and Don Francisco were confirmed on July 30th, 1804, Doña María Luisa and Don Buenaventura on July 28th, 1809.[155]    Again I have not come across María de la Encarnación's confirmation.

More will be told about Don Antonio de Portolá y de Requena, the heir, in the next chapter. The second son of the marriage, Don Francisco de Portolá y de Requena, lived at Balaguer, where he filled the office of town attorney, and married Doña Francisca Garcés, of Gerri. I have no information as to the existence of children of this marriage. Doña Francisca de Portolá y de Garcés died at 63 years of age on August 29th, 1870, having made her will before the Balaguer notary Don Bernardo Sala.[156]  Four months later her surviving husband, the Honorable Don Francisco de Portolá, 68 years of age, was to marry again, with Doña María Ana Puig, spinster, daughter of Don Juan Puig, a native of Pons, and of Doña María Escribá, a native of Balaguer. The wedding took place on December 31st, 1870, in the Church of the

152.  Ibid. (1800-1813), fol. 133.
153.  Ibid., fol. 211.
154.  Ibid., fol. 294.
155.  Ibid., Confirmations, fols. 51 verso, 59 and 60.
156.  Ibid., Deaths, fol. 220.

Don Buenaventura de Portolá and Rodeja, last Earl in direct
line, deceased in Figueras in 1944.
(Drawing by Eduardo Rodeja, lent by the author).

Holy Hospital in Balaguer city.[157]   Don Francisco de Portolá y Requena died on March 24th, 1874, 72 years of age, having made his will before the notary Manuel Quer, and without succession.[158]

Doña María Luisa de Portolá y de Requena had married a brother of the lady who was to become Don Francisco's second wife, a match which must have given rise to problems in the family, since there exists an order from Don Carlos, Prince of Spain, Captain-General of Catalonia, authorizing the marriage. It was celebrated in the Church of El Milagro at Balaguer on December 9th, 1813, the entry in the register declaring that Don Antonio de Puig Escrivá, of Pons, son of Don Juan Puig y Franquesa and Doña María Escrivá is espousing Doña Luisa de Portolá y de Requena de Balaguer, daughter of Don Antonio de Portolá y de Vilallonga, Baron of Castellonu de Monsech, Knight of the Royal and Distinguished Order of Charles III, and of Doña María Luisa de Portolá y de Requena y Santisteban, a native of the City of Guayaquil in the parish of the Americas.[159]   Their marriage agreement was drawn up before the Castelló de Farfaña notary Don Antonio Escrivá on October 9th, 1832.[160]   A daughter born of this marriage was named Luisa de Puig y de Portolá.[161]

The second daughter, whose birthdate and place we do not know, is known to have married the lawyer Don José Banquells, a native of La Guardia and resident of Balaguer, after a marriage agreement drawn up on December 31st, 1834, before the Zaragoza notary Don Joaquín Tomeo Villalba.

The son named Don Buenaventura de Portolá contracted marriage with Doña Teresa Alós de Balcells on October 6th, 1830.[162]   Contrary to the somewhat hasty opinion expressed by Don Domingo Carrobé in Father Sanahuja's *Historia de Balaguer*, the name of Alós clearly comes to be connected by blood with the Portolás. Given the importance of this point, I shall dwell further on it at the end of this chapter; besides clarifying matters, it will lead us to the last male descendant of the Balaguer branch of the Portolás.

---

157.  Ibid., Marriages (1870), fol. 339.
158.  Ibid., Deaths, fol. 291.
159.  Ibid., Marriages, fol. 140.
160.  Balaguer Notarial Archive, notary Raurés, vol. 404, fol. 70 verso.
161.  Ibid., notary Florejachs, vol. 412, fol. 130.
162.  Balaguer Parish Archive, Marriages, fol. 162.

Let us for the moment continue with the wedding of Don Buenaventura and Doña Teresa Alós de Balcells y Florejachs, as witnessed and sponsored by Don Vicente de Sangenís, a representative of the family whom the Portolás felt themselves closest to in the last years of their history in Balaguer. The matrimonial agreement between the contracting parties had been drawn up before the Balaguer notary Don Tomás Giró on December 30th, 1831, as Doña Teresa herself tells us in her will made at Figueras (Gerona).[163]

Doña María Luisa de Portolá de Requena y Santisteban died at Balaguer on February 4th, 1853, aged 75 years, having made her will before the notary Luis Florejachs, in terms similar to the will she had drawn up long before, in 1818.[164] Her last will, given under seal in the year 1852, named her oldest son Don Antonio as heir, and orders that the sum withheld reserved in his marriage agreement should be divided among her other children, who are named in order as follows: Don Francisco, Doña Luisa, Don Buenaventura and Doña María. To her grandchildren Don Luis de Portolá y Alós and Doña Luisa de Puig y Portolá she leaves twenty-five silver *duros* apiece.[165] The wording of the will conveys her grief over the Portolá family's altered circumstances, her great love and respect for her husband Don Antonio, and a rare sort of feminine sensitivity worthy of Doña María Luisa, great lady that she was.

Her husband Don Antonio de Portolá y de Vilallonga seems to have survived her by some years. Together with his sons, he presides over the liquidation of Portolá properties and their final departure from Balaguer, caused by the loss of family reputation brought on by new circumstances. The properties are sold off to Don Pablo de Veciana, a native of Tarragona, in order to pay off old family debts as well as the new ones incurred by trying to keep up a life-style which is being altered and left behind in Spain's normal course of development. In the end, Don Antonio de Portolá sells on a contract of redemption, to the businessman Don Juan Salat, on November 4th, 1852, the mezzanine and part of the main entrance of his residence on the Plaza Mercadal, for opering a shop.[166] Don Pablo de Ve-

---

163. Figueras Notarial Archive, notary Ramón de Pagés (1868).
164. Balaguer Notarial Archive, notary Luis Florejachs, vol. 412.
165. Ibid.
166. Ibid., vol. 411, fol. 259.

ciana buys, on contract of redemption, half of La Fulioleta, five hundred *jornales* in area.[167]   No doubt wishing to put an orderly finish to the family catastrophe, and under pressure from his sons, unable to take over the crushing debts, Don Antonio orders an inventory of the Portolá possessions, covering all his properties with the extent of each specified, its buildings and furnishings, including personal chattels and even the titles of the books in his library in the Balaguer house.   From this time onward, the selling off of the inheritance proceeds steadily, in orderly fashion, and with the heir's express permission.[168]

Let us now turn back to Don Buenaventura de Portolá y de Requena, who married Doña Teresa Alós de Balcells.   This member of the Alós clan was a daughter of Don Francisco Alós, a native of the town of Cubells, and Doña Luisa de Balcells, of Balaguer, who had been married on November 7th, 1807,[169] following a dispensation for consanguinity in the fourth degree and a timely authorization for the wedding to be celebrated in the Balcells house at Balaguer.   The offspring of this marriage were Doña Teresa Alós y Balcells, who was to marry Buenaventura de Portolá, Doña Ignacia Alós y Balcells, who became the wife of Ramón Balcells y Pocorull, and Don José Antonio Alós y Balcells, who married Doña Gertrudis de Berenguer; these last had four sons whom certain Balaguerans of mature age can still recall: Don Francisco Alós y de Berenguer (died in 1905), Don Manuel Alós y de Berenguer (died 1907), Don Luis Alós y de Berenguer (died also in 1907), and Don Calixto Alós y de Berenguer, who died in 1915 and was the last inhabitant of the Portolá House.   He is still remembered by many adults in Balaguer.[170]

Don Buenaventura de Portolá and Doña Teresa de Portolá y Alós left Balaguer and moved to the town of Borrasá close to Figueras in Gerona, of which he had been named a notary by a Royal Decree of 1833, as appears in the Figueras registry office. The young couple's move must have been made late in 1833 or in early 1834; he had taken possession of his notaryship at Borrasá by June 23, 1833, and he continued signing documents there until the 8th of January, 1872, on which date he fell grav-

---

167.  Ibid., notary Raurés, vol. 404, fols. 87-89 verso.
168.  Ibid., notary Armengol Sala, fols. 36 verso-61 verso.
169.  Balaguer Parish Archive, Marriages, fol. 350.
170.  Ibid., Deaths, fol. 154 verso.

ely ill. Don Buenaventura died on January 21st of that year at Borrasá.[171]   His wife, Doña Teresa de Alós y de Balcells, lived to be 81 years of age; her will was made at Figueras before the notary Don Ramón de Pagés on August 3, 1868, but she died January 25th, 1891.[172]

A great many children, of whom only two survived, were born of this marriage. The first-born was a girl-child named MARÍA DEL CARMEN, who entered the world at Balaguer in 1832 and died at Borrasá March 31, 1837.[173]

A second daughter, called MARÍA DOLORES, was born at Borrasá on April 1st, 1834, where she lived later, married to Don Juan Bonal y Pujol, a native of Terradas, of which marriage were born Don Joaquín, Don Buenaventura, Don José, Don Pedro, Don Luis, Doña Mercedes, Doña Loreto and Doña Cristina Bonal y de Portolá. The Bonal family is still living in Borrasá, and the eldest son of the line frequently occupies the family house of the Bonal y de Portolás.[174]

Another daughter of the Portolá-Alós marriage was named ANTONIA at her baptism on March 6th, 1836, sponsored by Don Francisco de Portolá y de Requena, resident of Balaguer, and Doña Antonio de Portolá y de Guinart, of Agullana (Gerona).[175] Afterwards a son was born, named LUIS, sponsored by Luis Antonio de Alós, of Balaguer, on May 1st, 1838.[176] This Luis died at Borrasá at the age of twenty-one,[177] and is the same Luis de Portolá y Alós to whom his grandmother left twenty-five silver *duros*. After him there come a son named MIGUEL on May 30th, 1840, another boy named JOAQUÍN on November 1, 1842, another named JUAN on February 12th, 1845, a girl named MARÍA CONCEPCIÓN on December 7th, 1847, and finally ILDEFONSO, in 1849.[178]   All of the children of this marriage died before reaching the age of confirmation, except for María Dolores, Antonia, and Juan, who were fifteen, thirteen, and four years old respectively when in

---

171.  Borrasá Parish Archive, Deaths, Book III, p. 61.
172.  Ibid., p. 154.
173.  Ibid., p. 84.
174.  Ibid., Baptisms, Book IV, last page.
175.  Ibid., Book V, p. 8.
176.  Ibid., p. 16.
177.  Ibid., Deaths, Book IV, p. 53.
178.  Ibid., Baptisms, Book V, pp. 23, 32, 54, 61.

1849 they were confirmed by the Bishop of Gerona, Don Floren-
cio Llorente, in the parish church of San Andrés at Borrasá.[179]

We have already learned of the marriage of the daughter
Doña María Dolores to Don Juan Bonal, with their numerous
offspring. With the death of the other daughter, Antonia, at an
unknown date, we only have left to follow the other surviving
child, named Don Juan de Portolá y Alós.

We have learned that he was a practicing physician for
some forty years in the city of Figueras, where at the age of
forty he married Doña Dolores Rodeja y Gay. From this marriage there sprang a male child, named "Buenaventura, Salvador, and José, legitimate and natural son of Don Juan de Portolá y Alós, native of Borrasá, and Doña Dolores Rodeja y Gay, of
this city of Figueras; the paternal grandparents being Don Buenaventura de Portolá y Requena, native of Balaguer (Lérida), and
Doña Teresa Alós y Balcells, native of Cubells (Lérida), both deceased; maternal grandparents Don Eduardo Rodeja y Nadal, a
native of Vilanant, and Doña Ana Gay y Boya a native and both
residents of this." The entry is dated November 4th, 1892.[180]
We shall speak a bit further of this Don Buenaventura de Portolá y Rodeja. Don Juan de Portolá y Alós died at the age of
sixty-nine in his Figueras house, 19 Calle de Avinyonet, now called
Calle de Pep Ventura, on November 2nd, 1914.[181] He is buried in
Figueras municipal cemetery next to his wife, who died in 1920.[182]

Don Buenaventura, the child of this marriage, bore his grandfather's name. He studied at the University of Barcelona, where
he took a degree in pharmacy and became well known among
his professors and companions for his great kindness and extraordinary knowledge of botany. He settled in the city of Figueras, and carried on his profession in the pharmacy located in
what was then the hospital, but was to be partly destroyed during the civil war. His kindly nature, his aristocratic descent
and his religious convictions led to his imprisonment for a period
of several months. During this time his pharmacy was so poorly
looked after that the upstairs room, a sort of pesonal retreat for
the pharmacist where all of the Portolá family documents and

179. Ibid., Confirmations, p. 46.
180. Figueras Civil Registry, Book 41, p. 64.
181. Ibid., Book 57, fol. 52, n.° 104.
182. Ibid., Book 62, p. 138.

papers of nobility as well as a great many valuable botanical books were kept, was totally destroyed by a fire, all of his personal treasures being lost in this odd blaze.

Here, then, let it be stated that Don Buenaventura de Portolá y Rodeja, known familiarly in Figueras as Don Venturita, was the last male descendant of the noble Portolás of Balaguer in direct line, and with him perished the family name of the House of Portolá, since he had remained unmarried. The sons born to Don Antonio and Doña María Luisa at Balaguer either had no children, or had only had daughters.

Don Buenaventura, sick, grief-stricken and feeble despite his not very advanced age, abandoned his pharmacy and sought a refuge with the honorable family of his lady mother, where he lived until his death on September 10th, 1944, in the town of Vilanant, on the estates of Don Eduardo Rodeja. He was buried in Figueras cemetery next to his parents.[183]

My most profound thanks go to the Señores de Rodeja, sons of the Ampurdanese historian Don Eduardo Rodeja, a faithful companion of the last Portolá's bitter hours. With his love for history, he was able to understand and to ease Don Buenaventura's grief. If I have spent pleasant hours in the old city of Figueras, capital of Upper Ampurdán, at the end of this genealogy which began at Artíes, continued at Balaguer and finishes at Agullans, it is above all thanks to the friendliness of the Ampurdanese, who treat their visitor with proper kindness, not overdone, and the same courtesy and respect which all still hold toward the last Don Buenaventura de Portolá.

---

183. Figueras Municipal Cemetery, division 3, niche 96, level 3.

IX. *Don Antonio de Portolá y Requena, married to Doña Antonia de Guinart.*
*Issue: Doña María Luisa, Doña Rosa and Doña Dolores.*

In the light of all that has been said above, the first Don Buenaventura's settling as a notary in Borrasá, a country settlement near Figueras, marks a point which must be further brought out. Just as the Portolá family had removed its roots from Artíes when the founder Don Gaspar de Portolá y Pont abandoned it in 1658 to settle at Balaguer, so now it became Ampurdanese upon the heir's taking up residence permanently at Agullana and the youngest son's move to Borrasá. After six generations of Portolás at Balaguer, with the changes undergone by all families, two of its sons left their native city, the hearth of their ancestors, and began a new existence, perhaps rather a new life, in new surroundings where they could once more achieve peace, respect and the regard of their fellows.

The Portolás must have had strong reasons for leaving Balaguer, where their family name had upheld, for many generations and as part of the small group of local aristocracy, the prestige of a house which produced honors and great deeds for its people and its country. But we have seen how economic difficulties had been sapping for years past at the family life, so that little by little it was necessary to turn to selling off more and more of the patrimony; and how the life led by the last Antonios had reduced the family's prestige, and how in the end the wars destroyed both prestige and the economic basis. The family responsibility fell upon the shoulders of the oldest son, and it is not surprising that once the inheritance had been mortgaged, there was no other way out than selling out and donations to cover the debts that were owed.

At twenty-three years of age, Don Antonio de Portolá y de Requena, lawyer, contracts matrimony woth Doña Antonia de Guinart y Pi, daughter of the nobleman Juan de Guinart, de Bruner y Pagés, Honorary Intendent of the Army, and Doña Rosa de Guinart y Pi, deceased—so reads the marriage record preserved in the parish church at the town of Agullana.[184] A marriage agreement between the parties was drawn up before the Figueras notary Don Miguel Sans y Oliva on July 10th, 1824.[185] Don Antonio was the first of the brothers to marry, and in moving to Agullana upon his marriage, he openly broke with the family policy of attempting to keep on at Balaguer, a decision which was also made by whatever sons Doña María Luisa and Doña María de la Encarnación may have had, and by Don Buenaventura, settling at Borrasá with an appointment as a notary.

The first child of the Portolá-Guinart marriage was christened María, Luisa, Ana at Agullana on July 30th., 1828, her godparents being Don Juan de Guinart and Doña María Luisa de Requena.[186]

On January 28th, 1830, the second daughter was born and baptized Rosa, Margarita, and Cristina, her sponsor being Don Buenaventura de Portolá y de Vilallonga, Mayor of the town of La Bisbal.[187]

And finally, April 19, 1833 saw the birth and baptism of the third and last offspring of the marriage, named María Dolores,

184. Agullana Parish Archive, Marriage, Book IV, fol. 50.
185. Balaguer Notarial Archive, notary Raurés, vol. 404, fol. 57.
186. Agullana Parish Archive, Baptisms, Book VI, fol. 25 verso.
187. Ibid., fol. 43 verso.

General view of the town of Castellnou de Montsec, with the fortified house and the chapel. The direct heirs had the title of «Baron of Castellnou de Montsec».

Margarita, and Francisca, godparents Don Francisco de Portolá, bachelor, native of Balaguer and Doña Margarita Guinart, widow of Buenaventura de Viñals of the town of Flassá.[188]

Don Antonio de Portolá y Requena no longer employed either the title of Baron of Castellnou or the right of succession granted to him by the Royal and Distinguished Order of Charles III. The presence of female children in the line of succession would have called forth the Portolá entailment created by the first of the family to reach the aristocracy, but there is no proof that any attempt in this direction was made, and of course the entail was connected to the baronage of Castellnou de Monsech.

Doña María Luisa de Portolá y Guinart lived at Agullana and at Figueras, where she wed Don Gerónimo Morell y Orlandís, a native of Palma (Balearic Islands), and died of pulmonary tuberculosis at the age of fifty-four, leaving no descendants.[189]

I should like to state that from this point onward, all of the information has been given to me personally by Don Ignacio Parellada, who is a worthy and enterprising figure, thoroughly attached to his family traditions, and a connection of the Portolá family, as the following will show.

Doña Rosa de Portolá y Guinart married Don Casimiro de Gomis, from which marriage there sprang a daughter named Doña Dolores de Gomis y Portolá, who married Don Luis Mariano Vidal but left no descendants; and a son, Don Luis de Gomis y Portolá, who married Doña Teresa de Pallejá y de Basa of the family of the marquesses of Monsolis, but also left no heirs. He died at Barcelona on January 6th, 1890.

This leaves the third daughter of Don Antonio, a lady named María Dolores, who contracted matrimony with Don José de Bach, a marriage from which sprang three sons, Francisco, Antonio, and Joaquín, who in turn married three Fontcuberta sisters. The marriage between Francisco de Bach y de Portolá and Dolores de Fontcuberta y de Dalmases of the house of the marquesses of Vilallonga produced no children. That between Don Joaquín de Bach y de Portolá and María Pilar de Fontcuberta y de Dalmases produced a son, Don José de Bach y de Fontcuberta who died in the Battle of Codo (Civil War. 1937) a

---

188. Ibid., fol. 78.
189. Figueras Civil Registry, Book 21, fol. 104.

brevet ensign in the Tercio of Nuestra Señora de Montserrat. Finally, from the marriage between Don Antonio de Bach y de Portolá and Doña María de Fontcuberta y de Dalmases were born four children, still living, named Don Mariano, Doña Antonia, Doña Dolores, and Doña Carmen de Bach y de Fontcuberta, who are in my opinion the heirs and successors of the House of Portolá.

Don Luis de Gomis y de Portolá's widow, Doña Teresa de Pallejá y de Basa, entered upon a second marriage with Don José Parellada y Faura, and the two became parents of the above-named Don Ignacio de Parellada, who conducted me through his Agullana residence, where, in an extremely fin-de-siècle chamber, I came across the arms of the houses of Gomis, Portolá, Pallejá and Basa, and from whom I have obtained the preceding information, which I have not attempted to check with official records, because of my informant's direct acquaintance with the facts and persons involved, most of which would be easily accessible to research. Some day, it may be, I shall decide again to take up the threads of what I here lay down as ended, though not necessarily completed.

Not everything was destroyed in the burning of the Portolá archives in the back room of Don Buenaventura's pharmacy at Figueras, for the most part records which had come to him from the widow of Don Luis de Gomis y de Portolá, the natural heir of Don Antonio de Portolá y de Requena. And time, God willing, may yet bring much to light to surprise and to instruct us about the family of the explorer and founder of California.

# CHAPTER I

Born in Balaguer (1717). - Childhood. - Military Service. - Nomination as second lieutenant of the Villaviciosa and Numancia regiment. Lieutenant of the same regiment and campaigns in Italy and Portugal. - Nomination as Captain of the «España» Dragoons Regiment. - Incorporation into the Viceroyalty of New Spain. - Nomination as Governor of the Californian Peninsula and Expatriation of the Jesuits. - The missionaries of Fray Junípero Serra. - Nomination as Commander-in-Chief of the Expedition into upper California. - Preparations and march through the Peninsula towards San Diego harbor.

The genealogy of the Portolá family of Balaguer, from its founder, that first Gaspar de Portolá y Pont who reached the ranks of the nobility in 1682 and established the entail of the Barony of Castellnou de Montsech, to the last descendant in the male line, named Buenaventura de Portolá y Rodeja, who died without successor in the city of Figueras, has been completely traced in the preceding section. There we have also documented the circumstances surrounding the birth of that other of the name, Don Gaspar de Portolá y de Rovira, he whom we might have styled "de las Californias".

For years we had hoped to come by specific documentary evidence for his birth in the city of Balaguer, which, for reasons developed below, seemed likely to have been his birthplace, but could not be seriously assumed as such until at last the document that is given below turned up.

Our Gaspar de Portolá's father, the holder of the title of Baron of Castellnou de Monsech, was Don Francisco de Portolá y Subirá, who had been previously espoused to Señora María Bardaxí y Lussan; of this marriage three children had been born, all of whom died, together with their mother, leaving Don Francisco a widower, some time before the year 1710. Don Francisco de Portolá afterward contracted marriage with Señora Teresa de Rovira y Sanispleda, herself a widow, in 1710 in

the city of Solsona.  Of this union there were a number of
children.

The lack of baptismal records for Don Francisco's and Doña Teresa's family has often been blamed upon his political
opinions, which were decidedly in favor of the Archduke Charles of Austria and against Philip the Fifth, and forced him to
stay out of Balaguer for long periods of time.  This may have
been the case, since we do know that his eldest son Antonio
was born at the monastery of San Cugat del Vallés, where the
parents were then staying under the protection of the wife's
uncle, Don Gaspar de Sanispleda, the prior of the monastery,
and also of her brother fray Francisco de Rovira, who had
officiated at the time their wedding took place in the city of
Solsona.[1]

The first fruit of this marriage, then, was born in a monastery, and there is no question that this was because his parents
were fleeing the horrors of war and Don Francisco de Portolá's
personal danger during the troops of Philip the Fifth's troops'
invasions of the terirtories of Balaguer and Lérida.  It stands
in Antonio's baptismal entry: his parents had been fleeing the
French, *"per haver-se retirat dels francesos."*  The record's date
is January 21st, 1712.

Later came a daughter whose name was Francisca and who
entered the convent of Santa Clara in Balaguer, taking the name
of Sister Rosa.  Her birth must have been in the year 1714, since,
she became a novice in 1730.  We do not know the place of
her birth, though the documents which mention her always
refer to her as "of Balaguer."

On October 2nd, 1716, a male son was born at Balaguer and
christened Antonio, as Father Sanahuja and the historian Domingo Carrobé have shown and as the records confirm for us.[2]
Remembering that the eldest son, the one born at San Cugat, was
also named Antonio, we must conclude that he had died before
the same name was used for the third child of the marriage.
The same entry shows that the Portolá family must already have
settled at Balaguer by the year 1716, and this seems reasonable,
since the harsh measures adopted by the victorious Philip the

---

1.  Archive, Solsona Cathedral, vol. II, fol. 314.
2.  Sanahuja, fray Pedro, *Don Gaspar de Portolá, gobernador y explorador
de la Alta California*, «Ilerda» n.º (1945), p. 71.

Fifth had actually not lasted very long or affected the Balaguer aristocracy except by removals from public office and heavy losses in property and possessions.

Afterward come the children named GASPAR, Francisco, Benita, Josefa, Benito, Ramona, and finally José. For all except the first two, we have records of their births at Balaguer, city of the Counts of Urgel, between 1720 and 1726, so that obviously only the period between 1717 and 1719 is available for the birth of GASPAR and Francisco.

The first born of the two was Gaspar de Portolá, since he is the first of the brothers named, at their confirmation at Balaguer by the bishop of Lérida, with Francisco afterward— a sure indication.[3] The ceremony was held when the brothers were about three and two years of age, respectively. Notice also that the name Gaspar, used repeatedly over three generations for the second sons of the House of Portolá, is again being employed in the same way since Gaspar de Portolá i de Rovira is the second living son of the marriage.

To clinch the question of the birthplace, I need only to present the following documentation from the Simancas General Archives, published here for the first time, in which the man himself declares that he is a native of Balaguer. The document, which is given in full later in this section, reads in part:

«Lieutenant Don Gaspar de Portolá, 46 years of age, a native of Balaguer in Catalonia, of robust health, status nobleman, unmarried...»

The statement could not be clearer; it is a declaration based on documents exhibited by the interested party and touching not only his quality of nobleman and bachelor status but also his birth and, as will be seen, his military services. Furthermore, since the document seems to have been drawn up in the year 1762, his age of 46 years would indicate that he had been born in 1716. Another document practically the same as the preceding comes from the Mexican archives through the courtesy of the Bancroft Library, University of California, Berkeley; dated July 1st, 1764, at the headquarters of the Numancia Regiment, it has all of the previous information and says that Don Gaspar de Portolá is 47 years of age, which would place his

---

3. Balaguer Parish Archive, Confirmations (1720), fol. 22.

birth at Balaguer in 1717. Now, if his brother Antonio was born in October 1716, he himself could not have been born before August of 1717.

The documents under discussion are military service records, and will be further used below. The other source which mentions a Balaguer birthplace is found in a book, *Cosas Viejas de Lérida*, published in 1893. The author, Agustín Prim y Tarragó, tells us in connection with the founding of the Hospicio (p. 32) that the will of "Don Gaspar de Portolá, a native of Balaguer," was signed at Lérida on May 29th, 1786. No doubt the author, who was the first to publish a full study of the charitable institutions of Lérida, had seen the very text of Portolá's will; his extensive account of its contents is the source to which all of us who have studied the constitution of these charitable foundations have had to turn, since the damage of the Civil War and the later conflagration in the Lérida notarial archives have destroyed the volumes of official registers which held not only the recording of Portolá's will but other records connected with his estate.[4]

We hold, therefore, that Don Gaspar de Portolá y de Rovira was born in Balaguer in 1717 or 1718 and received Confirmation in that city on June 9th, 1720.

We find him at Balaguer on four occasions later than this date. On April 23rd, 1733, Don Gaspar de Portolá and Doña Josefa de Portolá, of *Balaguer*, stand as godparents to the baptism of the child Gaspar, José, Jorge, son of José Samanta and María Samanta de Calaf.[5] On July 6th, 1734, he stood sponsor to the confirmation of his own brother, José de Portolá, child of Don Francisco and Doña Teresa de Portolá.[6] December 11th, 1734, as the nearest brother of Don Antonio de Portolá, he stands sponsor to the latter's first male child, given the names Mariano, Gaspar, Francisco, and José, the godparents being Don Gaspar de Portolá and Doña Mariagna Sulla.[7] And finally, in 1744, he sponsors the confirmation of José Farreny, son of the married couple Francisco Farreny and Theresa Trepat.[8]

4. PRIM Y TARRAGÓ, Agustín, *Cosas viejas de Lérida* (1893), p. 36.
5. Balaguer Parish Archive, Baptisms.
6. Ibid., Confirmations (1715-1779), fol. 56.
7. Ibid., Baptisms (1734-1760), fol. 10.
8. Ibid., Confirmations (1744), fol. 85.

El Th.e D.n Gaspar Posada de edad de 46.a. natural de Balaguer en Cathaluña, de Salud robusta, de Calidad Noble, Soltero, sus servicios y circunstancias las que se expresan y justifican por sus Papeles.

| Tiempo que empezò à servir los emplos | | | | Tiempo q.e ha servido y q.to en cada empleo. | | | |
|---|---|---|---|---|---|---|---|
| Empleos | dia | Mes | año | Empleos | años | mes | dias |
| De Alferez en los R.os de Drag. de Villaviciosa, yer. cia de Tum... | 31. | Julio | 1734. | de Alferez ......... | 8. | 8. | 26. |
| De Th.e de Drag. y de Gran en este eng. con antiga | 26. | oct.bre | 1743 | de Theniente ..... | 19. | 8. | 5. |
| Total hasta fin de Diciembre de 1762 ...... | | | | | 28 | 5 | 1 |

## Funcion en que se ha hallado.

Sitios de Demon, Cuneo, Fortona, y Valencia del Poò; Batallas de la Asama del Olmo (en la que fue herido) y de Plavencia, reencuentros del paso del Tanaro, y del Adone, y Campaña de Portugal.

G. M. L.g: 2486 - C. 31 - 16

## Informe del Coronel.

Desempeña lo que se le manda, y tiene Valor y Conducta.

paso d Capitan aumento en America

Service sheet of Gaspar de Portolá from his enrolment in the King's Service until his transfer to America. (Arch. Gral. Simancas).

By this last date, he was already a lieutenant of grenadiers in the Numancia Regiment, as will be seen when we turn to his military career. On February 4th, 1752, he is mentioned in the matrimonial contract involving his brother's heiress, Doña María Francisca de Portolá y de Valls, who declares that she enters into it with the consent both of her mother Doña Francisca de Portolá y de Valls and of her guardians, who, as we know and as stated in the document, were Don Pedro García de Arteaga, his wife Doña Josefa de Portolá (Gaspar de Portolá's sister), Señor Don José Tarré y de Subirá, and the girl's uncles Don José de Portolá and Don Gaspar de Portolá.[9]

Gaspar de Portolá is present in person at Balaguer on April 14th, 1756, being then a lieutenant of dragoons in the Numancia Regiment. On this date he acts as attorney for his brother José de Portolá, at that time an ensign of grenadiers in the Savoy Regiment. The matter is a lawsuit between these two and Doña Francisca de Valls, widow of Don Antonio de Portolá, and her daughter Doña María Francisca de Portolá de Rubalcava with her husband Don Antonio de Portolá de Rubalcava y Magarola. The record, drawn up at Balaguer, includes powers of attorney from Don José de Portolá to his brother Gaspar for the latter to represent him in this tangled lawsuit by joining in naming two persons to hear, arbitrate and impartially resolve all claims upon certain properties once belonging to their father Don Francisco de Portolá y de Subirá, to avoid on both sides the costs and delay likely to arise if the suit were heard in the Audiencia court in Barcelona; the arbitrators chosen were Rev. Dr. *utriusque legis* Don Gaspar Salvia and Don José Borrell.[10]

Meanwhile, on 30 August, 1742, Don Gaspar had been named guardian of his own father Don Francisco de Portolá y de Subirá, by reason of the latter's insanity, sharing the guardianship with Don Pedro and Don José Terré y de Subirá; he was stated to be absent from Balaguer as of this date.[11]

The final document which we have to discuss here is one of the most interesting and appealing ones, and at the same time one of the most important of all. This is his Military Service Record, which I was lucky enough to discover in the Archivo General de Simancas; I have already referred to it once above.

9.  Balaguer notarial Archive, Sales y Novell, vol. 64, fols. 170-180.
10.  Ibid., Sociats, vol. 149, fol. 82.
11.  Ibid., Rosinyach (1743), fol. 32.

In addition to Don Gaspar de Portolá's individual enlistment, it contains a series of data as to the number of years spent in his various ranks and positions, specifying the date upon which each was achieved.   Likewise here are recorded the services which he performed while in the army, especially all the military actions in which he took part.   At the end comes the evaluation of the Colonel of the Regiment, and a note as to Don Gaspar's departure to America as **Captain.**

It had long seemed obvious that the military career of Gaspar de Portolá y de Rovira, a man who rose to such heights in the history of American conquest and settlement, must have had some European background, in view of Spanish military activeness in the years between 1740 and 1760.   The constant military campaigns throughout the Mediterranean provinces on the Golfe du Lion, in the islands of Corsica and Sardinia, all over Italy and Portugal must surely, it seemed, have at some time involved the professional activity of our fellow-townsman.   By means of the documentation which I shall set forth here, we can reconstruct a number of years in the life of Don Gaspar de Portolá, years certainly not lacking in interest either in themselves or in the importance which they undoubtedly had in shaping his personal and professional character.   But first let us look at the text of this service record as a whole, before making some particular comments upon it:

Lieutenant Don Gaspar de Portolá, *46 years of age, native of Balaguer in Catalonia, robust health, status nobleman, unmarried; service performed and qualities are as expressed below and verified by his records.*

*Dates at which he began to serve in rank:*
    As Ensign in the Villaviciosa Regiment of Dragoons and in this Numancia Regiment, July 31st, 1734.

    As Lieutenant of Dragoons and Grenadiers in this regiment, his present one, April 26th, 1743.

*Length of time served in each rank:*
    As Ensign: 8 years—8 months—26 days.
    As Lieutenant: 19 years—8 months—5 days.

*Total to end of December 1762:*
    28 years—5 months—1 days.

*Actions in which present:*

Sieges of Demón, Cuneo, Tortona, Valencia on the Po; battles of Madona [Modena] on the Olmo (in which he was wounded) and Plasencia; skirmishes at the crossing of the Tanaro and the Tidone, and the Portuguese campaign.

*Report by the Colonel:*

He executes the orders given him, and possesses valor and conduct.»

At the end a note is added to the effect that he had "gone as Captain de Regimiento in America." [12]

Apart from the enlistment record which we referred to above as proving that he was born in Balaguer, it appears from this document he must have been born in 1717 or 1718 if forty-six years old in 1762 when his years of service as ensign and lieutenant were tallied—if we can assume this to be the date of the report.

The actions and battles in which he took part can be dated between 1744 and 1750. The action of Cuneo was fought between Charles Emmanuel, King of Sicily, and Spanish-French forces commanded by the Infante Don Felipe and the Prince de Conti, at the north-Italian city of that name. Valencia is a town upon the right bank of the river Po, and the Tanaro is one of its tributaries. The Battle of the River Tidone occurred on the 10th of August, 1746, and the battle of Piacenza on June 16th, 1746. The Portuguese campaigns took place later, in 1762, during the Seven Years' War: it would not be surprising if at that time he first came in contact with Lieutenant Fages and his Volunteers of Catalonia, somewhere in the south of our country, since they were also taking part in that difficult and indecisive campaign. Later they were to be under his command in California.

I do not think that we can draw any far-reaching conclusions from the report drawn up by the colonel of his regiment; to me it sounds like mere army routine. Nonetheless I would like to point out that when Portolá's superior states that "he executes the orders given him, and possesses valor and conduct," these stereotyped phrases were to be realized and find a factual projection in the Californian action. Fairly often, people have

---

12 Archivo General de Simancas, G. M. Legajo 2486, C. II - 16.

attempted to convert this bit of military jargon of 1762, this "executes orders given him," into a lack of personal initiative on Don Gaspar's part, when in fact the knowing how to obey the discharge of one's duty, and doing it with the degree of valor, straightforwardness and punctuality which has been laid down, are the worth and honor of the military. We will see excellent indications of how he was given a free hand to solve unforeseen problems according to his own skill and understanding, yet always under the written instructions that were issued to him. The courage that he demonstrated during these earlier years is sufficiently expressed by the wounds he received and the pains and privations he suffered. And we shall find plenty of further evidences as to his conduct, personal and professional, in the pages which follow.

Don Gaspar de Portola's commission as Ensign of the Villaviciosa Regiment was signed by the King at San Ildefonso de la Granja on the 31st of July, 1734, at which date he must have been 17 years of age. This document gives Don Gaspar's full name, and reads:

THE KING.

Forasmuch as I have named Don Gaspar de Portolá y de Rovira as Ensign of the Company of the Colonel, one of those in the Regiment of Dragoons to be raised under the name of Villaviciosa upon the offer of Don Juan Manuel de Semmanat y Oms, whom I have chosen as its Colonel...

The document is recorded at Barcelona on the 6th of October, 1734, where it is declared that Don Gaspar de Portolá is one of twenty men presenting themselves to make up part of this Villaviciosa Regiment.[13]

On April 23d, 1742, the Ensign of Dragoons in the Villaviciosa Regiment was transferred Ensign to the Numancia Regiment, and into Don Francisco Farrus's Company, an appointment signed by the King at Aranjuez.[14]

Portolá's next promotion comes at the hands of the Infante of Spain, Don Felipe, "Admiral-General of Spain and of the Indies and Generalissimo of the Arms of the King, my Lord and my Father, which are now ordered upon the Italian expedition..."

---

13. Bancroft Library, University of California, U.S.A., Portolá Papers, M-M 1811, Part II.
14. Ibid.

By this we learn that the Infante, in virtue of the powers he held, had named Ensign Don Gaspar de Portolá as Lieutenant of the Numancia Regiment in Don Juan José Pereda's Company on the twenty-fifth April 1743 at the Chamberí Government Barracks.[15] In view of what I have mentioned above about the Italian campaigns, this new documents shows us Don Gaspar de Portolá ready to leave for Italy in the Numancia Regiment as part of the Spanish army led by the Infante Felipe and the Prince de Conti; we have already learned of the actions and battles in which he took part during the campaign.

His return to Spain must surely have taken place at the beginning of the year 1749, since on the 20th of February of that year the King names him Lieutenant of the Numancia Regiment at Barcelona, where the appointment is recorded on the 28th of that same month.

From the above-mentioned service sheet covering the period from 1734 to 1762, and ending with the note that he is being transferred captain to America, we learn that he must have remained a lieutenant during these years. But on the first of July, 1764, His Majesty King Charles the Third issues the following commission as Captain, which I shall transcribe in full:

Don Carlos, by the Grace of God King of Castile, of Leon, of Aragon, of the Two Sicilies, of Jerusalem, Navarre, Granada, Toledo, Valencia, Galicia, Majorca, Seville, Sardinia, Cordova, Corsica, Murcia, Jaen, of the Algarves, Algiers, Gibraltar, the Canary Islands, of the Eastern and Western Indies, the Isles and Mainland of the Ocean Sea, Archduke of Austria, Duke of Burgundy, of Brabant and Milan, Count of Habsburg, of Flanders, Tyrol and Barcelona, Lord of Biscay and of Molina, etc.

Forasmuch as, considering the merit and services of you Don Gaspar de Portolá, Lieutenant of Grenadiers of the Numancia Regiment of Dragoons, I have determined to bestow upon you the command of a company in the new Regiment of Dragoons of Spain:

Therefore I command the Commandant-General of the Forces of the Realm of New Spain to issue the proper orders to set you in possession of the aforesaid Company, and to the Officers, Sergeants, Corporals and common Soldiers in it, that they recognize and respect you as their Captain, obeying the orders which you shall give them in my service by writing and by word without discussion or delay,

---

15.  Ibid.

and that both they and all other higher and lower commanders, officers and soldiers of my Armies observe and cause to be observed all privileges and perquisites due to you, for such is my will; and that the Officers of the Chests of my Royal Estate [Treasury Office] at Vera Cruz shall open the proper account for you, noting the fact at the foot of this Commissions, and shall pay you the salary and allowance specified by the Regulations, commencing from the day in which you take possession as shown by the first Review that shall be made of the sums to be expeded upon the forces of war in the aforesaid Realm, at such time and in such manner as shall be determined; the law of Half-Annate in no way applying to your position, which is purely a military one.  And a record of these presents shall be taken at the General Accountancy Offices of my Royal Estate and of my Indies Council.

Given at San Ildefonso, the thirty-first of July, one thousand seven hundred sixty four.

I THE KING.

Having had his commission recorded in the accountancy offices and by the Council of the Indies, Don Gaspar de Portolá proceeded to New Spain—Mexico—in order to take possession of the company granted him by the King, so that on the 19th of April, 1765, he had been entered upon the books of the Captaincy-General and with the Royal Tribunal of Accounts, according to the order of the Viceroy himself, the Marqués de Cruillas.[16]

At that period, the northern provinces of New Spain were in danger of being overturned by serious uprisings on the part of their native Indians, who had caused grave damage to the Missions located there, and had attacked the few other civilized outposts.  The areas inhabited by the Pimas, Seris, and Apaches—Indians of Sonora and Sinaloa—had come to hold centers of rebellion which must at all costs be broken up, if the work of years were not to be brought to naught.  The Jesuit Order had established rudimentary missionary centers there, the main cradles for the growth of civilization brought by Spain.  It was therefore urgently necessary that the zone should be completely pacified, and that the Interior Provinces of New Spain should be allowed to recover under military protection.  The expeditions undertaken in the course of past years had been mere punitive actions, producing only partial results, and sometimes none,

---

16.  Ibid.

since it was often necessary to abandon one danger zone that had been pacified in order to come to the aid of others where the battle was raging.

The presence of Visitor-General José de Gálvez in New Spain, and the replacement of the Viceroy, the Marquis de Cruillas, by another marquis, Don Carlos Francisco de Croix, began a new era, one fortunate to witness the qualities of these two great organizers, active and intelligent representatives of the King. After making great reforms in the government and economy of the Vicerealm of New Spain, Don José de Gálvez set out in person upon the imperative mission of pacifying the provinces of Sonora, Nueva Vizcaya, and New Mexico, those worst affected by the inroads of the Indians mentioned above.

The Visitor-General, claiming that the great cost of these expeditions would not fall upon the Royal Treasury, succeeded in collecting vast sums from individual contributions of the citizens and inhabitants of the provinces ruled by the Viceroy. His methods included even the spreading of fantastic and untrue stories about the fabulous wealth and beauty of the lands and peoples to which he was headed, and thus he managed to attract a great many greedy investors who hoped to recoup their share by profits in the lands to be won.

On the military side, he was able to count upon the forces set under the command of Col. Don Domingo de Elizondo, including dragoon regiments and, also, Don Pedro Fages and his Volunteers of Catalonia, in the company commanded by Captain Don Agustín de Callis. Most of these troops, including Gaspar de Portolá's company of dragoons, had marched as far as Tepic, near the west coast of Mexico, and were quartered there while waiting for the ships to take them north, at the moment when the Visitor-General called Don Gaspar to take up the position of Governor of Californias.

The campaign which had been planned out by the Visitor-General and the Marquis de Croix was so broadly conceived and elaborately worked out that it was said to be the most ambitious and best planned undertaking since the conquest of Mexico by Cortez. The Visitor-General set out from Mexico City in April, 1768, going via Guadalajara and Tepic to the harbor of San Blas, and thence crossing to Lower California, where he set up his headquarters at the mining camp of Santa Ana and commenced his acquaintance with the northern lands, their special needs and

customs, as well as completing the preparations for his Sonora
and Monterey expeditions.

Here Visitor-General Gálvez may have first met with the
newly-appointed Governor of the Peninsula of California, Don
Gaspar de Portolá. At San Blas The Royal Writ ordering the
conquest and securing of Spanish discoveries on the Upper California coast had just reached the Visitor-General one more
aspect of the grand campaigns that he had prepared, but a
conquest that was to crown the Visitor's fame, and provide the
opportunity for the colonization to be led by the Franciscans
under Fray Junípero Serra and by the Governor and Captain of
Dragoons Gaspar de Portolá y de Rovira.

Portolá himself had reached the Lower California peninsula
the year before, when he had taken up residence as governor at
the Presidio of Loreto, this being nearly the only outpost of civilization beside the missions, and therefore having the best advan-
tages for defense and administrative purposes. Portolá's appointment to the post in the year 1767 would seem on the face
of it to have been due to the Visitor-General's proceedings in
accordance with the secret instructions sent for the expulsion
of the Jesuits, a decree signed by the King on February 27th, 1767.

It was the Jesuit Order—the Company or Society of Jesus—
that held exclusive control over all the missions founded upon
the peninsula, and this upon the very remarkable terms of total
independence from the viceregal authorities, from whom the
Order received a contribution toward each one of the missions
established, but otherwise was granted total administrative responsibility over the territories thus occupied; the Jesuits' only
other duty was to meet the expenses of the military forces quartered at the Presidio of Loreto. Thus there can be no doubt that
these conditions, unique in the history of the settlement of New
Spain, required special attention in view of the expulsions decreed by the King. From the year 1697, when the first Lower
California mission was established, onward through the eighteenth century, the work the Jesuit missionaries had been of really
great importance, both in the number of missions established
and in the civilizing effect upon the natives; and even more
so upon the Sonora side of the Gulf, at least until the hostilities
arose there. The other colonizing activities included agricultures,
stock-raising and mining, contributing to a very respectable poli-
tical-social-economic development. The constant quarrels which

General view of the town of Ager, place where some members of the Portolá family settled down and where they had great properties. In the highest point of the town one can see the famous XI century Abbey, built on a Roman fortress.

Se continue lo llibre de les confirmats per lo S.or 25
I.m Señor Don Simeon de Guinda y Apeztegui Bisbe
de Urgell en 10 de Juny 1720 en S.t Salvador part
y part en Son Balasó en la Ciutat de Balaguer essent
Cange de Viari p.or de la Igl.a Collig.ta en S.ta Maria
de Balaguer lo R.nt Joseph Roger y Comissari del
S.t Offici

| Padrins | Confirmats | Pares | Mares |
|---|---|---|---|
| D.r Ramon Nogues | D. Joseph Nogues | D.r Joseph Nogues | D. Petronilla |
| D. Theresa Portola | D. Theresa Montaner | D. Gaspar Portola | D. Maria |
| D. Theresa Portola | D.na Theresa Nogues | D. Joseph Nogues | D. Petronilla |
| Anthon de Reuert | Ventura de Reuert | Joseph de Reuert | Theresa |
| Anthon de Reuert | fran.co Rubies | D.r Joseph Rubies | D.a Innes |
| D. Anthon Portola | Carlos de Reuert | Joseph de Reuert | Theresa |
| D. Anthon Portola | Joseph Tomsina | | |
| Ignasi May | Joseph Nadal | Vicens Nadal | fran.ca |
| Joseph auero | Joseph Gra | Pere Gra | Margarira |
| D. fermin Montaner | Miquel Valli | | |
| D.n fermin Montaner | D.r Gaspar Portola | D.r fran.co Portola | D.a Theresa |
| D.n fermin Montaner | D. fran.co Portola | D.n fran.co Portola | D.a Theresa |
| D. Caetano Berenguer | D.r fran.co Corco | D.r Anthon Corco | |
| Geroni Xifrer | Joseph Torra | Simo Torra | Antonia Torra |
| Geroni Xifrer | Pau farras | | |
| Geroni Xifrer | Joan | | |
| Margarida Mer | Theresa May | fran.co May | Theresa |
| Margarida Mer | Isabel farras | | |
| fran.ca Pla | Theresa May | | |

Confirmation Certificate of Gaspar de Portolá and of his brother Francisco in the Balaguer Parish in 1720.

the Jesuits had with the military stationed near their mission posts, the anti-Jesuit "legend" constantly chorused by 18th century politicians of liberal and Masonic stripe, the special conditions under which the Lower California missions functioned, and popular imagination, all gave rise to the belief that these missions must possess uncommon wealth and to tales of vast possessions of lands scarcely less imaginary than those sown with the trees of golden fruit.

In fact, the fifteen missions that the Jesuit order possessed in Lower California in 1768 were set in the midst of one of the most inhospitable and barren territories in the whole realm of New Spain, with rains almost non-existent, and natives difficult to civilize. Few were the riches that the missionaries had found, and great the abnegation and self-sacrifice that they could demonstrate, when Portolá and the Franciscan friars arrived to inventory and take over their temporal possessions: mission buildings many years old, with such scanty means of support that the Visitor-General himself immediately suppressed three of them as lacking even the minimum resources needed for missionary purposes.

However, the Spanish government was deeply engaged in the suppression of the Company of Jesus, and every means was sought to keep the Jesuit legend alive by playing upon the passions of greed, envy and ignorance, to the extent that even the Visitor-General, well-informed and knowing the situation at first hand, sees fit to blame the expelled Jesuits for the wretched state of the missions, of their inhabitants, and even of the country itself.

What was needed in 1767 was the presence at Loreto of a man and a military force capable of taking charge of the Jesuits' departure in the short time allowed, and seeing that it was done according to the intent of the Royal Order. And there is no doubt that it was foreseen that this order might unloose trouble throughout the Vicerealm in view of the great affection for the Fathers of the Company among all the people; especially it was to be feared that under the special circumstances in California, there might be a popular movement against their leaving and at the same time against the authority of the King. The instructions given to Portolá were quite concrete on this point, enjoining on him, besides various special details connected with the internal affairs of the Peninsula, to maintain that Province in obedience to the Sovereign, to keep it in peace, and to give and account of any occurrence of another sort.[17]

Such fears, felt throughout New Spain were what caused the order of expulsion to be kept secret, and to be conveyed to the superiors of the various convents only a few hours before they were to be forced to leave. The Visitor-General himself took a personal part in this action, and in putting down the demonstrations in favor of the Jesuits which the expulsion had caused at San Luis de Potosí and other places. At that time a proclamation was put forth that became notorious; in it the rebellious defenders of the Jesuits were told,

the vassals of the great Monarch who possesses the throne of Spain were born to be silent and obey, not to debate or discuss the affairs of Government.[18]

The reasons which led to Portolá's appointment as Governor of California, including his detachment from the dragoon forces being readied for the pacification campaign against the Seris Indians in Sonora, are not known to us; it is possible indeed that they were purely accidental. In any case, Don Gaspar set out in accordance with his orders for California, stopping with the soldiers under his command at San Blas.

At San Blas harbor lay the ships *San Carlos* and *San Antonio*, being outfitted for the expeditions by which Gálvez hoped to put down the Indian troubles. At Tepic nearby, where the troops of the new Governor of the Peninsula were quartered, Father Serra and his sixteen Franciscan missionaries from San Fernando College at Mexico City and from the Sierra Gorda were awaiting the completion of the same ships, one of which was to carry them across the Gulf to Lower California and the fifteen missions being abandoned by the Jesuits there.

The lack of ships was not allowed to affect Portolá's mission, the fulfillment of the Viceroy's command to carry out the Royal Decree of expulsion. Unaccompanied by the Franciscans, but with a total of fifty of his dragoon soldiers, Portolá set out by sea from San Blas. He was beaten back to port by the late-summer and autumn storms in the treacherous Gulf. The second attempt at a crossing in a small ship was successful, after

---

17. CARNER RIBALTA, J., *Els Catalans en la Descoberta i Colonització de California* (Mexico City: Ed. Bibl. Catalana).

18. HERNÁNDEZ SÁNCHEZ-BARBA, Mario, *La última expansión española en América* (Madrid: Instituto de Estudios Políticos, 1957), pp. 150-151.

a total of forty-four days at sea.   He landed at San José del Cabo on the thirtieth of November, so that he must have left San Blas on October 16th.

Portolá's arrival at the Cape, many miles from his intended destination of Loreto, provided a good start for his difficult mission, for the Jesuit priest in charge of Mission Santiago, close to the landing-place, came out to greet him and his men and accompany them to the Mission, where they could rest.   Father Türsch himself tells us that the Governor's reception was cold but correct, and that he observed the new leader of the Californias to be nervous and on edge.   Apparently Portolá's information about the state of mind of the Indians and Jesuits of the Peninsula had been totally misleading, and he had been expecting scarcely anything less than a real revolt.

"With tears in his eyes," we are told, the Governor conveyed the sad news of the expulsion to the missionary, and asked to be put in contact with his superiors.   Shortly afterward, Portolá and his soldiers began the first long march through Lower California, toward Loreto 150 leagues away.   Travelling with them was Captain Don Fernando de Rivera y Moncada, whom they had also met at Mission Santiago.   Concerning this march, on his arrival at Loreto, Portolá was to write:

> ...I regard the uniform worn by the California Buff-coat Company as extremely useful; our Soldiers [his dragoons] can't continue to wear the uniform they do now, for our first excursion abroad has just left everyone stripped of it—I more than anyone reached here torn and scratched to pieces by the terrible Thorn-trees [cactus] along these same trails in this Country... Certainly, Sir, a man must have more Cowherd than Soldier in him in order to serve in this land... Today I have despatched for Matanchel harbor the ship *Loretana* that belonged to the Jesuits; I am conducting an inspection and review of the Presidio Company here.[19]

Once at Loreto, he ordered the rector of the Mission there to write to the Jesuit superior living at Mission Guadalupe to be so kind as to come to Loreto Presidio, and at the same time to inform the rest of his missionaries all over the country of the Royal Order of Expulsion.   The arrival of the superior of the Company of Jesus, and the notifying of the rest, were handled by Portolá with a correctness and courtesy which, together with

---

19.   Mexico, Archivo General de la Nación, ramo de Californias, t. 76.

the Governor's other kindnesses and his decision that the planned
drastic measures against the Company were unneeded, won him
the gratitude of everyone involved.  This really generous procedure on his part calls forth the following phrases from the Jesuits' chronicler Father Ducrue:

> This Officer of the King arrived full of false prejudice against
> the Company caused by ridiculous accusations.  But then he saw the
> truth about California, and how false these slanders had been.  He
> never ceased to deplore the disagreeableness of his orders, which
> notwithstanding he fulfilled in every detail, yet with every kindness,
> and sympathy for ourselves.  And though never able to disregard
> these orders, he made plain the embarrassment they caused him.  For
> these causes, we must feel be grateful to this Catholic gentleman and
> considerate judge, who lightened our sufferings with his compas-
> sion...  The Governor not only treated us with all kindness ordered
> by the King, but supplied us most generously with everything needed
> for the Voyage... bewailing the fact that his position required him
> to carry out the order of expulsion.[20]

There can, I think, be no finer praise than this for the figure
of Don Gaspar de Portolá, nor any doubt that he carried out
the order for the expulsion of the Company with the highest
sense of responsibility.  Father Omer Englebert is right in calling him the "splendid Portolá".[21]

The departure of the Jesuits took place on the 4th of February, 1768, and thanks to favorable winds, within a few days
of sailing they had reached Matanchel, next door to where the
new port of San Blas was rising.  The unexpectedness of Portolá's arrival, and the expulsion of the Jesuits, had left the missions
unmanned by ministers, and without supervision for their lands,
schools, and socializing functions.  The Governor had no recourse but to appoint local military personnel to take temporary
control and run them—a control which continued on this unsat-
isfactory basis even after the Franciscans had arrived.  This
type of administration—during the few months which fortunately were as long as it lasted—proved so calamitous that the
scandalous plundering of property, slaughter of cattle, and other
despoiling reached an extreme which caused Visitor-General Gálvez in person to remove the administrators from the posts given

20.  BURRUS, Ernest J., S. J., *Ducrue's Account of the Expulsion of the Jesuits
from Lower California* (Jesuit Historical Institute), 1967, p. 68.
21.  ENGLEBERT, Omer, *Fray Junípero Serra* (Mexico City: Gandesa, 1967),
p. 112.

them by the Governor, and to turn control of the missions' worldly goods back to the missionary priests.[22]

By this time, the missionaries on the scene were Father Serra and his Franciscans. Their attempts to send their own advance representatives across the Gulf had been repeatedly frustrated, first by the storms, and then by a government order rescinding their assignment to the California missionary field. Serra, on receiving the news of this setback, had been forced to disembark in haste from the ship which he had just boarded with Portolá in order to make the crossing in October. The change of assignment was finally reversed after a successful appeal to the Visitor-General and the Viceroy, and with the arrival of the ship bringing the expelled Jesuits, the six months' delay characterized by one of Serra's group as "plaguy" came to an end. The new missionaries set sail for Loreto and landed at the harbor there on Good Friday, April 1, 1768, to be "greeted by the Governor" —Portolá—"and all the other officers and inhabitants, with every sign of satisfaction and pleasure." [23]

Here, apparently, Portolá's assigned task was about to end. In reality, unknown to anyone, the lucky chance of his being ordered to Lower California was to become the start of a greater undertaking and wider and nobler purposes.

What exactly Visitor-General Gálvez's plans for Upper California ad been at the time in 1767 when he named Portolá governor of the Peninsula and chose Serra to take over the mission properties left by the Jesuits is difficult to say. When he left Mexico City for San Blas on the 9 th of April, 1768, a royal writ ordering the governor appointed for California to be placed on the alert for possible intrusions by Russian explorers was already on the way from Madrid. This document, which Gálvez was to use and to cite repeatedly in developing and defending his own plans for the exploration and settlement of Upper California, was brought to him by special courier on his road westward, and provided the occasion for a council of officers which he convoked on reaching the new harbor and shipyard at San Blas. There it was decided that ships should be sent with troops

22. Barcelona, Biblioteca Central, Noticias de la Península de California, Ms., p. 80.
23. GEIGER, Maynard J., O.F.M., «The Arrival of the Franciscans in the Californias-1769-1769, According to the Version of Fray Juan Crespí, O.F.M.,» The Americas, VIII (1951), p. 215.

to found a military post at te harbor of Monterey, reinforced, if at all possible, by an overland expedition that would redezvous with them. The decision as to the practicality of the land expedition, as well as the final dispatching of the ships, is left to the Visitor-General himself, whose further journey over to the Lower California peninsula is spoken of as already decided on.[24]

Bearing what he interpreted as his new instructions, Gálvez reached the other side of the gulf and set foot in Lower California on the 6th of July, 1768, where, installing himself in the mining camp of Santa Ana about a hundred Leagues south of Loreto, he proceeded to set in motion all the preparations for the expedition to the north. So swiftly did all his projects unfold that he sought, during his journey, to provide for the establishment of a school for seamen and the building of a city next to La Paz harbor, sent off dozens of letters on all sorts of subjects, and while not neglecting his main purpose—the Sonora campaign—organized the settlement of Monterey down to the last detail.

Father Serra is called in for consultation, and from this time onward will have no rest from their joint planning of mission station for the new territories. Ten new missions are foreseen as founded between San Diego and Monterey, with six others between Santa María, at the moment the northernmost of Lower California, and San Diego Bay. One ought first to be founded at San Diego, named Mission San Diego, another at Monterey, to be named San Carlos Borromeo, and a third on the Santa Barbara Channel, named San Buenaventura. The rest will be granted as time goes on. (Though the fact was not foreseen at the time, many of these were founded with the Franciscans first sent to the Lower California missions, after they had been replaced by missionaries of the Dominican order).

Portolá is called in, and after a general study of the status of the Peninsula, Gálvez lays before him the plan for the occupation. First, the expeditions are to be double, one by sea and the other overland, the former locating the harbors and carrying the necessary material for a settlement, while the land forces are to survey the country and provide the settlers for the Presidios to be established at the two harbors of San Diego and Monterey.

---

24. Treutlein, Theodore E., *San Francisco Bay: Discovery and Colonization, 1769-1776* (San Francisco, 1968), pp. 1-8, gives the best documentation and account of the events leading up to Gálvez' arrival and council at San Blas.

Don Gaspar de Portolá is to be named Commander in Chief of the land expedition, as Governor of all the Californias.

The veteran Captain Fernando de Rivera y Moncada is called upon to be the Expedition's second commander, and is ordered by Gálvez to get quickly together all the horses, mules, cattle, equipment, weapons, provisions and supplies that will be needed. To find them, Rivera turns to the Missions, and before long strips them of most of the contents of their stables, which is to say their most valuable possessions. A receipt is left at each mission for what has been taken, since by the Visitor-General's order it is to be replaced immediately.[25]

The ships "San Carlos" and "San Antonio" are to be provisioned with everything needed for the Presidios and missions to be founded; their normal crew of sailors is to be increased by twenty-five soldiers, the so-called Volunteers of Catalonia, who have come over from Sonora under the command of Lt. Pedro Fage. Carner-Ribalta, in his book *Els catalans en la descoberta i colonització de Califòrnia,* provides a full study of Catalonian participation in the California enterprise of colonization, noting that here for the first time an expeditionary body under the name of "Free Company of Volunteers of Catalonia" figures in a Spanish conquest. The company's complement was of twenty-five men commanded by Lt. Don Pedro Fages, an illustrious Leridan and native of Guissona. This is not the place to examine the circumstances which for so long forbade Catalan participation as such in America, though certainly those individuals who were active in the colonies had to do so by enrolling under false names in the Indies companies of Seville and Cadiz, until the time that the prohibition was lifted.

That Pedro Fages did indeed command a company of Catalan Volunteers is beyond all doubt, since we have seen and shall see "the Catalans" referred to very frequently as taking part in the Expedition. And it is also certain that this Company was to be so stricken by the scurvy that of the twenty-five who embarked at San Blas for the journey to San Diego, only six were able to take up the march north with Governor Portolá, and of those who stayed behind ill at San Diego, thirteen died. Carner-Ribalta is especially concerned to give the correct form

---

25. Seville. Archivo General de Indias, Audiencia de Guadalajara 417, instructions placing Rivera under Portolá's orders and naming him second in command of the Expedition

of the Catalan names, which always appear in the documents of
the period in Castilianized forms; though we find some errors
in his lists like the name of Captain Rivera, who was born in
Celaya, Mexico, or that of Surgeon Prat, whom Fray Junípero
Serra calls a Frenchman.

And together with this troop of Volunteers of Catalonia,
such soldiers as seemed proper were to be chosen from the Loreto
Presidio company.

The total distance covered by the land expedition was to
prove to be some seven hundred kilometers, counting from San
Diego onward, in addition to another six hundred kilometers
separating that position from the last mission, Santa María in
lower California.  To this add the journey up through the entire
Lower California peninsula, which the troops had to traverse
in order to reach their jumping-off place at Vellicatá, just beyond
Santa María.

With the preparations all made for the march—with written
orders issued to the commanders of the packets "San Carlos"
and "San Antonio," with the officers named for the assigments
which would arise in the course of the Expedition, with the
objects to be achieved spelled out down to the least detail, with
the troops, the supplies, and the provisions all chosen, and the
various tools and utensils assembled that were need for establishing the Presidios, as well as all the Franciscan property for founding the missions—everyone was awaiting the order to set forth.
Don Gaspar de Portolá, as Governor and Expedition Commander,
received a memorandum of instruction which will be described
when the time comes; in it were set forth the immediate reasons
for this march toward upper California, as well as the most
minute instructions upon the manner of carrying it out.

But first, before we follow the Expedition in its way, let
us pause a moment to consider the true reason for the order
for the occupation of Monterey.  And, together with this, let
us quickly review the history of these "famous", and unknown,
harbors.

Until the 18th century, the Spanish presence in the Pacific
Ocean, or South Sea as it was then called, was so unquestioned
that in could be regarded as a private lake.  The sea-trade between the Philippines and New Spain, and the expeditions sent
out along the coast of California for geographical rather than

Uniform of the «buffcoat soldiers» native skilled horsemen,
great warriors and had walkers. They came from different
military detatchments of the territories of New Spain.

expansive purposes, provided the only ships that sailed the Ocean Sea. . And although, by the time the seventeenth century was on its way, there were challenges to Spain's right to a complete monopoly rule over those waters, Spanish power was so great, and other nations' forces and interests at stake so small, that these political debates were scarcely able to cross the threshold of reality.

With the coming of the eighteenth century, the radical changes and developments in the balance of power, with the decline of Spanish influence and the exigencies of the commercial expansion of the European nations, gave rise to a series of enterprises, more or less tolerated by Spain, aimed at the establishment of "factories," ports of call, and commercial stations on what to that time had been regarded as Spanish South Sea shores.

The English penetration into the northern Pacific was apparently limited to the desire of setting up trading posts in order to begin trafficking with the natives for furs. The first point of contact was to be the harbor of San Lorenzo de Nootka, discovered and named by the Spaniard Juan Pérez on August 9th, 1774. The physical occupation of the place and the diplomatic consequences brought about by the seizure ot the British company's representative were, later on, to end in the near-total abandonment of the harbor ty the Spanish.[26]

As for the Russians, once they had reached the end of their eager expansion in the wake of their Siberian explorations and settlements, they were bound to impinge upon the Pacific and, only a short distance away, the shores to the north of the land known as California. Russian expeditions under Behring pointed the way to the establishment of a colony on these Pacific shores, a way repeatedly followed by other explorers who, however, never achieved any positive results. Nonetheless, Spain's ambassadors at St. Petersburg sent continual reports to the Spanish Crown about Catherine of Russia's designs, and the consequences which the Russian landings might entail for Spanish prestige and the safety of the Philippines trade.

The Crown envisaged the creation of ports of refuge, harbors to serve as a protection for the Philippine galleons, for the construction of Pacific fleets, and in addition as commercial centers.

---

26. BARREIRO, R., *El primer encuentro entre españoles y rusos en América,* «Revista General de la Marina», CLXII (1962).

9

Presidios, schools of navigation, and so forth. But the fact that
the ambassadorial reports from Russia insisted on the necessity
of taking formal possession up as far as 47° latitude at the least,
and the difficulties which arose in New Spain, including Gálvez'
mental illness, were to limit these projects to the occupation
of the California harbors and the improvement of San Blas
as a naval base.

In time past, Juan Rodríguez Cabrillo had coasted the California shores as far as what was later known as Cape Mendocino.
From the year 1565 onward, the pilots of the Phillipine galleys
had carried out summary reconnaisances, and later Carmeñón,
Arteaga, Vizcaíno, and even the Englishman Drake had explored
and partially surveyed the Pacific and the coasts of America.
But it was Vizcaíno who in the years 1596 and 1602 led genuine
exploring expeditions along the coasts, expeditions inspired as
much by the desire of geographic knowledge and the call of the
far horizon as by the wish to establish bases in order to hold
the lands discovered.

With a good-sized squadron under his command, and pro-
mises of rewards and status, Vizcaíno achieved an historic feat
that made known under their present names the islands of Santa
Catalina and San Clemente, the Santa Barbara Channel, San Diego harbor, Point Concepción, the Carmel River, Point Pinos, and,
next to these last, Monterey Bay, so christened in honor of the
Viceroy, Don Gaspar de Acebedo y de Zúñiga, Count of Monterrey. The description which Vizcaíno, carried away by a deliberate exercise of the imagination in hopes of honor and rewards,
gave of this harbor was the direct cause of the failure of the
first land expedition led by Gaspar de Portolá.

One hundred and sixty-five years after the discovery of Monterey Bay, the Spanish sovereign Charles the Third dictates the
order leading to the occupying and founding of a Presidio and a
Mission at Monterey and at San Diego, in order to oppose the
claims of Russian expansion by a vigorous act. The *Historical
Journal* of Miguel Costansó opens with a very firm statement of
the reasons:

The High Government of Spain being informed of the repeated
Attempts of a Foreign Nation upon the Northern Coasts of California
with views nowise well-intentioned toward our Monarchy and its
interests, the King commanded the Marquis de Croix, his Viceroy

and Captain-general of New Spain, to initiate effective measures to protect [that] part of his Dominions against any Invasion or Attack.[27]

We have already seen how this Royal Order overtook Gálvez on his way to San Blas Harbor, and we have learned of the preparations afoot in the Lower California Peninsula to carry it out successfully.  Gálvez was able to count upon Father Serra and Portolá, who it seemed had "come to the south of California only in order to discover Upper California." [28]  The first phase of the Expedition had now been fully organized and the trailbreaker Captain Rivera was setting out from the Missions with his "Buffcoat Soldiers" (those belonging to the Loreto Presidio), the stock he had collected, trusted Indian bowmen, and supplies for the long marches awaiting them ahead.

Governor Portolá and Fray Junípero Serra were to follow soon behind him, reaching the frontier at Mission Santa María, and from there onward following in his footsteps as the second section of the land expedition toward the Harbor of San Diego, the first stage in the whole expedition to Monterey.

Rivera, on reaching Santa María with his large herd of cattle, found himself forced to search for a place richer in pasturage; having ridden some twelve leagues farther north, he found it at a point called Vellicatá, where he set up camp.   Don Fernando had left the Santa Ana mining camp in September, 1768, and was at Vellicatá in February, 1769.  Leaving the cattle and some of the men here, he set out on March 24th for San Diego, where he arrived on the 14th of May.  Completing this journey of fifty-two days with him were Father Crespí, twenty-five buffcoat soldiers, three muleteers, a junior-grade sailing-master, and a band of Indians serving as trail-makers, muleteers' helpers, and for other labor; they bore bows and arrows.  Total, some fifty men, allowing for desertions among the Indians.  Let us look at the description that Costansó gives of the buffcoat soldiers:

The Soldiers of the Californias Presidio, of whom equity and fairness require us to own that they labored endlessly in this Exped-ition, employ two kinds of arms, offensive and defensive: The de-fensive ones are Buffocat and Targe; the first of these, whose cut is similar to a sleeveless Coat, is made of six or seven plies of white

27. Madrid, Museo Naval, Colección Navarrete, Ms., California, Historia y Viajes, t. I, n.º 3 (Also printed, Mexico, 1770).
28. GEIGER, Maynard, O.F.M., *Palou's Life of Fray Junípero Serra* (Washington, D. C, 1955).

worked deerskin, impenetrable to Indian arrows unless shot from
very near by. The targe consists of two facing of rawhide, it is
managed with the left arm, and they use it to deflect arrows (*jaras*
as they call them), the horseman thus defending himself and his
mount. They employ besides these, a sort of apron of cow-hide
leather pinned to the head of the saddle and falling down on both
sides, that they call *armas* or *defensas*, covering their legs and thighs
so as to keep them from injury when galloping through brush.
Their offensive weapons are the lance, which they handle deftly a
horseback, the broadsword, and a short musket which they carry put
up and fastened in a sheath. They are men of great hardiness and
endurance in their work; quick to obey, determined, nimble, and, we
do not scruple to say, the best Horsemen in the world and among
those Soldiers who best earn their Bread from that August Monarch
whom they serve.[29]

At San Diego, the first land section was reunited with the
two packet-boats, which they descried already at anchor in the
bay upon their arrival.

Don Gaspar de Portolá left the Loreto Presidio on the 9th
of March, 1769, heading for the Vellicatá camp, where he was
to find the supplies and personnel left by Captain Rivera. At
Mission San Ignacio he was joined by Father Campa, who was
also assigned to establish the new missions. Fray Junípero, who
was to have set out with Portolá, asked his authority to follow
along immediately afterward, both because of his own desire to
say farewell to his friends at the missions along the way, and to
allow himself to recover from the badly ulcerated leg with which
he was suffering, by taking the journey in less extended stages.
Thus Father Serra set out on March 28th from Loreto, accompanied by his faithful servant José María and two others, including
a soldier; at the mission of Santa María de los Angeles, close to
Vellicatá camp, they caught up with the Governor, and all reached
the camp together on the 13th of May.

At Fray Junípero's instance, the Mission of San Fernando
Rey de España, a name suggested by Portolá, is established here
at the camp, and Father Campa is left in charge of it, with a
corporal and a left-over few of the buffcoat soldiers and some
muleteers to take care of the remaining cattle while awaiting the
outcome of the expeditions. Setting out for San Diego on May
15th with the Governor and Father Serra are Sergeant Ortega,

29.  COSTANSÓ, Miguel, *Diario Histórico* (see note 26).

fifty buffcoat soldiers, two servants, and some Indians and laborers: total, some seventy men.

The very day of their departure, early in the morning, a
troop of curious and placeful Indians, totally naked, appeared at
camp and were well treated by Father Serra and the Governor.
Gifts were made them of dried figs, raisins and tobacco-leaf.
Seeing a man among them who stood out as the one whom they
feared and obeyed, "acting as a Chief," Portolá "said to him that
if until then he had held this title only by the choice or intent
of his own people, from this day forth he was making him and
giving him the power of Chief in the name of our lord the King." [30]
This act constituted the first confirmation by the King of Spain's
representative of authority to a native—an act whose signifi-
cance is not merely anecdotal, but a genuine delegation of powers
from the conquistador to the colonized.

It is here also that Portolá and Serra show us the mutual
affection and respect between them by the special consideration
which the Governor attempted to thrust upon the friar, who was
suffering a serious ailment in his leg, forcing him to hobble as
he walked and to endure great trouble and pain.   Insistent as
Portolá became in trying to get the Franciscan to accept some
special treatment, Serra would not even use a sort of litter which
the Governor had had made up in order to have him carried.

The march to San Diego lasted forty-six days; they reached
the harbor on July 1st.   Portolá's arrival among the forces now
stationed there was greeted with shouts of joy and thunderous
salutes of musketry, for with the presence of their "headman"
(as Father Palou calls him), the serious plight in which the Expedition now found itself might be solved.

Here let us leave Portolá and his men at San Diego, facing
the desperate situation just referred to, and which we will shortly
learn more about, and let us turn first to one of the most interesting and original documents which have turned up to my surprise;
this is clearly the first time it has been published.   A facsimile
of a portion of it appears in this work.

In my visit to the Public Library of Toledo, to research the
documents kept there, especially those connected with the former
Archbishop of Mexico, Francisco de Lorenzana y Buitrón, later

30.  GEIGER, *Palou's Life of Serra*, p. 66.

Cardinal-Archbishop of Toledo, I found in the Borbón-Lorenzana Collection an exhaustive account of all the personnel and materiel sent by land and sea in the search for the Harbor of Monterey. The reader can form his own opinion as to its importance and interest. The document is a fold-out, some forty by sixty centimeters in size, divided into five columns each containing the list of materiel; it is headed by a description of the contents and of the personnel taking part in the expeditions.

(CENTRAL COLUMN)

"A General Table containing the Persons, Armament, and Spares, Vestments and Altar Service, Ration Supplies and Extra Stores, Tools, Instruments and Utensils, Wares and Effects sent in the two Expeditions by Sea and overland exploration to the two Harbors of San Diego and Monterrey, situated upon the Western Shore of the Peninsula of Californias in Latitude 33 and 37 degrees, for the Founding of a Fort, or Presidio, at the Second of the Said Harbors, and of New Missions among the Heathens dwelling beyond the last Frontier Reduction (which has just been established at Villacatá in 32° latitude) as far as Monterrey aforesaid.

First: A handsome Image of Mary Most Holy, given by the Visitor-General for Patroness of the Expedition.

### PERSONS

| | | | |
|---|---|---|---|
| Governor Ad Interim don Gaspar de Portolá . . . | 1 | An Engineer-draftsman . . | 1 |
| The 3 captains of the 3 Packets . . . . . . | 3 | A Captain of a Presidio . . | 1 |
| | | Seven Missionary Priests . | 7 |
| Their Masters' Mates . . | 3 | A Surgeon . . . . . . | 1 |
| A Master Junior Grade . . | 1 | Troops, Petty O f f i c e r s, crews and [other] posi- | |
| A Lieutenant of Infantry . | 1 | tions . . . . . . . . | 231 |

(FIRST COLUMN)

*Armament and spares for Land and Sea*

The three Packet-boats *San Carlos*, *San Antonio* and *San Joseph*, careened ashore, rigged, with Masts and Sails for navigating.
Twenty-three brass Cannon large and small.
122 Fusils and muskets with Bayonets and straps and pouch corresponding.
109 Brush Machetes, new.
Six Swords with *Bericues* (?).

25 Boxes of Cannon Loads with Powder, ball and wadding.
2½ Boxes of Musket Loads with Powder and ball.
 8 Chests of Gunpowder.
12 *arrobas* [300 lb.] of same.
21 *arrobas* [525 lb.] Cannon Balls.
41 *arrobas* 2 lbs. [1.027 lb.] musket-ball and charge.
 2 Bullet-moulds.
 6 Wadding-worms.
 1 Bag of Flints.
All the Munitions required for the Cannon of the three Packets.
 5 Topmasts and four yards.
 4 Suits of Sails of Spanish Canvas.
[1 ditto of Duckcloth.]
 4 pieces of Spanish Canvas, another of Duck.
30 pieces fine Bramant.
 3 Pieces thread Bramant.
 4 ditto of Frieze.
22 clews Oakum yarn.
 6 cording Mallets.
27 Sailmaking Meedles.
 9 cables, new and used.
 2 new Stream-cables.
17 new Hawsers of different thickness.
 5 pieces of Cordage, new.
32 pieces of Rigging, new, of all sizes.
 2 *tercios* of rope-yarn.
 1 *tercio* Wick.
 1 *tercio* of *Pita*.
 1 ditto of *Ixtle*.
 7 Anchors of brass and iron.
 3 brass Kedges.
 9 Sea-Compasses.
 2 Silver Reflectors.
 5 Glass Lanterns
 1 Lamp.
 3 arrobas of Sulphur.
20 Flags.
 5 Pennants.
 1 piece of Chinese silk.
A complete outfit in the three Packet-boats of Pulleys, Tackle,
    Blocks, Cableguards, Hooks, Marlinspikes, Splicing-fids, Buckets,
    Sailmaker's Palms, Tallow, Lead, and whatever is required for
    a Boatswain's other tasks.
Boatswain requires for other tasks.
Double sets of Caulkers, and Sea-Carpenters' tools and other utensils
    connected with these functions.
370 Barrels of water, closed and beaten down.

2 large barrel of water.
3 Bells.

### Sacred Vestments and Altar Service

Seven statues of Saints and one Nativity.
13 Engravings of various appellations [of the Virgin and saints].
 1 Silvergilt Monstrance.
 1 Sunburst for a Monstrance.
 4 Ciboria.
10 Silver Chalices, 5 of them gilt with Patens and Cochlearia.
 5 Silver Shells for Baptizing with.
 4 Silver Chrismaries.
 1 Silver Cross.
 3 Silver basins for the Lavabo and St. John's Gospel.
 6 large Silver Candlesticks.
10 ditto of Brass.
 2 little Candlesticks of Silver.
 6 ditto of Brass.
 6 Copper Candleholders.
 6 silver Thuribles with incense-vessels and ladles.
 2 silver Lecterns.
 2 ditto of Wood.
 6 Missals.
 4 Roman Ritualia.
 3 Betancourt's Handbook.
 7 pair of silver Cruets with the saucers for them.
 1 ditto of Glass.
Eight Altar bells of Silver and Copper
 8 church Bells large and small.
31 Vestments, various materials and colors.
 8 Chasubles with Stoles and Maniples.
 7 Amices.
28 Frontals with Palls and Hangings.
 6 Copes.
 3 Cassocks.
 2 Musettes.
 3 Dalmatics.
18 Albs with girdles for them; 2 ditto of silver cloth.
13 Altar-cloths.
22 Corporals.
 5 Surplices.
11 Acolytes' Robes.
12 Rochets for the same.
 7 Manuterges.

27 Purificators.
11 Consecrated Altars.
 5 Carpets.
 2 Holy-water pots with Sprinklers.
 3 Altarhorns.
 2 Irons for making Hosts.
20 Hoods for christening adults, Children, and those of an age
   between.
 5 yards of Red Damask.
 5 ditto of Chinese silk.
 3 ditto blue Taffeta.
 3 Sets of Curtains with Valance.
Several cloth remnants, Silver and Gold Point-lace, and lace.
 2 Towels.
One tinplate Wafer-box.


(THIRD COLUMN)

## Ration Supplies, Extra Stores, and Mounts

734½ *arrobas* of white and ordinary Ship-bread.
  20 *fanegas* of wheat.
1.030 *arrobas* 11 pounds of Flour.
  97 *arrobas* 11 pounds Pinole.
 364 *fanegas* ten *almudes* new Maize.
1.035 *arrobas* 11 pounds salt meat.
 306 Cows and heifers.
   6 Ewes and 2 sheep.
 153 Chickens and Cocks.
 34½ *arrobas* of Hams.
 119 *arrobas* 15 pounds Salt Fish.
  75 *arrobas* 18 pounds lard and tallow.
  22 Jars of Oil
 105 *arrobas* Rice.
 188 *arrobas* 11 pounds Chikpeas.
 117 *arrobas* 10 pounds Lentils.
 118 *arrobas* 27 lbs. Beans.
  68 *fanegas* of the same.
  94 *arrobas* 11 pounds Chocolate.
  35 *arrobas* 8 lbs. Sugar.
 125 *arrobas* 7 lbs. Brown loaf sugar.
   2 *arrobas* of candies.
 139 *arrobas* Dates, figs, and Raisins.
  43 *arrobas* 6 lbs. Cheese.
   9 pounds of cloves, cinnamon and Pepper.
7½ lbs. of ground Pepper.
  29 *arrobas* chile pepper.

   23 *arrobas* Garlic.
  270 *arrobas* Salt.
   14 jars of Californias Brandy.
   26 jars of ditto Wine.
   17 jars of ditto Vinegar.
   35 sacks of Bran.
   41 bags of Charcoal.
As many *arrobas* of firewood as thought necessary for 8 months' sail
     by the three Packets.
    3 sacks of slaked Lime.
   18 *arrobas* Tallow Candles.
  525 individual ditto.
   30 *arrobas* rendered tallow.
  262 Horses and Mules.
    2 female Burros.
  105 pack-saddles fully accoutred.
   73 Sheepskins and Mats for Saddle-pads.
   11 *cargas* of Bags.
   53 Saddlebag Blankets.
1.000 *pesos* cash in *reales* in each of the Packet-boats for any emer-
     gency that may arise.


(FOURTH COLUMN)

*Tools, Instruments and Utensils*

   17 Hammers large and small.
   62 carpenter's and woodsman's Axes.
    8 Hatchets.
   11 Bricklayer's trowels.
    6 files.
   12 picks and *picaderas*.
   12 Chisels and Augers.
    1 Carpenter's Plane.
Nine Saws large and small.
    9 tongs.
    2 complete Blacksmith's Forges with double set of Tools and
      Utensils.
    7 iron Shovels.
   14 Hoes.
    8 Wedges, shod.
  101 Mattocks.
    4 Ploughshares.
   20 Crowbars, shod.
   47 Copper pots, Kettles, and pans
Twenty Copper Stew-Ladles.
    6 Brass Syringes.

6 Brass Chamberpots.
54 Latches and Padlocks with Keys for them.
2 steelyards.
2 pairs of Scales with weights for them.
24 hinges.
3 pairs of Iron Fetters.
2 Cushions.
4 trivets.
4 large Copper Cauldrons.
2 Gaff-hooks for extracting Rations.
6 copper measures for rationing Water.
7 ditto of wood.
16 pairs of Cups.
137 Plates, Dishes, and cups, China and ordinary ware.
2 Drinking glasses.
25 Wooden Plates.
54 tablecloths and napkins.
16 metates [grinding-stones] with grinders for them.
3 iron Griddles.
5 Strainers and sieves.
5 yards of Metal Sieve material.
2 Campaign Tents.
2 Metal Coverings.

(Fifth Column)

### Wares and Effects

4 dozen Crucifixes.
15 dozen Medals.
7 gross Huasteca rosaries.
47 Bundles Assorted Beads.
3 ditto Coral, assorted.
60 ditto Smalt and Milk-colored.
12 dozen Mock Pearls.
18 Packets of Earrings.
7 Metal Rings with Stones.
50 Pair of Earrings ditto.
9 Dozen Barcelona handkerchieves.
2 dozen of Puebla.
3 dozen handsome Shawl-cloths.
4 Blankets *conquillas*.
996 yards of assorted ribbon.
2 pieces of Cloth for the crews' use.
2 of Flannel for the same.
18 *tercios* Tobacco Leaf.
2,272 Packages of Cigars.

 56 *arrobas* Soap.
  6 *quintales* of Steel.
 30 ditto of Round-Iron.
  4 reams fine white Paper.
  3 *arrobas* Wax Candles.
 30 dressed Cordovan goat and Sheepskins.
 10 Brass Candleholders.
 17 pair Snuffers.
323 Cutlasses or Knives.
 12 Machetes for Belt.
27½ dozen Clasp-knives of several sorts.
  4 dozen Awls.
  8 bundles of fine thread.
  1 pound Pack-thread.
 16 pounds of *Pita*, loose and spun.
 50 hanks of *Ixtle*.
 16 Papers of Sewing-Needles.
 26 Matting-Needles.
 13 pair Matting Shears.
121 pair scissors of various sorts large and small.
 23 Thimbles.
 12 dozen Combs, various sizes.
 12 Helves.
  7 *arrobas* of tarpauling and shingling nails.
800 nails of various gauge.
7.000 tacks *de Bomba* (?)
 16 pounds of Wick.
 12 Catechisms.
  4 Inkstands.
 97 Tie-ropes.
 18 Halters.
  4 lbs. of Glue.
  5 skeins of Wire.
 10 dozen Shoes.
  2 Boxes containing various Vegetable, garden and flower seeds, for planting.
  3 *fanegas* of Rice.
  3 ditto of Wheat, and 2 of Millet, for sowing.
  3 pounds *Quina* [chinchona bark].
 10 of Quicksilver for Assaying.
  3 volumes of the History of California.
  7 Tanned local Cowhides.
210 Cowhide Bags.
162 yards Canvas and coarse linen for packing [?].
294 pair Horseshoes with nails for them.
 35 yards coarse Blue Cloth.
  2 kitchen Grinding-bowls.

18 spare Girths.
 9 Packsaddle covers.
12 fine Bridles.
119 yards of Homespun.
12 pair of Petticoats.

Real de los Alamos, August 1st, 1769.[31]


The importance of this document needs no comment; its perusal suffices to show how completely and minutely the Expedition was organized. It is noticeable that only one name is mentioned, that of the Governor Don Gaspar de Portolá, all other officers and ship captains, even the missionaries headed by the President of the Missions, going unnamed. The number of men in the Expedition is given as 250, totalling all those referred to. By putting together various sources, we ourselves have arrived at the number of 50 belonging to Captain Rivera's section and 70 in Portolá's at the real start of their march overland, that is, at the place called Vellicatá or Mission San Fernando, before the meeting at San Diego, as we have shown. At the moment we still have not yet told the events of the sea expedition, how many men were in their contingents, the dates they weighed and how the voyage to San Diego unrolled—all of it absolutely necessary to put together the exploits of Portolá's Expedition to Monterey. To learn about this, let us turn back to the South, where preparations for these sea expedition were drawing to an end.

At San Blas, as already indicated, they had finished building the two Packets which were to take part in the Expedition. These weighed anchor, one after the other, for La Paz harbor, where the Visitor-General was directing preparations from the nearby Santa Ana Camp. The *San Carlos* was inspected so closely that the Visitor, unhappy with the shape her keel was in, ordered her unloaded and careened once more in order to protect the hull and prevent possible leaks. Lacking tar for caulking, he cleverly substituted various plant secretions and mortars which worked to every one's satisfaction, and the ship was reloaded with her own cargo and wares sent earlier from San Blas which had been waiting at the landing. Also shipped were the vestments and altar

31. Toledo, Biblioteca Pública, Papeles Borbón-Lorenzana, t. 64, n.° 21; Seville, Archivo Genera de Indias, Aud. de Guadalajara 417 (reel 355/39 on Bancroft Library microfilm; duplicate copy in Aud. de México 1369, reel 216/43-46 on Bancroft Library film); San Marino, Huntington Library, Ms. GA 532.

furniture for the missionaries and the utensils for their missions-to-be.   Visitor-General Gálvez', involvement and interest reached unheard-of extremes when he in person helped load the packets with the articles he had selected.   From the list given above, notice that these included everything from sewing needles to inkstands to flower seeds, besides the provisions for the forces, the tools for various jobs, the glass beads, the tallow candles—even chamberpots.

When all was set and the crew had received the Sacraments at the Mass celebrated by Fray Junípero, the *San Carlos* weighed anchor, January 9th, 1769.   On board her were Lt. Fages and twenty-five Volunteers of the Free Company of Catalonia; Engineer Miguel Costansó; Surgeon Pedro Prat; Father Fernando Parrón; second ship's officer Don Jorge de Estorace, twenty-three crew, two servants ,four cooks and two blacksmiths, all under the command of Captain Vicente Vila, acting as commander of the expedition by sea. The ship's complement thus consisted of sixty-two persons.

The Visitor-General's orders to the Captains were specific: The *San Carlos*, leaving first, was to sail to San Diego and wait twenty days at most for the *San Antonio* to arrive.   Should it fail to do so, the *San Carlos* was to continue toward Monterey, to await and aid the overland expedition.   The packet *San Antonio*, on its own arrival at San Diego, was to go on to Monterey whether or not it had met the *San Carlos*.   For assistance later, the packet *San José* would sail from La Paz directly to Monterey.

The *San Antonio*, also named *El Príncipe*, weighed from La Paz on February 15th, carrying Father Vizcaíno and a total complement of thirty-two persons, twenty-eight of them crew; her captain was the Mallorcan Don Juan Pérez.   And to complete the flawless plans that had been drawn, the packet *San José*, laden with supplies and wares, set sail toward Monterey on June 16th.

The *San Carlos* reached San Diego Bay on the 30th of April, and found there the *San Antonio*, which had sailed later from Cape San Lucas, had had better winds, and had been able to make the run faster.   The *San Carlos's* own sail had been less than fortunate, with unfavorable winds which held her along the Lower California coast in heavy gales. The water barrels on board were made leaky by the battering, so that they had to look for watering-places ashore, having vast trouble in finding any springs large enough for their pressing requirements, so that twice they had to delay, with the ship lying to against the winds out at sea, while ashore Lt. Fages and his few soldiers labored to fill the ship's empty butts.  As if this were not enough, the scurvy had begun to strike among the crew and weaken it, four persons perishing before they made port.  They reached San Diego in a terrible condition, with barely enough hands well to handle the ship.

Let Captain Vila, himself, tell of their situation on the arrival at San Diego Bay, while the log keeps repeating the sad refrain, "no improvement among the sick."

Saturday 29 to Sunday 30 of April.

Searching for the Harbor with all sail set, head to the east, wind fresh from the north-northwest, flat sea.  At four in the afternoon I furled and stowed the Main, fore, mizzen and topgallant-sails, one league off the point which I named *Punta del Vallado* as the hill standing over the harbor resembled a breastwork.  Here we commenced to enter a seaweed-bed floating so thickyl that though the ship had been making over two knots, she was brought almost to a halt and lost steerage-way.  I took soundings until passing entirely out of it very close to the point, in 14 or 15 fathoms, bottom black sand and gravel in spots...

At this time I discovered the Packet *San Antonio* anchorel at Guijarros Point, (Ballast Point) and we unfurled our pennant; she broke out hers and fired a cannon to call her boat, which had gone ashore.  I continued on the task and, with the wind fallen nearly still, I lowered the topsails and anchored in six fathoms, loose black sand.  At this hour the ebb-tide was setting outward.

At eight o'clock in the evening the *San Antonio's* boat came up with her second, Don Miguel del Pino, who told us the news of her voyage and how she had arrived this harbor on the eleventh of April with half her crew infected with the scurvy, only two of them having died, and they had no men fit for work other than the seven in the boat, of whom some were feeling the symptoms of the same disease.  Their Captain Don Juan Pérez was in poor health, only the missionaries were well.

I sent the boat off with orders to come back at dawn, on the chance that the on-land breeze would allow us to come inside and reach shelter once for all.

Sunday 30th to Monday May 1st.

...At twelve o'clock at night the tide stood higher and in a total calm I weighed and with the boat out ahead towing succeeded in dropping anchor at five in the morning under the shelter of Point Guijarros next to the *San Antonio*. At seven o'clock the *San Antonio* saluted us with six guns; Mass was said aboard us, and I answered her afterward with five. At ten o'clock in the morning, Don Juan Pérez came aboard with the Rev. Fr. Missionaries Fray Juan Vizcaíno and Fray Juan Gómez. At a half past ten in the forenoon the *San Antonio's* boat stood away with Don Pedro Fages, Don Miguel Costansó, Don Jorge Estorace my second, and the same missionary fathers, all of them being in stronger health, intending to explore the land and look for a good watering place, since what the *San Antonio's* crew had been able to get by digging wells was brackish and undrinkable.

Don Juan Pérez having given me an account of the condition of his crew, the few men he had left capable of continuing the voyage to Monterrey as he had been ordered to do on the last of April on the *San Carlos* failing to arrive (Pérez having been convinced that I had reached San Diego first and had gone on to Monterey); in view also of the state of the *San Carlos*, this ship having only two seamen who were well, the rest being ill, and over half the troops in the same case, with no medicines nor fresh meat to treat them with, it all having been used up during the sail, and seeing in addition Surgeon Don Pedro Prat incapable of attending them because he was gravely ill himself, I determined to postpone the *San Antonio's* voyage ... and to set the sick men ashore with due caution, in the hope that by the use of medicinal herbs and plants which the land commonly bears in many places, and by breathing better air than that in the hold, a good many of them might become better, recover their health, and be able to continue the voyage to Monterey according to our orders; and should these measures fail to produce the good effect for which we wished, I decided as a last recourse to send one of the two packet-boats with four to six men in her (though it seemed rash merely to think it) off for San Blas with reports for the Most Excellent Lord Viceroy and the Most Honorable Visitor-General, informing them of our sad plight, and begging them to send us the help we needed without loss of time. We had better-founded hopes in the arrival of the overland expedition in charge of the Governor and the Captain of the Californias Presidio, and in the coming of the Packet *San José*, which we supposed already under sail for San Diego; and by means of her crew, who would be in less sad state than our own, we promised ourselves both to continue on to Monte-

# Personas. Armamento, y respetos, ornamentos,

y útiles, gerreros, y efectos que han ido en las dos Expediciones de mar, y ___ de Californias a los 33, y 37 grados de latitud para ___ estable___ ___ de la ultima reducción de frontera que acaba de establecerse en ___

Primeram.te una ___ imagen de maria s.sma q.e ___ el S.r Virrey son d.n Jose Sarmona de la Expedi.n

## Personas

| | | |
|---|---|---|
| El Gover.r ___ Arzen ___ ___ ___ 1 | | ___ ___ Delineador ___ 1 |
| ___ cap.n de ___ ___ 3 | | el Cap.n de ___ 1 |
| ___ segundo ___ 3 | | ___ P.e ___ 7 |
| On ___ 1 | | On Cirujano 1 |
| On Then.te ___ ___ 1 | | ___ ofic. ___ man.a Cap. y ___ 231 |

| ___ y ___ Sagradas | ___ ___ ___ repuestos, y Caballerías | Herram.tas |
|---|---|---|
| ___ y un Nacimiento | 73 ___ ___ ___ blanca y ___ | 17 ___ |
| ___ ___ ___ Custodia ___ | 20 ___ ___ | 62 ___ |
| ___ ___ ___ Corona | ___ ___ ___ de mar ___ 376 1 ___ | 8 ___ |
| ___ los 3 ___ ___ ___ | 36 ___ ___ ___ ___ | 11 ___ |
| ___ Conchas de plata p.a Baut. | 10 8 ___ ___ 11 ___ de ___ ___ | 6 ___ |
| ___ una ___ de plata | 306 ___ ___ 5 obo ___ y 2 ___ | 1.a ___ y ___ |
| ___ de la___ y otro ___ | 183 ___ ___ y ___ | 12 ___ y |
| ___ Dios ___ ___ | ___ ___ 106 18 ___ de ___ | ___ ___ |
| de plata ___ ___ ___ | ___ 181 ___ de ___ | nueve ___ |
| ___ ___ de ___ | y de ___ | 2 ___ |
| y ___ Dos ___ | 22 ___ ___ | 2 ___ |
| ___ ___ ___ | 10 ___ ___ | 2 ___ |
| ___ Tres ___ | 18 ___ 11 ___ de ___ | ___ |
| ___ para ___ ___ | 117 6 ___ ___ | 7 ___ de ___ |
| ___ Seis ___ | 111 ___ 27 ___ de ___ 68 ___ ___ | 14 ___ |
| ___ de ___ de plata | ___ ___ de ___ | 8 ___ |
| ___ grandes y ___ | 35 8 ___ de ___ | 101 ___ |
| ___ ___ y ___ | 11 ___ ___ de ___ | 4 ___ de |
| ___ ___ | 2 ___ ___ ___ de ___ y ___ | 20 ___ |
| ___ y ___ | ___ ___ | 6 Ollas ___ |
| ___ Palos, y ___ | ___ y ___ | 20 ___ |
| ___ Dos ___ | 2 ___ de ___ 2 ___ ___ 270 ___ | 6 ___ de ___ |
| | 14 ___ ___ de Californias | 8 ___ de |
| | 25 ___ de ___ | |
| ___ ___ ___ | 41 ___ ___ ___ | 88 ___ |
| | ___ ___ ___ | 2 ___ |
| ___ de plata ___ ___ | ___ ___ | 2 ___ |
| ___ | 18 ___ ___ ___ sebo | 24 ___ |
| ___ ___ ___ | 50 ___ ___ | 3 ___ |
| ___ Dos ___ | ___ ___ ___ sebo ___ | 2 ___ |
| ___ ___ ___ | 26 ___ y ___ ___ | 4 ___ |
| ___ ___ Cinco ___ | Dos ___ | ___ ___ |
| ___ ___ una ___ | ___ ___ ___ ___ | ___ |

List of the persons, objets, material and equipment which were sent
to Monterey in Portolá's expedition. Document detailed in the text.
(Bibl. Lorenzana. Toledo).

rey and to send one of the ships to San Blas for the purpose above mentioned, asking the properly assessed reinforcement of men, provisions and other effects in order to complete the undertaking we had begun.

### Monday the 1st to Tuesday May 2nd.

...At nine o'clock at night, the boat arrived successfully alongside, and the gentlemen and missionary fathers who had gone in it related how they had gone about three leagues along the shore, at which distance they encountered a village of heathens on the banks of a river of excellent water, the Indians consisting of thirty-five to forty families living scattered in several lodge-huts, and very friendly and well-behaved. The country was fresh and pleasant, with all sorts of sweet-smelling plants, wild grapevines, and plenty of game.

### Friday the 5th to Saturday 6th May.

...At three o'clock in the afternoon four of the sailors who were least affected set off in the ship's boat with Don Pedro Fages and some soldiers bearing arms. The *San Antonio's* boat with her Captain and some soldiers went out to survey how far the Harbor extended...

At eight o'clock in the morning the *San Antonio's* boat departed with Don Pedro Fages, Don Miguel Costansó, Rev. Fr. Juan Vizcaíno and those soldiers who seemed strongest, to set about building barracks.

### Saturday the 6th. to Sunday the 7th. May.

...At sunset the boat with the missionary father and the officers came back; they had decided to make the barracks for the sick men upon a small knoll next to the shore, a cannon-shot away from the ships; to this end they had got together a lot of brushwood bundles, to be used with sod in providing cover for those who would be moved into the barracks.

### Monday the 8th. to Tuesday the 9th. May.

...At eight o'clock in the forenoon the boat went ashore laden with two cannon from the ship's artillery with the carriages and everything else needed to work them, two chests full of loads for the cannon and musketry, with a satchel of musket-balls of all calibres for canister-shot, eight days' ration of maize, pease and dried meat for the soldier guards ashore, and cabin biscuit for sippets in the sick men's gruel.

Lodgings and barracks having been thrown up, the unloading of the sick men began, and at four o'clock in the afternoon all of them were ashore, I myself staying aboard along with the boatswain, who was ill, and a Galician seaman and a cabin-boy, they also affected by the scurvy. I was unable to take a step, and Rev. Fr. Fray Fernando Parrón was in no good health either...

TUESDAY THE 9TH. TO WEDNESDAY 10TH. MAY.

...This day I placed the artillery on board ship so as to be able to protect the people ashore, laying the cannon to bear upon either side of the lodgings.

...At eight o'clock in the morning, sent the boat to land with the mizzen and spritsail to be used in setting up another barrack for ten sick men from the San Antonio...

This same day four soldiers fell ill and Engineer Don Miguel Costansó told me there were no more than eight men capable of any work left ashore.[32]

Of the hundred and some men aboard the two ships at their sailing from La Paz, only eight men were left "capable of any work." The ocean had witnessed the death of some, and now at San Diego Bay, within the rocky cliffs of Point Loma, those who perished day by day were being steadily interred. The two ship's crews were totally unable to manage even one vessel, and supplies and medicines were exhausted. The only hope lay in the change of climate and Surgeon Prat's herbs. They did not know, though they could hope, that the first section of the land expedition was four days' march away, under Rivera; sea and land contingents met on the 14th of May. None of Rivera's men had died, though some were ill. Gathered together at San Diego Bay, they waited with awakened hope for the Governor's expedition and the ship *San José* which should be coming only a few leagues behind. In the shelters at the shore's edge, however, the sick became worse and worse, and slowly the count of the dead rose to over thirty-one sailors, four Catalan soldiers, and eight of the *San Antonio's* men. Fifty men living, eight of them capable of useful work; a few others ill and being cared

32. VILA, Vicente, *Diario de Navegación del Paquebote San Carlos...*, Madrid, Museo Nacional, California, Historia y Viajes, t. I, n.º 1; another copy printed by R. S. Rose, *Publications of the Academy of Pacific Coast History*, II (1911), pp. 1-119.

for by the eight, but still themselves useful for a few jobs.   The rest, dying.

At Portolá's and Father Serra's arrival, the camp is overwhelmed with joy; cannon-discharges and the rattle of musketry stun San Diego Bay, and the soldiers dash out to clasp their companions in the expedition.   But joy quickly becomes pain for the newly-arrived as the situation is made clear to them. Let Father Serra be the one to tell us what happened, and the decision reached by the Governor with the overland officers and sea-captains:

...God be thanked, day before yesterday, the 1st of this month, I reached the harbor of San Diego here, beautiful indeed, and rightly famous.   This is where I caught up with all those who had set out first, both by land and sea, less those who had died.   My companions Fathers Crespí, Vizcaíno, Parrón and Gómez are here with me, all well, thank God.   The two ships are here; the *San Carlos* has no sailors for they have all died of Loanda sickness, and only one of them and a cook are left.   The *San Antonio* alias *El Príncipe*, whose captain is my countryman Don Juan Pérez from the shores of Palma, reached here twenty days before the other though sailing a month and a half later.   As she was about to set out for Monterey, the *San Carlos* arrived here and on aiding the latter with her crew she caught the infection as well and eight died and in fine what they have decided is that this *San Antonio* is to return to San Blas and bring back seamen for herself and the *San Carlos* and then both will go ahead.   We shall see what shape the packet *San José* is in when she arrives; the last shall be first when it comes to going on.[33]

Father Palou makes the situation clear and adds other facts not mentioned by Father Serra:

At this place both Commanders [Portolá and Vila] called a meeting to discuss and decide what was to be done in view of the few seamen left alive and untouched by that plague in the flagship, —whether her crew and the troops sent from California in her— since this was the reason it was no longer possible to fulfill the Visitor-General's instructions to them.[34]

---

33. *Relación Histórica* of the life of Junípero Serra by Francisco Palou, ch. XVI, in Manuel Ballesteros Gaibrois, ed., *Viajes por Norteamérica* (Biblioteca Indiana, Viajes y Viajeros; Madrid: Aguilar, 1958), pp. 672-673); GEIGER, *Palou's Life of Serra*, p. 70.
34. Ibid., pp. 674-675; GEIGER, *Palou's Life*, pp. 72-73.

Carrying all the personnel at their disposal at San Diego who might learn anything of navigation or be of any use to Captain Juan Pérez, the packet *San Antonio* set out bound for San Blas on the 9th of July. When she reached there with Portolá's and Serra's dispatches and Captain Vila's report, it seemed the arrival of a ghost ship, for only two men aboard could stand, four were at death's door, and nine others had perished and their bodies were entombed in the sea.

Governor Gaspar de Portolá, Don Vicente Vila, Lieutenant Fages, Captain Fernando de Rivera and the missionary fathers once more turn to analysing their situation and the orders the Visitor-General had given the leader of the Expedition. No longer is it possible to follow them as written, but there is no compelling reason either why they should sit still at San Diego waiting for the *San José* to arrive, or for possible further instruction from San Blas.

...Provisions and everything else judged necessary for an unknown but, in the opinion of everyone, likely a lengthy journey were made ready  Supplies and loads of utensils designated for mission church, household and field purposes and brought by the expeditions were to be left at San Diego with eight buffcoat soldiers to guard them.[35]

Portolá's decision as he made it known to his comrades was that "the unexpected disaster with the ships did not excuse him from continuing his journey to Monterey by land," and so it was that the march to Monterey was begun on the 14th of July, Governor Portolá himself in command, and with him the expedition, consisting of sixty-three person in all:

...The Governor, in Command, with his servant; Captain Ribera and his servant; Lt. of Volunteers Don Pedro Fajes and six of his Soldiers; Engineer Don Miguel Constanzó; twenty-seven Buffcoat soldiers; seven Muleteers; fifteen Christian Indians from our California Missions; [and] myself [Father Juan Crespí] together with Rev. Fr. Fray Francisco Gómez.[36]

---

35. Ibid.

36. Manuscript Journal of Fray Juan Crespí, under July 14, 1769. Mexico, Archivo General de la Nación, Archivo Histórico de Hacienda, Documentos para la Historia de México, ser. I, t. 3, fol. 52 verso (Bancroft Library Microfilm); Rome, Curia generale dei Frati Minori, antico archivio Collegio San Antonio, t. 60, under §96. Cf. Geiger, *Palou's Life of Serra, ibid.*

Father Palou adds that the mule train

carried all the provisions thought to be sufficient to keep them from undergoing hunger or deprivation, in accordance with the repeated injunctions of the Visitor-General.[37]

As has already been indicated several times, the organizing ability of this oft-mentioned Visitor, Don José de Gálvez, was so careful and extreme that in addition to his taking personal part in arranging and inspecting the expeditions, he issued each of the ship captains as well as Captain Rivera and Governor Portolá written instructions, containing all sorts of cautions about the marches and laying out in detail all the decisions that could be anticipated in their course.   Here are Governor Portolá's:

*Instructions which are to be observed by Captain of the Dragoons of Spain Don Gaspar de Portolá, Governor and Commander in Chief of this Peninsula of Californias, during the Expedition and journey overland to the Harbors of San Diego and Monterey, situated upon the South Sea shore in latitude 33 and 37 degrees.*

1.   In view of the fact that this expedition's chief object is that of spreading Religion among the Heathens dwelling in the North of this Peninsula through the peaceful means of founding Missions to achieve the spiritual Conquest at the said Harbors of San Diego and Monterey and in other locations lying between that may now be discovered and judged the more fertile and best suited for the aforesaid purpose of erecting missions settlements [*reducciones*] as well as for that of introducing the rule of the King our Lord, I instruct the said Governor to set forth, with all possible swiftness and a small escort, in company with the Rev. Fr. President of the Missions, for the frontier at the [Mission] of Santa Maria, and after reinforcing his escort at Villacatá with part of the troops settled there by Presidio Captain Don Fernando de Rivera, to follow his [Rivera's] march as far as the aforesaid San Diego Harbor, along the course and routes that the same Captain shall have left marked out.

2.   The Governor shall cause to be carried only those provisions needed for the journey as far as Villacatá and thence to San Diego, inasmuch as Captain Rivera has been sent plenteous supplies for this overland expedition by means of the Boats and Canoes which I have ordered to go to San Luis Gonzaga Bay, located inside the Gulf in latitude 31°, and which are now sailing there for the second time; in

---

37.  Palou, *Relación Histórica*, ibid.; Geiger, pp. 73-74.

addition, His Majesty's two Packets *San Carlos* and *San Antonio*, sailing by the South Sea, and as I suppose already at San Diego Harbor, at least the first of them, are carrying a large amount of all sorts of foodstuffs, in order that those travelling by land shall want nothing; I having indicated the same place, San Diego, in my orders and Instructions to the Sea expedition and to Captain Rivera, as their first point of rendezvous, so that he may take whatever supplies he shall think necessary for getting to Monterey from those shipped in the Packet-boats. And since it is to be expected, following the instructions I have given, that both parties will send me advice of their arrival, the Governor shall see to it, if he meets couriers on the way that their messages reach me wherever I am with all speed.

3. Among the considerations which will engage the Governor's full care and attention as leader of a journey with the highest aims and requiring the most careful leadership in order not to negate or ruin its success, I charge him with zeal and watchfulness to cause the Soldiers in his party and the Muleteers in its train to maintain the strictest discipline, especially when beyond the Frontier of the present Missions; recommending to all, as an unbreakable article of regulations, good treatment of the Indians, and announcing that it will be punished as an unforgivable crime if any of them should offer insult or violence to the women, for beside the offenses to God which they would be committing in such outrages, they might endanger the whole of this Expedition.

4. If Captain Don Fernando de Rivera, in consequence of my previous instructions and the directions I have recently sent him as a result of the departure of the Packet-boats, shall have gone on ahead with a lightly-equipped party to explore and survey the Country in between San Diego and Monterey, the Governor is to wait with his own division at the first of these Harbors until the Captain shall return or shall send an escort of his own men with whom to continue the march; and while they are staying at San Diego, he shall by his presence and active command endeavor to promote the founding of the Mission and the guard-post which are to be established at that point to serve as refuge and Stopping-place for the Packets on their return voyage and for the parties of troops returning overland from Monterey.

5. If, on the contrary, the Captain has not passed beyond San Diego, both Divisions of the land journey shall proceed onward to Monterey, the Governor travelling always with the last section and allowing the Captain to continue with the first one at one or two days' marches ahead, according as they shall see fit in the light of actual events which cannot be foreseen in advance and given rules for; and so I leave it to the said Governor's wisdom, and to the Captain's as well in what concerns him, since he is to go ahead as the

first explorer of the Country through which the Expedition is to pass, how they are to judge and determine what measures seem best to them according to actual circumstances; though it must ever be their principal concern not to exasperate or antagonize the Natives, but to do everything possible to attract them and gain their good will by treating them well and making small shows and gifts of trinkets or of food that will not be missed in sustaining the Troops in both Divisions.

6. These are to come together whenever events require, as there are grounds to fear some opposition from the Heathen Indians at whatever place or point on the march, always observing as an invariable rule—the safest one among unknown peoples and in unknown lands—that of journeying with every caution, and not relying upon any friendship or indifference shown by the Indians, since these may be feigned, or where real may prove to be unlasting because of their natural inconstancy in all their doings.

7. Before reaching Monterey, a distance of only two or three leagues from it, is the mouth of the Carmel River, which old and recent accounts set down as full-flowing and swift. As I have directed, in special instructions to the Engineer-Draftsman Don Miguel Constanzó sent with the *San Carlos*, that he endeavor to make a survey of the best and safest places where the land expedition may cross that river, and if there are none such that there shall be Boats provided for the Men, and Rafts or Flatboats for getting the stock across, the Governor shall take care, upon this advice, to cause Captain Rivera to inform himself in detail, upon reaching the banks of the aforesaid river, of the results of the Engineer's examinations, by drawing close in order to search for its mouth upon sea and signaling with gunfire or however he shall judge appropriate to tell the men of the sea expedition of his arrival, supposing he has not first come across troops or sentries or lookouts posted in the neighborhood of the Carmelo, as it is likely they will have been by the leaders of the sea expedition in keeping with their instructions and with the directions I have given them.

8. As soon as the Governor shall have succeeded in reaching Monterey with his Expedition and there have joined the Sea expedition that has gone with the Packet-boats, he is to perform the solemn act of possession in the name of His Majesty, issuing the proper document which he is to forward at the first opportunity to the Most Excellent Lord Viceroy, sending the duplicate of it later along with the journal which he is to keep of his journey and the report of whatever he had noticed and judged worthy of His Excellency's attention.

9. While a Presidio and Mission with temporary buildings are being established at Monterey, in keeping with the instruction I have issued to the Engineer upon this point, the Governor shall remain at that

Harbor with all the Men in his and Capt. Don Fernando de Rivera's parties, and during his stay there is to attempt, by agreeableness, sagacity, and wisdom, to draw the Indians of that District and surrounding ones, making them to understand by whatever means possible what great good will come to them from living in brotherhood with the Spaniards under the sovereign protection of the King our Lord; but without purposely upsetting arrangements of Subject and ruler with those from other Dictricts who may come in, drawn by curiosity, rather merely proposing mutual trade and friendship to them and issuing some sort of document in the event of your striking agreements with them or any kind of treaty.

10. As the most appropriate means of achieving the laudable and proper goals to which both the Sea and land voyages are aimed are most surely those of treating the Indians with gentleness and love, not however having them believe that we fear them, the Governor is to put special study and care into reconciling both extremes and causing everyone else to follow his example, and seeing that the natives be given no just cause for antagonism or fear. But if after all prudent recourses have been exhausted, there should be Villages or Towns in any of the Provinces the Expedition shall go through which obstinately oppose its passage, force will then be used, taking such measures that at the first demonstration of them, they shall be made to recognize the superiority of our weapons, nonetheless not causing bloodshed once those who have been showing themselves hostile cease or yield, and granting them forgiveness and good relations freely and as a matter of course; in this and any similar cases which may arise, allowing the Reverend Father Missionaries to do everything that their charity, love and Apostolic zeal dictate to them in dealing with the Natives so as to undeceive them and draw them to us; but you are never to allow them, upon the impulse of their fervor and ardent wishes, to be unprotected amid the savages.

11. On passing by Mission Santa María, which is located upon unfavorable and barren territory, the Governor will, in accord with the Rev. Fr. President of the Missions, who is to be with him, cause that Mission and the Guard of soldiers stationed there to be moved provisionally, and as swiftly as possible, to the place named Villacata, where Captain Rivera has been with his detachment, and where he will have posted another Guard in keeping with my orders; as during this Expedition these pickets should not be duplicated unnecessarily, thus wasting the soldiers for nothing, nor can Mission Santa María be left in its present location, the more so as the country at Villacatá is fertile and has plentiful rain and thus is suitable for a Mission's being founded there.

12. As soon as the Mission settlement and the Presidio have been established with reasonable surety at Monterey, the Governor will

assign there the number of Soldiers belonging to the Company of this Peninsula whom he shall not absolutely require for his return, which he is to make with Captain Rivera, and he shall leave the political and military command of Monterey and the surrounding other new settlements in the charge of Don Pedro Fages, liutenant of the Company of Volunteers of Catalonia, to whom it properly belongs by his position as Commander of the regular troops sent in the expedition by Sea, until such time as the Most Excellent Lord Viceroy, informed of everything, shall take such action as he is pleased to do. And the said Governor shall proceed back to Loreto along the same Route as that by which he is now to journey, or by such other one as may then be thought better, always, upon the way up or the way back, inspecting for the most suitable and fertile spots in which to found the new Missions.

Cape San Lucas, February the 20th. one thousand seven hundred sixty-nine. — *Don Joseph de Galvez*.[38]

Spain's move upon Upper California was marked by her need to affirm and defend territories theoretically belonging to the Crown. Its ownership, as has been shown above, lay more in geographical knowledge than in fact, since the sole result of earlier explorations had been to place two harbors and a number of islands upon the maps,—no more than a few known spots upon the shores of the South Sea. Not even the Manila galleons, from which such rich profits were realized, ever were able to put in to these harbors, lacking any of the installations that would have been required. All really that was needed, as King Philip the Third had proclaimed in 1606, was support-points for the Manila ships, so that storms or freebooters would not slow the development of their trade. But never were the King's wishes clearly enough expressed nor the requirements for the step sufficiently demanding for it to reach the stage of reality. And so San Diego and Monterey remained "famous"—and unknown.

Only the Russians' push of expansion on the shores about Bering Strait made the need of regularizing Spain's ownership clearly felt. Seen in this light, the reasons for the occupation of the two bays were undeniably primarily political. But there

---

38. Seville, Archivo General de Indias, Aud. de Guadalajara 417, n.º 6 (reel 354 on Bancroft Library mcrofilm). Earlier translated and annotated by Maynard Geiger, O.F.M., *Southern California Quarterly*, XLVII (1965), 209-218, with a somewhat different rendering of the paragraph on treatment of the Indians (the original wording, on which the present translation is closely based, can of course be found in the Spanish edition of the present book).

can be no doubt either that, if the moving force behind the occupation of the new shores was the need to secure them politically and militarily, the most efficient means to this end was the missions, which worked together in a very curious way with the Presidios, perhaps protecting them somewhat more than, as in theory was the case, being protected by them.

The missionary effort in California remained dependent on the Viceroy for many years, the authorization for new settlements cash payments, and later support almanys coming from the government. There are constant proofs of this interdependence of politics and religion. Father Junípero Serra is constantly in touch with the political power in Mexico, both in order to report the news of events in his missions and to set forth their needs and desires. And when, owing to various collisions between captains and missionaries, waves of misunderstanding seem to arise, it is Father Serra who turns to the political authorities to have the offenders called to account or even removed.

This mingling of religious with specifically political operations should not, I think seem startling or upsetting to anyone, for it was certainly the case that Spain's civilizing work was upheld by bringing in the missions to spread the Gospel at the same time that the neophytes were being introduced to work and agriculture. It was fitting that the Viceregal government should underwrite the new missions, since once they were set up and a nucleus of neophytes introduced into the new society, the adjacent military settlements benefited by their flourishing presence would become more valuable in the government's eyes.

It is possible—I only say possible—that Fray Junípero, "the pacifier of the Sierra Gorda," having enough to keep him busied in Lower California, might never have spread the Gospel to Uper California had the military expedition not been launched on the orders of the King. But it is also possible—and in fact there are well-known episodes, such as the near abandonment of San Diego in March, 1769, which suggest—that without the joining of missionary endeavor with the explorations, the settlement would never have taken root or endured. And I cannot doubt the sincerity of the Visitor-General when, in a great many documents connected with these explorations, he gives spiritual welfare the place of preference over material, places the mission ahead of the presidio. These views of his, clearly and repeatedly expressed in Portolá's instructions, are in my opinion authentic and no product of hypocrisy; if the Visitor-General was a born politician, he was still a Spanish Visitor-General, and such a man does not indulge in mental contortions while presenting the expedition with an image of the Virgin with the request that it be returned to him after the venture is over, or while taking a tender farewell of the expeditionaries before the sailing of the ships, or while speaking with Father Serra and addressing him as "most beloved Father," of finally while crying out "How I would like to go with you to plant the Cross in that new Realm!" as the caravans set out.

From San Blas in August 1769 the news of the state of the San Diego expeditions spreads out: men learn of the vicissitudes of the voyage by sea, the crews stricken by illness, the preparations being made despite everything by Governor Portolá, and everyone's hope pinned on help from the Visitor-General and the Viceroy. The latter writes the Minister of the Indies, Knight-Commander Don Julián de Arriaga, this letter summarizing both the explorers' situation and the actions about to be taken to get the requested aid to them.

*"The Viceroy Marquis de Croix to Minister of the Indies Don Julián de Arriaga.*

Most excellent sir.

My Dear Sir:    Attached you will find the letter and Report addressed to me from the Harbor of San Diego in the province of California by the master of H. M. Packet *El Príncipe*, and Commander of the Expedition by Sea to Monterey, Don Vicente Vila, wherein your Excellency will be informed of all that happened during the Voyage and of the reason for their having remained at the above-named Harbor, where they are awaiting the coming arrival of the packet *San José*, upon whose despatch I refer to the Visitor's letters of which I have sent copies previously to your Excellency and those being enclosed with another letter of mine of this date, especially those from the aforementioned gentleman in which tables and accounts are drawn up of the said Packet-boat's lading.

Together with these reports, and upon the 10th of this month, I received others sent to me from the aforesaid San Diego Harbor and from San Blas by Don Gaspar de Portolá, Don Miguel Costansó, Don Pedro Fages, Don Fernando de Rivera y Moncada, Don Juan Pérez and the Commissioner at the new Settlement and Navy Yard of San Blas, the substance of which is the same as that reported by Don Vicente Vila, with their unanimous agreement and resolve to

send back the aforementioned Packet *El Príncipe* and to continue the expedition to Monte Rey by land; to which they were all
setting out very willingly, in confidence they would achieve a complete cure of their debilities upon the way, as Constansó and Fages
particularly assure me. With the same letter, Portolá and Rivera
report the success of their own journeys by land, and the care being
given to attending and treating the sick in the shelter of the New
Mission and through the care and devotion of the Rev. Fr. President,
for which purpose Surgeon Pedro Prat was to remain there.

With the same unanimity of opinion, they describe the pleasure
and willingness with which they were undertaking their decision to
continue the Journey overland because of the circumstances mentioned and because of this being the only season for travelling in those
parts, as well as their hopefulness of finding at Monterey, as described
by the old accounts, the fertile land and other conditions needed for
their support and favorable to the success of praiseworthy a purpose,
for which happy result they would spare no effort. As soon as I had
received these news, and in view of the said Commissioner at San
Blas having assured me that he had communicated them also to the
Visitor-General, I issued direct and most pressing orders and instructions to the effect that without wasting a moment the Packet *El
Príncipe* be readied for sea well provisioned, and return to her destination without any avoidable delay; whereby, through the favorable weather for the sail and trusting above all in the assistance of
Heaven, I hope by Its Mercies to see the desired end of this enterprise
attained, since it is directed to the spiritual and worldly good of the
unhappy dwellers of those lands.

God keep Your Excellency the many years I desire him to.

Mexico, August 27th, 1769. — Kissing Your Excellency's Hand,
Your obedient servant, — *The Marquis de Croix.*

To His Excellency Knight-Commander Julián de Arriaga." [39]

Don Gaspar de Portolá has begun the overland march to Monterey, leaving the missionaries and the sick at San Diego; he
has left there also all the hopes for the arrival of the packet *San
José*, which will never come; he trusts that the *San Antonio*,
back from San Blas, will fill out the *San Carlos's* crew so that
both vessels together will be able to provision and store the
presidio he is ordered to found at Monterey Bay. God's protect-

39. Toledo, Biblioteca Pública, Col. Borbón-Lorenzana (papeles americanos),
t. 65, n.º 5: Archivo General de Indias, Aud. de Guadalajara 417 (reel 354/14-19
on Bancroft Library film; duplicate copy, ibid., Aud. de México, reel 214/6-7
on Bancroft film).

tion went with them on their journey, but their own forecasts failed to come true, as we shall see in what follows.

The journey is begun toward the unknown: they set out in the hopes of being about to grasp it, looking ahead to a succesful march, with their pioneer calling and the boldness of conquest beckoning to them through the hard moments that await them, as they dream of a new world nearby, an Arcady and Paradise-for some of them a goal, for the rest merely so many miles of trail to be travelled.

They open paths and set up camps in lands that have never known tread of European feet; they raise stockades and chapels, they receive and bestow honors, the ancient races of the natives fraternize with the oldest blood of Spain, they baptize using the fresh waters of unexplored rivers, they dine on seeds and fish from unknown seas and lands, and they leave behind them as they go new friends, admirers, and subjects, new towns bearing the sonorous new names of the saints.

They have now left the San Diego shores, seeking only the horizon ahead.  In front marches Captain Rivera with his buff-coats, the trailbreakers and those who with spade and crowbar open the way and protect the main body of the expedition.  They seek out watering places where, beside the good grasses in the river bottoms, the little shelters of the soldiers will be pitched. Often they are followed at a distance by the Indians of nearby villages, half fearful and half admiring, viewing wonderstricken these amazing horsemen like mythological gods.

Using their precise instruments, the explorers take the positions of the new routes, and upon the blank maps of Californiა sketch the lines which soon will become the *Camino Real* of the Franciscan missions.

Here now follow, day by day, the entries of a journal kept during the march to Monterey, written down by the light of dawn upon the fresh grass of the fields.  Here are set down in full all the details of the occupation of the vast territory lying along the Pacific—details which historians condense into a note.  We will come to know the adventure which began on July 14th., 1769, through the hand of Miguel Costansó of Portolá's Expedition.

# CHAPTER II

First Expedition by land towards Monterey
harbor. - His failure. - Discovery of San Francisco harbor. - Return of the Expedition to
San Diego mission.

Instruccion que deberá observar el Capitan de Dragones
de España D.ⁿ Gaspar de Portola, Governador, y Comandante en Gefe de esta Peninsula de Californias en la expedicion y viage por tierra à los Puertos de S.ⁿ Diego y Monterrey, situados sobre la Costa del mar del Sur à los grados 33,
y 37 de latitud.

1º .......... En consideracion à que el principal objeto de esta
expedicion, es el de extender la Religion entre los
Gentiles que abitan el Norte de esta Peninsula
por el medio pacifico de establecer Misiones que
hagan la Conquista espiritual en los dichos Puertos de S.ⁿ Diego y Monterrey, y en los demas parages intermedios que ahora se descubrieren, y regu-
laren por mas fertiles, y à proposito, asi al fin expresado de exigir Reducciones, como para el de in-
troducir la dominacion del Rey mi Señor,
prevengo à d.ho Governador que con la brevedad
posible, y una pequeña escolta se ponga en camino con el R.ᵐᵒ P.ᵉ Presidente de las Misiones
para la frontera de la de S.ᵗᵃ Maria, y que refor-
zando su Escolta en Villacatà con parte de la
que hà establecido alli el Capitan del Presidio
D.ⁿ Fernando de Rivera, siga sus marchas hasta
los referidos Puertos de S.ⁿ Diego por el rumbo, y

Instructions from Gálvez to Portolá for the expedition to Monterey.
Document detailed in the text. (Arch. Gral. de Indias. Sevilla).

# THE MIGUEL COSTANSÓ JOURNAL
# OF PORTOLÁ'S EXPEDITION.*

---

* Translated from eight manuscripts, whose variations are referred to in the footnotes, as follows: "early draft copies"=Tulsa, Thos. H. Gilcrease Inst., Conway papers 66, fols. 268-335, and Mexico, Biblioteca Nacional, Californias, legajo 53. 659-764 (consulted via typescript in Bancroft Library, Bolton papers, Item 88, folder 1); "corrected draft copy"=Madrid, Museo Nacional, Ms. 56'. (Virreinato de Méjico, t. 1, n.º 22; consulted via microfilm); "signed final copy"=Mexico, Archivo General de la Nación, ramo Historia, t. 369, fols. 25-104; other "final copies"=Seville, Archivo General de Indias, Audiencia de Guadalajara 417 (reels 357/27 through 361/28 on Bancroft Library microfilm); same archive, Papeles de Estado 43 (reels 5260-5262/46 on Bancroft Library film); San Francisco, Sutro Library, Memorias de Viages, fols. 234-322; "Palou's version"=Mexico, Archivo de la Nación, Historia, t. 22 (the composite journal put together by Palou under Juan Crespí's name but containing much of Costansó's journal from a version agreeing in different places with both the draft and the final versions and perhaps containing original material).

*A journal of the overland voyage made to the north-
ward of California at the order of His Excellency, the
Marquis de Croix, Viceroy, Governor and Captain-Gene-
ral of New Spain, etc., etc., by the direction of the Most
Honorable Don Joseph de Gálvez, Councilor of the
Chamber in His Majesty's Supreme Council of the In-
dies, Visitor - General of all His Majesty's Tribunals,
Treasuries and Branches of Revenue in the same realm,
and Intendant of His Army, etc., etc., carried out by
troops detailed for this purpose, commanded by the
Governor of the aforesaid Peninsula, Don Gaspar de
Portolá, Captain of Dragoons in the España Regiment.**

---

* This title is found in three manuscripts of the final version of the journal
(though in one it is added by a later hand). One copy has instead: "A journal
of the expedition made overland from the Harbor of San Diego to the northward of California, to discover that of Monterrey, A.D. 1769 and 1770." Copies
of the draft version have no title, though one has the marginal note: "Treats of
the fruitless ["fruitless" added] expedition overland in search of Monterrey Harbor by Don Gaspar Portolat [sic], Governor of California; he reached San
Francisco Harbor; they underwent many toils and suffered from lack of provision; the Engineer Costansó determined several locations."

Our departure having been set for July the 14th, the Governor ordered six soldiers under a corporal to go out to scout the country for the first two days' march ahead. They set out in the morning of the 12th and returned the following day in the afternoon with the report of having come across a watering-place at six or seven leagues' distance with enough for the men and the mounts.

## Friday, July 14th. 1769

From San Diego to the like-named hollow, 2 leagues.

Distance made from San Diego, 2 leagues.

After watering our animals (as we knew that there would be none for them where we were to spend the night), we set out in the afternoon and went two which we named [Cañada] de San Diego.

## Saturday, July 15th.

To Osuna's Pool,
4 leagues.

From San Diego,
6 leagues.

We raised camp from this spot in the morning and came to the place surveyed earlier by the scouts, which was named Poza de Osuna [Osuna's Pool] as well as San Jácome de la Marca—the first name given by the soldiers, the second by the missionary fathers. The spot is a very handsome pleasant hollow, which must be over two thousand yards wide in places, all covered with grass, and with some trees and a great deal of water, standing in pools. Next to one of these, at the west of the place, we made our camp at one o'clock in the afternoon. Upon our way we had met with two heathen villages, the first one more or less halfway along, the second within the same hollow as our own campground. All the country we travelled through was plentiful in grass and not at all steep; we bore northwestward always [and north-northwestward],[1] however the land allowed, consisting as it did of middling high knolls with drops down into several hollows all ending upon the sea, whose waters reach up into them in inlets in which quantities of salt gather.

The Indians of the hollow at once came over to see us, approaching little by little, vastly afraid, until, on being well treated and presented with string of glass beads, they gave way and became so familiar with us as to be bothersome.

In the afternoon the scouts were sent out, and returned the next day in the morning with news of having found water at the right distance.

---

1. Added in the final version.

# Sunday, July 16th.

To San Alejos,                                          From San Diego,
3 leagues.                                              9 leagues.[2]

In the afternoon we shifted camp, and directing our way northward and north - northwestward over high land with knolls like those before, we crossed two very pleasing hollows. We saw, in the first one, a heathen village where they came out to meet us as we passed by; one of them made the usual speech, to which when he was through we answered only with gestures and signs of thankfulness, not, however, stopping any further. They came with us for a long way, pointing out some small-sized sources of water along one side of the route. We stopped at the second hollow, next to a small-sized heathen village and close to the watering place that had been scouted out; this was a spring of good water located upon the hollow's eastern slope, and as it was a little scanty it was necessary to dig out a pool in front of it to catch the small flow, and wait for it to fill, in order to water the animals.

The countryside showed itself well-favored, growing brushwood and a few trees called sycamores,[3] and exceedingly plentiful in grass. The hollow here was named [Cañada] de San Alexos.[4]

2. Altered from "10" in the draft copies.
3. [Alisos.]
4. Spelled San Alexos in the final version (San Alexo in one copy), San Alejos in the draft copies.

## Monday, July 17th.

To Santa Sinforosa,                              From San Diego,
2 leagues.                                          11 leagues.

In the afternoon we set out from the aforementioned spot, the countryside having been already surveyed by the scouts. Travelled three leagues, with the same sort of country as before, that is, grass-covered knolls of black soil, very easy to go through and over. We came to the watering-place, which was located within a middling wide hollow; the water was collected into pools and rose from two separate springs, around which it made swamps or marshes covered with rushes and grasses. We placed our camp upon a slope [5] of the hollow on the western side; we named it Santa Sinforosa.[6] A heathen village upon the top of a knoll was in view from our campsite here; advised by their neighbors the San Alexos people of our coming, they deputed two of them to ask our permission to come visit us. By using signs we conveyed that they should wait till the way back to their village, shortly afterward all its dwellers came over. There must have been as many as forty men, fine appearing and of good stature; their headman or leader at once commenced the usual speech, using loud tones and curious faces; but giving him no chance to finish, we made a present of a few beads to him and his folk, and took leave of them.

In the morning they were back, spending the time quietly among us until we left.

---

5. "The slope," in the draft version.
6. Here and below spelled Sinforosa (once Simforosa) in the final copies; Zimforosa, Sinphorosa, etc., etc. in the draft copies; the Z is altered to and replaced by the S in the corrected draft.

# Tuesday, July 18th.

To San Juan
Capistrano,
2 leagues.

From San Diego,
13 leagues.

The watering-place which had been surveyed by the scouts was a little over two leagues away from Santa Sinforosa, a march which we made during the afternoon. The countryside we passed was again low hill lands; the place where we stopped was an exceedingly pleasant and agreeable one, a valley of remarkable size, thick with trees and covered with the finest grasses; it must have been close to a league in width, with various hollows running into it along the north and northeast side. The watering place consisted of a large-sized pool or swamp; we camped upon a little knoll located toward the west within the same valley, and named it San Juan Capistrano.

The heathens in its area, who had been informed of our coming, turned out to meet us, apparently so assured and certain of our friendliness that they brought along all their women. The chiefs or headmen made us their customary speeches.

# Wednesday, July 19th.

We lay by here, and the scouts were sent out early, with orders to survey the country as far along as they could go, yet so as to return to camp not later than nightfall. Seven men set out for this purpose under the Sergeant of the Californias Presidio. The heathens visited our lodgings very early in the day, in larger numbers than yesterday: there must have been over two hundred souls of both sexes.   They dealt just as familiarly with us as they could have done with their own countrymen and friends.   We treated them well and made them presents; but the experience made such an impression upon them that however much we tried to tell them goodbye, they would not leave, but stayed watching and gazing at us until very late.


## Thursday, July 20th.

To Santa Margarita,                                    From San Diego,
2 leagues.                                             15 leagues.


Very early in the morning we took up our march, following through one of the hollows that gave upon the north side of San Juan Capistrano Valley; then in turned northeastward, and we left it so as not to be turned from our course, and, after putting some hills behind us, we came down upon another pleasant spacious hollow, thick with trees and covered with grass.   It was two leagues' march; we named this spot Santa Margarita.

The water was plentiful, sweet and good, standing in pools at the watering-place, notwithstanding that there was a large lake of brackish water within the same hollow.   The heathens belonging to the closest villages at once came over to greet us, numbering some seventy souls [7] of both sexes; we gave the women a present of some beads, and took leave of them all.

---

7. "Persons," in the final version.

# PORTOLA'S EXPEDITIONS

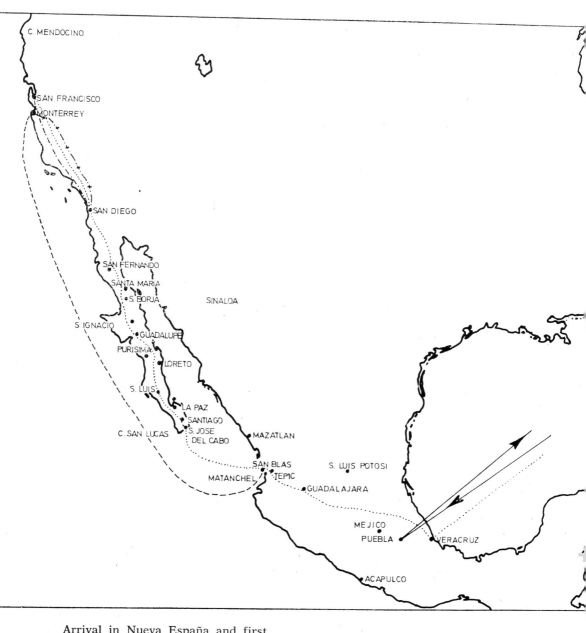

Arrival in Nueva España and first expedition to Monterrey.

Return to San Diego.

Second expedition to Monterrey.

Return to San Blas.

Portolá was the Governor of Puebla de los Angeles in México (Nueva España) from 1776 to 1785.

Diario del Principal de Mejico [...] el dia [...] de [...]

Resuelta, ya la salida, para dia 4 de Julio, mandó el Gobernador, fueran dos Soldados, y un Cabo à explorar el terre-
no para las dos primeras Jornadas; salieron esta dia
12 en la mañana, y volvieron el dia siguiente en la tarde con noticia de haver encontrado un Aguage à
distancia de seis ò siete leguas suficiente para la Gente y Caballada.

### Viernes 3 de Julio.

Despues de dàr agua à la bestias, por saber q[ue] no la ha-
via en el parage en q[ue] habiamos de dormir, salimos en
retaile, y andubimos dos aguas, paramos dentro de una
Cañada abundante de pastos à la que pusimos nom-
bre de S[an] Diego.

### Sabado 4 de Julio.

Levantamos el Campo en la mañana, dellicaurge[?]
dia, y llegamos al Sitio reconocido ~~anteriormente~~
antecedentem[en]te por los Exploradores, que recivio nom-
bre àcia Josa de Osuna, y tambien del S[an] Jacome
en Marca, el primero se lo pusieron los Soldados, el segun-
de los S[eñores] Misioneros; es este parage una tierra muy
liesca, y amena, en parte tendrà mas de dos mil
yaras de ancho, toda cubierta de Pastos, con alguna Arboleda, y mucha agua rebalzada en pozos,
à la parte del Occidente, junto à una de ellas senta-
mos nuestro Real, à la una de la tarde, encon-
tramos de nuestro camino dos Rancherias de
Gentiles, la primera, en la mediania del que mas
ò menos, la otra dentro de la propria Cañada de
nuestro Campamento; todo el País que transitamos
era abundante de pastos, y nada aspero: dirigimos
siempre al noruesre, conforme lo permitia el terre-
no, formad de Lomas, de mediana altura con pendien-
te à varias Cañadas, q[ue] todas iban à terminarse al Mar,

[marginal notes left:]
para
de la exp[edicion]
p[o]r mar
en busca
del Puerto
de Monterey
p[o]r D[o]n Juan
Portolà Gov[ernad]or
de California
que el [...]
en [...]
penitencia
[...]
[...]
[...]
[...]

A la Josa de
Osuna

9 leguas

[marginal notes right:]
a S[an] Diego

el agua,

Diary of Portolá's expedition to Monterey and San Diego, written by
Miguel Constansó. (Museo Naval. Madrid).

## Friday, July 21st.

To Los Rosales,
2 leagues.

From San Diego,
17 leagues.

In the morning we shifted camp, and, taking a north-westerly course, set out from Santa Margarita hollow; the way was one of middling high knolls, and at two leagues we stopped upon the [sic] hollow's western slope; with a watering-place amounting to some pools, and with grass enough. We saw some heathens' wives here, but very few of the Indian men showed themsel-ves. We named this place the Cañada de los Rosales [Rose-patches] because we saw such an extreme plenty of them here.

## Saturday, July 22nd.

To the Cañada
del Bautismo,
3 leagues.

From San Diego,
20 leagues.

We set out from los Rosales, and by keeping on our northwestward course along a way of knolls and streams, came to a watering place about three leagues away from the spot we had left. There was standing water in a pool that was of small compass but some depth, within a hollow upon whose eastern slope we set our camp, on level ground with plentiful grass.

There was a small-sized heathen village next to the camp; the people spent most of the day with us, all very happily and peaceably. Here the reverend missionary fathers baptized two of these heathens' little children who were dying, wherefore the place was named the Cañada del Bautismo, Christening Hollow.

## Sunday, July 23rd.

To Santa María                           From San Diego,
Magdalena,                                  23 leagues.
3 leagues.

We went on from the Cañada del Bautismo to another hollow which was named [Cañada] de Santa María Magdalena, located to the north-northwestward of the first; the way, though over low hill land and a bit broken, was not very hard going. The spot was plentiful in grass, lush with willows and other trees; the water plenteous and abounding at the watering-place, standing in pools among rushes and reeds.

## Monday, July 24th.

To San Francisco                          From San Diego,
Solano,                                     26 leagues.
3 leagues.

We set out on our way and, taking a north - northwest course in through another hollow that runs into the Santa María Magdalena one, we turned westward at the end of it; by topping some knolls and then crossing over a large [8] stretch of level land, we came down upon another very pretty hollow running at the foot of a high mountain range, with a stream of water and a great deal of trees. We placed our camp on level ground at the eastern side, and immediately were paid a visit by the Indians of a village living in the same hollow. They came over unarmed, with unmatched friendliness and peaceableness, made us a present of their poor seeds, and were treated by us with ribbons and trinkets.

---

8. "Good-sized," in the final version.

# Tuesday, July 25th.

We lay by at the aforesaid hollow, named San Francisco Solano. The scouts left early to survey the country, and came back in the afternoon with news of having found [9] water, though at six leagues' distance or a bit more.

# Wednesday, July 26th.

**To the Aguage
del Padre Gómez,
3 leagues.**

**From San Diego,
29 leagues.**

After midday we set out from San Francisco Solano, being careful first to water our mounts; we aimed our way to the northwestward, over middling high, easily travelled knolls with soil, until we came down to a very spacious plain whose limit was lost to our view. On going three leagues we stopped next to a very small-sized source of water, with scarcely enough in it for the men; it was named Aguaje del Padre Gómez [10] since this missionary father, one of our company, had been the one to discover it.

---

9. "Come across," in the final version and corrected draft.
10. Gomes in the drafts; the same altered to Gomez in a signed final copy. "Father" omitted after "missionary" in two final copies.

# Thursday, July 27th.

To Santiago,                                    From San Diego,
3 leagues.                                         32 leagues.

We shifted our camp from the aforesaid watering-place in the morning, and, crossing the plain on a north-west course, came at three leagues to the water, a very fine running stream of it; yet it was plain to see that it was dwindling with every day, from the dry season, and its waters sinking little by little into the sand.   The stream was coming down from the mountains, and is evidently a good-sized flood in the rainy season; it is very lush along its banks; this spot was given the name Santiago.

# Friday, July 28th.

To Río de los                                   From San Diego,
Temblores,                                         33 leagues.
1 league.

We went on from Santiago to another place the scouts had reported, not very far away at all, since we reached there in an hour's march.   It is a fine river, and one which carries large floods in the rainy season, as may be seen by the bed and the sands alongside it. There is a great deal of willow timber, and the spot has very good soil all of which can be irrigated for a great distance around.

We encamped upon the left of the river; upon its right side is a populous village of Indians who received us with great friendliness. Fifty two of their number came over to our camp, and their chief or headman told us, using signs easy for us to understand, and accompanying them with much pleading, that we should stay and live with them; that they would provide us for our sustenance with antelopes, hares, and seeds; that the lands which we could see were all theirs, and they would share them with us.

Here we experienced a fearful earthquake, which recurred four times during the day. The first quaking or shock ocurred at one o'clock in the afternoon and proved to be the most violent; the latest was about a half past four. One of the heathens, who must no doubt have filled the office of a priest among them, was at the camp at that juncture, and being [11] thunderstruck no less than we ourselves, with horrid cries and great expressions of fear he commenced imploring the heavens, turning himself about toward all quarters and acting as though conjuring the weathers. We named the place Río de los Temblores, Earthquake River. [12]

## Saturday, July 29th.

To the Ojitos                                              From San Diego,
Little Springs,                                               35 leagues.
2 leagues.

We set out at two o'clock in the afternoon leaving the Río de los Temblores, and travelled two leagues, leaving the plain and departing from the seashore in order to go into the mountains, for fear of a lack of water on the plain. We had no water for our mounts, but there was enough of it for the men in some little springs or

---

11. All except the signed final copy, which seems to have been altered, read *aturdidos*, literally "they being thunderstruck."

12. Two draft copies have a marginal note: "The quakes lasted for 15 leagues."

wells of a narrow hollow, close [13] by a heathen village. The Indians belonging to this village were holding a celebration and dance, to which they had invited their neighbors from the Earthquake River.


# Sunday, July 30th.

To San Miguel                                    From San Diego,
Valley,                                             39 leagues.
4 leagues.


We set out from the Little Springs—where a quake [14] had recurred, not so strongly—at a half past six in the morning, crossing the plain on a northward course and drawing steadily closer to the mountains.  We topped some fairly high, broken hills, only to descend at once into a very pleasant spacious valley with a plenty of waters, some running deeply in channels, others standing as in swamps.  This valley here must be about three leagues wide and in length a great deal more.

We seated our camp next to a channel of running water, whose banks were covered with watercress and cumin-plants: We named it Valle de San Miguel, Saint Michael's Valley; it must lie about four leagues away from the Little Springs.  In the afternoon still another earthquake was felt.

---

13. The draft version makes this word apply to the hollow, the final version attaches it grammatically (—os not —a) to the springs.

14. One draft copy reads "quakes", with the plural ending stricken out by a corrector, possibly Costansó himself.

# Monday, July 31st.

Through the same                                     From San Diego,
San Miguel Valley,                                        41 leagues.
2 leagues.

We left the aforenamed campsite at seven o'clock in the morning, and crossing the channel, which we had to throw a bridge over because of its depth, we travelled two leagues to the west - northwestward, in through clumps of straw and low brush which delayed us a long time, every step of the way having to be cleared. We crossed a very miry stream of running water, and made camp a little further on, in an open clear spot within the same valley, and next to a gap seen to the westward. We felt another strong quake at a half past eight in the morning.

# Tuesday, August 1st.

We spent this day lying by, and the scouts went out to survey the country.

The ground shook at ten o'clock in the forenoon; at one o'clock in the afternoon the quake recurred strongly, and an hour later we experienced another one. Some soldiers asked leave to go out ahunting on their horses, and others to go afoot, with a notion of shooting some antelope, many of which species had shown themselves: they are a kind of wild goat, armed upon the forehead with antlers a bit larger than goats'. At their return, these soldiers said they had seen a river of fine water sixteen to seventeen yards [15] in width rising next to the gap on the south side of the valley and at the foot of a hill in view from the campsite, half a league distant at the utmost.

## Wednesday, August 2nd.

To the Porciúncula
River, 2 leagues.

From San Diego,
43 leagues.

We shifted camp in the morning, and by travelling westward came out of the valley through a gap in between low hills; then we came into a fairly spacious hollow with a great deal of cottonwood and sycamore trees, among which, upon the north-northwest,[16] a handsome river ran and, rounding the point of a steep little height, continued on toward the southward.

Another river course or bed showed to the north - northeast, a sizeable torrent, but now dry: this bed joined with that of the river and thereby furnished us with plain proofs of the great floods it must carry in the rainy season, for there was a great deal of tree trunks and jetsam along the sides. We stopped at this place, which was named the Porciúncula. At afternoon and night three successive earthquakes were experienced here.

---

15. Spanish yards, therefore 44 to 47 English feet.
16. The draft versions read "north-northeast".

Uniform of the soldiers called «Catalonia Volunteers», regular troop
who for the first time takes part in an action of conquest and colonization
in America. (Drawing by V. P. Pallarés).

# Thursday, August 3rd.

To Sycamore Spring,                                    From San Diego,
3 leagues.                                             46 leagues.


We forded the Porciúncula River, flowing very swiftly down through the hollow by which it issues from the
mountains out into the plain.    We took up a west-southwesterly course over a high level country, and at three
leagues' march came to the watering-place, which was
given the name of Ojo de Agua de los Alisos [Sycamore
Spring].    This was a large source lying in a bottom,
out of which sprang extremely wide-girthed trees of this
variety; it was covered with grass-clumps, sweet-smelling plants, and watercresses.    The water ran off to
the southwestward in a deep channel.    All of the soil
which we saw on this day's march seemed admirably
suited to yield all sorts of grain and crops; along our
way here we came across a whole village of heathen
Indians out gathering their seeds across the plain.

Quakes were again felt during the afternoon; we
were astonished at how they kept on, and some among
us were convinced that there must have been large vents
in the mountain range running westward ahead of us:
we found a number of such indications upon the way
between the Porciúncula River and the Sycamore Spring,
for the scouts saw large swamps of a pitchlike material,
boiling and bubbling, up close to the mountains.

# Friday, August 4th.

To Antelope Spring,                                    From San Diego,
2 leagues.                                             48 leagues.

We made our way from the Sycamore Spring,
skirting the mountains [17] over a good, level, grass-covered route, to the Ojo de Agua del Berrendo [Antelope
Spring], so named by us from one of these creatures
being taken alive—one of the Volunteer soldiers having
broken its leg by a musket-shot the afternoon of the
preceding day and having been unable to overtake it.
The watering place lay in a depression surrounded by
low knolls close to the seashore.   At this place we
found a village of heathens, very friendly; at once they
visited our quarters with bowls full of seed foods, nuts,
and acorns, a present we returned by our strings of
glass beads, which they greatly esteem.

# Saturday, August 5th.

To the Sta. Catalina                                   From San Diego,
or Los Encinos                                         51 leagues.
[Live-oak] Valley,
3 leagues.

The scouts, having gone out to survey the coast and
a way along the shore, soon came back reporting they
had come to a very high cliff at the mountains' end,
abrupt to the sea and utterly shutting off any way past
along the seashore; this forced us to look for a way
through the mountains, and, though steep and difficult,
a way was found.

---

17.  Instead of *sierra,* one draft copy reads *tierra*—"the country."

Thus in the afternoon we set out from the Antelope Springs, and, heading northwestward toward where country mountain seemed to afford a pass, we went into the range through a canyon made by steep heights on both sides; but at the end of it, they were a little easier, allowing us to take to the hill slope and toil up to the summit, whence we had a view of a very pleasant spacious valley.   We went down to it, and stopped next to the watering place, a very large pool.   Close by it was a populous village of very friendly well - behaved heathens; they offered us their seed foods in bowls or baskets made of rush, and came over to the camp in numbers that, had they been armed, might have given us cause for alarm, for we counted as many as two hundred and five of them altogether, between men, women and children.   Each of them would present us with a bit to eat, and we responded with our own beads and ribbons.   On this day's march we made three leagues, and we named the valley Santa Catalina; [18] it is about three leagues in breadth and over eight in length, all surrounded by heights.

## Sunday, August 6th.

We lay by on this day, receiving countless heathen visitors who came from various directions to see us. They had heard the news of the packet boats sailing along the coast and Santa Barbara Channel, and drew upon the ground the shape or plot of the Channel with its islands, showing us the route of our ships; they also said that once before a bearded folk, dressed and armed like ourselves, had come into their lands, pointing as they showed that they had come from the east.   One man

18. Spelled Cathalina in the draft copies, and Catharina and Chatarina (sic; in the marginal note) in some final copies. Francisco Palou spells St. Catherine's name Catarina here.

related how he had travelled to their country and there
seen places or settlements made up of large houses,
where each family occupied its own building.   Besides
this, he added that in a few, about seven or eight, days'
march northward, we would come to a large river running among steep mountains, and uncrossable; beyond,
we would see the sea, and it would prevent us from pursuing our journey further in that direction.   But we
left these geographers' reports to be verified by the witness of our own eyes.


## Monday, August 7th.

**Through the same**                                    **From San Diego,**
**Live-oak Valley,**                                         **54 leagues.**
**3 leagues.**


We went across the Santa Catalina Valley, three
leagues in width,[19] to camp at the foot of the mountains
which we were to essay on the following day.   There
was water enough and to spare for the men, little enough
for the animals, in among rushes and reeds.


## Tuesday, August 8th.

**To the Ranchería**                                    **From San Diego,**
**del Corral,**                                              **58 leagues.**
**4 leagues.**


We went into the mountains, with the route already
prepared by the pioneers sent out ahead in the early
dawn.   We made part of the way through a narrow
hollow, part way over extremely high hills of bare

---

19.  This phrase is lacking in the draft version.

ground, hard going indeed up and down for our beasts, then went down to a little valley with a heathen village whose folk had sent messengers over to the Santa Catalina Valley for us and guides to teach us the best way through the mountains. Here these poor Indians had a large repast all laid ready for us, and seeing that we purposed to go onward so as not to lose our day's march, they made the most earnest entreaties to require us to come to their village, which lay to one side of the road. In order not to slight them, we had to yield to their requests, gaining their good will and a present consisting of seeds, acorns and nuts; besides, they gave us more guides, to bring us to a watering place which they told us of. It was late when we reached it, after a day's march of four leagues.

The country between the village and the watering place is handsome and pleasant in the plain, though this is surrounded by bald steep heights; we saw a great deal of very large stout cottonwood and white-oak trees upon the flat. The watering place proved to be a stream with a great deal of water flowing within a middling wide hollow, with a great many willow and cottonwood trees; close by the place where we camped was a populous village of Indians living without any shelter save that afforded by a slight booth shaped like a cow-pen, so that the soldiers named the whole spot the Corral Village.

## Wednesday, August 9th.

Before our eyes lay enormous chains of mountains, into which we should have perforce to enter were we to attempt to continue on our northward or northwestward courses, the best and most direct routes for our journey; but we were afraid instead that the farther we might go inland, the greater might be the obstacles, and

that we might be departing too far from the shore.    It
was decided therefore to follow along the hollow in
which we were then camped and downstream, if possible,
to the sea; for which purpose the scouts, sent out early
in the morning, bore orders to press on as far as they
could, in order to survey any hindrances that might face
us along the way, while the men and the pack-train therefore lay by here during this day.

A crowd of Indians came over to the camp with a
present of seeds, acorns and canegrass-honeycomb, a
very friendly, affectionate folk; they expressed their
meaning admirably well by the use of signs and understood everything which we would tell them in like language: in this fashion they gave us to understand that
the way inland was very mountainous and steep, while
the one along the shore was level and easy; if we went
through the interior of the country we should cross five
mountain ranges with as many valleys, and on going
over the last range we should have to pass a swift full-
flowing river running down through a canyon.

The scouts came back at night-time saying that there
was level country with plenty of water and grass affording a way through to the seashore, though they had been
unable to have a sight of the sea itself despite having
gone about six leagues onward following the lead of the
hollow.

## Thursday, August 10th.

Through the Cañada                          From San Diego,
de Santa Clara,                                61 leagues.
3 leagues.

We made three leagues within the hollow, which ran
west-southwestward this whole way.    We stopped on the

bank of the stream, which was running a good-sized [20] flow of water at our arrival, but at once under the hot sunshine dried up, just as the scouts told us they had found it to do on the day before: a peculiarity we afterward noted at other streams which were flowing at night-time and ran dry during the day.

This hollow's soil is all very soft, loose, and whitish, and our animals sank into it with every step they took. The hollow here was named Santa Clara.

## Friday, August 11th.

Through the Cañada                                  From San Diego,
de Santa Clara,                                          64 leagues.
3 leagues.

Early in the morning we set out on our way; the hollow still ran in the same west-southwesterly direction; at three leagues we stopped close by a populous village upon the bank of another stream of running water issuing out of the mountains through a narrow gorge and emptying into the Santa Clara Hollow, which here has a greater breadth. This village must have had over two hundred souls, and they were living with no more in the way of shelter than those at the Corral, that is, within a booth like the other.

In the afternoon, seven chiefs or caciques came over with a numerous suite of Indian bow and arrow men, who however had their bowstrings loosened in token of peace; they were bearing a bountiful present of seeds, acorns, nuts and pine-nuts which they spread before us. The chiefs, taking care to learn who was in charge, made

---

20. One of the draft copies reads "plentiful"; all other versions, including Francisco Palou's, have "good-sized."

a special offering to ourselves,[21] the Commander and his officers, of various necklaces made of little black and white stones whose consistency is a great deal like coral, differing from it only color. The number of heathens showing themselves today must have been perhaps over five hundred men.[22]

## Saturday, August 12th.

Through the Cañada                                From San Diego,
de Santa Clara,                                      67 leagues.
3 leagues.

We shifted camp in the afternoon, and, keeping still on through the hollow over a rough way past streams and gullies made by water draining from the mountains in the rainy season, we stopped upon one of these which was still carrying a good deal of water. In this day's march we made three leagues.

A few heathens came over from a village which we had in sight here, bringing the usual bowls full of seeds and pine-nuts, which they offered us with the same freeness and goodwill as those before.

## Sunday, August 13th.

Through the Cañada                                From San Diego,
de Santa Clara,                                      69 leagues.
2 leagues.

Made two leagues, still going on down through the hollow, anxious to reach the shore, which we had been

---

21. By a different placing of a comma, some copies of both versions read "in charge of us, made a special offering to the Commander and his officers."
22. Altered from "souls" in the draft copy revised by Costansó.

supposing to be near at hand. We seated our camp a short distance away from the stream, which henceforward we shall more fitly term a river, from the size of its flow by this spot, contributed by various streams that give into it upon both sides of the hollow.

Beyond this spot we could make out a spacious level, extending south and westward out to the sea, grass-covered with a few trees. Close to our camp-site was a very small-sized village of heathens, dwelling in their spherical-shaped (like a half orange) grass-covered huts with a vent atop to let the light in and the smoke out.

## Monday, August 14th.

To Pueblo de la
Asumpta,
2 leagues.

From San Diego,
71 leagues.

In the morning we shifted camp, aiming our way west-southwestward for a space of two leagues. We came to the shore, and were faced with the view of a regular town, the most populous and well laid out one that we had seen up to that time, located upon a strip or point of land at the very shore, overlooking it and appearing to dominate the waters. We counted as many as thirty well - built grass - roofed and spherical - shaped large roomy houses; and by the large numbers of people who came to greet us and later gathered at camp, we reckoned there must not have been under four hundred souls.

These are heathens of a fine figure and frame, very active and quick, diligent and clever. Their skill and dextrousness is especially evident in the framing of their

canoes, which are built of good-sized pine boards well
lashed and tarred together, and beautifully shaped: they
handle these with the same degree of skill, with three
or four men setting out to sea afishing in them, while
they are roomy enough to hold up to eight or ten; they
make use of long paddles with two blades, rowing with
unspeakable swiftness and speed. Everything which they
execute is remarkably fine and well finished; but what is
most worthy of astonishment is the fact that they have
no other tool than flint to work the wood and stone with,
being either unacquainted with the use of iron and steel,
or knowing very little of the extreme usefulness of these
substances, for [23] we did indeed see some fragments of
knives and sword-blades among them, which however
they did not use for anything save [24] cutting up meat or
cleaning fish taken from the sea. By means of our glass
beads and other trinkets, we purchased from them some
baskets or bowls which we saw, made of rush, with several wooden carvings, dishes and cups made all in one
piece, of various shapes and sizes, that could not have
been more handsomely made upon a lathe.

They presented us with quantities of fish, especially
the kind called "bonito"—to judge by how easily they
caught them, it was fishing season then with them—, as
well tasted and delicately flavored as the catch of the
eastern Cartagena and Granada fisheries.

The Engineer with this Expedition [25] observed the
latitude of this town, upon the shore using the English
octant, by the meridian height of the sun, facing the solar

---

23. The draft text: "or knowing it very little... although."
24. The draft: "which however they use only for."
25. This phrase is in only one of the draft copies, added in a handwriting
that looks exactly like Costansó's.

disc, the height of the lower limb of which
    was found to be . . . . . . . . . . 69° 42'
Solar semidiameter, add   . . . . . . .   16'
Height of observer's eye above the water,        13'
    six to seven feet, subtract . . . .   3'
Meridian height of sun's center . . . . . . 69° 55'
Zenith distance   . . . . . . . . . . . 20° 05'
Solar declination for the meridian here, 106° to
    107°. West of the Island of Fierro, due at
    noon [26]  . . . . . . . . . . . . . . 14° 08'

Latitude of the said town . . . . . . . . 34° 13'

We believed this to be the same town which the first
Spanish sailors, Rodríguez Cabrillo among others, named
*Pueblo de las Canoas,* Canoe Town. We ourselves gave
it the name of the Assumption of Our Lady or La Asumpta,[27] having reached here the eve of that feast.

We seated our camp a short distance away from the
town, upon the banks of a river carrying its waters down
to the sea, and issuing out of the mountains upon the
north in a gorge.

Some chiefs or caciques from the mountains came
in the afternoon with their people to greet us; various
islanders of the Santa Barbara Channel who happened
to be here at La Asumpta Town also came over.

---

26. The last phrase is not in the draft copies.
27. The name is spelled variously in the different copies: La Asumpcion or
La Asunción de Nuestra Señora; La Asumpta or La Asunta or (incorrectly) La
Absumpta, La Absunta. The same variations occur further on.

# Tuesday, August 15th.

In the afternoon we set out, after watering the animals, the scouts having told us we would be unable to reach the watering place, which lay a considerable way from the place which we were leaving, in a single march. We made two leagues along the shore, and placed our camp next to a temporary village of Indian fishermen who made us a present of more fish than we could eat.

These folk, during the night, serenaded us upon highly discordant shawns or pipes which did nothing save to annoy us and keep us awake.

# Wednesday, August 16th.

In the morning we made two leagues or a little more, keeping alongside the seashore.   We came to a village or what we shall rather call [28] a populous heathen town situated upon the very shore at a point of land, next to which ran a small [29] stream of good water.

The heathens belonging to this village resorted immediately [30] to the camp which we set up upon the other

---

28.  This phrase is found only in the final copies.
29.  Only in the final version.          ‘      ‘
30.  Only in the final version.

side of the stream, and brought us barbecued or grilled fish to eat, the while that their canoes out fishing at the moment returned with fresh fish; they landed a little way from us and brought up a plenty of bonito and sea-bass which they made us a present of, offering us such quantities that we could have laden the entire pack-train with fish had we had the means to prepare and salt it.   They gave us besides some unsalted dry fish (they employ no salt in their foods) which we added to our provisions, and it came in very helpful during the journey.

One of this town's chiefs or caciques had happened to be at the Asumpta town when we passed by, and had been one of the most [31] eager to entertain us: a robust man of good figure and features [32] and a great dancer, in regard to which we named his home the Dancer's Town. It seemed even more populous than the Asumpta; the houses are of the same size and structure.

## Thursday, August 17th.

To the Carpintería,                                   From San Diego,
1 league.                                             76 leagues.

We continued our march for a short way along the edge of the shore, then over high knolls above the sea, stopping round about a quarter-league away from it close to a stream of excellent water, issuing out of a hollow in the mountains, with a great deal of willow trees.   In sight of us was another heathen village or town consisting of thirty two houses, and as populous as [33] the ones before.   Men, women and children all came over to the camp with fresh [34] and barbecued fish, all of them greedy

---

31. In the draft version, "the most".
32. In the draft, "physiognomy."
33. In the draft, "no less populous than."
34. The draft reads "dried."

for glass beads and necklaces, which are a better cur-
rency and more highly valued among them than gold and
silver.

The soldiers called this the Carpenter-shop Town, *La
Carpintería,* since at the time they were building a canoe
there. It is no more than[35] a league distant from the
Dancer's Town.

This seemed to us all a very fit place for a mission,
both in regard of the countless heathens dwelling along
these shores in an interval of only six leagues, and because of there being a great deal of soil capable of yielding a great harvest: a claim that can also be made in the
mystical sense, for the tractability of these folk gave us
great hope that the word of God will likewise yield its
fruit within their hearts.

## Friday, August 18th.

To Pueblo de la                              From San Diego,
Laguna,                                          79 leagues.
3 leagues.

We went on from the Carpintería town to Lake
Town, three leagues beyond the former. We encamped
upon a lake whose fresh waters are a source of supply to
the heathens possessing and living in its neighborhood:
namely the most populous town yet seen; we supposed
there must be over six hundred souls. They offered us
as much barbecued and fresh fish as we might wish and
came with their women and children over to camp, more
friendly and affectionate than we had found them anywhere before.[36]

---

35. In the draft "only."
36. In the revised draft copy, the passage "more friendly... before" is substituted, in what seems to be Costansó's own handwriting, for the following: "as
much at ease among us as among their own relations and friends."

Along our way found two villages that had been destroyed; we were unable to ascertain the reason why, but were persuaded it must have been the result of wars and feuds that commonly arise so easily amongst them.


## Saturday, August 19th.


We shifted camp, less for the sake of making a day's march than in order to escape the bothersome attentions of the heathens, for we scarcely made half a league, departing from the shore which was cliffy and lined with high hills here, before [37] stopping in a hollow with running water, though it sank into the sand not far from its source. The hollow was clothed with handsome live-oaks and cottonwoods; pine trees were not wanting upon the mountain tops.

Despatched in the morning, our scouts came back in the afternoon with news of having seen large settlements and a great number of heathens, proclaiming how well received by them they had been everywhere. Ten heathens came over to the camp unarmed at night, for the purpose (they said) of leading us to their village on the morrow; they were allowed to spend the rest of the night at a little distance from the camp, with a few people sent to keep them company and entertain them until daybreak.

---

37. Some slight errors in some of the copies suggest that something may have been lost from the previous two or three phrases conceivably the words "before noon".

## Sunday, August 20th.

**To the Pueblos**                                          **From San Diego,**
**de la Isla,**                                                    **82 leagues.**
**3 leagues.**

We went from the hollow here to the Island Towns, distant it must be some three leagues [38] from Lake Town over a level way between the mountains and some knolls stretching along the seashore. We came in view of a long bare point of land, on the eastern side of which a large inlet comes in through two separate mouths (or so some said, for not everyone could make out both of them), half a league, more or less, apart. Upon its northern side [39] the inlet is hemmed in by a hillock and middling large strip of land, declared to be an island by those who claimed to have seen the two inlet mouths—as indeed it must be, if the two mouths are actual. From the hillock, whose greenery and trees afforded a remarkably handsome prospect to the eye,[40] rose and extremely populous heathen settlement with innumerable [41] houses, so that there were some who claimed to have counted over a hundred of them. This inlet spreads through the plain eastward, turning into marshes and lakes of considerable extent, upon the shores of which there are two other towns smaller than the one on the island. We passed through the midst of one of these to get the watering place next to which we set out our campsite; and shortly thereafter the heathens belonging to the three towns came over with barbecued and fresh fish, seeds, acorns, porridge or mush and other foods, insisting we should eat them, and making plain by their looks the satisfaction they received

---

38. "Distant round about three leagues," in the draft version.
39. This phrase—which is in fact confusing—is not in the final version.
40. "To the view," in the draft.
41. The draft version says only "a great many."

«San Carlos», Captain ship under the command of Vicente Vila,
in the sea journey to Monterey. (Drawing by V. P. Pallarés).

from our presence among them. We treated them all, and made them presents of glass beads, ribbons and other trinkets, which we also used to trade for curios in the way of baskets, skins and featherwork.

The whole country which we examined, whether along the way or from our campsite, is most highly favored, plentiful in grass, and covered with live-oaks, willows and other trees, giving signs of fecundity and of yielding everything that might be wished, or planted.

The heathens, not content with presenting us with their foods, wished to entertain us as well, plainly showing how obstinately and jealously each town sought to excel the others in winning our approval and praise by their presents and entertainments. The headmen and caciques came over from each town in the evening, one after another, decked according to their custom, painted and laden with feathers, carrying split canes in their hands by the shaking and noise from which they marked the beat of their songs and the measure of their dance, which they kept so well in unison and time as to cause no discord.

The dancing lasted all afternoon, and we had great trouble getting free of them: finally we sent them off, recommending them earnestly by signs not to come back and bother us at night; but all in vain, after nightfall they returned with a great train of buffoons or minstrels, all playing pipes whose tone grated upon the ears. They were in danger of scaring our animals, and so the. Commander went out to meet them with his officers and a few soldiers. They were given a few beads, and it was suggested that if they should break into our sleep again they would not be our friends and we would take it ill of them. The measures was sufficient to make them withdraw and leave us in peace for the rest of the night.

## Monday, August 21st.

To S. Luis Obispo,                                    From San Diego,
2 leagues.                                                84 leagues.

This coast runs nearly west-northwest between the Asumpta town and the one we left this morning [42] named Lake Town, as has been said. From here onward, the coast runs almost [43] west, on which course we made two leagues in sight of the sea over high hills broken by gulches draining from the mountains, which come close to the sea in places leaving not much land in between; elsewhere the heights draw further back, leaving a bit of plain, up to half a league or a little more, between themselves and the sea. We crossed through a considerable live-oak wood and came to our watering place, a stream of good water within a hollow upon whose flanks close to the shore the heathens were occupying a village that must have had over a thousand souls. We stopped on the righthand side of the hollow not far from this village, the inhabitants of which at once came to greet us and to give us a great deal of fresh fish and the dried kind cured without salt; nor did they spare entertaining us with dancing and celebration, like those at the Island.

The place here was named San Luis Obispo.

---

42. Either this remark belongs in the last entry, or "Island Towns" should have been written instead of "lake town".

43. "Toward the west," in the draft version.

## Tuesday, August 22nd.

The scouts, having set out in the morning, returned at one o'clock in the afternoon with news of having found water and a good road along the shore at low tide, in order to take advantage of which we found it necessary to delay the march till the following day; so men and packtrain lay by and rested here.

## Wednesday, August 23rd.

To San Güido,
3 leagues.

From San Diego,
87 leagues.

By using the hour of low tide in the morning, we travelled round about a league by the shore, then left it and made the rest of the march, three leagues, over high hills that were abrupt to the sea and broken frequently in places by ravines and gulches through which the mountains shed their drainage; nealy all of these had running water in them.

We came to our stopping place, a town of eighty houses and about eight hundred souls on both sides of a hollow with running water in it, where they again entertained us with dancing and a bountiful present of fish and seeds.

We placed our camp upon the left hand of the stream in a high open spot: we named the whole place here San Güido, St Guy.

## Thursday, August 24th.

To San Luis Rey,                                    From San Diego,
3 leagues.                                          90 leagues.[44]

Today's march was as hard going as yesterday's, with road and terrain of the same nature, requiring the pioneers to be thrown out ahead every moment in order to prepare hard places a toilsome task wich created a great deal of delay.   We came to the stopping place, a hollow where a salt-water inlet thrust in, on the banks of which an Indian town of fifty hearths greeted and entertained us as te ones before had. The heathens here have scant firewood, and any good water must be gotten up above in the hollow where a stream comes down, before it mingles its waters with those of the inlet.

In the afternoon, from this place, named San Luis Rey, we made out the last three islands of the Santa Barbara Channel: San Bernardo, the westernmost; Santa Cruz, next to the east; and Santa Barbara, for which the stretch of sea and shore which we are discussing is named, is easternmost of the three. This day we made three leagues.

## Friday, August 25th.

To San Zeferino                                     From San Diego,
Papa, 2 leagues.                                    92 leagues.

We began the march from San Luis Town and travelled four hours in order to make two leagues over high

---

44. The figures for the distances are left blank in the draft.

very broken land above the seashore; one of these clefts completely cut us off from our way, because of its steep western slope: we had to take the shore road, over rocks at the foot of a cliff, laved by the sea waves, and no more passable than they, save at the ebb of the tide. This cliff lasted a quarter-league, and them we went up over high hills until the stopping place, which was called San Zeferino Papa, St. Zephyrinus the Pope, a heathen town of twenty houses and two hundred souls, more or less, where they received us in friendly and affectionate manner. Their locations is a rather gloomy one: they live within a hollow girt about with not very high, totally bare hills without any trees on them; other of an equally gloomy look are in view up within the country. But there is no want of grass, and the soil is good and friable. In through the mouth of the hollow comes an inlet which provides a landing place for the Indians' canoes; like all the others along these shores, they live by fishing. Here in the hollow is fresh running water, but it must be taken further up before it mingles with the inlet.

While at this spot [45] we suffered cold blustery north winds, from which we feared baleful effects harmful to health.

The altitude from the horizon of the sun's lower limb, observed with the English octant facing toward the solar body, was found at noon to be . . . . 65° 47'
Solar semidiameter, add . . . . . . 16'

Inclination of line of sight on account of height of observer's eye the water, six to seven feet substract . . . . . 3'   13'
Horizon altitude of center of solar body . . . 66° 00'
Resulting zenith distance . . . . . . . 24° 00'
Solar declination at that hour . . . . . . 10° 30'

Latitude of the town . . . . . . . . 34° 30'

---

45. "While still upon these shores," in the draft version.

# Saturday, August 26th.

To Pueblo                                    From San Diego,
del Cojo,                                        94 leagues.
2 leagues.

We made our day's march, a short one, in the afternoon, making two leagues over high knolls that were a
bit easier going than the ones before.  In the midst of
the way we passed by a village of twenty houses set beside the sea at a wide and spacious spot on the shore;
we came into sight of Point Concepcion, which ends the
Santa Barbara Channel.

We encamped above a hollow, on the eastern side;
there was a heathen town within it, consisting of twenty
four houses, where they received us like all the others
and made us the same sort of presents.  They have the
usual canoes, and live by fishing.  The countryside they
inhabit is likewise scarce in wood, but the soils of a good
quality and plentiful in grass.  The chief of the town
here was lame, and therefore the soldiers dubbed his
town Ranchería del Cojo, the Cripple's Village.

By observation of the noon height of the sun, the latitude of Point Concepcion was determined as thirty four
degrees thirty minutes, being the same as San Zeferino
Town.

# Sunday, August, 27th.

To Ranchería                                    From San Diego
de la Espada,                                      96 leagues.
2 leagues.

The way ran on in sight of the shore over level land on a westward course as far as Point Concepción, and beyond this point, which lies a little over a sea-mile away from the Cripple's Town, we turned northwestward because of the coast's trending about in this way.

We went two leagues and a half, stopping upon the northwest side of a hollow within which was a heathen village of twenty hearths and two hundred fifty souls more or less.[46]

Into the hollow reaches an inlet which catches the water of a stream and keeps it from reaching the sea, although it issues from the mountains with a good-sized flow. The village heathens here are very poor, have no canoes, and live in want; the country they inhabit is of little regard—steep, gloomy, and scant of wood.

While at this spot a soldier lost his sword,[47] by letting it be stolen from his belt; though he afterward got it back, as the Indians who had seen the deed done ran after the thief themselves, and the village therefore got the name of la Ranchería de la Espada, Sword Village.

---

46. The phrase "more or less" is added in the final version.
47. "A sword" in the draft version.

## Monday, August 28th.

To Los Pedernales,                                    From San Diego,
2 leagues.                                                98 leagues.

We travelled for two leagues over land high above
the shore but good and easy going; the watering place
next to which we stopped was a spring of very good
water, with close by a small-sized poor heathen village
of ten huts and sixty souls.   There was a strip of land
running out into the sea, in view from our campsite and
a musket-shot away at most.   Here we gathered a great
deal of good flint stones for our firearms, and consequently the spot was called *los Pedernales*, the Flints.

By observation of the noon height of the sun, it appeared we were in thirty four degrees, thirty three minutes.[48]

## Tuesday, August 29th.

To the Cañada                                         From San Diego,
Seca, 2 leagues.                                       100 leagues.

We set out from the Flints in the afternoon, and
went two leagues north-northwestward over land high
above the sea and through sand-dunes, stopping within
a hollow where there was grass aplenty for our animals
but scarcely any water, which was gathered into a pool.
The soldiers called it the Dry Hollow.

Before coming to the dunes here, the coast is bluff
and abrupt, with a great many ledges of rocks running
out into the sea.

---

48. Two of the draft copies mistakenly read "three minutes."

# Wednesday, August 30th.

To the big San
Verardo River,
1 league.

We went from Dry Hollow to the big River of San Verardo, news of which we had received from some heathens, by signs, upon our arrival at the Dry Hollow, but which we had been unwilling to believe could be so short a way from there; nor did we finally believe them until we saw the whole village belonging to the river, men, women and children, all looking for us at the hour of loading the pack train in the morning, and then reached the place itself at a littlde under a league's march.

The river mouth here is entirely stopped by a sand-bank over which we crossed dry shod; its waters seemed still and currentless, though some flow could be seen by going a little farther up, a sure sign that the water sinks into the sand and finds its way out into the sea in this manner.

Here along the river there is a very handsome flat, with a good deal of willow trees and a great deal of soil capable of yielding all sorts of grain. There were some extremely large bears seen, and great numbers of these creatures' tracks.

# Thursday, August 31st.

To the Rancheria
del Baile de las
Indias, 2 leagues.

From San Diego,
103 leagues.

In the morning we set out from the San Verardo River; travelled two leagues northward over flat land much overgrown with a wild rosemary and other sweet-smelling bushes, till we came to a hollow with grass in plenty; crossed through the midst of it, and on topping its northern slope discovered a heathen village upon a middling sized lake surrounded by knolls of little height. These were poor heathens; they had no houses, and we doubted whether this could be their permanent abode. They entertained us with dancing, and it was the first place where we had seen the women dance. Two of these stood out over all the others, holding tufts of flowers in their hands and adorning their dance with various pretty gestures and motions without dropping the measure of their songs.

We called the place Squaw Dance Village.

# Friday, September 1st.

To the Laguna
Larga, 3 leagues.

From San Diego,
106 leagues.

We took an inland route from Squaw Dance Village northward, departing from the shore in order to avoid the crests of dunes with which it is lined and other hard places; however, we found it impossible to escape a chain of them which reached out from inland and lay across our way. This sandy ground, however, was soon past;

then we went through high hills and hollows with very good soil and good grass. We camped within a large valley, next to an extensive freshwater lake that must have been some two thousand yards in length, and as much as five hundred in breadth,[49] perhaps more in places. We named the whole valley Laguna Larga, Long Lake valley; it is three leagues away from the spot we set out from in the morning.

There were two heathen villages in this valley, one of them small-sized and wretched, the other a bit larger, containing several huts.

## Saturday, September 2nd.

To the Laguna                                    From San Diego,
Redonda,                                          109 leagues.
3 leagues.

The scouts came back in the morning from their survey, removing the worry they had caused us over their failing to return to camp the evening before. The cause of their tardiness was having missed their way because of the thick fog which came on, and obligated them to spend the night in the valley on their way back to camp after scouting the march we were to make. This proved to be three leagues, across the valley (which is two in width, on the north-northwest course which we pursued) and the rest of the way over high tablelands, which we followed up to the watering place, another large lake nearly circular in shape, lying within a hollow shut off by sand dunes that held back the water and kept it from emptying into the sea. All of the hollow was covered with rushes and reeds, absolutely impenetrable, over-flowed and waterlogged soil. It all stretched eastward to westward.

---

49. A little over 1.800 yards and 450 yards, respectively, in English measure

As a great many bear tracks had been seen, in the afternoon six soldiers set out ahunting on horseback, and managed to shoot one dead. It was a fearsome beast, fourteen palms [50] from the soles of the rear paws to the head, the paws over a *tercia* [51] long, and the whole weighing what must have been more than fifteen *arrobas*. [52] We ate some of the meat, and found it well flavored and good.

We named the whole place here the Round Lake.

## Sunday, September 3rd.

The men and pack-train lay by here today, while the scouts, who set out to look for a way through the mountains, came back in the afternoon stressing the troubles they had had even to get to their foot. We had recognized the fact already by viewing the land ahead: enormous dunes upon the sea-shore and lakes, inlets and marshes making a positive labyrinth of the plain.

We judge the mountain range in view nearby to be the same one that we had been keeping constantly upon our right ever since leaving San Diego; in some places it draws back from the sea, in others it approaches it and entirely shuts off any way along the shore, as is the case here.

---

50. Apparently about 9 feet 8 inches.
51. About a foot, since the *tercia* is about 11 inches.
52. Say nearly 600 pounds.

## Monday, September 4th.

To the Ranchería del Buchón, 4 leagues.

From San Diego, 113 leagues.

To avoid the marshes on the plain and the inlets reaching to the foot of the mountains, we took a westward course over the top of the dunes, which we crossed through at the narrowest spot discovered by the scouts, only half a league across. At once we struck upon the shore and went round about a league north-northwestward along it, then turned back inland again eastward, crossing the dunes at another half-league-wide narrow neck, and then regaining firm ground over a strip of land between two waters: we had upon our right a fresh-water lake with the dunes guarding its rear and keeping it from draining to the sea, and on our left an inlet reaching into the plain. We got around its head by going north-northeastward, and then recovered our northward course and went into the mountains through a gap or hollow lined with live-oaks, sycamores, willows and other trees. We placed our camp in the same hollow on the bank of a stream covered with watercresses. We went four leagues in this day's march.

Along the whole way we met with no more than one poor, small-sized heathen village; this country is rather empty.

The Indians belonging to the village here, which was only a short way from our lodgings, came over to visit us in the afternoon with a present of seeds and a little fish which they offered to us. The person of their chief was disfigured by a large growth hanging from his neck, at the sight of which the soldiers nicknamed him the Goitre, *el Buchón*, the name which was likewise given to his village and the whole spot.

## Tuesday, September 5th.

To the Cañada
Angosta, 2 leagues.

From San Diego,
115 leagues.

We pursued our march through the same hollow, which began turning northwestward; shortly beyond there, we left it and took our way over hills and high knolls not far from the seashore: steep and hard going, constantly up and down, but a well-favored country grown over with live and white oak trees. We saw not leagues. We placed our camp within a very narrow hollow girt about by extremely high hills, with running water and grass enough for our mounts.

The place was named the Narrow Hollow.

## Wednesday, September 6th.

The scouts came back stressing how hard and steep the way was which awaited us upon our next march; their report heard, it was decided to lie by here while sending pioneers out ahead to repair the troublesome spots in the mountains, a task which took them the whole day.

## Thursday, September 7th.

To Cañada de los
Osos, 4 leagues.

From San Diego,
119 leagues.

We set out from the hollow over the top of high beetling hills, a bad road which lasted over three leagues

until coming down to another spacious hollow with a
great many freshwater lakes in it, where our mounts
were unable to water because the banks were so miry;
which obliged us to prolong the march as far as a stream
of very good water encountered on our way a league farther down; we encamped upon its banks.

In the hollow here we saw troops [53] of bears, who
keep the ground ploughed up and full of the holes dug
while seeking their sustenance from roots yielded by the
soil; the heathens also feed upon these, there being some
which are well flavored and tasted.   A few soldiers got
onto their horses, attracted to this big-game hunt because
twice before it had worked out well for them; this time
they managed to shoot one dead, but had a lesson of the
ferociousness and fury of these beasts.   The instant they
feel themselves wounded, they charge full tilt upon the
hunter, who can only escape by spurring his horse, for
their first rush is swifter than could possibly be supposed from the outer appearance and awkwardness of
such brutes.   Their toughness and strength is not easily
overcome, and only good aim or good luck on the hunter's part can bring them down on the first shot, by
hitting head or heart.   The one they succeeded in killing
here took nine musket-balls before it dropped, and this
only when they shot it in the head.   Some other soldiers
were so rash as to bait one of these beasts while riding
mules: they shot six or eight times at him, and the bear
certainly must have died from the shots; but he maimed
two of the mules, whose riders were only too lucky to
escape with a whole skin.

This was named Bear Hollow.

_____

53. "A troop," in the draft version.

# Friday, September 8th.

Through the Cañada                                    From San Diego,
de los Osos,                                            121 leagues.
2 leagues.

We made our march through the same hollow, following it down to the sea, as it tends constantly westward. Along our way we had some obstacles in the
form of deep gullies which had to be prepared in order
for the pack-train to cross. At two leagues we stopped
upon a knoll in sight of the sea and close to a stream
of very good water, covered with watercresses. The
country was pleasant and well favored, plentiful in grass
and nowise scant of trees.

Not far from our lodgings was a small - sized,
wretched heathen village, scarcely amounting to sixty
souls, living in the open without house or hearth. They
came over to visit us, offering us a sort of gruel made
out of parched seeds which we all thought tasted well,
with a flavor of almonds.

Upon the south side there reaches up into this hollow an inlet of enormous size, which we thought must
be a harbor; however, its mouth, which opens southwestward, is covered by reefs that give rise to a raging surf.
A short distance northward of the mouth, in front of our
campsite, was seen an extremely large rock shaped like
a round head [morro], which, at high tide, becomes an
island separated from the shore, though by less than a
musket-shot. Beyond this head the coast trends west-
northwestward as far as a big point which we could make
out, abrupt to the sea, the coast making, between this
point and another point of the mountains which we had
left in back of us, a large bight, with shelter from the
south, southwest and western quarters, if only there is
sufficient depth.

Scene reflecting the daily life of the Californian Indians
and their peculiar huts.

# Saturday, September 9th.

To the Estero,                                    From San Diego,
3 leagues.                                         124 leagues.

Went three leagues along the shore, which abounds
with streams of living water shed from the mountains,
which lie not far away from the sea in this stretch. We
stopped within a middling wide hollow into which shot
an inlet with a stream of good water emptying into it out
of the mountains. The knolls bounding the western side
of the hollow ran to the sea and cut off the way along
the shore, but left open the way to the north and the
north-northwest, where two branches of the hollow ran,
leaving us the choice of which direction to take.

Horizon height of the sun's lower limb, obser-
   ved with the English octant, facing the solar
   disc, found at noon to be . . . . . . . 59° 21'
Solar semidiameter, add . . . . . 16'
Inclination of line of sight on account
   of height of observer's eye above the         13'
   sea, 6 to 7 feet, substract . . . . 3'
Horizon height of center of solar body . . . 59° 34'
Zenith distance . . . . . . . . . . . 30° 26'
Declination at that hour . . . . . . . . 5° 01'

Latitude of the place . . . . . . . . . 35° 27'

This place was named the Inlet, *el Estero.*

## Sunday, September 10th.

To the Cañada                                    From San Diego,
del Osito,                                        127 leagues.
3 leagues.

We took the arm of the hollow that bore to the
north-northwestward and followed it for three leagues'
distance, then left it because it was turning northward.
On a northwest course we topped some knolls,[54] from
which we could descry the mountain country covered
with pine trees, and, beneath in a very deep hollow
wooded with willows, cottonwoods, pines and other
trees, a little river with a good deal of running water,
which some of us would have had to be the Carmelo
River.

We placed our camp on the height above the hollow,
which was named Little Bear Hollow, *el Osito*, because
some mountain Indians coming down to visit us brought
along a cub of this species which they were taming, and
offered it to us.   They must have amounted to sixty men.

## Monday, September 11th.

To the Cliff,                                    From San Diego,
[el Cantil],                                      128 leagues.
1 league.

We went down to the sea and along the shore, bearing off to the northwestward, and made a league and a
half of good road with watering places every inch of the
way.   We stopped upon a cliff at the edge of the sea

---

54. This clause is omitted from the draft version.

on the northwest side of a hollow with a stream of very good water debouching through it, and grass and firewood enough and to spare.

Here the meridian height of the sun was observed, by which we learned the latitude to be thirty five degrees, thirty five minutes.

## Tuesday, September 12th.

To the deep
stream valley,
2 leagues.

From San Diego,
130 leagues.

By following the seashore over high knolls and broken country, with the way constantly interrupted by gullies and streams (all with plenty of water in them), to repair which kept the pioneers busy using their axes and machetes to clear brush and their pickaxes and crowbars to open the way through, we came to a point of land abrupt to the sea and left it upon our left hand, turning in through a gap which the mountain range afforded us, and continued our march north-northwestward crossing various hollows and streams.

We stopped upon a knoll, high up above a hollow or deep stream valley where there was water enough in a pond. On this day's march we travelled about three leagues.

## Wednesday, September 13th.

To the foot of the
Santa Lucía
Mountains,
2 leagues.

From San Diego,
132 leagues.

We travelled two leagues, partway in the aforesaid hollow or stream valley, partway above cliffs in sight of the sea.   We camped between two streams of good water and at the foot of the mountains, which are very high here, and fall abrupt to the sea, albeit they seemed to grant a way through by a gap seen toward the east.   We believed this might be the range referred to in the rutters of shipmasters who had sailed these seas, particularly those with Sebastián Vizcaíno's expedition, as the Santa Lucías; wherefore our commander, wishing to ascertain whether this were so and for the purpose of scouting the country at whatever length was needed, rigthly supposing that this woul be the hardest spot in our entire journey to win past (to judge by how the old accounts dwell upon how steep it is), decided to lie by here and to despatch the most knowledgeable scouts to survey it to their satisfaction by going as far upcountry as they could, without any limit of time being set for their return.   The scouts in effect set out, eight in number under Captain Don Fernando de Rivera,[55] after midday.

## Thursday, September 14th.

The scouts arrived back at nightfall, and confirmed all that we had been fearing as to the roughness and difficulty of the mountains; we took comfort, however, from the news they gave us of having found a way through, though one that must be opened by plying pickaxe and crowbar.

## Friday, September 15th.

The pioneers were sent out very early in the morning to commence the work.   They came back after dark, having levelled the way for the first day's march we were to make into the mountains.

---

55. The revised draft copy alone spells the name Ribera.

# Saturday, September 16th.

To the Santa                                    From San Diego,
Lucía Mountains,                                    133 leagues.
1 league.

We went into the hollow which was to grant us a
way through the mountains, following it first along one
slope,[56] then the other, however the terrain allowed.   This
was a very narrow hollow here: the mountains which
girt it about rose in places abruptly straight up, and were
all of them insurmountable for goats and deer, let alone
for men.   Through the midst of the hollow there ran a
stream of water, crossed over many times before we
reached the spot where we camped: here it split into two
branches, one heading to the east-northeast, the other to
the north; a bit more northwestward a hill not quite so
overhanging as along the rest of the hollow showed; we
were to climb up the skirts of this, after first opening
the way.   We made little more than a league in this
day's march.

As soon as the men had dined we set about the work,
everyone turning to, without exception of persons;[57] they
were divided into several parties between camp and the
place proposed for the end of our day's march, and we
managed to complete the whole section in the afternoon.

# Sunday, September 17th.

To the Hoya de                                    From San Diego,
Santa Lucía,                                    134 leagues.
1 league.

We topped the grade and then, by following the ridges
of the hills forming the flank of the northward-head-

---

56. "Side," stricken out, in the draft copy.
57. I. e., without distinction of rank; the final version says merely "without
exception."

ing hollow of which we spoke, came down another very long grade and camped within a hollow where there were some heathens living at large without house or hearth.   There could not have been over sixty souls of them, tractable and exceedingly obliging folk.   We made a league at most in this day's march, and called the spot the Santa Lucía Hollow.

## Monday, September 18th.

The men went out very early in the morning upon the task of preparing the way, very few remaining behind at camp.   But though they toiled at it all day long, they had to return without completing the stretch to be made on the next march.

## Tuesday, September 19th.

The whole day, and the larger part of the men, were employed upon the same road work, which was finally achieved.

## Wednesday, September 20th.

Through the same                                From San Diego,
Sta. Lucía Mountains                            136 leagues.
to the Real de los
Piñones, Pine-nut
Camp, 2 leagues.

We started the march in the early morn and began by climbing a pretty steep grade, then went along the

side slope of a deep and narrow hollow in which there
was running water, went down to it and crossed the
stream two or three times in the same hollow, which is
a bit wider in this portion, and then climbed anew up
an extremely long grade. From the top of the grade we
could overlook the mountain country stretching in all
directions with no end to be seen to it on any side: a
gloomy prospect indeed for so many poor travellers as
we, tired and wayworn with the fatigue of the journey,
with levelling rough places and opening paths through
hills, woods, dunes and marsh. The cold weather began
to be felt, and we now had a great many soldiers affected
with scurvy and unfit for duty, thus increasing the toil
for those left on their feet. On this day's march we
made two leagues, stopping within an exceedingly narrow
little hollow where there was scarcely the ground for us
to camp on. The watering place was a small one, with
the water standing in pools, the grass extremely scanty.
In this vicinity and round about there were three heathen
villages, a wandering folk without house or home; at
the moment they were busy harvesting pine-nuts, which
the great many pine trees in these heights yield abun-
dantly.

The scouts, having set out in the afternoon to inspect the country, brought back news of having seen a
suitable stream and hollow for shifting our camp to,
with enough grass for our mounts, who needed it sorely.
They also told us that the mountains had been becoming a bit more manageable where they had gone, toward
the east-northeast, far off our proper course though it
was; they assured us however that farther on the country
gave signs of being easier to travel through in a better
direction.

# Thursday, September 21st.

To the Arroyo
de las Truchas,
[Trout Creek],
1 league.

From San Diego,
137 leagues.

To reach the hollow which had been inspected by the scouts, several bad spots had to be repaired, and the pioneers set out early in the morning to prepare them; our march, in order to give them time to finish the task, being delayed till the afternoon.

After the men's dinner the march was begun, and we went a league over broken country, though less steep than that before. We placed our camp upon the bank of a small river with a great deal of running water, and a good many trout and other sorts of fish in some pools or backwaters.

We named the place Trout River, *Río de las Truchas.*

# Friday, September 22nd.

We lay by at this place in order to give the scouts time to inspect the land fully, and for our mounts, who were beginning to be sorely tried, to recover a bit.

# Saturday, September 23rd.

The scouts returned after nightfall from their surveying with pleasing news. They said they had advanced twelve or fourteen leagues ahead and had followed down a hollow to its mouth upon the sea. However, as later became plain to everyone, they had been signally deceived by all the fog filling the hollow in the direction of the sea, and thought they had seen the shore, while it was still quite a long way off. Within the hollow ran a river which they took to be the Carmelo, as they saw stout trees along its banks, cottonwoods, willows, live and white-oaks and several other sorts. The men were a great deal cheered by this news; everyone took heart, supposing that not far away lay the goal of our travels, whither our wishes had been forestalling our own arrival.

## Sunday, September 24th.

Through the same Sta. Lucía Mountains, 2 leagues.

From San Diego, 139 leagues.[58]

We started the march and went round about two leagues through rolling hill lands, course northward and sometimes northeastward; we went down a grade at the foot of which was a stream with a good deal of water running in it, flowing toward the east and then, as we were given to understand by the heathens, turning northward and joining Trout River. All the country we crossed through, and the more so [59] from this stream onward, was covered to right hand and left with white-oaks and live-oaks as tall and stout as any in the forests of Europe. All of them were laden with acorns, though not yet ripe ones, a harvest of mast enormous enough to feed many a herd of swine: the Indians use it in making mush, which we have eaten of in several places, and they also barbecue it and eat it like bread.

58. The distances are miscopied in the corrected draft.
59. The draft version reads "especially."

In this stream-wash there was a village of wandering Indians, very poor ones but showing themselves friendly and obliging.

## Monday, September 25th.

Through the same                                    From San Diego,
Sta. Lucía Mountains,                                 140 leagues.
1 league.

Forewarned that we would find no water until the river the scouts had informed us of, we watered our animals before setting out in the afternoon. We stopped in the midst of a hollow, a little over a league northeasterly of the place we had left. The soil in this hollow is stony; [60] there is a great deal of white-oak and live-oak trees.

## Tuesday, September 26th.

To the Real del                                     From San Diego,
Chocolate,                                            143 leagues.
3 leagues.

We travelled through the same hollow we had followed the day before,[61] on the same [62] northeasterly course; little by little it became narrower, while the heights girding it about, stony and white-colored,, drew completely [63] together at its end; nonetheless, they granted us a way through that was nowise difficult in going down to the hollow of the river which the scouts had taken to be

---

60. "Very stony," in the draft.
61. "... we ... before" only in the final version.
62. "Same" only in the draft.
63. In the draft version, "almost entirely."

the Carmelo, as we were faced by a grade of small account thickly overgrown with brush of various sorts, among others wild chestnut-bushes with very bitter-tasting fruit.    There was a village of wandering Indians at the foot of the grade, over two hundred souls, it must have been, houseless and living in the open next to a fallen live-oak, so that it was named [64] Fallen Tree village, *rancheria del Palo Caído*.    The heathens here offered us quantities of pine-nuts and seeds; we stayed a while among them and then went onward in order to get to the bank of the river believed by most of the people to be the Carmelo, and camp there.

The borders of this river are overgrown upon both sides with willows, cottonwoods, live-oaks, white-oaks [6] and other timber, and the whole bottomland laved by it is exceedingly lush.    The soil seemed well friable, yielding a variety of sweet-smelling plants, among them an abundance of rosemary, sage, and rose-patches laden with blooms.

This day's march was three leagues, and the camp which we located upon the river bottom was later known as Chocolate Camp.

## Wednesday, September 27th.

To Real del
Alamo,
4 leagues.

From San Diego,
147 leagues.

Once the pioneers had effected the clearing of the river-bottom, we crossed where the stream was split into three branches below a backwater off it where there were large pools with a great many fish in them; some

64. In the draft, "whence came its name of."
65. "White-oaks" is not in the draft version.

of the soldiers said they saw fish that might have weighed eigth or ten pounds.

We left the river bottom, to continue the march over level unwooded land, approaching slightly toward the hills bounding the hollow along its northern side, until we came once again to the bluff of the river bottom slanting over toward the hills and bending northwestward, forcing us then to take to the slope of the hills we had had to our right.[66]  As soon as the terrain permitted, we pursued our way again over level land, not departing very far from the river,[67] and placed our camp close to some pools [68] at a spot well supplied with grass, which is not plentiful everywhere in the hollow.  There was a cottonwood tree here which we enclosed within our encampment, so that it got the name Cottonwood Camp; it lies four leagues away from Chocolate Camp.

This day we saw a great many antelopes moving in bands over the plain, but none of them provided us a shot at it.

## Thursday, September 28th.

To Real Blanco,                              From San Diego,
4 leagues.                                   151 leagues.

There was no better road, nor could we have wished for one, than the same hollow, opening northwestward and widening out apace as we approached nearer the seashore, following the course of the river as it bent about unchecked from one side to the other between the hills girding it about.

---

66. A version of this entry copied by Francisco Palou reads "hills we had had in sight of us to the right hand," possibly the original wording.

67. "From the way following the river," in Palou's version.

68. "A pool," in the draft version.

It was four leagues' march; we camped within the river bottom amid a patch of live-oaks. The soil here was whitish, whence came the name of White Camp for the place. During the march we again saw several bands of antelopes, but they had gotten up into the hills far beyond gunshot.

## Friday, September 29th.

To Real de los Cazadores, 3½ leagues.

From San Diego, 154½ leagues.

This day's march was hardly less than the preceding one; we went three leagues and a half over soft whitish soil which our animals sank into, though it was a bit more plentiful in grass. We stopped next to the river, flowing here more boldly and noisily. A great many antelope were seen in the course of the march.[69]

This was named the Hunters' Camp because at it we surprised some heathens who were so steeped in their chase that they did not see us until we were atop of them, and then startled, took to flight, no efforts of ours being enough to draw them back.

---

69. The space for this paragraph (found only in the final version) is left blank in the corrected draft, and other draft copies also show signs of the omission.

# Saturday, September 30th.

Following the                                        From San Diego,
same hollow,                                          158 leagues.
3½ leagues.

We made another three leagues and a half down-
river, course northwestward and west-northwestward.
The hills bit by bit were lowering themselves and by
drawing away apace were widening the hollow out; here,
in sight of where the hills turned into two low points, it
must have been over three leagues across.   The land was
of the same nature as described above, the soil soft un-
derfoot, crossed by open cracks running in all directions,
whitish and scant of grass.

From camp, we could hear the noise of the sea, with,
however, no shore in sight; wherefore, wishful as we
were of learning what part of the coast we were upon,
and persuaded we could not be very far away from the
wished for Harbor of Monterrey and that the mountains
we had put behind us were without question the Santa
Lucías, as we had concluded from the history written by
Father Torquemada treating of the expedition and voyage of General Sebastián Vizcaíno, and from the rutters
of the sailingmaster Cabrera Bueno, our commander determined that the scouts should set out early to survey
the shore and river mouth.

Back they came saying that the river emptied into an
inlet coming up from the sea through the hollow; that the
shore, seen both to north and to south, was surrounded
by dunes, with the coast-line making an enormous bight;
that to the south was described a hill running out into a
point out at sea, covered with trees that looked to be
pines.

On hearing this news, some began to suspect that we must have left the harbor we had been seeking behind us, because of the great circuit we had made in crossing the mountains, having cut across them northeastward and northward, until coming down to the hollow which allowed us to regain the shore way by going northwest and west-northwestward.   They added, that the point of pines discovered on the south side was a strong token of the fact, since it is one of the marks given by the rutters for Monterrey Harbor; and, they asserted, the large bight reported by the scouts was doubtless the one that lies between Point Año Nuevo and the aforesaid Point of Pines.

These arguments made some way with everyone; to which could be added the fact that we were in over thirty six degrees and a half of north latitude, so that it seemed indispensable to proceed to survey the point before undertaking anything else.

## Sunday, October 1st.

By the same
hollow, 1 league.

From San Diego,
159 leagues.

We approached a bit nearer the shore by following the river's course for round about a league, then some officers with the engineer went on to examine the shore. What they observed there was the large bight seen by the scouts, the northern point of which, running a considerable way out to sea, bore northwestward of them a distance of over eight sea-leagues, or so they judged; the point on the south side made by the pine knoll, southwest by south; they could not see the inlet mouth, as its connection with the sea does not occur where they stood but much farther to the northward.

It proved impossible to observe the sun's meridian height with the octant, in order to determine the latitude, as the coastline offered no free horizon, either to southward or to the north.

## Monday, October 2nd.

Early in the morning the scouts set out eagerly on the way to survey the Point of Pines, convinced that they could not fail to meet with the Harbor of Monterrey, which we [70] were supposing to have been left behind us.

As it had not been possible to observe the meridian height of the sun while at the shore on the previous day, this measure was performed at camp by means of the gnomon.  The hypotenuse of a right triangle was measured as 8,000 of the equal parts commonly shown upon the scale of a pantometer or proportional dividers from a surveyor's kit, and the shadow at the meridian was 4,338 when measured, yielding a calculated angle for the sun's meridian height of 57 degrees 10 minutes, a zenith distance of 32 degrees 50 minutes, while its declination was 3 degrees 54 minutes, and the latitude of the place therefore 36 degrees 44 minutes.

## Tuesday, October 3rd.

The scouts came back in the afternoon, saying they had seen never a harbor, either on the north side of the Point of Pines or the south, but only a small-sized bight lying between the said Point of Pines and a point a little farther south, where there was a stream of water coming

---

70. The draft version says more specifically, "which they were supposing".

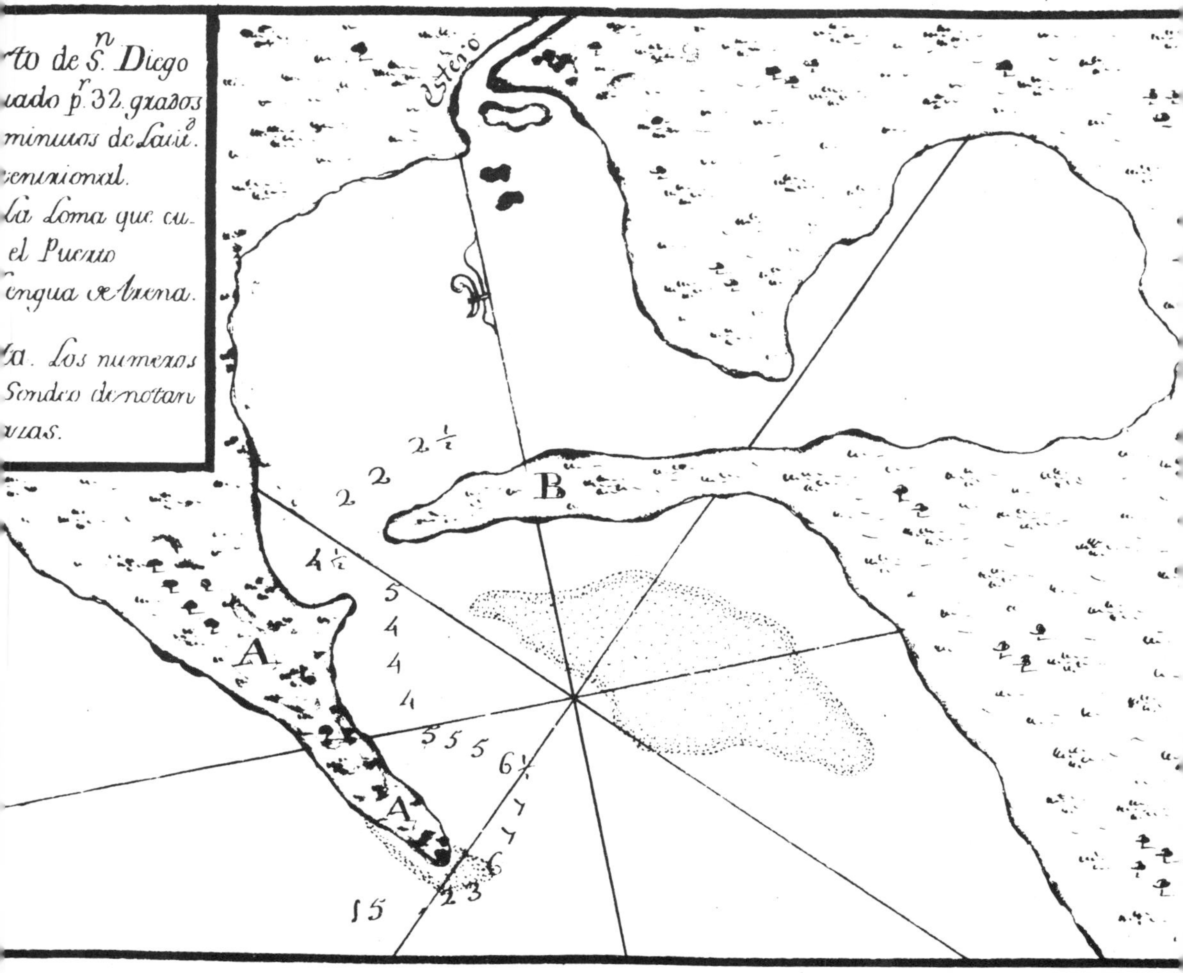

rto de S.<sup>n</sup> Diego
uado p.<sup>r</sup> 32. grados
minutos de Latit.
eridional.
la Loma que cu.
el Puerto
engua de Arena.

a. Los numeros
Sondeo denotan
zas.

Estero

2

2 ½
2 2
2

B

4 ½
5
4
4
4

A

5 5 5
6 ½

A

6

15    2 3

1 5

San Diego Harbour in 1769, from the original drawing by Vicente Vila.
(Arch. Gral. de Indias. Sevilla).

down from the mountains and an inlet into which it emptied. Beyond, the coast ran in cliffs south by west; [71] the insurmountable steepness of it forced them to turn back, convinced furthermore that the cliff which they had in view was the same one by which we had been forced away from the shore and made to take the way through the mountains.

## Wednesday, October 4th.

Confounded a bit by this news, our commander determined to call a meeting of his officers in order to deliberate upon the most suitable course to be taken in the present straits. He set forth the short supply of our provisions, the number of our sick (seventeen men being half crippled and unable for any duty), the lateness of the season, and the excessive toil endured by those who were still well in caring for the mounts, in watching them by night, in guard duty at camp, and in constantly sallying out to survey and explore. The meeting was held after hearing a mass of the Holy Ghost, and the officers all voted as one to continue the journey, as the only course left to us—in hope of meeting through God's grace with the long wished for harbor of Monterrey and there finding the packet "San Joseph" [72] to relieve our necessities. And should God allow us all to perish while searching for Monterrey, we should have fulfilled our duty to God and to man, by striving till death to complete the undertaking upon which they had sent us.

---

71. So in all the copies.
72. Spelled *San José* in the corrected draft copy.

## Thursday, October 5th.

The scouts went out in the morning to survey the country, in order to pursue the journey.

## Friday, October 6th.

The scouts returned in the afternoon with very flattering news. They had come across a river with a great amount of lush growth and trees of Castile, and thought they had seen another point of pines to northward of it (though it was afterward realized that they had been deceived by the cloudy weather). They had seen, as well, tracks of large animals with cloven hooves, which they supposed must have been buffalo, and a populous village of heathens living camped in grass-covered huts, where there must have been over five hundred souls, so they said. These Indians had had no notice of our coming to their lands, as was seen by the consternation and terror our men's presence caused: for some, amazed and confounded, scarce knowing what they did, ran to their weapons; others shouted and cried out; the women dissolved into tears. Our people did all they could to quiet them, and the sergeant of Loreto Presidio, who was in charge of the party, managed it with great difficulty by getting down from his mount and approaching them with signs of peace. The Indians would not let him come as far as their village; they made signs to them for him[73] to stop, and all at once seizing their arrows, they drove them all point downward into the ground, as they also did with other darts and feathers which they brought

---

73. In the draft copies, "to him."

out upon the instant. After this they withdrew; and as the scouts recognized that this had been arranged as a sign of peace, several of them got down and collected a few of the arrows and devices set out. The heathens were very happy with this, approving our men's behavior, who then, the better to assure them that their [74] intent was not to do them harm, but rather that they wished for their friendship, asked them by signs for food. At this the Indians grew better pleased, and at once their women set to grinding seeds from which they made some dough-balls, and made them a present of them. The sergeant gave them a few beads, which left the Indians very well satisfied and pleased.

## Saturday, October 7th.

To Laguna de
las Grullas,
2 leagues.

From San Diego,
161 leagues.

We went two leagues over the plain, in which we were a little delayed by having to prepare a passage across two swampy gullies we found upon our way, by putting earth and faggots for the pack train and mounts to cross upon. We located the camp among some low knolls close to a lake where we saw a good number of cranes, the first this journey has afforded us a sight of.

The holy oils were administered during the night to one of the sick men, who had turned very ill.

This place was named Crane Lake.

---

74. "Our," in the draft version.

# Sunday, October 8th.

To the Bird
Village, Ranchería
del Pájaro,
4 leagues.

From San Diego,
165 [75] leagues.

We continued upon our way through higher knolls than those we had left, with lakes of greater or less size filling every low spot in the terrain and forcing us to fetch a great many circuits around them. We came at four leagues' march to the village of which the scouts had informed us, which we found deserted, contrary to what we had expected, for when setting out from Crane Lake we saw various arrow and darts which had been driven into the ground close to camp and some shellfish placed at the foot of them, which the Indians had planted there in the afternoon or night of the day before, without showing themselves to us. We had been persuaded by these signs of peace that they would let us find them and treat with them at their village; yet suspicion or fear made these savages abandon it instead, a circumstance we were all sorry for, as we missed them extremely, principally for the purpose of acquiring information about the country, and for going with the scouts on their explorations, from which we [76] had been profiting very much. We placed our camp upon the bank of the river discovered by the scouts and not far from the village, which was next to its very lush pleasant bottomland full of cottonwoods, sycamores, and tall white-oaks, live-oaks, and another kind we did not recognize.

At this place we saw a fowl that had been killed and stuffed with grass by the heathens, which appeared to

75. Altered from "164" in the corrected draft copy.
76. The draft reads "they."

us to be a royal eagle; it was eleven palms [77] from wing-tip to wing-tip, and the river on account of this find was named Bird River, *Río de Pájaro*.

## Monday, October 9th.

The short cloudy days had been leaving the scouts no chance to survey the country, more especially since we reached here rather late. This obliged us to lie by at this place in order to give the scouts time to carry out their exploration by setting out early in the morning and being given the full day's limit for the purpose.

They surveyed the country for two days' march of the pack-train ahead, and came back with no news of any importance: a thing which dismayed us considerably, because of the shortness of supplies and the hindrance of the sick unable to shift for themselves, whose number was increasing every day.

## Tuesday, October 10th.

To the hollow
of the small
Corral Lake,
1 league.

From San Diego,
166 leagues.

We set out from Bird River [78] and went a league over level land, being unable to continue the day's march further as the sick men were extremely ill, and falling to the ground off their mules. We stopped next to a small lake [79] among knolls: a country very plentiful in wood, water and grass.

---

77. About 7 feet 7 inches, apparently.
78. The revised draft copy reads *Rl.* ("Bird Camp") instead of *Rio.*
79. Underlined as if a proper name in one of the final copies.

## Wednesday, October 11th.

The sick men were so very ill and near to their end that, with several of them having been given the sacraments, it became clear to us that failing to give them some surcease and rest was to risk their dying upon the way. Hence our commander determined to let them rest here, with a view to continuing onward as soon as they should receive some improvement; but in order not to lose time, and to the end of getting some news of Monterrey harbor, which we all [80] supposed to be close by, he ordered a party out to go as far onward as the animals (now becoming much weakened with the cold [81]) would allow. The sergeant of the presidio set out upon this exploration with eight men, each of them taking a relay of three mules.

## Thursday, October 12th.

This day passed without anything remarkable, with some improvement on the part of the sick.

## Friday, October 13th.

No particular occurrence.

---

80. "Everyone," in the draft version.
81. In the draft, "becoming weakened with the great cold."

# Saturday, October 14th.

We had been anxiously awaiting the scouts, who came back in the afternoon. The sergeant reported he had advanced some twelve leagues without getting any news of the harbor we were seeking, and had got to the foot of a high white mountain range.

# Sunday, October 15th.

To the Lagunilla,[82]
1½ leagues.

From San Diego,
167½ leagues.

We set out from the Laguna del Corral, Pen Lake, so named on account of a piece of fence built in between the lake and a knoll in order to keep the mounts penned in at night with only a few watchmen. We performed the march very, very slowly, so as not to unsettle the sick men, whom we contrived to transport upon saddle-supports,[83] the way women travel in Andalucía. We made a league and a half, stopping next to another small lake in the midst of a very pleasant narrow little [84] hollow with plenty of wood and grass.

The way proved rather hard going than not: we bore a north-northwestward course, not departing very far from the shore, from which we were separated by high [85] hills all grown over with trees which they said were sa-vins, the thickest, tallest and straightest ones we had

---

82. One draft copy has *las Lagunillas* in this marginal note.
83. *Xamuas*, i. e. *jamugas*.
84. "Little" is omitted in the draft version.
85. "High" does not appear in the draft.

seen until that time.   Among them were some of four and five yards' diameter.[86]   Their wood is of a rather dull, dark red hue, very soft, brittle and full of knots.

This hollow got the name of the Little Lake.


## Monday, October 16th.

To el Rosario,
2 leagues.

From San Diego,
169½ leagues.


We moved on from the Little Lake to the edge of a stream of good water which lay two leagues away to the west-northwestward, travelling in sight of the seashore; we were faced with two hard places to be prepared, the first at a very woody deep creek, the other a gulch where the way down and up was opened.

The place here was afterward known as the Rosary.


## Tuesday, October 17th.

To the Río de
San Lorenzo,
St. Laurence River,
2 leagues.

From San Diego,
17½ leagues.


At two leagues away from The Rosary, we forded a pretty big river, with water up to the beasts' girth-bands. The pioneers were kept busy in clearing the way down to the river and up from it across the ford and breaching a way through a low wood covering its bottomland.   It had been the same at another stream which we crossed short-ly before.   We encamped upon the righthand side of the river, which was called San Lorenzo.

---

86. Up to 13 feet nine inches in English measure.

# Wednesday, October 18th.

To las Puentes,                                    From San Diego,
2 leagues.                                         173½ leagues.

We followed the run of the coast, west - northwestward over knolls making high cliffs on the side toward
the sea; there is very little beach along the shore in the
whole of the two leagues' distance which we travelled.
We were faced with three hard spots to be prepared, at
as many hollows with running water at the bottom of
deep gullies, over which bridges needed to be thrown,
made of poles [87] covered with earth and faggots, for the
pack-train to cross.  We encamped upon a knoll at the
edge of the sea and at the east side of a hollow coming
out of the mountains, with a stream of good water.   This
place was called The Bridges.

# Thursday, October 19th.

To the Alto                                        From San Diego,
del Jamón,                                         176 leagues.
2½ leagues.

Our way this day was hard going because of the
constant ravines which we were faced with, seven or
eight in number, all giving the pioneers much to do, particularly one of them because of its depth and the
straightness of its sides.  At this ravine the mule carrying the cooking-pot fell over, wherefore it became Pot
Ravine, the *Barranca de la Olla*.

---

87. This phrase is missing from the corrected draft copy.

The coast now turns more to the northwestward [88] and is all in cliffs, save where a little bit of beach is formed at the outlets of the ravines. We had upon our right hand some bare whitish hills, gloom-inspiring, and for days past had lacked the comfort of seeing any heathens.

We stopped upon a very high knoll, in sight of the white mountains discovered by the scouts, on which were descried some clumps of pine trees. At the foot of the knoll, to left and right, ran fairly copious streams of water. We made two leagues and a half this day, and the place was called by the name of the Ham Height.

## Friday, October 20th.

To the Cañada
de la Salud,
Healing Hollow,
1 league.

From San Diego,
177 leagues. [89]

Upon setting out from camp, we were faced with a very long grade to climb, after crossing the stream running at the foot of the knoll on the north side. A way for us had to be opened by plying crowbars, in which task our whole morning was spent. Afterward we travelled a long way upon the ridge of a chain of gullied hills dropping to the sea, and stopped at the very shore at the outlet of a very deep creek coming out between very high hills of the mountain country. This place, named Healing Creek or Hollow, lies a league or a little more away from the Ham Height. In this short distance the coast runs northwest by north; the hollow lay open to the north-northeastward, running inland around about a league in that direction.

---

88. The corrected draft copy alone reads "to northward."
89. The marginal notation of distances is missing in the draft.

From the shore's edge a strip of land could be made out lying a short distance off to the west by north; it was low, with rocks scarcely elevated above the water.[90]

## Saturday, October 21st.

We lay by here at the hollow while the scouts employed the day surveying the country.

Observed with the English octant facing the sun:

| | | |
|---|---|---|
| Meridian height of its lower limb . . . . | | 41° 41½' |
| Astronomical refraction, subtract . . . | 1' | |
| Inclination of visual horizon on account of height of observer's eye, three to four feet, subtract . . . . . . | 2' | 13' |
| Solar semidiameter, add . . . . . . | 16' | |
| Height of center of solar body . . . . . . | | 41° 54½' |
| Zenith distance . . . . . . . . . . | | 48° 5½' |
| Declination at the above hour . . . . . . | | 11° 2½' |
| Latitude of this place . . . . . . . . | | 37° 3' |

At evening and night of this day heavy showers fell, driven by a hard south wind which raised a storm at sea.

## Sunday, October 22nd.

At daybreak it was overcast and gloomy, with our people wet and sleepless because they had had no tents, so that it was necessary to give them a day of rest. But what was remarkable upon this occasion [91] was the fact

---

90. The draft version reads, prehaps more correctly, "low and rocky, scarce-ly" etc.

91. "Upon this occasion" missing in the uncorrected draft copies.

that all of the sick men, for whom we were fearful that
their having got wet would prove harmful in the highest
degree, found themselves relieved of their pains between
night and morning; this was the reason for the hollow's
being named "la Salud."

## Monday, October 23rd.

To the Ranchería                                    From San Diego,
de la Casa Grande,[92]                              179 leagues.
Big House Village,
2 leagues.

We shifted camp two leagues from Healing Hollow,
camping again close to a heathen village which had been
discovered by the scouts, and situated in a pleasant pretty
spot at the foot of the mountains, opposite a gorge covered with pine-trees and savins, among which ran down
a stream of which the Indians availed themselves.   The
land, covered with grasses and nowise scant of wood,
was plainly well-favored.   Part of the way we made
along the shore, and the remainder, beyond the point of
rocks spoken of above, as far as the valley, was over
high level ground with a plenty of water standing in
lakes of more or less size.

The heathens, who had been warned by the scouts
of our coming to their lands, received us with a great
deal of affability and kindness, nor failed to make the
usual present of seeds kneaded into thick dough-balls;
they offered us also bits of honeycomb of a kind of syrup
which some said was wasp-honey: they brought it elaborately wrapped up between cane-grass leaves, and its flavor was not to be despised.

---

92. Spelled *Casagrande, Casa-grande* in some copies.

In the midst of the village there was a great house of spherical shape, very roomy; while the other little houses, which were of pyramidal form and very small-sized, were built of pine splints. And because the big house stood out so above the rest, the village was so named.

*Note:* The point of rocks, which we left behind on the way, is the one known as Año Nuevo, New Year's Point; its latitude, with but slight difference, the same as was observed at Healing Hollow.

## Tuesday, October 24th.

**To the Valle de
los Cursos,
4 leagues.**

**From San Diego,
183 leagues.**

The Big House Indians gave us guides for the way ahead. We travelled northward over high knolls not far from the sea-shore; we were faced with a few rather hard grades that had to be prepared, as did the crossing of two creeks with a great deal of woods, before reaching a village two leagues away from the place whence we set out. We found it less its inhabitants, who were busied at that season in harvesting their seeds; we saw six or seven of them so employed, who advised us that there was another more populous one a little farther on, whose people would attend to us and furnish us with whatever we should need. We took their word for it, and though it was rather late, continued onward and went another two leagues of broken country before reaching it. The route, though hard going over high knolls and hollows, was agreeable; the soil seemed to us remarkably good and friable, with frequent watering places, and the heathens the best for character and wit that we had yet seen.

The village lay within a valley surrounded by high knolls, with the sea discovered through a mouth opening to the west-northwest.   There was a very copious stream of running water, and the soil, through burnt off about the village, was not scant of grass upon the hills.

## Wednesday, October 25th.

A great many of the pack mules had given out upon the previous day's march, and they were rested this day to restore them.   The scouts were despatched to survey the country, with guides from the same heathens here. They came back at night with no news of consequence, having gone ahead four leagues or so north-northwest-ward along the coast.

## Thursday, October 26th.

Because of the captain of the Californias Company, Don Fernando de Rivera y Moncada,[93] being indisposed with the general ailment of scurvy and with a flux of the bowels which attacked a good many people, we were ob-liged to put off the march.

---

93.  The corrected draft copy, alone, omits "Company," and spells the name Fernando Ribera y Moncada.

# Friday, October 27th.

**To the Flea
Village, Ranchería
de las Pulgas,
2 leagues.**

**From San Diego,
185 leagues.**

We set out from the valley, called *los Cursos,* Diarrhea Valley, by the soldiers, on a northward course, and then followed along the coast over high knolls north-northwestward, making a scant two leagues and stopping next to a stream of little account. The land bore a gloomy appearance, bare knolls with no trees on them and accordingly lacking in firewood. Upon the northern side of the stream here there were some abandoned heathen huts, where everyone who was so curious as to visit them became covered with fleas.

On the way here were faced with a very long grade to prepare in order to get down to a stream at its very outlet on the sea.

# Saturday, October 28th.

**To the Llano de
los Ansares,
2 leagues.**

**From San Diego,
187 leagues.**

Went two leagues along a way like the previous day's, upon the same course above the shore, stopping next to another stream and close by the beach. The spot was lacking in wood. Many heathens visited our camp; most of them however belonged to the villages [94] we had left

---

94. "Village" says the draft version, perhaps more correctly.

behind, a wandering folk throughout this country, which is very little inhabited.

Northwestward [95] of our campsite there was a point of high land ending in the sea with two very irregularly shaped, sharp-pointed big island rocks in front of it. [96] What to make of these marks we could not tell. We were now above 37 degrees 20 minutes north latitude, [97] yet unable to say whether we were far away from Monterrey, or close upon it. It rained upon us constantly; our provisions were running out and the men's ration reduced to a mere five flour and bran cakes a day, no grain, no meat (four bags of it that were left being saved for the sick); the decision was made to slay mules for the soldiers' rations, but they refused this recourse until a time of greater want, since they still had been managing to shoot a duck or two and were all very capable of eating the gruel and seed foods which they had been getting from the heathens, though in small amount. [98]

Our commander, by the more misfortune, had fallen ill; the captain of the presidio as well; and indisposition and disorder of the bowels was well-nigh universal and common to all, [99] the author of these records having hardly escaped it either. But as it is an ill wind that blows none any good, so is it certain that this was the chief reason for the easing and improvement experienced by the sick men with the aid of no other medicine, nature by these means dissolving the humors which had caused the mal-

---

95. "North-northwestward," in the draft copies.

96. "In front of it" is an addition in the final version.

97. The draft version, reflecting Costansó's knowledge before he took an observation on the way back, reads "We had been considering ourselves in nearly 37 and a half degrees."

98. In the draft, "Our men were reduced to eating only five flour and bran cakes daily; no meat, no grain remained, save for a little being kept for the sick..."; the last portion of the sentence from "since..." onward is not found.

99. The draft version reads, "Our commander, to complete our misfortune, had fallen ill; the captain of the Californias Presidio as well; and many were suffering from a running and flux of the bowels which sapped their strength."

Fray Junípero Serra, President of the Californian Missions and founder
of the first Missions in California which would be the origin
of the immense task done by the Franciscans.

ady,[100] and the same purpose being also served by the change in the weather, with the northwesterlies and fogs ceasing and land breezes commencing to blow after rains had purged the atmosphere and in some wise renewed it.[101] Little by little, the swelling and constriction in the sick men's limbs that had as good as crippled them vanished, the sharps pains they had been feeling in every limb at the slightest movement also disappeared apace, and their mouths cleared, gums firming and teeth becoming solid-symptoms, all of these, very characteristic of that most evil disease the scurvy, and an illness which made more inroads among those who had come by ship.[102]

## Sunday, October 29th.

It rained all the night before, with a south wind. at dawn it was still raining, with extremely dense cloud,[103] and impossible for us to leave the place, which was afterward, for the reason which we shall tell, named the Goose Plain.

---

100. The phrases "with the aid... malady" have been removed from the final version.

101. The draft version reads, "with the ceasing of the northwesterlies, the benefit from the rains, and the land breezes springing up which purged the atmosphere and in some wise renewed it." The final version: "with the northwesterly winds and fogs ceasing and land breezes commencing to blow after rains." Compare the entry for October 22nd.

102. In the draft version: "Their legs began to be less swollen, the sharp pains they had been feeling in every limb at the slightest movement ceased, the swelling of their gums vanished symptoms very characteristic," etc. Final version: "Little by little... vanished, their pains also disappeared apace, and their mouths ceared, gums firming and teeth becoming solid all symptoms of the scurvy." The draft adds "This spot was known as the *llano de los Ansares*" (as *los Ansares* in the corrected draft), instead of mentioning the name in the next entry.

103. This phrase was removed from the final version.

# Monday, October 30th.

To the Rincón de                                    From San Diego,
de las Almejas,                                     188½ leagues.[104]
1½ leagues.

The day dawned looking fair, with a cold north wind [105] and clear sky. We broke camp and, by following the shore until we left the point with island rocks which we previously spoke of to the westward of us, passed over the top of some knolls and across several small hollows with rather deep gulches with water, at which we were delayed by having to throw little bridges over them for the pack-train to cross on.[106] We stopped not far from the sea-shore, along which the way was entirely shut off by a cliffy height, at the foot of which there ran a small stream of good water; this issued from a pocket in between various elevations, at the end of which, up against the heights and sheltered from the north, we placed our camp.[107] This day's march was one league; the place afterward became known as Mussel Headland.

In the afternoon, the sergeant of the presidio was ordered out to seek a way to pursue our next march.

---

104. The final copies make the day's march only "1 league," and consequently leave the fraction out of the following totals.
105. "A very cold north wind," in the draft.
106. «Which we previously spoke of,» «several small», "rather," "having to," and "for... cross on" are found only in the draft; "little" only in the final version.
107. The draft version reads: "We stopped not far from the shore, and at the foot of heights which denied us a way along the sea; these formed a pocket sheltered from the north, from which issued a stream of very good water, upon which we camped, while a way was sought to pursue our next march." The next sentences are not in the draft.

# Tuesday, October 31st.

To the Bay or
Harbor [108]
of San Francisco,
1 league.

From San Diego,
189½ leagues.

The heights which forbade us the way along the sea-sore, easy to climb though they were everywhere [109] on the way up, had a very abrupt steep descent upon the opposite side. The pioneers set out very early in the morning to fix it, and with them the Sergeant of the Presidio to speed the work; and afterward we followed along with the pack-train and the remainder of the men at eleven o'clock in the forenoon. [110]

From the summit we descried a large bay lying to the northwest under a point of land reaching far out to sea, over which there had been much disputing the day before as to whether it was an island or no, it having been impossible then, because of some horizon-mist covering it, to mak it out as clearly as now. [111]  Out beyond, about to west-northwest with respect to us, were seen seven white *farallones* [island rocks] of various sizes, and looking back toward the bay there were abrupt white bluffs made out more to the northward; while turning around northeastwardly, the mouth of an inlet was discovered which seemed to make inland. [112]  On sight of these marks we turned to the sailing-directions of pilot

---

108. Only "Harbor" in the draft.
109. "Everywhere" only in the draft.
110. "To speed the work," "and... men" only in the draft.
111. The draft has only "...reaching far out to sea and looking like an island, a matter about which a great many people had been mistaken the afternoon before."
112. "Of various sizes" is added from the draft, which continues, "Following the shore of the bay along the north side, white bluffs were distinguished, and turning northeastward an inlet mouth was seen," etc.

Cabrera Bueno, and thought that beyond all doubt what
we were looking upon was San Francisco Harbor, and
so were persuaded that Monterrey Harbor lay behind
us,[113] an opinion accepted by most because of the agreement between the marks given by that pilot in his rutter and the ones which we were now observing.   The
latitude we were in, by the engineer's reckoning, of
thirty seven degrees thirty three or thirty five minutes,[114]
indicated the same.   And so the point seen outside,
which many had thought an island, must be Point Reyes;
although the said pilot locates it in thirty eight degrees
thirty minutes, that is, a degree farther north.   But this
writer's authority was of little weight in the judgment of
those with any skill or of those who were guided by them,
owing to our previous experience of his latitudes, which
generally prove too high.   And so what is there to be
surprised at in his laying down Point Reyes a degree
farther north than it in fact is, if he does the same with
Point Concepción, locating it in thirty five degrees and a
half, whereas repeated observations have established it
as lying in thirty four degrees and a half, while San
Diego harbor, according to the same author, lies in thirty
four degrees, yet its latitude indisputably exceeds thirty
two and a half by only a few minutes.[115]

We went down to the harbor and placed our camp
a short way from the shore, close to a stream of running
water sinking into the ground and turning into a marsh
of considerable extent that reached nearly to the sea.

---

113. "And recognized that what we had in view was no doubt San Francisco
Harbor, an opinion accepted," etc.—this is the reading of the draft version, from
which the last part of the sentence is added.

114. Less precisely stated in the draft: "The latitude we were in, of 37-1/2
degrees, tended to indicate the same."

115. In the draft, "But this author had no effect upon us in this particular,
since we had had experience that all his latitudes, whenever he describes these
shores and their harbors, are in error on the high side: for example, he lays
down San Diego harbor in 34 degrees, Point Concepción in 35-1/2, whereas repeated observations have established the latitude of the former as not exceeding
32-1/2 by [more than] a few minutes, while that of the second place is not over
34-1/2 degrees, and so we were not surprised to find this harbor of San Francisco
as well lying a degree less far to the north than the said Pilot relates."

The country was plentiful in grass and all surrounded by very tall heights making a deep hollow that opened only toward the bay northwestward.[116]   We had gone one league.

## Wednesday, November 1st.

There were a few who were not yet fully persuaded that we had left the harbor of Monterrey behind, nor would they believe either that we were at San Francisco harbor.   Our commander ordered the scouts out to survey the country for a certain distance, assigning them a three days' limit for their return and hoping that in this survey they would perhaps bring back information to remove the skeptics out of the perplexity they were in.[117]

From the inner coast or shore of the south side of the bay, the *farallones* were found to bear west by south; Point Reyes, which is the point upon the north side of the bay, west sixteen degrees north; and some white bluffs farther in, northwest by west.[118]

---

116. In the draft: "We went down the grade and placed our camp in the midst of a very lush little valley laved by a stream of good water that turned into a marsh of considerable extent covered with cane-grass, bordering the southern shore of the bay." There follow the bearings which in the final version are given in the next entry.

117. Altered from the draft version, which reads "information to remove him out of the perplexity he was in."

118. The draft reads "From the shore here"; "which... bay" is added from the draft, which gives the bearing less precisely as "west by north" (nearly 5° more westerly).

# Thursday, November 2nd.

Several soldiers asked permission to go out ahunting, since a great many deer had been seen.[119]  Some of them went a good way from camp and so far up into the heights that they came back after nightfall.  These men said that they had seen to the northward an enormous sea-arm or inlet shooting as far inland as eye could see toward the southeast;[120] that they had made out handsome plains all thick with trees; and that the quantity of smokes they had made out rising from all over the flat did not allow them to doubt that the land must have been well peopled with heathen villages.[121]

This could only confirm us more and more in the opinion that we were at San Francisco harbor, and that this was the inlet mentioned by the pilot Cabrera Bueno, the mouth of which we had seen while coming down the slope toward the bay, in among some bluffs, and of which this pilot speaks the following words in his rutter:[122] "By the middle bluff there enters a salt-water inlet without any breakers; once within, you will find friendly Indians, and will easily make fresh water and wood."[123]

From their news, we also suspected that the scouts could not have got across to the opposite shore that was viewed to northward, and consequently must not have got

119. In the draft: "ahunting on the heigh, since a great many antelope had been seen." Either "antelope" or "deer" may be a miscopying for the other word (*berrendo, verrendo, benado, venado*).
120. The final version adds, a little confusingly, "to the northward *of the bay*." "As far as eye could see" is missing from some earlier draft copies.
121. The draft versions reads "smokes seen everywhere" and "exceedingly well peopled."
122. In the draft, "This confirmed us further" and "while coming down to the harbor."
123. "And wood" is not in the original printed rutter of Cabrera Bueno, so the words seem to be quoted from memory.

so far as to survey Point Reyes, as it was no few days'
affair to make their way, as they would inevitably have
had to do, around the head of the inlet, whose extent was
so dwelt upon by our hunters.[124]

# Friday, November 3rd.

At night the scouts returned to camp firing off their
guns.[125]   They had us in great suspense until, all turning
out to meet them, we commenced to satisfy our curiosity
by questioning them and getting their replies.

The reason for their rejoicing proved to be none
other than their having concluded, from the uncertain
signs made by the Indians, that there was a harbor, and
a ship in it, at two days' march from the place they had
reached (which was at the end or head of the inlet).
Some, upon this mere hint, became fully persuaded they
were already at Monterrey, and tried to convince the
rest of the fact; and they made no doubt that the packet
*San Joseph* was at that appointed spot, waiting for us.[126]

---

124. From the draft, since the final version shortens the paragraph: "could
not have got across to the opposite farther side of the bay, nor was it any
three days affair to get around the head of an inlet the extent of which," etc.

125. "And letting us know in advance what good news they were bringing,"
adds the draft.

126. "And tried... fact" was removed from the final version; it is supplied
here from the draft, which says "Many," not just some, "thought themselves
already at Monterrey." The parenthesis mentioning the end or head of the inlet
is also taken from the draft (the earlier copies of which have, by a senseless
error, *Serro* "the height" for *Estero* "inlet").

## Saturday, November 4th.

To the Cañada de
de San Francisco,
San Francisco Hollow,
2 leagues.[127]

From San Diego,
191½ leagues.

With this news, our commander determined to continue the journey in search of the harbor and vessel of which the scouts had been informed by the heathens, and in the afternoon the march was begun,[128] along the southern shore or beach of San Francisco harbor; we at once went into the mountains steering a course to the northeastward, and from the height of a hill descried a great inlet drawing to the southeast and south-southeastward.[129] Leaving it to our left hand turning our backs upon the harbor, we took a hollow open to south and south-southeastward, and at sunset stopped in the shelter of a cluster of live-oaks bordering the skirts of the heights upon the western side. It was two leagues' march.[130]

---

127. This and the similar marginal notes for the next two entries are not found in the draft copies.

128. From the draft; the final version begins simply, "We set out upon the march in search of the harbor."

129. In the final version: "the southern San Francisco shore or beach till we took to the mountains on a northeasterly course; from their height we descried the great inlet," etc.

130. The final version: "turning our back upon the bay, we travelled southeastward through a hollow in which we stopped at sunset."

# Sunday, November 5th.

**Through the San
Francisco Hollow,
3 leagues.**

**From San Diego,
194 [131] leagues.**

We skirted the inlet along its western side though without seeing it, since the hills of the hollow which we were following to the south-southeastward stood in the way. We went three leagues and a half. The country was well-favored; the mountains upon our right hand [132] showed themselves crowned with savins and scrub-oaks, with other lesser trees. There was grass enough. We stopped at the edge of a stream of good water; some heathens showed themselves and invited us to their villages, offering us their usual presents of seeds and fruits.

# Monday, November 6th.

**Through the same
hollow, 3 leagues.**

**From San Diego,
197 leagues.[133]**

We travelled another three and a half [134] leagues upon the same course without leaving the same hollow, through ever more favored country more wooded with savins, white-oaks, and live-oaks laden with acorns. Two populous villages of heathens came out to meet us with

---

131. In the draft version, "194-1/2"; but the reckoning is askew.

132. The entry to this point is from the draft version, which continues "showed themselves grown over with handsome live-oak and savin trees," does not mention grass, and is somewhat wordier in the rest of the entry. The final version says "We went three leagues; ...the heights to the western side of the hollow," etc.

133. This is the reckoning of the final version, wich is at least consistent. The draft reads "197-1/2" (properly 198-1/2).

134. "Three" in the final version.

presents of seeds parched and made into dough [135] and large bowls full of mush or white porridge, which very largely supplied the want our people were in. [136]   These heathens made earnest entreaties for us to come to their villages, offering us many presents if we would accept a lodging there, but were much saddened when we would not accept their offers. [137]   Our people asked a thousand questions of them, using signs to usurp the office of the tongue, in order to get news of the harbor and ship being sought; and some simple souls were well pleased with certain vague laughable faces and pointings by which they were answered; but truth to tell, the rest of us were left at sea and unable to make anything, of their gestures. [138]

In the meantime, we came to the end of the hollow, where the knolls or chain of heights which we had been bearing upon our left hand between ourselves and the inlet ended, while those upon our right swung eastward apace, closing off the valley which held the waters of the inlet. [139]   We, also, directed our way to the east, went a short way upon that course, and stopped upon the banks of a deep creek whose waters came down from the mountains and rushed headlong to their rest in the inlet.

135.   In the final version "presents of gruel."

136.   The draft version adds, "who were reduced, as was said above, to five flour and bran cakes as their entire daily ration."

137.   Reworded in the final version.

138.   In the final version: "Some asked them several questions using signs in order to get the news they wished for from them, and were well pleased" etc.; "a dumb-show from which in truth very little could be understood, and most remained at sea."

139.   The signed final copy inserts "the heights" for "those," and the other final copies follow suit; the draft version reads: "while those upon the right hand, which, with the first ones, formed the hollow through wich held the waters in a spacious valley."

## Tuesday, November 7th.

The scouts were despatched from this place in order to acquire definite news of the harbor and ship which the heathens had made signs about, for which purpose they were given a limit of four days, and carried a provision of flour for the time assigned. The sergeant of the presidio was the head of the party, and some Indians went with him to act as guides.[140]

## Wednesday, November 8th.

Nothing remarkable occurred in our camp.

## Tursday, November 9th.

Our men, for want of meat and grain, hit upon eating acorns from white-oaks; most, however, underwent serious harm to their health, [with] indigestion and fever.[141]

---

140. The draft version: "The scouts set out anew to survey the country in order to acquire definite news of the harbor and ship of which they said the heathens had given them advice. They were given four days' limit in which to achieve their purpose, and set out in the afternoon with guides from the Indians themselves, carrying their flour ration for the time assigned.

141. In the draft version: "for want of meat and other provisions hit upon eating acorns, but underwent most serious harm," etc.; the interpretation of "most" is partly a matter of punctuation, but the final version makes it clear.

# Friday, November 10th.

The scouts arrived again at night, very downcast, finally unpersuaded of the notion that Monterrey harbor might lie further on, and disenchanted with heathen reports and sign language, which at last they admitted to be unununderstandable.[142]

They said that all the country they had been over to northeast and north could not be travelled, from want of grass, which had been burnt off by the heathens,[143] and, more than anything else, from the fierceness and ill will of the latter, who received them very badly and tried to stop them from going further on. They had seen no marks to indicate that the harbor was near, and they had been faced by another enormous inlet to the northeastward which also reached a great way inland and was connected with the southeastern one, and, like it, would require a search to find how to get around it.[144]

# Saturday, November 11th.[145]

Return from
San Francisco
Harbor,
2 leagues.

From San
Francisco Inlet,
2 leagues.

The scouts' reports having been heard, and weighed against the state we were in, our commander determined

---

142. The draft copies read "understandable" (*inteligibles*), an obvious miscopying for which the final version substitutes "scarcely understandable at all."

143. This clause is not in the draft version.

144. In the draft, "the native Indians" "received them very spitefully," etc. "They also related that they had seen another inlet equal in size and extent to the one we had in view, and connected with it, and that it would be neccessary to go many leagues to get around it; ...and that the land was rough and ill favored."

145. Here the final version adds a descriptive heading: "Return from San Francisco Harbor in search of the Point of Pines and Santa Lucía Mountains."

to call his officers together in order to choose, on the basis of their opinions, whatever was most suitable to the service of God and the King and to the welfare of all.[146]

On assembling, the officers gave their views in writing, and unanimously agreed it had become necessary to turn back, for they recognized that Monterrey harbor must lie behind us, and they held it mere rashness to go onward after we had seen the marks observed upon the coast, which agreed perfectly with those for San Francisco harbor. The meeting was also attended by the reverend missionary fathers, whose decision was especially prayed of them, and they seconded what they felt to be the wisdom of the officers' choice.[147]

The decision was no sooner taken than put into effect, and in the afternoon of this day camp was shifted two leagues from the place at the inlet, going backward along our way from San Francisco harbor.

## Sunday, November 12th.

| To the Cañada de San Francisco, 4½ leagues. | From San Francisco Inlet, 6½ leagues. |
|---|---|

Made four leagues and a half to north-northwest-ward and north,[148] stopping next to a small lake within what was named San Francisco Hollow.[149]

---

146. This is from the draft version. The final version: "in order to decide in concert what choice was most fit to be taken in the present circumstances, bearing in mind the service of God and the King and their own honor." (Portolá's actual charge to the council had said that "our honor, and even our lives" were involved.)

147. From the draft; the final version avoids the question of going farther and the specific identification of San Francisco harbor, and adds of the missionaries that they "owned it indispensable to go back in search of Monterrey harbor, which they also recognized must lie behind us."

148. "And north" is removed from the final version.

149. "Within the hollow that we had followed when coming from San Francisco Harbor," says the final version.

# Monday, November 13th.

To San Francisco                                              From San
Harbor,                                                Francisco Inlet,
2 leagues.                                                8½ leagues.

Went two leagues and came to San Francisco Harbor.

# Tuesday, November 14th.

To las Almejas,                                               From San
1 league.                                              Francisco Inlet,
                                                          9½ leagues.

Shifted our camp to the Rincón de las Almejas,
Mussel Headland, so named earlier by our people because of the plentifulness of this shellfish upon the
rocks of the shore laved by the sea.[150]

Here there was proper opportunity for observing the
meridian height of the sun, using the English octant,
facing the solar disc; which was,

Lower limb . . . . . . . . . . . . . 33° 50'
Being atop a cliff around about 40 feet above
   the water level, the inclination of the line
   of sight above the horizontal was 6 min-
   utes, to be subtracted . . . . . .      6'
Astronomical refraction, subtract . .      1'          9'
Solar semidiameter, add . . . . .         16'
Height of center of sun . . . . . . . . 33° 59'
Its zenith distance . . . . . . . . . 56° 01'
Declination by equations . . . . . . . 18° 30'

North latitude of the place . . . . . . . 37° 31'

---

150. The final version greatly shortens this wording, but adds the following
calculations for the latitude, only the final result being given in the draft.

The southern shore or beach of San Francisco harbor is distant about four sea-miles to northward of here; thus its latitude must be 37 degrees 35 minutes.

## Wednesday, November, 15th.

As our people were in want of any provision, except for the meagre ration of flourcakes, a rest was ordered here in order to allow them a chance to lay in some supply of mussels, which, as said before, were very plentiful in the rocks along the shore.[151]

## Thursday, November 16th.

To the Llano
de los Ansares,
1 league.

From San
Francisco Inlet,
10½ leagues.

Between the day we first caught sight of San Francisco Harbor and the time we left it, we had had constant clear fair weather without cloud or fog; this day, however, a thick mist obscured the horizon, with the wind southerly, making us fear rain. We nonetheless set out from Mussel Headland and made a little over a league,[152] as far as the place which the soldiers now christened Goose Plain; such quantities did we see of these creatures that some soldiers on going out to hunt shot twenty two of them, Divine Providence being pleased in this wise to provide a remedy for the want they were in.

---

151. Shorter in the draft: "This was made a day of rest for our people, in order" etc.

152. In the draft: "a league and a half's march."

# Friday, November 17th.

**To the Deep
Creek, 3 leagues.**

**From San
Francisco Inlet,
13½ leagues.[153]**

When we raised camp the sky was very cloudy, and hardly had we begun the march than the south wind came up, very strong,[154] followed soon afterward by rain, lasting the whole march.   We made three leagues before coming to a deep creek of good water, a little farther south than the Flea Village.[155]

# Saturday, November 18th.

**To south of the
Diarrhea Village,
Ranchería de los
Cursos, 3 leagues.**

**From San
Francisco Inlet,
16½ leagues.**

Travelled three leagues, passing Diarrhea Valley, where we found the village deserted; we stopped in a spacious hollow next to a stream of good water,[156] so spacing our march as to reach Big House village upon the following day.

---

153.  The draft version lacks the marginal distance-reckoning from November 12th through 15th, and when it does commence it is two leagues behind the correct reckoning of the final version (given here), apparently because the November 11th marginalia, which appear in the draft, were overlooked.

154.  "Very strong" is not in the draft version.

155.  In the draft: "a deep creek upon whose banks we halted."

156.  "In... hollow" is added from the draft, which reads further "upon a stream with a good deal of water."

EL Exmô. SEÑOR DON JOSE
DE GALVEZ MARQUES
DE SONORA.

Don José de Gálvez, General Visitor of the Territory of New Spain
and organiser in every detail of the expedition to San Diego and Monterey.

## Sunday, November 19th.

**Further south than Big House Village, 4 leagues.**

**From San Francisco Inlet, 20½ leagues.**

We passed one league beyond the Big House village, which likewise we found abandoned, and stopped upon a cliff close to the shore and to a stream of good water insight of New Year's Point.[157]  Made four leagues.

## Monday, November 20th.

**To Alto del Jamón, 4 leagues.**

**From San Francisco Inlet, 26½ leagues.**

Went from New Year's Point to Ham Height, four leagues away.[158]

## Tuesday, November 21st.

**To las Puentes, 2 leagues.**

**From San Francisco Inlet, 26½ leagues.**

Made two leagues in this march,[159] as far as the place called the Bridges, where we stopped.  A great

157. In the draft: "at the bank of a stream emptying ingo the sea at the same spot."
158. The draft reads "a scant two leagues," which is more in accordance with the estimates made upon the way up.  The actual distance would be three leagues.
159. The draft again differs, "two leagues and a half," in conformity with the earlier estimate; the actual distance is in between the two different estimates.  After November 22nd the draft omits the marginal distances until December 10th.

number of geese were shot in this and the last few days, boundless flocks of these creatures being in sight at every step; one of the soldiers' messes laid in a supply of over a dozen of them.[160]

## Wednesday, November 22nd.

To el Rosario,
4 leagues.

From San
Francisco Inlet,
30½ leagues.

We forded the San Lorenzo River, not pausing at the spot, and continued the march as far as the Rosary Creek, four leagues away from the Ham Height.[161]

## Thursday, November 23rd.

To Corral Lake,
3 leagues.

From San
Francisco Inlet,
33½ leagues.

This day's march was to Corral Lake, three leagues and a half away from the Rosary, leaving behind the spot called the Little Lake, past which we went without pausing.[162]

---

160. The last clause is from the draft; the final version says only "so that no hunger was felt in camp."

161. The draft adds, "again a great many geese were shot in the course of the march."

162. From the draft; the final version omits the mention of the Lagunilla (Little Lake).

## Friday, November 24th.

To south of
the Pájaro,
or Laguna
del Macho,
2 leagues.

From San
Francisco Inlet,
35½ leagues.

The scouts departed from us at Corral Lake, on their way to surveying the coast carefully all over again, since the road to be followed by the pack train and the rest of the people went a little inland here. We passed the Bird Village and River and stopped a league farther on, upon, a lake named el Macho, Mule Lake; wood is scant at the spot, and the land consists of rolling knolls covered with grass.[163]

## Saturday, November 25th.

In order to have the shore inspected carefully and at length, we lay by at Mule Lake.

At night the scouts came back with no news of any account. They did say they had found out that it was not buffalo tracks we had seen upon the way up to San Francisco Harbor, but rather ones made by very large stags,[164] of extraordinary stature, twenty-two of which they saw in one band close to the seashore. They said the heads of these creatures were furnished with very thick, branching, tall antlers, their color white between

163. The final version omits mentioning the Pájaro Village, as well as the description of the countryside.

164. *Ciervos* (later the usual Californian word for elk).

breast and chin and the rest of the body a light chest-
nut, except for the hindquarters also being wite.[165]


# Sunday, November 26th.

**To the Carmelo
River,
5½ leagues.**

**From San
Francisco Inlet,
41 leagues.**

After a five leagues' march from Mule Lake we
stopped at our old camp ground at the river and hollow
mistakenly thought to have been the Carmelo.   Along
the way we came across a new heathen village, where
their spherical-shaped houses or huts were forming into
a well-designed town; these were the same Indians who
had previously been occupying the banks of the Bird
River.[166]


# Monday, November 27th.

**To the Punta
de Pinos,
5 leagues.**

**From San
Francisco Inlet,
46 leagues.**

We went around about a league up the river and
forded it at a spot where its waters, unmixed with those
of the sea, allowed a crossing.   We then took up a southerly course until very close to the shore, which was lined
with dunes along the skirts of which we continued our
march, coming about to the southwestward, which is the
lie of the coast; all the land we crossed through was

---

165. The entire description of the animals is found added in the final version.
166. From the draft, which alone mentions the village; the final version has
5-1/2 leagues, as in the marginal notation, but despite the latter, has the remark
about the river (though with the word "mistakenly" removed).

sandy,[167] covered with brushwood and a bit scant in grass, with some clusters of woods of undersized live oaks. We rounded a middling-sized freshwater lake [168] by crossing upon some dunes between it and the sea. We placed our camp in sight of the Point of Pines, which had been explored earlier, as was said, and close to a small lake whose water we found a bit thick for us; there was grass and firewood aplenty.

Here, next to the mountains, we lost sight of the geese, the succor which had lasted us until today. It was five leagues' march.[169]

## Tuesday, November 28th.

To the Ensenada
de Pinos,
Bight of Pines,
1½ leagues.

From San
Francisco Inlet,
47½ leagues.

In the morning we shifted our camp, and, with the coast to one hand, began to climb the hill of pines; the pine-wood had already commenced before we reached its skirt. We went over to the other side, where there is again a [170] bight sheltered from the north and northwest quarters by the same point as it stretches east-southeast to west-northwestward.

On the south side of this bight is another point, protecting it from the south and southwest. We cannot

---

167. Up to here from the draft; the final version, probably because of the mistaken "southerly," has only "We took up a southwesterly course over level land."
168. "Freshwater" from the draft; "middling sized little lake" in the final version.
169. No indication of the distance is found in the draft.
170. The draft: "entered into a very large pine-grove, before going up the hill of pines, which we at once climbed over to the other side, where there offered itself to view a middling-sized," etc.

promise a good anchorage in the shelter of these points; rather, there are a great many ledges and rocks visible in the water and toward the shore, and no beach at all, unless along the eastern side, where a saltwater inlet shoots in, receiving the fairly copious flow of a little river coming out through a valley seen in that direction. Neither can we vouch as to the kind of bottom found in this bight, nor as to the soundings in it.[171]

We crossed the inlet and encamped beside the seawater upon the south side of the bight, not far from a little stream of very good water.[172]

## Wednesday, November 29th.

This day was dedicated to letting the men and the pack-train rest and lie by, and well they needed it. The men, however, were much worse off here than the beasts; for the land, with grass aplenty for the latter, proved miserly in everything for the former, and the sea no less grudging, affording not a single mussel, though abounding with gulls and pelicans, the lone fishermen of these shores. They were given no quarter by our men, who ate all that they could shoot of them.[173]

It was decided to lie by here and to despatch the scouts to survey the coast, skirting along the mountainside, with the purpose of following the same way ourselves, according to whatever account of it they might

---

171. The draft adds: "since there was no means of ascertaining, for lack of a boat or canoe by which to carry out these measures."

172. In the draft: "encamped upon the shore next to another stream of good water at a spot very plentiful in grass and wood."

173. In the draft, these remarks appear in the next entry: "We were all poorly off here, the hunt proving of little avail and fishing less, the shore affording not a single mussel; only some gulls and pelicans were shot, which our soldiers' appetite did not spare."

give us on their return: still believing and hoping that they would come across the harbor which we were seeking.[174]

## Thursday, November 30th.

The scouts were to have set out this morning, but some hindrance arose and their sally was put off.[175]

This day the meridian height of the sun was observed with the English octant, facing the astral body, and was,

| | | |
|---|---|---|
| For the lower limb | | 31° 23' |
| Semidiameter, add | 16' | |
| Correction to subtract by reason of height of observer's eye above sea level | 3' | 11' |
| Astronomic refraction, subtract | 2' | |
| Height of center of solar body | | 31° 34' |
| Its zenith distance | | 58° 26' |
| Declination | | 21° 50' |
| Latitude of the Bight of Pines | | 36° 36' |

The City and Bay of Cádiz is located under the same parallel.[176]

The cold was setting in, keenly felt, and during two whole days the land wind blew quite hard from the northward; as we were learning, these squalls usually last forty eight hours, more or less, without interruption.[177]

From the aforesaid Point of Pines, the coast swings around from south to southeastward, the part of it in

174. This paragraph is found only in the draft version.
175. Found only in the draft.
176. The calculations are not given in the draft, only the result.
177. The draft: "there were constant northwesterlies, in squalls lasting forty-eight hours more or less without interruption, like those experienced on the coasts of the Gulf of Mexico."

view beyond the southern point of the bight running south by east.[178]

Some ten or twelve heathens came over in the afternoon of this day, saying that they had their village within the valley of the river emptying into the inlet.  They brought and offered us in the name of their village a considerable amount of gruel and seeds that was shared out among our men.[179]

## Friday, December 1st.

The scouts, ten men in number, were despatched in the morning of this day, the captain of the Californias Presidio, Don Fernando de Rivera, going with them in person, with six Indian pioneers.  They carried a few days' provision of griddle-cakes.  Although there was a mule butchered for the men's rations, few of them would eat it, with the exception of some of the European soldiers and the Indian allies.

## Saturday, December 2nd.

Two mulatto mule-drivers, missing from camp for three days after asking permission to go out ahunting and still not returned, had us greatly worried, suspecting they had received some harm from the heathens or had deserted.

---

178.  From the draft version, with "southeast by south" emended to "south by east" according to the final version: "Beyond the aforementioned point on the south of the bay the coast runs," etc.

179.  The paragraph is found only in the draft version; the word "considerable" only in the early draft copies.

## Sunday, December 3rd.

As long as the land-winds lasted, the weather stayed fair, but during this afternoon it turned to a southerly, with clouds and rain.

## Monday, December 4th.

In the night the scouts arrived back, tired out from the steepness of the mountains, where they had had to walk most of the way on foot, as far as their exploration went. The upshot of this survey was to assure us that these are the Santa Lucía Mountains, from the marks they found agreeing with those given in pilot Cabrera Bueno's rutter; such as a high white slightly sloped hummock on the coast that can be seen many leagues at sea, and a headland shaped like a top, appearing as an island rock, about six leagues distant from Point of Pines.

They related that two of the six California Indians they had taken with them had deserted.

## Tuesday, December 5th.

In view of what had been happening to us, we were at a loss. How can we claim that so famous a harbor as Monterrey, one so much praised and cried up in its day by men of repute, by able, well-informed, skilled sailors who had come expressly to survey these coasts by order of the monarch then ruling the Spains, has not been found despite the most exquisite, earnest efforts practised at the expense of a great deal of sweat and toil? Or will it be allowed that it has become sealed off and destroyed by the passage of time?

Accounts by General Sebastián Vizcaíno and historians contemporary with him locate Monterrey harbor in thirty seven degrees.  Not only do we see no sign of it there, but not even a possibility of any such harbor's having ever existed at that latitude, for the shore is bordered by a range of extremely tall mountains falling abrupt to the sea, as any sailor will see.

It would not indeed have proved surprising had we found Monterrey harbor in a latitude greater or less than that mentioned by the old accounts, this being a failure or mistake which we have noted at most places along the coast between Cerros Island and San Francisco harbor, and must be attributed to inadequacy of the instruments at that time used by navigators for ascertaining horizon elevation of heavenly bodies.  The commonest and the one then generally used by sailing-masters at sea, the forestaff, is an instrument crude and difficult to employ, useful only for taking heights with one's back to the heavenly body, since in facing it the observation, already rough, becomes of no practical worth.  However, upon shores which afford no northward horizon (the case with these of which we are speaking), there is no way of taking the sun or any body whatsoever whose declination is larger than the latitude of the observer's location, other than face to; ergo, such observations made with a forestaff must necessarily lead to error—let alone all the possible mistakes arising from using poor tables of declination; and who can doubt that in modern times we have calculated and ascertained the declinations and right ascensions of heavenly bodies with greater refinement and exactness than two centuries ago, both from the advances made in astronomy in the course of this time and because of the improved construction and precision of present-day instruments.

So that we shall positively affirm that Monterrey harbor does not exist at the latitude indicated by the old rutters of thirty seven degrees, nor indeed beyond these thirty seven degrees northward as far as [180] thirty seven degrees forty four minutes, which is the latitude we estimated Point Reyes to lie in, having first happened across San Francisco harbor, with marks varying (as far as we could tell) not a jot from those mentioned by pilot Cabrera Bueno; and since according to this sailing-master and all others who have surveyed these shores, the said San Francisco harbor lies northward of Monterrey, what hope remains that the latter can be found farther to windward? Nor does this harbor exist south of the same parallel of thirty seven degrees, whether within the Santa Lucía Mountains or without them, for after exploring the whole coast step by step, we have not the slightest suspicion left that it could have eluded our efforts and investigations.

We have also to say that in the entire journey we have not seen any lands more uninhabited than those which are located in the aforesaid latitudes, especially upon issuing from the Santa Lucía Mountains, nor a wilder and more savage folk than the natives there. What then of the populousness so dwelt upon by the old writers, and the extremece tractability [181] of its inhabitants?

Our commander, upon the return from the mountain exploration, laid before his officers the gloomy state we found ourselves in, with no more supplies than sixteen sacks of flour, and with no hope of finding the harbor or consequently any ship to aid us to remain in the country; and he called them to a council.

---

180. A number of the preceding words seem to have been dropped in all of the existing draft copies.

181. "Goodness" in the draft (a near quote of the old sources); Francisco Palou's copy of this material adds here: "yet this is more easily removed than a harbor as famous as Monterrey was in past centuries."

## Wednesday, December 6th.

The meeting was to have been held this day but was put off to the following, in order to give everyone more time and opportunity to think over a subject of such importance.

## Thursday, December 7th.

At the meeting the opinion of some was for remaining at Point of Pines until our supplies had been entirely used up, and beginning the return afterward, by planning to eat mule meat for the rest of the journey.[182]   On further consideration, however, in view of how little we had left, of the excessive cold, and above all of the snows now beginning to cover the mountains, our commander took it upon himself to decide for returning, arguing that if the way through the mountains became closed to us, we must necessarily all perish.

A violent south wind arose in the afternoon, causing a great tempest at sea and blowing us about a good deal on land.

## Friday, December 8th.

The weather remained raw and stormy, not allowing us to stir from the spot.

---

182.  Palou's version of this entry adds the information that others wished to divide the expedition into two parts, one to stay and the other to return south, but that "a number of obstacles were raised to both opinions."

## Saturday, December 9th.

The storm still continued, the weather not clearing until evening.[183]

## Sunday, December 10th.

**To the Pine-wood,**
**1½ leagues.**

**From Bight**
**of Pines,**
**1½ leagues.**

Before leaving the bight here,[184] we set up a cross upon the shore with a [185] legend carved into its timber, saying *Dig at the foot you will find a writing*[186]—the one which we shall insert here, copied letter for letter:

The overland expedition which set out from San Diego on July the 14th, 1769, under command of the Governor of Californias Don Gaspar de Portolá,[187] entered upon the Santa Bárbara Channel the 14th of August,[188] passed Point Concepción on the 27th of the same, reaced the foot of the Santa Lucía Mountains the 13th of September, entered into that range on the 17th of

---

183. To this entry, Palou's version adds the following: "The Californian Indians with the Expedition found on the shore quite a large iron hoop, much rusted, which must have weighed some *arrovas* [quarter-weights, multiples of 25 pounds; though elsewhere Palou mistakenly writes *arrova* for Costansó's "pound"] when new; we judge it must have come from some ship's mainmast."

184. In the draft, "the Bight of Pines."

185. The word "large" occurs here in the draft version, but is stricken through in the corrected draft copy and removed from the final version.

186. Not punctuated in the draft, and wrongly divided in the final copies. Palou's version of the same material adds that the message was put into a flask *(limeta)*.

187. "Don Gaspar Portolat" in the draft copies—a common misspelling.

188. "The ninth of August" in the final version and Palou's copy incorrectly.

the same month, finished crossing the range or rounding it entirely upon the 1st of October, and the same
day sighted the Point of Pines, and on the 7th of the
month, having explored the Point of Pines and the bights
on its northern and southern sides without seeing any
signs of Monterrey harbor, determined to search further
on for it.   On October 30th the Expedition caugh sight
of Point Reyes and the *farallones* of San Francisco harbor, seven in number; on its trying to reach Point Reyes,[189] however, enormous inlets shooting an extraordinary way inland and requiring an immense circuit to
be made around them, together with other hindrances
(the principal one being the lack of provisions), forced
it to turn back again in the belief that Monterrey harbor
might perhaps lie within the Santa Lucía Mountains[190]
and have been passed by without being seen.   It turned
back from the end of the San Francisco Inlet on November 11th, passed New Year's Point the 19th of the same,
and came once more to the Point and Bight of Pines here
on the 27th of the month.   Between that date and the
present December 9th, it took measures to search for
Monterrey harbor within the mountains by skirting them
along the sea despite their steepness, but in vain.   At
last, having lost all belief or hope of finding it after all
this endeavor, effort and toil, it is setting out today for
San Diego, without any more provisions than fourteen
sacks of flour.   It prays for God Almighty to guide its
way, and for His Providence to bring thee, sailor, to thine
own safe harbor.

Here at the Bight of Pines, December 9th, 1769.

*Note:*[191] Engineer Don Miguel Costansó observed the
latitude of several places on the coast, of which the main
ones were as follows:

---

189. In the draft, "On trying to reach there."
190. The draft: "within the mountains."
191. The draft copies suggest an original wording: "Note by the engineer..."

| | | |
|---|---|---|
| San Diego, at the camp occupied by the Expedition ashore . . . . . . . . . . . | 32° | 42' |
| Easternmost heathen town upon the Santa Barbara Channel . . . . . . . . . . . | 34° | 13' |
| Point Concepción . . . . . . . . . . . | 34° | 30' |
| Beginning of the Santa Lucía Mountains on the south . . . . . . . . . . . . | 35° | 45' |
| Their end here at the bight of the Point of Pines | 36° | 36' |
| New Year's Point, which is low, with rocky reefs | 37° | 04' |
| Upon land close to San Francisco harbor, the *farallones* bearing west by north . . . . | 37° | 35' |
| I judge Point Reyes, seen to the west-northwestward from the same place, as in . . . . | 37° | 44' |

The officers in command of the packets, whether the *San Joseph* or the *Príncipe,* are implored, should they touch shore here within a few days from the date of this writing, after informing themselves of its content and of the Expedition's sad state, to endeavor to sail close along the coast toward San Diego, so as to aid the expedition with provisions if at all possible, if it should be so fortunate as to sight one of the vessels and be able to signal its own position to them by flags or by musket fire.

Praise be to God.

We started our march in cold fair weather, went a league and a half, and camped upon the other side of the Point of Pines.

# Monday, December 11th.

To the Carmelo                                    From Bight
River,                                               of Pines,
4 leagues.[192]                                  5½ leagues.

We took the plains road, course northeastward as far as the river, which we forded; we placed our camp a little above the ford, on the same ground we had occupied on September 30th. A great many geese were shot, remedying the want we all were in. It was four leagues' march.

# Tuesday, December 12th.

To los Cazadores,                                From Bight
3½ leagues.                                         of Pines,
                                                       9 leagues.

We shifted camp, and by following the hollow up river, stopped at three and a half leagues at th' same spot we had occupied on September 29th, called The Hunters.

---

192. Beginning here, the marginal notations naming individual camps are found only in the final version, with the exception of the December 30 entry.

# Wednesday, December 13th.

**To Real
Blanco,
3 leagues.**

**From Bight
of Pines,
12½ leagues.**[193]

We went a day's march from The Hunters to White Camp, three and a half leagues from the former spot. Shot a great many geese and saw large bands of antelope.

# Thursday, December 14th.

**To Real
del Alamo,
4 leagues.**

**From Bight
of Pines,
16½ leagues.**

Went four leagues, as far as Cottonwood Camp. A few heathens showed themselves, offering us mush made from acorns.

# Friday, December 15th.

**To Real
del Chocolate,
4 leagues.**

**From Bight
of Pines,
20½ leagues.**

We went on from the Cottonwood to Chocolate Camp, four leagues away from the preceding camp.

---

193. At this point (because of the marginal entry of 3 instead of 3-1/2 leagues) the total league-count of the final version begins to diverge from the draft, whose more accurate reckoning is given here, or supplied where omitted; the final version again ignores half-leagues at December 29 and January 3. See note to January 5.

## Saturday, December 16th.

To Palo                                          From Bight
Caído,                                             of Pines,
4 leagues.                                   24 [½] leagues.


We left the river hollow and made toward the Santa
Lucía Mountains through another hollow which opened
from northeast to southwest and in which the Fallen
Tree village had been; we found it deserted at present.
Four leagues' march; we stopped next to a very small-
sized watering place without enough to water the animals.


## Sunday, December 17th.

To Río de                                        From Bight
de las Truchas,                                    of Pines,
2 leagues.                                    26½ leagues.


We travelled on the same southwesterly course; on
leaving the hollow which we had been following [194] we
crossed another more spacious one where there is a
stream of running water. We encamped within the
mountains, on the Trout River, at the same spot as upon
September 21st. It had turned bitter cold, and a heavy
frost fell during the night of this day.

---

194. "The Fallen Tree Hollow," *Cañada del Palo Caído,* in the draft.

## Monday, December 18th.

To Real de los
Piñones,
1 league.

From Bight
of Pines,
27½ leagues.

This day's march was only one league, as far as the cramped Pinenut Camp.   As a result of the snows which had fallen at the beginning of the month, the mountain streams were flowing, so that we found plenty of water here.[195]

## Tuesday, December 19th.

To Hoya de
Santa Lucía,
2 leagues.

From Bight
of Pines,
29½ leagues.

A hard day's march over the steepest part of the mountains, the portion also which had given us the most trouble upon the way up, since most of the way [196] was opened up by plying pickaxe and crowbar.   At this place we found the heathens who had treated us so well the last time, and they did no less on this occasion.

---

195. In the draft, "plenty of water at the places which had most lacked it on our way up."

196. "Almost the whole of the way," in the draft, which also gives the name *Hoya de Santa Lucía* in the next sentence.

## Wednesday, December 20th.

The pack mules were so ill-used and in such poor condition that they must be given a rest.  We had only slight provisions left, and as there had been some small misbehavior among the soldiers on this account, in a number of them daring to steal flour out of the sacks, the commander determined to distribute what was left of it among them, and let everyone rule himself with respect to what fell to him.  This was done, leaving everyone equal and well pleased; the missionary fathers and the officers received a little biscuit and chocolate, with a ham for each for the remainder of the journey.

## Thursday, December 21st.

To the Muledriver's
Village, Ranchería
del Arriero,
3 leagues.

From Bight
of Pines,
32½ leagues.

We shifted camp in the morning and came out of the mountains along the same road which we had first opened, went down to the shore, following along it for the distance of a league and a half, and stopped close to a village of heathens who came out to receive us, having been advised by the mountain people of our coming. These Indians gave us to understand, by signs, that they had been harboring one of our deserters at their village, where he had been resting for the last three days.  We went over at once, and he, as soon as he caught sight of us, did what he could to save us a part of the way, by coming forward to meet us; his feet were swollen and he had difficulty walking.

*Questioned*, for what reason had he deserted? he *Answered*, he had never intended to desert, but that after they had set out to shoot geese along the shore, his fellow had suggested to him that they should keep on following the mountains along the shore in order to be the first to discover Monterrey Harbor and win the prize by returning to camp with the news. They had gone all that day and the next, thinking every time they sighted a point that they would find the harbor beyond it. Having by that time been absent from camp for two days without leave, they persuaded each other that the punishment would be no worse if they were to stay away another four or five, and that if they were so lucky as to discover the harbor they would be forgiven and still receive the reward. Thus they decided to pursue their journey until seeing an end to the mountains, which they got past with unspeakable trouble and toil, "maybe falling over some dropoff".[197]

*Questioned* about his companion and the two California Indians who had also deserted, *Answered*, that his fellow had been worse beaten about by the trip than he himself and had persuaded the California Indians to remain with him among some mountain [198] fishermen living encamped at the way into the mountains, until he could again have the use of his feet to travel on back to San Diego; which was where the subject himself was also aiming to go, as they were of no mind to cross the mountains again to look for us, both for fear of being punished and from the even greater fear they had contracted of the steeps of the mountains.

We went three leagues in this march.[199]

---

197. Presumably this last phrase is the mule-driver's own expression.
198. The draft version has "heathen fishermen" intead.
199. Only in the final version.

## Friday, December 22nd.

It was very cloudy at daybreak, and therefore impossible to continue the march.

## Saturday, December 23rd.

**To Arroyo
del Laurel,
3 leagues.**

**From Bight
of Pines,
35½ leagues.**

In the morning we shifted our camp, though with the weather threatening rain; we were lucky enough not to have any, however, before we reached the place known as the Laurel-tree Creek, so named because we had seen the first of these trees at this spot earlier.

On this occasion we found upon the stream a small-sized village of heathens who gave us of their gruels and seeds. We placed our camp upon a knoll close by the stream here; [200] it rained heavily in the afternoon and night of this day. We travelled three leagues by a more direct way than we had followed when coming up.

## Sunday, December 24th.

**To Real
del Osito,
3 leagues.**

**From Bight
of Pines,
38½ leagues.**

We went from the Laurel-tree Creek to Little Bear Camp, which we had occupied last September 10th and

---

200. In the draft, literally "the said watering-place," in the final version "this watering-place."

is three leagues distant from the former spot. A way which we had dug for ourselves past a cliff on the shore upon the way up had been carried away by the rains and left impassable; we had to search out another way, through a brushy hollow, with machete in hand.

## Monday, December 25th.

To the village
of Indian
fishermen,
3½ leagues.

From Bight
of Pines,
42 leagues.

Before we had set out from the Pines or Little Bear [201] Camp, over two hundred heathens of both sexes came by, many of them bringing basins of gruel and some fish, which we provided ourselves with, in exchange giving them strings of glass beads, which are already greatly esteemed in these parts.

This day's march was three leagues and a half; we stopped a little further south than the Inlet Camp, next to a small-sized village of Indian fishermen from whom we bought a good deal of fish, which was some help to our people. Shortly, a largue number of heathens visited our lodgings with basins full of gruel and mush.

## Tuesday, December 26th.

To Cañada
del Oso,[202]
4 leagues.

From Bight
of Pines,
46 leagues.

We went on from the Fishermen's Village to the Cañada de los Osos, Bear Hollow, and took up the same

---

201. The final version reads only *"del Real de los Pinos."*
202. So in the final copies (despite the printed text).

campsite as on September 8th. We had rain all during the march and found it hard going; went four leagues.

## Wednesday, December 27th.

To the small-
sized stream,
3 leagues.

From Bight
of Pines,
[49] leagues.

We had been greatly wishing to reach this hollow here, intending to shoot some bears, in the opinion we would find as many here as the last time. Very early in the morning the chase was prepared, the soldiers catching horses and leading them in hand, all ready to saddle them and mount when the chance came. As we began the march, however, a hard shower came on which lasted all day and the following night without stop.

The pack train already had been loaded and, without provisions as we were, it was no time to lose a day's march. Therefore we continued onward up the hollow, making three leagues before coming to a small-sized stream on whose bank we placed our camp. There was wood and grass in plenty.

## Thursday, December 28th.

Our men lay by here because they were wet and sleepless and in order to dry out our effects.

Bronze statue of Gaspar de Portolá in his native city of Balaguer.
At its stone pedestal there is and inscription in bronze, given by
the people of California to commemorate the bicentenary of the State of
California (1770-1970). A copy of this statue was given by
His Majesty the King Juan Carlos of Bourbon to the City of Monterey
in January 1977.

# Friday, December 29th.

To Ranchería
del Buchón,
3 leagues.

From Bight
of Pines,
52 leagues.

Had we proposed to keep on the same route beyond Bear Hollow as that we had followed upon the way up, we should have had no few obstacles to contend with in crossing a branch of the mountain range that reaches over to the sea; however, we recognized that we could avoid it without going out of the our way, indeed saving ourselves distance, by going up through the hollow, where we would come out at the *Plan de los Berros* [Watercress Flat] or Buchon's Village. We succeeded thus without great trouble, the only hard spot that confronted us being at a stream covered with rushes which spread its waters among some knolls, turning into a considerable marsh, across which we found a way nevertheless. It was three leagues' march.

Scarcely had Chief Buchon learnt of our arrival than he came to pay us a visit in camp, bringing a plentiful present of gruel, mush and very good-sized tamales that looked as if made of corn and which our hunger made delicious. We returned his present with trinkets and glass beads, which he greatly esteemed, and so took leave of him.

# Saturday, December 30th.

To the Laguna
del Mégano,
2½ leagues.

From Bight
of Pines,
54½ leagues.

Before setting out from this place we were visited afresh by Chief Buchon, who, doubtless recognizing our need, brought a second, more plentiful and abundant present than the previous day's; it was distributed among the men, with everyone getting a good-sized share.

This day's march was two leagues and a half, to the Dune Lake; we shortened it considerably by the way along the shore, meeting with no other obstacle than an inlet where the Indians showed us the ford across, and thus missing the circuits which are unavoidable upon the inland route, which is a maze of lakes and inlets.

## Sunday, December 31st.

To the Laguna                                         From Bight
Larga,                                                of Pines,
3 leagues.                                           57½ leagues.

In the morning some heathens came to camp with a present of gruel, mush and tamales, which they sold us in exchange for beads. Then we took up the way to Long Lake, three leagues' march. The Indians belonging to the villages [203] close by came to the camp with a present like what we had received at Round Lake.

## Monday, January 1st., 1770

To the Baile                                         From Bight
de las Indias,                                       of Pines,
3 leagues.                                           60½ leagues.

From the Long Lake, we made a day's march to Squaw Dance Camp, three leagues from the former spot; though we failed to find the village of heathens here who had treated us so well the first time.

---

203. So in the early drafts and final version; the revised draft reads "the village." "Round Lake" seems to be synonymous with "Dune Lake."

The countryside does not want bears; along the way the soldiers discovered a large she-bear among some thickets, with three cubs following her. At once a few of them saddled horses and went out to hunt her. They managed to shoot the mother and a small cub, providing a fine feast-time for the camp. The meat of these beasts is well tasted and flavored; on that occasion, however, we thought it better than the richest veal.

## Tuesday, January 2nd.

**To the Cañada Seca, 3 leagues.**
**From Bight of Pines, 63½ leagues.**

We marched from Squaw Dance to the Dry Hollow, being sure to load with water at the San Verardo River, where we did not delay as it is a place scant of firewood. A three leagues' march.

## Wednesday, January 3rd.

**To Punta de los Pedernales, 2 leagues.**
**From Bight of Pines, 65½ leagues.**

Some heathens came over early from the San Verardo River, bringing a little bit of gruel and mush for us. We then shifted camp toward Flintstone Point, a two leagues' march.

From Flintstone Point, Point Concepción, the easternmost of the Santa Barbara Channel, is discovered to southeast 8 degrees east; the westernmost point of San Bernardo Island, to south thirty-three degrees east; Santa Cruz Island, western point, by the southeast.

# Thursday, January 4th.

To the Pueblo                                            From Bight
del Cojo, the                                             of Pines,
Cripple's Town,                                          70 leagues.
4½ leagues.

We set out from the Flintstones, passed by the
Sword Village without stopping, and reached the Crippled *Temi*'s (or Chief's) Town, four leagues and a half
away from the first place.

The Indans of this town presented us with quantities of fresh and dried fish, a great deal of sardines and
bonitos, so that we began, thank God, to see plenty prevail in our camp.

And on the other hand the soil, which was covered
with handsome verdure, afforded excellent grazing to our
mounts, so that we had the pleasure of seeing them every
day visibly recovering their strength.

Ever since we had left Bear Hollow the weather had
held very fair; the nights alone were cold, the days however were more like spring than winter.

*Bearings of the islands from this spot*

San Bernardo,
    western point . . . . . . . . . .     S    12°    E
    eastern . . . . . . . . . . .          S    17°    E

Santa Cruz,
    western point . . . . . . . . . .     S    30°    E
    eastern . . . . . . . . . . .          S    41°    E

Santa Barbara,
    western point . . . . . . . . .      SE     8°    E
    eastern . . . . . . . . . . .         SE    22°    E

In the language of these natives, the island of San Bernardo is called *Toa;*[204] Santa Cruz, *Lotolic;*[205] Santa Barbara, *Anajup.*

# Friday, January 5th.

To San
Zeferino,
2 leagues.

From Bight
of Pines,
[72] leagues.[206]

In the morning we left the Cripple's Town or Concepción at the Point, made two leagues eastward, and stopped close to the town that was named San Zeferino Papa. There was enough fish at this village here for all of the men.

*Bearings on the Islands*

San Bernardo,
    western point . . . . . . . . . S   5°   W
    eastern . . . . . . . . . . . . S   1°   W

Santa Cruz,
    western point . . . . . . . . . S   5°   E
    eastern . . . . . . . . . . . . S   25°   E

Santa Barbara,
    western point . . . . . . . . . S   35°   E
    eastern . . . . . . . . . . . . SE   9°   E

False Sail, center . . . . . . . . . SE   28°   E

A bearing was taken to the sun's center, using the same compass, at sunset, West 36° South; its declination at that hour was 22° 32' near enough; the latitude of the

---

204. So in the draft version; *Thoa* in the final copies.
205. So in the early draft copies and final version, *Latolic* in the corrected draft.
206. Beginning here, the draft version lacks marginal notations of distances. However, with January 7 the final version's league-count is brought into agreement with the earlier figures in the draft.

spot, by observation made August 25th, is 34° 30'; therefore the sunset amplitude must be 27° 42'; which, subtracted from the magnetic amplitude, yields a variation of the compass needle of 8° 18' easterly [207] upon these coasts.

## Saturday, January 6th.

To San Luis,                                        From Bight
2 leagues.                                            of Pines,
                                                    [74] leagues.

It is two short leagues from San Zeferino Papa to San Luis Rey; we made them before noon, and stopped at the same place as last time.

*Bearings on the Islands at this spot*

San Bernardo,
    west end . . . . . . . . . . . S 23° W
    east end . . . . . . . . . . . S 8° W

Santa Cruz,
    western end . . . . . . . . . . S 3° W
    eastern end . . . . . . . . . . S 8° E

Santa Barbara,
    western end . . . . . . . . . . S 13° E
    eastern end . . . . . . . . . . SE 2° E

Point la Conversión . . . . . . . . . SE 23° E

---

207. Literally "N. E.," added only in the corrected draft.

# Sunday, January 7th.

To San Güido,
2 leagues.

From Bight
of Pines,
76 leagues.

We went on from San Luis Rey to San Güido Town, two short leagues' march on a poor way which we made in the morning,

*Bearings*

Point Concepción, to . . . . . . . . W   5   S

San Bernardo,
    western end . . . . . . . . . S   28   W
    eastern end . . . . . . . . . S   22   W

Santa Cruz,
    western end . . . . . . . . . S   12   W
    eastern end . . . . . . . . . S   10   E

Santa Barbara,
    western end . . . . . . . . . S   21   E
    eastern end . . . . . . . . . SE

# Monday, January 8th.

To San Luis
Obispo,
3 leagues.

From Bight
of Pines,
79½ leagues.

We shifted camp in the morning from the place called San Güido to that of San Luis Obispo, three short leagues away from the former.

*Bearings*

| | | | |
|---|---|---|---|
| Point Concepción to the . . . . . . | W | 1° | S [208] |
| Santa Cruz, | | | |
| western end . . . . . . . . | S | 25° | W |
| eastern end . . . . . . . . . | S | 4° | W |
| Santa Barbara, | | | |
| western end . . . . . . . . | S | 2° | E |
| eastern end . . . . . . . . . | S | 42° | E |
| The False Sail . . . . . . . . . | SE | 2° | E |
| Point la Conversión . . . . . . . | E | 26° | S [209] |

# Tuesday, January 9th.

To the Pueblo                                     From Bight
de la Isla,                                          of Pines,
Island Town,                                    81½ leagues.
2 leagues.

Went from San Luis Obispo to the Island Towns, a march of two leagues and a half over a somewhat way through countryside grown over with liveoaks and other trees; we stopped in an open clear spot upon the east side of these towns.

# Wednesday, January 10th.

To Pueblo de                                     From Bight
la Carpintería,                                     of Pines,
5 leagues.                                        86½ leagues.

We set out from the Island Towns wishing to get to Carpintería town five leagues and a half away, in the

---

208. The final version provides an entry, left blank, for San Bernardo.
209. In the draft version, apparently "E 2° S," with a peculiar "2."

intent of putting all the obstacles of the Channel behind us while the ground was still dry and firm. We passed through the Lake Town without pausing there and arrived late at Carpintería Town, taking up the same campsite next to it as we had on August seventeenth upon our way up through these lands.

There was no fish either at this town or at Lake Town, whether because the Indians had not been dedicating themselves to fishing or because it is scarce upon this coast during this season.

# Thursday, January 11th.

To la Asumpta,
5 leagues.

From Bight
of Pines,
91½ leagues.

We went on from the Carpenter-shop to the Asumpta,[210] the last Channel town, passing through the Dancer's Town without pausing. All of the ones here where they had had such quantities of fish and made us a present of such a deal of it were now without any and, it was plain to see, were suffering great need, so that had we not laid up some supply at the towns behind, we should have founds ourselves all very poorly off. This was five leagues' march.

The westernmost islands of the Santa Barbara Channel can no longer be made out from here, that of the same name[211] being the only one upon which a bearing was taken:

---

210. So in the signed final copy; others read *Asunta*, a spelling which obviously lies behind the error *Punta* in the draft copies.
211. I. e. "Santa Bárbara Island"; a false punctuation of the wording of the draft version has led to an awkward sentence in the final version.

| | | | |
|---|---|---|---|
| Eastern point of it, to . . . . . . . . | SW | 22° | W |
| Western point . . . . . . . . . . | S | 35° | W |
| The False Sail [*Falsa Vela*] . . . . . | S | 6° | W |
| The *mesitas* [little tablelands], three in number . . . . . . . . . . | S | 4° | E |
| A low sand point three miles away . . . | S | 33° | E |

*Note:* The *mesitas* are islets of middling height above the water, level on top, to westward of the False Sail, which is another isle of greater elevation which we took for a ship the first time we sighted it.

## Friday, January 12th.

To the Sierra de la Conversión, 6 leagues.

From Bight of Pines, 97½ leagues.

Upon leaving the Santa Barbara Channel we came into the Santa Clara hollow, which we crossed by a southeasterly course so as to go into the Conversión Mountains, intending to pass over into what is known as the los Encinos or Santa Catalina hollow.[212] We thought we ought to be able to get through the mountains[213] by a gap which we had in sight in the same direction.

We forded the Santa Clara River and took a guide from the heathen village located close to its banks, the one next to which we had camped upon August 13th; followed a low hill range and came down upon a good-sized plain ending to the west side upon the sea and to the eastward up against some other hills, which we went

212. In the final version, *La Cañada de los Robles o Encinos* (White- or Live-oak Hollow); in the early draft copies, *Santa Catharina, Catarina,* is the spelling.
213. The draft version adds, "without difficulty."

over and then came into a spacious hollow which we followed southeastward, stopping next to a heathen village of sixty souls, more or less, a very stunted and poor folk. There was water, wood and grass enough at the place; it was six leagues' march.

## Saturday, January 13th.

Through the same
mountains,
2 leagues.

From Bight
of Pines,
99½ leagues.

We took a guide from the village who led us through an easily-travelled gap by which we crossed a large part of the mountains. We then went up a grade with a stream dropping down it which rose out of a very large spring covered with water-cress. At the top of the slope we found ourselves let out upon another very pretty hollow covered with grass and live-oak trees. This hollow ended in another slope, a bit of a hard pitch at the foot of which was a small-sized village whose dwellers gave us barbecued mescal-heads in trade for beads. This whole countryside has pretty and pleasing landscapes, with water in plenty.[214] We climbed the slope and from its top made out still another very handsome flat, with another heathen village upon it, next to which we stopped. At hand we had a great deal of water, wood, and plenty of grass for the mounts. It was two and a half leagues' march.

214. A sentence added in the final version.

# Sunday, January 14th.

**To el Triunfo,**
**2 leagues.**

**From Bight**
**of Pines.**
**101½ leagues.**

Two of the oldest heathens in the village[215] offered
to act as our guides to bring us out of the mountains.
At the outset they took a southeastward course, the one
best to our purpose for shortening the way, but half a
league or a little more away from camp they began leading us into the steepest most tangled part of the range.
We realized, too late, that we could not take the pack-
train past those steeps; turning back and passing close
by their village again, we took other guides who led us
by a better way along a very different course indeed,
namely north-eastward.  They brought us through some
easy knolls; on putting these behind us we fell upon
level land eastward, and on going a scant two leagues[216]
stopped next to a small-sized village whose people pled
with us to stay there and not go onward, as it was a
long way to water and too late to reach it by daylight.

We were not displeased by the notion of halting at
this spot, which was named el Triunfo, the Triumph:[217]
it is a flat of great agreeableness and extent, with live
and white oaks growing upon all sides and a great deal
of grass and water.

---

215. "Town," in the draft version; "The two oldest," in the corrected draft
(probably by an error).

216. The draft has been somewhat reworded here: "the road, between rolling
knolls, was much better," etc.

217. A religious name; spelled *Triumpho, Triumfo* in various copies.

# Monday, January 15th.

To Real de
los Robles,
6 leagues.

From Bight
of Pines,
107½ leagues.

At the Triunfo we took guides, as far as another small-sized village that was a league and a half away; here they gave us others, who made us extremely uneasy by leading us northeastward, yet make signs, as we would for them to guide us to the east our southeast, they continually refused, saying the country in those directions was not passable.   They gave us no cause to regret having trusted them, for shortly afterward they made to the eastward, going up a long low slope, from whose height we discovered what we had been in search of, namely the White-oak or Santa Catalina Valley.   We went down to it, and by travelling southeastward arrived late at our old White-oak camp which we had occupied on August fifth and [218] sixth.   Six and a half leagues' march.

# Tuesday, January 16th.

To the Llano del
Ojo de Agua
de los Alisos,
3½ leagues.

From Bight
of Pines,
111 leagues.

By this time we had a better acquaintance with the country, and, by knowing whither we were bound, were able to judge more surely as to the course we ought to

---

218. In the draft, "or."

follow; besides which, the mountains provided us with well-marked places and points of reference [219] by which to find out our position, so that we were able to shorten the way considerably.

We continued southeastward beyond the White-oaks [*los Robles*] without leaving the same valley; and instead of going through the mountains bordering its eastern [220] side by the way we took last time, cut through them upon the southeast without losing ground.  Luck also favored us in discovering a gap which granted us a way through unhindered to the Sycamore Spring plain,[221] haying now won free of all mountain obstacles, for it is all level land between here and San Diego.[222]    We made three leagues and a half in this day's march, and stopped among some knolls where we issued from the mountains, a little way off from a small-sized stream which ceases among its own sands not far from where it first rises.

## Wednesday, January 17th.

To Valle de                                             From Bight
San Miguel,                                              of Pines,
5 leagues.                                             116 leagues.

On coming into the plain we saw to the eastward a mountain chain covered with snow which we had also seen when going into the Santa Clara hollow.  From the knolls which we were leaving we could also discover the Porciúncula River or at least the fringe of trees lining its banks, so that all that was required was to head for it,

---

219. The draft has "as it were"; "places and" is added by the final version.
220. Sic; should be "western."
221. In the draft, "Sycamore Plain," *llano de los Alisos.*
222. The draft: "for there is not another range to be crossed between here and San Diego."

southeastward across the plain. We reached and forded it, noting by the sand, trash, fallen trees and pools alongside it that there had been a big flood a few days earlier, when it had overflowed its bed. We went three leagues further, as far as San Miguel Valley, and there stopped at the same spot we had occupied on July 30th.

## Thursday, January 18th.

| To Río de los Temblores, 6 leagues. | From Bight of Pine, 122 leagues. |

We set out through the mouth of the San Miguel Valley, which is all grown over with trees. For a long while we kept on to the southwestward, alongside the river, which already deserves that name at the point where it rises out of a copious spring just at the valley mouth; its bottomland is covered with willows and a few not very big cottonwoods. We forded the river and set off over level land southeastward all the way to Earthquake River, which we forded also; it was carrying more water than the Porciúncula. We made a long six leagues in this day's march.

## Friday, January 19th.

| To Aguaje del Padre Gómez, 4 leagues. | From Bight of Pines, 126 leagues. |

Went from Earthquake River to Father Gómez' Water; the whole way is over a plain; there is little wood at the spot. A four leagues' march.

## Saturday, January 20th.

To Santa María
Magdalena,
5 leagues.

From Bight
of Pines,
131 leagues.

Between Father Gómez' Water and San Francisco
Solano three leagues away, the way lies through knolls.
There is a stream here which, when we passed by upon
July twenty-fourth, was carrying a great deal of water,
while we were struck with wonder to see it now entirely
dry, when there has been a good deal of rain throughout
the area; it was attributed to the fact that the stream
here must receive melt water from some of the snowy
mountains seen inland, and presumably flows only in the
seasons when they thaw.   The phenomenon gave no excuse for pausing here; we continued two leagues further
on, to the hollow named [Cañada] del Incendio, Wildfire
Hollow, or Santa María Magdalena; the stream here had
also dried up, but there were pools left with enough
water for men and mounts.   Some of the soldiers had
been suffering cramps and diarrhea (a general illness
during this journey); two of them became worse during
the night, worrying us a good deal.[223]   There is wood
enough here.[224]

## Sunday, January 21st.

March to
water,
4 leagues.

From Bight
of Pines,
135 leagues.

We went from Santa María Magdalena or Wildfire
Hollow to Christening Hollow, found the watering-place

223. Shortened in the final version: "During this night some soldiers who
had been ill with cramps and diarrhea became a good deal worse."
224. Only in the final version.

there dry, and had to keep onward in search of water: we found some in a stream within a hollow a little over a league from the Christening [*el Bautismo*], with grass and wood enough.

## Monday, January 22nd.

To Valle de
San Juan
Capistrano,
6 leagues.

From Bight
of Pines,
141 leagues.

We went by the Rosepatches [*los Rosales*] and Santa Margarita Hollow, not stopping till the San Juan Capistrano Valley, a six leagues' march over rolling hill lands. In the hollows that run down into the valley we saw several lakes not seen upon our way through in July of last year, made by the rains which had fallen in the meanwhile.

## Tuesday, January 23rd.

To San Jácome,
7 leagues.

From Bight
of Pines,
148 leagues.

Went from San Juan Capistrano to San Jácome de la Marca, a seven leagues' march which was three stages' worth of our journey up, these being the stretches between San Juan and Santa Simforosa,[225] two leagues; two more to San Alejos;[226] and three to San Jácome.

---

225. *Sinphorosa, Zimphorosa* in draft copies, *Sinforosa* in final version.
226. *Alexos* in the early draft copies.

## Wednesday, January 24th.

We were coming to San Diego, and the opinions among us were several as to what state we would find the new settlement in, left by us in its very beginnings over six months ago.    Every one argued according to the promptings of his own nature and mood: one man would expect to find every help and comfort there, judging matters favorably, while another would fall gloomy, thinking how weak and poorly supported we had left it.    Truth to tell, everyone had a dread that if the grip of disease and death had continued among the men, nothing might be left of the settlement but a waste.    Again, there was everything to dread from the perverse character of the San-Diegan [227] Indians, whose greed for plunder can only be checked by awe of superior force, and we feared their having attempted some outrage upon the mission and its small guard.    The fact that we had been unable to acquire news along the coast about the ships, despite our efforts to do so, had been making us apprehend that we should find none of them at San Diego either.

Still entertaining these concerns and arguments which had been weighing upon us for days past, we were forestalled by the happiness of seeing fresh tracks of men and horses, over half a league from the Presidio, which we caught sight of shortly afterward.

The minute we saw its stockade enclosure and the lowly structures inside, we hailed it by firing off our

227. *Indios Dieguinos.*

weapons, which was the first news of our arrival for its dwellers; and out they came at once with greatest rejoicing to meet us with open arms. We found the reverend missionary fathers, fray Junípero Serra, president of the Missions, fray Juan Vizcaíno,[228] fray Fernando Parrón, in good condition, the first and third of them still recovering from the general illness of scurvy, which was still afflicting several soldiers, both of the regular troops which we had left behind here and the men from the Presidio and Christian Californian Indians. From their mouths we learned how God had taken to Himself all of those whom we had left sick abed, a few weeks after our departure; those however in whom the disease had not become so rooted during the time at sea had recovered, through the endeavors of Surgeon Don Pedro Prat's tireless and charitable zeal, while those who had fallen ill later—everyone, indeed, since the outbreak spared no one—had also been cured; experience thus proving, in this case, how correct were the wise measures of him [229] who had sent a man of this profession with such praiseworthy abilities, and how useful citizens of this sort are in any colony or new settlement.

They also related to us how, on the 15th of August, the Indians of the nearest village attacked the camp,[230] driven only by their greed and leanings to thievery; they awaited a suitable occasion to throw themselves upon it, intending to seize and carry off whatever they might; finding some resistance from the few men who happened to be there at the time, since most of the garrison was

228. Variously spelled *Biscayno, Bizcayno* (early draft copies), *Viscaino, Viscayno, Vizcayno* (corrected draft and final copies).
229. [José de Gálvez; the passage is in Gálvez' own style rather than Costansó's.]
230. The final version omits "attacked the camp," making the main verb "awaited." A poor final copy reads "villages" (blotted).

away, they tried force, resorting to the use of their weapons. With their first volley of arrows, they slew a mule-driver and wounded Reverend Father fray Juan Vizcaíno; then those of our men capable of taking up their weapons fired upon them, killing three of the heathens and wounding several, which forced them to withdraw, having been given a lesson. Since that time, however, they had not left causing occasional harm, killing a horse or mule now and then and shooting arrows into others, though by night and unseen.

At the Harbor and Presidio of San Diego, February 7th, 1770.[231]

Miguel Costansó

---

231. The date-line is found only in the final version, the following original signature only in one copy; another final copy prefixes *Don* to the name.

# CHAPTER III

Comments on the first Expedition in the search for Monterey harbor. - Difficulties and heroism of the expeditionaries. - Foundation of the San Diego Mission by Fray Junípero Serra. - History of this Mission during Portolá's absence. - Desperate situation of the land and sea Expeditions. - Plan for abandoning San Diego. - Arrival of supplies and reinforcements from San Blas.

Second expedition to Monterey by land and sea. - Taking up possession of California in Monterey and founding of San Carlos Mission. - Governor Portolá hands over command to lieutenant Fages. - Return of Portolá to Mexico. - Extract from News of Monterey harbor. - Promotion of Gaspar de Portolá to the rank of lieutenant-colonel.

I have chosen to give a full text of Costanso's journal of this expedition—which is referred to as "fruitless" by an annotation in one of the manuscripts—because to my mind it is this account, among the many longer and shorter chronicles of the march, which comes closest to narrating the events in a concise way and in one which, if not absolutely free of literary flourishes, at least sticks to an orderly and factual presentation. From the various details given, it is clear that Engineer Costansó's task as relater or recorder of the expedition's progress was merely to take daily notes of whatever occurred in the course of the march, to record the places where the expedition's commander ordered camp to be made, to note down the number of leagues made and distances between points along the way, and to carry out measurements of latitude, so that the caravan's position could be known at every minute. Not only did he plainly succeed in all this, but his journal is also of genuine interest to the reader in both form and contents.

Miguel Costanó is also on record among historians as the author of a publication titled *Diario Histórico de los Viajes de Mar y Tierra, hechos al Norte de la California*, etc., or "A Historical Journal of Journeys by Sea and Land to the North of California", which covers not only the first part which I have given here in detail, but also the second march of the Portolá Expedition north in 1770, which resulted in their locating their long wished for Monterrey Harbor, and in the founding of the Mission and Presidio there. However, this "Historical Journal," significant, important and complete though it is, falls short of the immediacy, freedom and warmth which we get from the same chronicler's notes of daily life, scribbled down on the march. For all this, of course, we shall not refuse to employ and comment on the printed work an acquaintance with which has a great deal to contribute to the purpose of this work.

I have likewise seen the journal of Father Juan Crespí, an unwearied accompanier of both expeditions, and faithful friend of Fray Junípero Serra; in a long and fruitful trek through the Missions of California, he produced numerous accounts which are indispensable for a proper knowledge of the missionaries' wanderings and the beginnings of civilization in all this vast realm.    We shall often come in touch likewise with Father Crispí as a chronicler of the Expedition even though, for the reasons already set forth, my choice has usually been again to give selections from the Costansó journal printed in its entirety above. Should these reasons seem insufficient, the fact that a fuller version of Costansó's daily record than ever before is here given in print for the first time would be enough to justify its use. It was pure chance which led me to visit the Museo Naval in Madrid, where, among the many documents carefully preserved, there, I happened upon this copy, unknown and breathing with life—unknow not as far as its existence was concerned, but unknown to me because it had never been published in Spanish works which I had been able to consult.

As before, I shall follow the progress of Portolá's Californian expeditions, employing the classical sources of the better-known chroniclers, and thus we will frequently have recourse to Costansó's above-mentioned *Diario histórico*, to Father Fray Juan Crespí, to Vicente Vila and to Father Palou, all of whom will lend us their words as faithful witnesses for us of the events with which we are concerned.   I have put off mentioning Don Gaspar de Portolá's own journal till last, since not many tidbits of information can be gotten from it, though because he is the central personage of this book it will be published in full also at the end, as an Appendix.   It is not surprising if Don Gaspar's style and narrative form are spare; his position involving the complete overseeing of the expeditions, in addition to the military's notion of information, would keep him from adding frills and details.   His own psychology as a man may also have helped in keeping his narrative down to absolutely necessary matters; all these reasons together, at any rate, make his journal a cold unemotional account.   Personally, I see nothing wrong with this, indeed quite the contrary, since it gives

G. G.

9 Jun.º 76.

D.T.L. 185 = F. 210
nue 24.

D.n Carlos 8.º: Por quanto en considera_
cion delos meritos, y servicios de vos
el Theniente Coronel de Dragones
D.n Gaspar de Portolà, y atendiendo à lo que hicisteis en
el Govierno delas Californias, y primeras Expediciones
de aquella Peninsula hasta el Puerto de Monterrey, hè
venido por mi Real Decreto de veinte y tres de Mayo
proximo pasado, en conferiros (como por este mi Real
Titulo os confiero) el Govierno dela Puebla delos Angeles
enlas Provincias dela nueba España: Por tanto
mando al Gran Chanciller, y los demi Reyno delas
Yndias, tomen, y reciban de vos el nominado D.n Gaspar
de Portolà el Juramento acostumbrado con la
solemnidad que entales casos se requiere de que
bien, y fielmente servireis el expresado Govierno dela

First page of the Commission of Portolá as Governor of the City of La Puebla de los Angeles (México). (Arch. Gral. Simancas).

us a straightforward reflection of a perfectly planned military expedition's daily march, leaving the frills and descriptive detail for his companions to fill in.

This journal of Portolá's, together with the few letters of his which are known, has very often led to our subject's being judged as a man lacking in imagination, impoverished in expression, and even limited in mind. Supposing that all these points affecting his style were established, they would still have little to do with his personality: in the first place because they are so few, and in the second place because—I again insist—the Expedition to San Diego and Monterrey led by him had been planned in detail down to the slightest eventualities by the Visitor-General, who had issued exact and concrete orders individually to almost all of the Expedition's officers, indicating to each one his own functions, and showing his wish that each should proceed to keep his own journal separately from the official chronicler of the march. It may be that Don Gaspar's professional procedure had been cast into the style of the newly-proclaimed Army Regulation norms, in which case the conciseness and shortness of his account would be no vice but a virtue. Authors such as Professor Brown of Ohio State University show no hesitation in affirming that Don Gaspar de Portolá's long years of serving the King had made his personality that of a man terribly faithful to regulations, —"He would work 'by the book,' normally unwilling or unable to take responsibility beyond his literal orders": in my opinion, a creditable trait in view of the strict obedience and assignment of responsibility required by the military training of that age.

Leaving these questions of personality, let me now continue with the story of the Expedition which brought our men into the new lands of Upper California in search of the Harbors of San Diego and Monterrey—not so "fruitless" an expedition after all, since from its wanderings sprang the knowledge and exploration of the hard way later to be known as the *Camino Real* of the California Missions, and the discovery of the harbor of San Francisco. Fray Junípero Serra, conversing with the Visitor-General himself at the time plans were laid for the three new missions which were to be established in the territories about to be explored, had lamented that St. Francis, founder of his Order, should not have a mission in his name; now he rejoices in himself at the chance discovery of San Francisco Bay, seeing the saint's special intercession in the fact that, after

failing to recognize Monterrey Harbor, despite their being able
to "read all of the marks for it in the History," they had gone on
to such a high latitude.  On this point, Father Palou tells us:

When the venerable Father Fray Junípero treated with the Most
Honourable Visitor-General about the first three Missions which he
entrusted him to establish here in New California, seeing the list of
names and patrons he had given them, he said: "Sire: and is there
no Mission for Our Father St. Francis?"  To which he answered, "If
St. Francis wishes a Mission, let him let his harbor be found, and it
shall be put there."  The expedition went north, came to Monterey
Harbor, stopped there, and set up a Cross there without anyone in
all their number having recognized it, though they could read all of
the marks for it in the History.  Over forty leagues farther up, they
encounter the Harbor of San Francisco (our father), and they all
recognize it at once as agreeing with the marks for it which they
have with them.  What in view of this can we say, save that our
Seraphic father wished for a Mission at his Harbor? [1]

And so St. Francis got a mission at his famous harbor, or
at least at what the Visitor-General accepted as such, for he ordered ten missionaries sent in the ship *San Antonio* bound for the
new harbors, and if the vessel reached San Francisco Harbor before Monterrey and one of the Franciscans wished to remain
there, the promised mission might, he said, be founded.  Circumstances were to modify the plans of the zealous President of the
Missions, and San Francisco remained missionless for six years
longer.

The first march to the unrecognized Harbor of Monterrey
was rewarded by the recognition of that of San Francisco.

But let us pass on, now, to some remarks upon the journal
to which we have just been introduced—remarks which, im my
opinion, show that all the members of the Expedition *were
unanimously of the opinion that Monterrey Harbor did not in
fact exist;* and this show further the noble drive that led them
all to any sacrifice in order to reach the limit of the goal that
had been set for them.

In view of what had been happening to us, we were at a loss.
How can we claim that so famous a harbor as Monterrey, one so

1. PALOU, *Relación Histórica* of the Life of Serra, ch. XVIII (p. 678 as cited
in Note 32 to Chapter I above).

much praised and cried up in its day by men of repute, by able, well-informed, skilled sailors who had come expressly to survey these coasts by order of the monarch then ruling the Spains, has not been found despite the most exquisite, earnest efforts practised at the expense of a great deal of sweat and toil?    Or will it be allowed that it has become sealed off and destroyed by the passage of time?...

So that we shall positively affirm that Monterrey harbor does not exist at the latitude indicated by the old rutters of thirty seven degrees, nor indeed beyond hese thirty seven degrees northward as far as thirty seven degrees forty four minutes, which is the latitude we estimated Point Reyes...

Nor does this harbor exist south of the same parallel of thirty seven degrees, whether within the Santa Lucía Mountains or without them, for after exploring the whole coast step by step, we have not the slightest suspicion left that it could have eluded our efforts and investigations.

(Constansó, Monday, December 5th).


This is the critical review of the well-known engineer and explorer Costansó, with his well-earned reputation as a skilled geographer, who after these events long continued to set down on the maps of California the new discoveries and new observations of the many expeditions made in his time.    And with him we may set down the best part of the names belonging to the nascent history of California: Father Crespí, Father Gómez, Lt. Pedro Fages, seasoned Captain Rivera, brave Sergeant Ortega.

Could the famous harbor have been destroyed or filled up? Or were the skilled sailors who had located Monterrey Harbor at 37 degrees latitude, perhaps wrong?

Not filled in; nor were Vizcaíno's marks mistaken; it was only that Portolá's explorers were unable to see what lay before their eyes.   General Vizcaíno's journal of navigation located the harbor exactly north of the Santa Lucía Mountains, and said of it: 'Tis all that could be wished for as a refuge for ships bound from the Philippines.   'Tis a Harbor sheltered from all wind points and surrounded by Peaceful Tractable Heathens.   They possess hemp like that of Castile, cotton...

And here in reality at the latitude described, the weary men of the expedition saw a small cove, where a great well-sheltered harbor should lie; a trickling stream in place of the great Carmel River; ponds and little inlets in place of the great lake they expected to meet. The patient clever inhabitants become, in Costansó's phrase, "a wild savage folk," and the fertile cultivated lands the most unpeopled, especially upon leaving the Santa Lucía Mountains, which we have seen in the whole journey. It is not strange that, with these "marks for it in the History," Portolá and his companions did not recognize the marvelous harbor of Monterrey.

Hard suffering had already been the lot of the men of the expedition, and great the hindrances caused by sickness, hunger and fatigue. Look at some of these quotations from Costansó.

Wednesday, September 20th. ... From the top of the grade we could overlook the mountain country stretching in all directions with no end to be seen to it on any side: a gloomy prospect indeed for so many poor travellers as we, tired and wayworn with the fatigue of the journey, with levelling rough places and opening paths through hills, woods, dunes and marsh. The cold weather began to be felt, and we now had a great many soldiers affected with scurvy and unfit for duty, thus increasing the toil for those left on their feet.

Wednesday, October 11th. The sick men were so very ill and near to their end that, with several of them having been given the sacraments, it became clear to us that not to give them some surcease was to risk their dying upon the way. Hence our commander determined to let them rest here, with a view fo continuing onward as soon as they should receive some improvement; ...

Saturday, October 28th. ... It rained upon us constantly; our provisions were running out and the men's ration reduced to a mere five flour and bran cakes a day, no grain, no meat (four bags of it that were left being saved for the sick); the decision was made to slay mules for the soldiers' rations, but they refused this recourse until a time of greater want ... Our commander, to complete our misfortune, had fallen ill; the captain of the Californias Presidio as well; and many were suffering from a running and flux of the bowels which sapped their strength.

They had gone through troublesome days along the new roads, troublesome above all because, beyond their physical toil and illnesses, what weighed upon them was the expedition's failure, which might represent a long-term abandonment of the decreed Spanish expansion all the way to San Francisco Bay.

The soldiers did not pause long before agreeing to feast upon the old mules brought from the Lower California missions, and though at the start "the only ones to eat them" were the Catalonians "and our Indian allies," shortly the whole party began to feed and quiet their hunger pains on one butchered mule after another:

"...We ourselves, who have undergone hunger to the point of devouring our mules..." [Crespí];

"...At this point twelve mules from the pack train were slaughtered, on whose flesh our people fed all the way to San Diego..."
[Costansó, *Diario Histórico*];

"...«As you know, I am responsible for a hundred human lives», said [to Fray Junípero] the Governor, who himself had just beforehand been breakfasting and dining upon aged mule meat..." [Palou].

Let all these facts which I have just related and quoted suffice for a sample to show the state in which the men of the expedition returned to San Diego.

At every instant, Governor-Commander Don Gaspar de Portolá had to give an example of discipline and authority, giving orders and taking responsibility as the true leader of the march, but never failing to show his absolute command was no despotic absolutism; on the contrary, partaking in the same pains and privations as all of his men. It is interesting to note that during all of these six long months, in all of the existing accounts he is spoken of with admiration and respect as "our Commander," and shown the regard and affection earned by his humane nature and talents. On three ocasions, when their difficult plight suggested it, he took a drastic decision, though not without first listening to the opinions of all his officers and even the missionary fathers themselves.

On that despairing day in October when the expedition had been going in circles around the bight of Monterrey without recognizing it, Don Gaspar called a meeting for the first time.

... Confounded a bit by this news, our Commander determined to call a meeting of his officers in order to deliberate upon the most suitable course to be taken in the present straits. He set forth the short supply of our provisions, the number of our sick (seventeen

men being half crippled and unable for any duty), the lateness of
the season, and the excessive toil endured by those who were still
well, in caring for the mounts, in watching them by night, in guard
duty at camp, and in constantly sallying out to survey and explore.
The meeting was held after hearing a Mass of the Holy Ghost, and the
officers all voted as one to continue the journey, as the only course
left to us—in hope of meeting through God's grace with the long
wished for harbor of Monterrey and there finding the packet *San
Joseph* to relieve our necessities.  And should God allow us all to
perish while searching for Monterrey, we should have fulfilled our
duty to God and to man, by striving till death to complete the undertaking on which they had sent us.

This deeply-felt and sincere chronicle of Costansó's—possibly
one of the most moving passages to have been written down
in the whole long history of Spanish conquest and colonization—
reveals the deep devotion on the part of all the members of the
expedition to the service assigned them, and brings out the
heroic extremes to which their enthusiastic common labors
reached.  For the Governor, responsible for a hundred lives
under his leadership, this noble and courageous act must indeed
have been the cause of inner satisfaction and pride.  Along the
rocks and cliffs of the Pacific, he must have dwelt once more in
thought upon the kind of men who, at such moments, could
carry and unfurl the banners of their King throughout all the
oceans of Spain's empire.

This calling of officers' meetings, with the remarkable fact
that after all of their opinions had been set forth they went on
to vote, and vote in writing in such a way as to leave no doubts
nor let anyone avoid his responsibility, has struck me as a surprising thing.  No doubt this was the first time that leadership had
recourse to a vote, and it is a remarkable coincidence that this
should have happened in what is now one of the States of the
American nation.

Having reached the harbor or Bay of San Francisco, examined most of its extent, and having despaired of being able to
seek the long wished for, hidden Harbor of Monterrey farther
ahead, the officers of the expedition meet for the second time
on November 11th.

The scouts' reports having been heard, and weighed against the
state we were in, our commander determined to call his officers
together in order to choose, on the basis of their opinions, whatever

was most suitable to the service of God and the King and to the welfare of all.

On assembling, the officers gave their views in writing, and unanimously agreed it had become necessary to turn back, for they recognized that Monterrey harbor must lie behind us, and they held it mere rashness to go onward after we had seen the marks observed upon the coast, which agreed perfectly with those for San Francisco harbor. The meeting was also attended by the reverend missionary fathers, whose decision was especially prayed of them, and they seconded what they felt to be the wisdom of the officers' choice.

The decision was no sooner taken than put into effect, and in the afternoon of this day camp was shifted two leagues from the place at the inlet, going backward along our way ...

They had gone far beyond the latitude where the Harbor of Monterrey might lie, and come by chance to discover and explore San Francisco Harbor; and, since all the sea charts located San Francisco above Monterrey, logic required that the expedition should turn back in order to continue searching for it. They had little enough hope of finding it, for they had already surveyed the Santa Lucía Mountains and the surrounding country step by step, without locating it. But at the same time as unfavorable circumstances forced their return, they had in mind to make one more search for it: a futile hope, that would have worse results.

Tuesday, December 5th. ... Our commander, upon the scouts' return from the mountain exploration, laid before his officers the gloomy state we found ourselves in, with no more supplies than sixteen sacks of flour, and with no hope of finding the harbor or consequently any ship to aid us to remain in the country; and he called them to a council.

Wednesday, December 6th. ... The meeting was to have been held this day but was put off to the following, in order to give everyone more time and opportunity to think over a subject of such importance.

Thursday, December 7th. ... At the meeting the opinion of some was for remaining at the Point of Pines until our supplies had been entirely used up, and beginning the return afterward, by planning to eat mule meat for the rest of the journey. On further consideration, however, in view of how little we had left, of the excessive cold, and above all of the snows now beginning to cover the mountains, our commander took it upon himself to decide of returning, arguing that if the way through the mountains became closed to us, we must necessarily all perish.

There is no real need for me to discuss this subject further; it is plain that the officers' meeting called together by Commandant Portolá were genuine command advisory councils, and that the decision taken "on his own account" by the expedition's leader arose out of their reports and written votes, even where some of them upheld a differing opinion.

The reader may turn to the entry of December 9th, in order to appreciate the quiet bitterness of disappointment reflected in the written message which the expedition left buried below the sign of the cross, in case it should be found there by the packets *San José* or the *San Antonio* in their own search for Monterrey.

The way back, once begun, is traversed much more rapidly that on the march up toward San Francisco, since the route is now well known to them, and perhaps also because hunger and sickness are at the heels of the expedition's men, eager to find themselves back at San Diego and to rest and recover from the toil and trouble of the journey in the comfort of the mission and presidio that have been founded there.

But as they draw near to the point of their arrival, we find all of them recording worry over the companions they had left behind there at San Diego.

We were coming to San Diego, and the opinions among us were several as to what state we would find the new settlement in, left by us in its very beginnings over six months ago. Everyone argued according to the promptings of his own nature and mood: one man expecting to find every help and comfort there, judging matters favorably, while another would fall gloomy, thinking how weak and poorly supported we had left it. Truth to tell, everyone had a dread that if the grip of disease and death had continued among the men, nothing might be left of the settlement but a waste.

Gloomy thoughts, these, for weary expeditionaries who, all during a speedy and peaceful return trip, have been feeling a mixture of hope and fear over their arrival at their harbor of refuge But at last:

"The minute we saw its stockade enclosure and the lowly structures inside, we hailed it by firing off our weapons, which was the first news of our arrival for its dwellers; and out they came at once with greatest rejoicing to meet us with open arms." [Costansó, January, 24].

Portolá himself narrates their arrival with his accustomed terseness:

Today reached San Diego; thank God, not a man has perished in all of the toil, trouble and want we have been through; for we have been depending solely, during our return, upon God's great providence, without any recourse in the human sphere save that of slaying mules for food in our utmost extremity.

A later account also attributed to Portolá mentions the same turn of events:

In the meantime, to keep from perishing, I ordered an old weak mule out of those which carried our packs and ourselves to be slaughtered at the end of each day's march. We barbecued, or half-broiled, the meat over a fire kindled in a hole in the ground; and once the mule-flesh was thus cooked, without a grain of salt or other seasonings, which we had none of, we closed our eyes and fell upon the scaly carcass like starving lions (with what a hunger!). We devoured twelve of them in as many days, constrained to get all our nourishment and enjoyment from them, or from nowhere. At last we came to San Diego, stinking of mule. On greeting me, the Reverend Father President said, "You have come from Rome without seeing the Pope," referring to our having failed to find Monterrey harbor.[2] Let us pause here ourselves, halting the expedition at the gates of San Diego, and stopping to learn what had gone on inside there since Portolá and his men had left it exactly six months and ten days before now.

The Harbor of San Diego, which had been the end of the first stage of the expedition, had been turned into the first presidio in Upper California. The Father President had left the formal founding of the Mission until later, and during a few short days had worket with the Governor in planning and provisioning the expedition that was setting out to search for Monterrey. The

2. Viniegra, Juan Manuel, *Providencias de Gálvez*, Ms. Bancroft Library transcript ZE-4 from Archivo General de Indias, Papeles de Estado.

calamities that had stricken the "San Carlos" and the "San Antonio" caused a series of unforeseen measures to be put into effect at the moment when the expedition's departure was being prepared—the San Diego post had to be left supplied with troops and men to protect it and care for the large numbers of sick, the majority of them from the ships' crews and the Volunteers of Catalonia.

At San Diego a guard was left which seemed sufficient to protect the Mission and the sick men, with Surgeon Don Pedro Prat to continue attending them; he also left behind an adequate number of Horses and Mules for the use of all, and Fathers Fray Junípero Serra, Fray Juan Vizcaíno, and Fray Fernando Parrón all remained there for the purpose of establishing that new Mission station... and the Governor being of the opinion, that the unforeseen disaster of the ships did not excuse him from continuing his journey to Monterrey by land, in view of all of his own troops and other company being in good health, ... he determined to pursue his march in search of that Harbor, without waiting for the season to become too far advanced, in order not to risk having the way across the Mountains shut off by the snows... [Palou.]

Portolá and his men had originally reached San Diego from Vellicatá on the 1st of July. Father Junípero Serra, in a letter dated at San Diego on July 3rd, writes as follows to Father Palou:

As for the land expedition, the Governor, so he tells me, wishes to continue it together with the Captain [Rivera] three or four days from now, and will leave us eight buffocat soldiers here and some Catalonians who are ill, to serve if they get better. The Mission has not been founded; but as soon as they have left, I shall see we set it in hand. [And Palou himself later adds to this account: ] The day for the overland expedition's to march was decided upon, and the Commander set it for the 14th, when the feast of the Seraphic Doctor St. Bonaventure falls...

Our Commander paused for only a short breath at San Diego Bay, since having arrived on July 1st, he fixed the 14th of the same month to set out on the second stage of his march, and did as planned.

Left at San Diego, then, were the missionaries, Serra, Vizcaíno, and Parrón; the captain of the *San Carlos* packet; eight buff-coat soldiers, fifteen soldiers of the so-called Free Company of Catalonia or Catalonian Volunteers—most of them ill—, some sailors, also ill, nine Christian Indians, a blacksmith, a carpenter, two muleteers, and an Indian boy named José María who had been attending Father Serra since Loreto; and in addition, Surgeon Prat. Of these fifty men, the only ones in health were the buff-coat soldiers. Left behind also were munitions, horses, and mules, nearly all of the tools and other property of the expeditions, and all of the altar service and church furniture that the missionaries had brought to found their missions with.

Once the Portolá expedition had departed for Monterrey, the very small number of able personnel at San Diego Presidio set about the job of fixing and strengthening the flimsy awnings and tents which had been thrown up earlier. A stronger wall or stockade was built, on Surgeon Prat's orders the worst of the sick were separated from those who were still good for a little work, a new hut was built of trunks and branches for the missionaries' quarters, and finally the Presidio was set onto the footing of a tiny military encampment, with guards set over the horses, the stockade, and the *San Carlos* packet, which lay anchored close to the shore, waiting for the reinforcements from Mexico that would once more let her sail the Pacific waters. In the meantime, her cannons protected the camp installations, which were also covered by their own two pieces of artillery on land.

The moment long awaited by Fray Junípero Serra had arrived. Not once had the Franciscan's "missionary zeal... allowed him to forget the goal of his coming," and now he turned to the work which Father Palou mentions in these terms. On the summit of a small rise lying inside the Presidio, he set up a tall cross, and there, on the 16th of July, 1769, with the assistance of Franciscan Fathers Vizcaíno and Parrón, celebrated the first Mass, thereby founding the first of the missions whose far-stretching chain, in years to come, would cover the entire Californian coast. Father Serra skimped no detail in the solemnity of the service, which took place with all the soldiers in attendance, together with Captain Vila, Doctor Prat, and Christian Indians who, curious and interested, watched as the ceremonies were performed by Father Serra dressed in alb and pluvial cope. After the Mass, they all proceeded to the blessing of the Cross, the flimsy primitive church hut, the lands,

the waters, and the people; all the men took part in the ceremonies, singing the *Veni Creator Spiritus* as salutes of musketry fire rattled off.

The sound of the salutes was enough to cause the local
Indians, who had been coming around for some days to watch
the people of the mission and all that they were doing, and had
slowly been coming closer to the stockaded wall to peer through
the fence at the horses—those unknown creatures they had seen
for the first time with such fear and fright—to take to their
heels in flight; for a good many days there was no further sign
of them.

Nonetheless the Franciscans were able, little by little and
with many hindrances, to begin their missionary work. First
came gifts, the glass beads, the handkerchieves, the little pic-
tures, to draw the Indians to the Mission, where, once used to
the presence of these strange foreigners and confident of the
kindness of the missionaries, they began peering into the huts,
church, and tents, fascinated by the new world which met their
eyes. It was hard to get them to take part in the soldiers'
meals, since any food they were prevailed upon to take was
spat out again as if it were poison. "There was no doubt that
this was a special providence of the Most High: for if they had
taken the same liking to our foodstuffs as they had for the
clothing, the Spaniards would have had to starve." The Indians
nonetheless lost no time in showing the missionaries their extreme attachment for everything new; they carried off whatever
they could get their hands on, entering the sick men's tents and
pulling off their blankets, and even making off from the *San
Carlos* with a piece cut from one of the ship's sails. These
must have been among the first problems that began to arise
with these natives "of a haughty, insolent, greedy, mocking and
bullying nature, though cowardly." Fray Junípero gives us the
following anecdote about their desire for colored cloths and
tissues:

... the Governor feels most of them would make good grenadiers
because of their fine stature; for a piece of cloth, however, or any
rag, they are capable of tearing down the roof over their own heads,
as the saying goes. When I give them anything to eat, they usually
tell me clearly enough by signs, no, not that, but that I should give
them my habit, as they tug it by the sleeve. Had I bestowed it
on all of them who were claiming it as their vocation, we should have

had a large community of heathen Franciscans by now ... They asked
the Governor for his buff-coat, waistcoat, breeches and everything
else he had on ... they even pestered me to give them my spectacles,
and because I passed them to one whose gestures I thought only
meant that he wanted to borrow them to see what they were, God
knows the trouble it cost me to get them back.[3]

These naked, mocking, close-watching Indians knew nothing of
firearms and trusted in their bows and arrows, in their wooden
cutting-sticks, war-clubs and cudgels, "capable of great harm";
being both ambitious and greedy for everything they could see,
several times they attempted to take all of it, even at the expense of slaying the unhappy inhabitants of the encampment.

August 15th was a hard day for the Mission.   Immediately
after the celebration of Mass in honor of the glorious Assumption of Our Lady into Heaven, a troop of bow-and-arrow-armed
Indians broke in upon the Mission, boldly snatching everything
that came their way, pulling down the tents and beating the
sick.   The alarm spread through the camp; the buff-coat soldiers ran to seize their protective dress and their weapons;
against them the Indians shot a shower of arrows that fell upon
soldiers and other personnel alike, wounding one buff-coat as well
as the blacksmith, who, roused to bravery, gave back a war-cry
louder than the Indians themselves.   Also wounded were Father
Vizcaíno and the poor child José María, who died in Serra's
arms.

The damage inflicted on the other side by musket-fire and
the spectacular effects of these new weapons caused more fright
than fatalities; the bodies, such as there were, were hidden, but
some of the wounded Indians shortly came in and asked to be
treated by Surgeon Prat.   The sight of this man's unselfishness
and of the dedication of the missionaries, who managed to hide
any fear they felt and to show only affection and selflessness
"caused the Indians to regain some esteem for them; and the
gloomy experience of the failure of their attempt having put
fear and awe into them, they behaved in a different manner
than before, paying frequent visits to the Mission, but no longer
equipped with weapons." (Palou).

---

3. Tibesar, Antonine, O. F. M., ed., *Writings of Junípero Serra*, vol. I (Washington, D. C., 1955), pp. 112, 114

The Spaniards were saved from the Indian peril, but not from that of the scurvy. Surgeon Prat tried to make up for the lack of medicines by putting his knowledge of botany to use, scouring the country for herbs which might somehow alleviate the plague. Both Father Serra and Prat himself had been attacked by this "Loanda sickness," as the scurvy was known, and like the rest had suffered the awful pains in their extremities, swellings of the gums, and dysentery which had gradually been destroying everyone's health. During these six long months the missionaries buried four more sailors, eight Catalonian Volunteers, and six Indian bowmen. There was little anyone could do in these troubles, save to hope and pray. Months had gone by since they had had news of the rest of the Expedition, or of any ship. The *San Antonio* or *El Príncipe* had long since sailed for San Blas for reinforcements, and should have reached there and have been on the way back by now. The *San José* had not been seen either. Gloom and fear were beginning to take possession of everyone. Among the soldiers, talk turned more and more often to what had become of the Monterrey expedition; tales were woven about the imaginary lands which must exist north of the known latitudes; others suspected that the northern explorers' delay in returning must be due to the inroads of sickness, or perhaps they had encountered the Russian forces also trying to settle the California coasts.

In upon this melancholy camp, on January 24, 1770, crashed the sound of a salvo of musketry. The sentinels returned it: they had recognized the column returning from the north, with the Governor on the point, the two missionaries, Lieutenant Pedro Fages and his little troop of six Volunteers of Catalonia, the Indian footmen with their crowbars, pickaxes and spades, the buff-coat soldiers, the muleteers with their much-diminished number of scarcely-laden beasts, and as rearguard Captain Rivera and the rest of the Spanish troops. It was a stirring and heartfelt meeting, on both sides, between the new arrivals and those who had stayed at the Mission—hearty clasps and shows of friendship, and no doubt a good deal of unruly horseplay among the soldiers. For all of them the long-delayed moment of reunion had finally come. Don Gaspar de Portolá himself describes the state of the settlement at his arrival in these words:

We found San Diego, with exactly the same garrison of eight buff-coat soldiers we had left there; there were also the three Fathers; but of the fourteen Volunteers who had remained behind, eight were dead, and the *San Carlos* still at anchor in the place we had left her, neither the *San José* nor *El Príncipe* having appeared here...[4]

It was at this point that Fray Junípero asked him, "Have you been to Rome and not seen the Pope?"—for there was no hiding the Expedition's failure to find Monterrey, despite their surprising discovery of the great Harbor of San Francisco, a discovery which immediately led Fray Junípero to think of the Visitor-General's promise to found a mission at that bay if it could be located.

Portolá had brought his entire expedition back without the loss of a single man; at San Diego he found a population of about thirty souls, which, together with his own newly arrived group, added up to nearly a hundred men.

No time was lost in inspecting the state of their supplies and drawing up a full report of them. Here is the report, finished and signed on January 28th, 1770, four days after Portolá's return to the Mission:

A full list of the grain and flour remaining, including that belonging to all the Missions, as follows:

|  | Fanegas and sacks | Weeks' worth |
|---|---|---|
| Corn, good | 30 | |
| Corn, poor | 34 | |
| Flour | 30 | |
| Allowing a ration of one almud, the good corn, leaving out of account 20 *almudes* not worth the trouble of counting since so badly spoiled, will last | | 4 |
| The 34 *fanegas* of bad corn, at 1½ *almud* daily ration, will last three weeks, leaving 24 *almudes* over | | 3 |
| Thirty sacks flour, supposed to contain 10 *almudes* per sack, which may not prove the case, at one full *almud* will last | | 3½ |
| Leaving seventeen sacks of flour over, equal to two weeks' rations | | 2 |
| | 94 | 12½ |

---

4. See Appendix A.

*Note.* According to the account which I am presenting to the Meeting, the whole amount of existing supplies will last no longer than twelve and a half weeks; wherefore I am reporting the fact so that each one may take thought as to what matters most.

San Diego, January 28th, 1770.

GASPAR DE PORTOLÁ
[rubric]

*Note.* Out of this list of supplies, six sacks of flour are being given to the party that is setting out for Californias with the Captain.

*Note.* For the supplies contained in this report, there are 54 persons to be given rations, plus 14 Indians at one-half *almud* weekly.[5]

This time, the accounts of the Expedition's stores and the personnel to be fed from them are remarkably clear and complete. The report lists a total group of fifty-four Spaniards and fourteen Indians who are to remain at the Mission. Sixty-eight rations are therefore to be provided.

Possibly the ships which they are waiting for may arrive in the meantime, but the expedition cannot count on it. The Governor decides to go in search of provisions to the nearest place they can be had, to the Californias, meaning the last Missions founded in the uppermost part of Lower California, specifically Mission San Fernando at the spot called Valicatá. He organizes a party of about twenty-five men who are to set out in this expedition under Captain Don Fernando de Rivera y Moncada. By sending them, he hopes both to reduce the strain on their present supplies, and to obtain the provisions and livestock that had been left behind there. But it will be better for Portolá himself to tell as about this, in his letter written from San Diego right after making the final decisions, and directed to the Viceroy, the Marquis de Croix; in it he also reports his journey to Monterrey harbor.

Most Excellent Sir.

Sir:   From San Diego I had reported back to Your Excellency by the *Príncipe* that, notwithstanding the unhappy state of that ship as well as the *San Carlos,* which were unable to pursue their

---

5.  México, Archivo General de la Nación, ramo de Californias, t. 76; copy in Seville, Archivo General de Indias, Aud. de Guadalajara 417 (Bancroft film, reel 357/20-22).

Aerial view of Lérida with the Zuda Castle.
Portolá was King's Lieutenant of this city. (Photo A. Sirera).

voyage to Monterrey because of the death of nearly their entire crews, I had determined to continue onward with the Land Expedition, reckoning that since the San Joseph was supposed to have set sail in the month of June, she might reach that destination even before me, and with the successful completion of her voyage the Expedition would be achieved; and that it was not right to eat up provisions, sitting idle at San Diego. I therefore set out on the 14th. of July of the year last past, with every good fortune so far as 36 degrees latitude; at that place, however, the Scurvy or Loanda sickness attacked this Expedition so strongly that 21 out of the 27 Buff-coat Soldiers, including myself, fell ill, and the other six were crippled by it, and indeed given all of the last rites. For all of this, the Expedition did not fail to continue onward until reaching latitude 36 degrees forty six minutes, at which point I ordered a halt, both because I regarded it as the proper latitude, since we had found San Diego in 32½° and because we had passed the Santa Lucia Mountains, which had forced us to fetch a circuit around them because of their total impenetrableness; and the Captain, having sallied out to explore the part we had missed, reported on his return that he had found no Harbor, whether Carmel or Monterrey. We having been all agreed that, by the marks given by Cabrera, we would be sure to find these here, and what with the throng we had of sick men, I decided to go no further on without first calling a Meeting in order to decide what was most fit to do. By common agreement it was resolved to continue the march and search for the Harbor at a higher latitude: and so it was done, with the beneficial effect that, as we moved into a different clime, the sick men improved, though the harm was that it cost us forty-some days to travel what we afterward made, coming back, in eighteen. This Expedition, then reached 37 degrees 46 minutes and a bit farther on, noted the *farallones* which, according to Cabrera's landmarks, is San Francisco Harbor. Finding ourselves in such an excessive latitude, we halted the Expedition here, and for the second time I requested a meeting. It was decided by common accord that the Expedition should turn back fearing as we did that Monterrey Harbor must have been left behind us because of the constant fogs we had been undergoing; that it should be looked for with the greatest thoroughness and care, and that if it were not found, the Expedition should settle down at the Point of Pines, at the end of the Sant Lucia Mountains. During this period we had some very clear fair days, and no person was left with any doubts that the Harbor might lie anywhere in what we had travelled through. The Expedition having settled itself at the said Point of Pines, the Captain of the Presidio don Fernando de Rivera set out, as first Scout, as appointed by His Most Honourable Lordship, to survey the country, not alone that which he had already seen, but he went as far onward as the steepness of the Mountains would let him, and viewed as much as he could beyond; on his return he

reported that he thought the Mountains to be the Santa Lucias without any doubt (as did all the soldiers with him; nor have we found
any other that could be), with the landmarks given by Cabrera, a
headland, and a peak; but that there was no Monterrey or Carmelo
Harbor to be found.  For this reason we have supposed that a great
many sand-dunes here at this point (no other point than it has been
found, either) could have stopped up those Harbors; that the Harbor
might have been here, we find confirmed by the agreement with
almost all of Cabrera's Landmarks, even to the extent of our finding
iron Tires from a Ship's Mainmast here.  Having lost all hopes of a
Harbor, having seen no Ship in seven months, finding not even a single
Heathen dwelling on the shore between the end of the Channel and
the place we had reached—no doubt the wildness of the Coast does
not allow them a living—and finding our flour on the point of giving
out, I requested a Meeting for the third time.   By common accord
it was decided to have the Expedition return to the Santa Barbara
Channel; to this I agreed, not only because it was a better-supplied
country (the only hope for us now) and so that in case a ship should
appear it could give us provisions to take up the journey anew, if
not to Monterrey then to San Francisco Harbor; and in case of not
having this help, we could return to the San Diego Presidio or Mission; where the whole Expedition now is, not even one man having
been lost.  In sum, Sir, this is what occurred during my journey, as
will be testified by my Journal, which I cannot send at the moment,
having been totally occupied with other matters.  I shall provide it
on the next occasion that presents itself, and in the meantime the
lack may be supplied by the one which I believe is being sent by don
Miguel Costansó to His Most Honourable Lordship.  I am left only
with the comfort that this Expedition has lost nothing by making
this Journey, other than our extreme toil, and the severe wants undergone in the six and a half months which I have spent in going
and returning; and that the profit from it has been to have explored
as far the surroundings of San Francisco Harbor, to have surveyed
the mind of the Heathen peoples, to have learned how extremely
well-populated the Channel with its regular settlements and the num-
berless Heathens dwelling there is, and to have convinced ourselves
that Monterrey does not exist where we have travelled. All this, so
that Your Excellency with more information may the better determine as you think best; and to prove that by land there is no hindrance as far as the good treatment we have experienced from the
Indians is concerned; indeed the only obstacle I find is the certainty
of suffering from the scurvy, whether by sea or by land, although by
land we have learned by experience that it quickly disappears with
the ease of changing one's climate; but as for those who have caught
it at sea, rare is the man who does not die of it, for at the moment
of writing this, fifty persons have been buried at San Diego, among

them thirteen of the 25 volunteers. On my arrival at this Presidio or Mission of San Diego I requested an account of the provisions that are left aboard the *San Carlos,* including what was sent for all of the Missions, a note of which I enclose for Your Excellency. On this account I have requested a Meeting to decide on what is best fitting. I have thought it would be best to despatch the Captain with a strong party, for two reasons: first, to lessen the number of Rations, second, so that he may take measures to have the cattle there in Californias driven to us here; I myself to remain here with the necessary number of men, these being 15 buff-coats with a sergean, for protecting the Mission, and Lieutenant Don Pedro Fages with the twelve men of his troop; we have reached an agreement with the Naval Commander that these latter are to be assigned, in case the Ships are late in arriving, as crew for the Packet *San Carlos* (under his command) should he find it proper for her to sail, though this will never be until we find ourselves in the last necessity. I shall remain here at this Mission until Your Excellency's answer; only representing to Your Excellency that for whatever decision you may take, the party which has set off to Californias must be recalled, and more men if possible; and since that party is in Californias, if Your Excellency sees fit, you may write me to have a party despatched since those who are here know the way. Which is all that i have worthy of Your Excellency's attention.

Desiring that God our Lord may Keep Yr. Excellency's most excellent Person the many years that He may and I wish for,

San Diego, February 11th, 1770,

Most Excellent Sir;
Sir:
Kissing Yr. Excy's Hand
your most affectionate Servant and obedient subject,
GASPAR DE PORTOLÁ
[rubric] [6]

On the 12th of February, the courier set out bearing this dispatch, with its account of the state of their provisions, leaving Portolá and his men to await at San Diego the arrival of

---

6. Archivo General de la Nación, Californias, t. 76, fols. 66-68; copy in Archivo General de Indias, Guadalajara 417 (reel 357/13-20). In the latter copy, for unknow reasons, the number of those who had died at San Diego is given as «forty-six», no fifty, as in the autograph original.

word from the Marquis de Croix and from the Visitor-General. At the same time Captain Rivera and his men left for San Fernando and the other missions of the Lower California peninsula with the goal of bringing cattle back to San Diego. But the Expedition commander's responsibility could not rest with merely awaiting the outcome of the mail dispatch and Captain Rivera's return with provisions.

Meeting, therefore, with Father Junípero Serra and others of the Expedition, and giving calm consideration to their present straits and those they might soon find themselves in, if neither the Captain by land nor the hoped-for ships by sea should arrive in time to aid them, Portolá settled upon a final deadline beyond which they would leave San Diego, abandon the entire attempt, and retire to the long-established missions in the peninsula. The argument of the situation in which they found themselves was this: Rivera with a party of twenty-five was setting out for Velicatá; once they had left, the main party had provisions to last until the end of April. By that date, then, they would have to be back in Christian lands, and in that case they would have to leave San Diego by March 20, since forty days' march separated them from Velicatá. Therefore, decided the Commander, if either of the ships should enter San Diego Harbor before or on March 19th the journey would be made back to Monterrey; if by March 19th there should be no ship, the morning of the 20th everyone would start the withdrawal to Lower California, even though orders to return to the north might later be received there.

It cannot have been any pleasure for Portolá and the officers of the Expedition to plan the abandonment of San Diego and their almost empty-handed return to the place from which they had first set out. But the responsibility for the live under Portolá's care had to take precedence over vague chances that help might arrive. Just as he had been able to decide to keep onward toward Monterey in July, 1769, at the time when the sea expedition had suffered its severe losses, so now the Commander did not hesitate to decide on returning to San Fernando Mission, hoping to be able to regroup and reorganize the land section of the Expedition there before he once more set out to search for the long lost harbor.

Father Junípero Serra, seeing that the planned day of departure coincided with the feast of St. Joseph, named as patron saint of the expedition, requested Governor Portolá's permission to begin a novena in honor of the saint, certain that his intercession might work the miracle of solving their problems in the way and at the time they most wished for. Everyone joined in the program of prayer.

Meanwhile, the eager missionary, drawn on by his love for converting the heathens, had been planning ways to remain at San Diego in company with Father Crespí and Sea Commander Vila, should the day come for which the Governor had set the departure. It is said that before the feast of St. Joseph drew near, Serra had had a quiet interview with Vila aboard the *San Carlos*, and that Portolá, kept informed of these plans, deliberately helped keep the brave missionaries' intentions a secret. At least, Father Omer Englebert has affirmed so in a book, though I myself doubt that Portolá would have stood for such proceedings on the part of Serra and Vila, especially in view of the specific orders he had to take care of the lives of the missionaries. The same author elsewhere in his book denies Portolá this supposed degree of tolerance by writing that the least failure of discipline might lead to a massacre, and therefore that Portolá, fair-minded and kind though he was, could not afford to overlook anyone's lapses.[7]

Says Father Palou,

St. Joseph's day arrived, and the feast of this great saint was celebrated by a sung Mass and sermon, with everything packed and prepared for the whole Expedition's retreat for Old California on the following day. But on that very afternoon, God saw fit to fulfill the burning desires of His servant [Father Serra] by the intercession of the Most Holy Patriarch [St. Joseph], and to give all of them the comfort of their having sighted, clearly and distinctly, a ship, which, sailing out of view the next day, anchored in San Diego harbor only on the fourth day following.

Engineer Costansó adds,

On March the 23d, His Majesty's Packet the *San Antonio*, under her captain and pilot Don Juan Pérez, reached and anchored in San Diego Harbor. Having set sail at San Blas on December 20 of the preceding year, 1769, she had experienced heavy weather and contrary winds during her voyage, having been blown four hundred

---

7. ENGLEBERT, Omer, *Fray Junípero Serra*, pp. 86, etc.

leagues away from the coast and having been forced to sail back toward it in order to take on water; she made land in thirty-five degrees latitude, whence, turning prow southward and presenting her larboard rail to the shore in search of an anchorage, she fell upon Point Concepcion, in thirty-four and a half degrees north latitude, the westernmost land on the Santa Barbara Channel, under the shelter of which she managed to take on water, next to a settlement of heathens, who gave a detailed account of the Land Expedition, using unmistakable signs to show how the foreigners had passed through there going northward and had later come back, short of food, heading south, riding their horses—which they expressed by sitting in a similar fashion on the barrels which the sailors had brought ashore, and making other movements of a man on horseback. They also repeated the names of several soldiers, which, being known by some of the sailors, showed the sounds were not pronounced at random.[8]

Portolá's and Father Serra's reports had indeed reached the right quarters, for the *San Antonio*, sailing from San Diego on July 9, 1769 with Captain Pérez and a few sailors aboard, had reached San Blas in twenty days' sail, but with eight sailors gone who had died on the way. On her arrival at port, measures were quickly set afoot to outfit the same ship for returning north, directly to Monterey this time, since it was supposed that the Expedition must already be settled there. As Costansó's account shows, lack of water caused her to put in to where Captain Pérez learned that the land expedition had returned to San Diego. Even so, at the last minute Pérez had decided not to deviate from the orders he had received at San Blas from the Viceroy; he set out from the anchorage determined to go on to Monterey after all, but on sailing only a few sea-miles, the loss of his anchor determined him to return south to San Diego, where the *San Carlos* could supply him with a spare.

His arrival was the occasion of a celebration by all concerned. The despatches he brought from the Viceroy fitted well with Father Serra's and Vila's belief that harbors do not get "stopped up," and that the very spot where Portolá's men had driven in their cross and buried their message must have been the location of Monterrey Harbor. Everything worked together for one end; the official letters, the expeditionaries' own thoughts, their desire to fulfill their original instructions to the word, and the arrival of relief and reinforcement, provisions ad men, all

---

8.  COSTANSÓ, *Diario Histórico* (see note 26 to Chapter I).

produced an immediate bustle and preparation for the second march north to Monterey.

This time they could count on knowing the way the friend ship of the natives, and the certainty that somewhere at the end there was a harbor that would suit their purposes. When the *San Antonio* had been outfitted with everything needed and her crew brought up to strength, with the addition of Father Serra, Surgeon Prat, Engineer Costansó, and a few soldiers, she was ready to sail. The land expedition, this time, was to be composed of the Governor, Lieutenant Fages, Sergeant Ortega, and the Franciscan Crespí, together with some of the troops who had taken part in exploring these coasts the previous time.

The sea expedition sailed on April 16th; contrary winds blew the ship down to Latitude 30° before more favorable weather allowed them to make land at Monterey after forty-six days' sail. The land party followed on the next day, April 17th, and, knowing the country they travelled, this time they reached their destination in thirty-eight days from departure, eight days before the ship.

All reached Monterrey: those coming by land on May 23d, and the *San Antonio* on the 31st, of the same dropped anchor in the very same harbor and anchorage in which the Squadron of General Vizcaíno, sent by the Count of Monterrey upon the discovery of the Coasts by Order of King Philip the Third, had lain one hundred and sixty eight years before. The harbor, as has been said, lies in thirty six degrees forty minutes north latitude, at the dropping off of the Santa Lucia Mountains, upon their northern side. Its principal shelter is the Point of Pines, stretching Northwest to Southeast (not Northeast-Southwest, as it is located by Pilot Cabrera Bueno's guide), and upon its Northeastern side lies the Roadstead, where any Vessel may anchor in four, six, or eight fathom, bottom fine sand and a good holding-ground, depending upon distance from shore.

The Point of Pines, sheltering the Roadstead upon the Northwest, is all girt about with rocks and cliffs, but beyond the rocks begins a handsome Beach bordered by Dunes, in an easterly direction, turning at once Northeastward and North, as far as a very large Inlet with several branches distant over three leagues from the beginning of the said Beach. Beyond the Coast runs on back toward the Northwest and Westward, rather high land covered with trees, cliffy in places, till Point Año Nuevo, which lies out to sea in thirty six degrees three minutes latitude—the Roadstead [of Monterey] thus being surrounded by land upon all sides save the North-northwest, the only place where it is improtected.

This description of Costansó's, so firmly and clearly iden-
tifying the place, is written by the same man who a few short
months before had surveyed its shores, dunes and cliffs and had
roundly stated in his Journal under December 5th that the harbor did not exist in the given latitude, that it could not have
escaped their search and efforts.

At any rate, now we have the expeditions met at Monterey,
ready to set about the founding of the Presidio and mission,
which are to bear the name of San Carlos Borromeo, according
to the instructions drawn up so long ago now at San Blas.

Portolá, Fages and Crespí explore along the shore, until
they come up against the cross they had planted there earlier;
they find it still standing, surrounded by arrows and sticks
bearing feathers and food, still-fresh fish and seeds. From here,
with the pleasure of knowing they have reached their harbor,
they survey the bay with its silent peaceful waters. Two leagues
from the outer coast, they set up their camp upon the Point of
Pines, and settle down to await the sea expedition's coming.
Soon the ship is sighted.

On June 3d, Portolá and his men, wearing their best uni-
forms and full-dress trappings, bear the royal standard unfurled
to the spot chosen for taking possession of California in the
name of His Majesty King Charles III. A party from the ship
draws slowly toward shore to the beat of oars, while aboard the
San Antonio the guns are loaded and trained for firing salutes.

Ashore, under an ancient tree, where a church-bell has been
hanging and is being tirelessly chimed, the Franciscans are
standing in wait. Fray Junípero Serra vests himself in alb and
stole, and, everyone kneeling and facing the Pacific Ocean, they
sing the Veni Creator. Close by lies on the ground a large cross
which they will next raise and set up over the grave of a common seaman from the San Antonio who has just died; from
the ship come echoing the cannon salutes and the cheers of
the mariners left aboard. Solemn Mass is then celebrated, and
immediately afterward commences the ceremony in which the
first Governor of all the Californias, Don Gaspar de Portolá y de
Rovira, illustrious son of Balaguer, nobleman of the Spanish
military, repeats aloud, in a manner so as to be heard by all
present, that he, the Commander in Chief of the Expedition,

takes possession of these lands in the name of the King of Spain, for the greater Glory of God, the Safety of the Realm, and the good of the heathen population.

Loud salvos from the troops' muskets, and the soldiers' cheers echoing from the calm waters of the Monterey shore. Fray Junípero blesses the land in the direction of the four winds, and the shore at hand, while Governor Portolá and his officials tear up plants from the ground and cast them in the air, gather stones and throw them toward the shore, crying ¡Long live the Faith, Long live the King! Planted next to the old oak and flapping in the breeze, the flag symbolizes to all, present or distant, that Spain has increased by another empire her immense possessions in the Realm of New Spain.

A few days afterward and everyone was hard at work beginning to build the Presidio and Mission, to be christened with the name of San Carlos, the second settlement to be founded in Upper California.

June 14th was Corpus Christi day; work paused while they celebrated a solemn mass with a procession which, headed by Portolá with the soldiers formed up in file two abreast, trod the sands of the shore singing hymns and bearing the statue of the Virgin which had been entrusted to the Franciscans by the Visitor-General, to be returned at the close of the Expedition. Once more salvos from the packet *San Antonio* broke the silence, and cheers of Spaniards affirmed the people's faith and the hope of the spiritual and worldly winning of California.

Following this last ceremony, the Governor prepared to set in operation the last steps of the plan that had been drawn up at San Blas. First he wrote the Viceroy a long account of the second expedition to Monterey: his leaving San Diego after the *San Antonio's* lucky arrival there, and the journey along the routes found out the first time, with no problems along the way save for the wildness of the country. The natives had continued to greet them with the same signs of friendship and awe, especially the chieftains called the Buchón and the Bailarín, "Big-craw" and "Dancer," who were later to provide a great support for the long journeys of the missionaries. Portolá also informed the Viceroy that he would be departing from the Mission and Presidio in a few days, proceeding to Mexico City

via San Blas and Tepic, in order to come before His Excellency
the Viceroy and the Visitor General with a full account of the
expedition under his command.

Meanwhile, direct from Monterey Harbor, he was sending
the soldier José Velázquez overland with urgent orders to bear
the papers recording the taking of possession and the founding
of the mission-presidio of San Carlos to Their Excellencies.

A document found in the Central Library of Barcelona,
entitled "Accounts of the Peninsula of California and the first
expeditions made to win it...," a manuscript including a report
of the expeditions as well as a statistical table both of mission
possessions and of the missionary expeditions, contains on its
folio 86 a copy of a sight draft in which the Viceroy Marquis de
Croix orders his exchequer to pay the amount of 150 pesos to
the soldier José Velázquez, "who brought the papers of the discovery of Monterrey."   The march which had awaited Velázquez
in order to make this delivery was the whole distance back from
Monterey to San Diego and thence to Loreto, whence the news
passed on to Mexico. We shall see later that the despatches
sent to Viceroy Croix by Portolá, Costansó and Pérez from San
Blas Harbor arrived before those that went by Loreto.   Velázquez took a month and a half traversing overland the 570 leagues
between Monterey and the Lower California capital, the first
news coming to the hands of Father Palou from the Loreto
Presidio towards the second of August; thence the despatches
went by boat across the Gulf to San Blas, and on to Mexico
City, as has been said.

Meanwhile Don Gaspar, Commander in Chief of the Expedition, was still carrying out the Visitor-General's instructions.
With Mission and Presidio founded, he was preparing to turn
over command to Lieutenant Don Pedro Fages, another son of
Lérida now being made the next governor of California.   There
also were to remain Fathers Junípero Serra and Crespí, with
the task of beginning to preach the Gospel in the new land and
of establishing another mission, to be called San Buenaventura,
on the Santa Barbara Channel—a foundation which, for various
reasons outside the bounds of this study, did not take place
until 1782.

I should like to picture—if only for a moment or two—
the scene at the leave-taking of the missionaries, officers, and
soldiers from their leader Portolá.   They could perhaps hope,

most of them, that the future might offer chances for them to meet again, scattered through the deserts of the Californias or the other colonies; perhaps providence might even bring them together another time for another undertaking like the one they had just brought to an end, those men who had spent nearly two years travelling north and south along the Pacific coast. Father Serra was in ill health, his leg, from which he had suffered so much in the past, seeming likely to restrict the travels which his faith was nonetheless about to force on him. Captain Rivera had withdrawn to Lower California and requested to be retired from the army. Portolá himself was fifty-three years old and suffering from sickness.

There on the shores of Monterey, those who departed and those who remained must have told each other, more by mood than by words, how much friendship had been left by those hard days together, how many ineffaceable memories written in mutual consideration and respect. Gaspar de Portolá and his men, the officers and captains of the ships, the buff-coat soldiers and the Catalonian Volunteers, had begun their passage into the pages of world history by inaugurating the birth of Greater California; yet the only reward that any of them could be conscious of at that moment was his own pride at having well fulfilled his individual calling and duty.

From the ship rang out the salutes of the cannon, and the Mission's little bell chimed steadily, as the soft winds slowly pushed the *San Antonio* from the shore, separating forever Portolá and Serra, the true heroes and pioneers of this conquest.

They sailed from Monterey on July 9th, and reached San Blas on the first of August. Once in Harbor there, Portolá and Captain Juan Pérez send despatches which reach the capital on August 10. Portolá briefly repeats the facts about the successful occupation of Monterey, assuming that the report he had previously sent by an overland courier might have arrived first; copies of the legal oath of possession are enclosed for the Viceroy. To Gálvez, Portolá writes that he is returning to Mexico in accordance with the terms of the Visitor-General's instructions, though by ship rather than by land, in order to avoid draining the new settlements of any of their soldier-settlers who would otherwise have had to escort him. Gálvez is assured—in language which the Visitor-General will quote in his printed broadside announcing the success of the expeditions

—that the settlers have been left "as safe as if they were in Mexico City," with further supplies for them on the way from Lower California, and Father Serra immensely eager to found the next mission.

Portolá's letters are dated August 1, on which date the news of the occupation of Monterey was still unknown in the capital. From San Blas, accompanying the other expeditionaries' despatches, Don Juan Pérez also writes a note on the subject to Visitor-General Gálvez.

Most Honorable Sir.—Dear Sir: By the post despatched from Monte-Rey, which bore the news of the succesful putting-in and arrival there of all us who were bound for that Harbor by sea and by land, I reported the principal events of our sea voyage to Your Most Honorable Lordship, as well as what had been achieved in pursuance of your orders upon the land there, following the performance of the act of taking possession of it, without the slightest opposition on the part of its Natives, whose mannerly and well-disposed character does not belie that of their ancestors, so much praised by Vizcaíno's Spaniards formerly.

I boarded ship at that Harbor on the 9th of the present month, accompanied by Don Gaspar de Portolá, onto, the *Príncipe*, in order to return hither, where we anchored in the harbor today after twenty four days' sail free of hindrance or hardship, thanks be to God.[9]

At Mexico City, their lordships the Viceroy Croix and the Visitor-General received the despatch from Portolá, with such relief and happiness that they passed a message to the dean of the cathedral to sound out a peal from his bells, signalling the news to all the city's people. Startled by the loud sign of joy, they gathered, while the other churches and chapels took up the chime and passed it on, and soon the far corners of the city acknowledged the happy news that the domains of His Catholic Majesty had become greater by three hundred leagues of northern shores. The inhabitants of Mexico City thronged before the Viceroy's Palace, and the leaders of society entered to congratulate him upon the good news. Their compliments were received inside the palace by both Viceroy and Visitor-General, the latter of whom had organized the expeditions by his own hand,

9.  Seville, Archivo General de Indias, Guadalajara 417, n.º 10.

with the enthusiasm which he put into all of is activities,, even
to laboring personally over such details as the packing and loading of supplies and provisions which were to ko with the expeditionaries.

Both men, eager to give the news official standing, dispatched Madrid-ward the success of His Majesty's expeditions,
mentioning that the conquest had been achieved under the command of Captain Governor Don Gaspar de Portolá and other
sea and land officers. Likewise they ordered the government
printers to put out an *Extract of News* meant to be circulated
throughout the country and sent abroad to all courts and chan-
ceries, governors and tribunals, exchequers, viceroys and gov-
ernments of the entire world. This publication, a type very
well known at that time, has the defect of some exaggeration
in the way it paints the occupation, in claiming as accomplished
facts a number of measures which had not been completed and
never would be, and in describing as excellent and ample the
physical facilities and the supplies with which the presidios and
missions had been left. I have no doubt that such remarks
were deliberately planted in order to make it clear to the courts
of Catherine the Great and the King of England that Spain's
King had every intention of preserving and developing these
posts, which had cost so much time and sacrifice.

The pamphlet or broadside, dated Mexico, August 16th, 1770,
runs as follows:

AN EXTRACT OF NEWS OF MONTERREY HARBOUR, *of the Mission and
Presidio founded there under the appellation of* SAN CARLOS, *and
of the two expeditions by sea and land despatched for that purpose in the year 1769 last past.*

Following repeated costly expeditions made during the last two
centuries by the Spanish Crown in order to survey the Western
Coast of California along the South Sea and to occupy the important
Harbour of Monterrey, this undertaking has now been successfully
achieved by two expeditions despatched pursuant to Royal Order and
by disposition of the Authorities of this Realm, by sea and by land
from Cape San Lucas and from Loreto Presidio in the months of
January, February, and March of the year last past.

In June of that year both expeditions met at San Diego Harbour, located in latitude 32 degrees and a half; and the decision
having been taken for the packet *San Antonio* to return to San

Blas Harbour to recruit her crew and to bring fresh supplies, the command packet ship *San Carlos* remained at anchor in the same Harbour of San Diego because of a lack of her seamen, who had ded of scurvy; and, a Mission and Garrison having been established there, the land expedition pursued its journey up through the country, as far as 37 degrees 45 minutes latitude, searching for Monterrey; but, this having not been found by the marks given by earlier voyagers and coast-pilots, and fearing lack of provision, the expedition returned to San Diego, where, upon the fortunate successful arrival of the packet *San Antonio* in March of this year, the Commanders by land and sea made the opportune decision to undertake once again the fulfillment of the instructions they had been given.

In fact both expeditions set out from San Diego upon the 16th and 17th of April of the present year, and the expedition by land had the fortune, in this second journey, to find Monterrey Harbour and to reach there upon May 16th, while the sea expedition touched the same place on the 31st of the same month, with no misfortune or losses save that of a Caulker stricken by sickness.

That Harbour having been thus occupied by sea and land, to the especial gratification of the countless Heathen Indians who inhabit all the country explored and surveyed in these two journeys, the Act of Possession was celebrated upon June 3rd, with the legal Instrument thereof drawn up by Commander in Chief Don Gaspar de Portolá and certified to by the other Officers of both expeditions, all of them asserting it to be the very Harbour of Monterrey, with the identical marks described in the old accounts of General Don Sebastián Vizcaíno and the rutter of Don Joseph Cabrera Bueno, First Pilot of the Philippine Galleons.

Upon the 14th of that month of June last past, the aforesaid Commander Don Gaspar de Portolá despatched a post overland to Loreto Presidio, bearing the welcome news of the occupation of Monterrey, and of the Mission and Presidio of San Carlos having been founded there; however, on account of the great distance, the Government Authorities here have not yet received those Despatches, whereas on the 10th of the present month others reached this Capital that had been sent from San Blas Harbor by the same Portolá, by Engineer Don Miguel Constansó, and by Captain Don Juan Pérez, Commander of the aforesaid Packet *San Antonio* alias the *Príncipe*, which had set out from Monterrey on the 9th of July, and in spite of being becalmed for eight days made her long voyage so speedily and successfully that she anchored at San Blas on the first of this month.

At the new Presidio and Mission of San Carlos de Monterrey plentiful goods and provisions have been left, with a year's worth of supplies for founding another Missionary Post to be dedicated to San Buenaventura, at a proper distance away; and Lt. of the Volunteers of Catalonia Don Pedro Fages having been left there as well, as Military Commander of the new establishments, it is judged that by this date he will have been joined by the Captain of Loreto Presidio, Don Fernando de Rivera, with nineteen more soldiers and cowherds and muleteers, bringing two hundred head of cattle and a share of provisions from the new Mission of San Fernando of Vellicatá, which is situated out beyond the Frontier of the previously-won part of California, for they had set out from that place upon the 14th of April last, bound for the aforementioned Harbours of San Diego and Monterrey.

Notwithstanding the fact that at the latter, the storehouses already contructed for the new Presidio and Mission were left plentifully supplied upon the departure of the Packet *San Antonio*, and that His Majesty's two other Packets the *San Carlos* and *San Joseph* are believed to be at anchor in San Diego harbour, the Government Authorities here have ordered the *San Antonio* to undertake a third voyage from San Blas Harbour at the end of next October, carrying fresh provisions and thirty missionaries of San Fernando, from the mission lately arrived from Spain, to erect new Mission Stations in the extensive and fertile country surveyed by the land Expedition, from the former frontier of California as far as San Francisco Harbour, not much farther north from that of Monterrey, to seize the happy chance now offered by the mannerly and well-disposed character of the countless Indians inhabiting Northern California.

In proof of this fortunate disposition among that populous and extremely tractable Heathen folk, our Commander Don Gaspar de Portolá assures us (and the other Officers and Missionary Fathers all agree in the same) that our Spaniards dwell as safely at Monterrey as if in the midst of the Capital here, though the new Presidio has been left adequately fitted out with artillery, men, and plentiful munitions; while the Reverend Father President of the Missions, assigned to that of Monterrey, relates in great detail and with particular joy the friendliness of the Indians and the promise they have already made him to give him their children to be educated in the mysteries of our sacred Catholic Religion; and this exemplary and zealous Minister of it adds a full account of all the Solemn Masses held between the arrival of both of the Expeditions and the departure of the *San Antonio* Packet, as well as the Solemn Procession of the most Holy Sacrament held on Corpus Day, June 14th, together with other particulars testifying to the especial providence by which God has seen fit to favor the good success of these Expeditions, doubtless in reward of the ardent zeal of our August Sovereign, whose incomparable piety acknowledges the first responsibility of his Royal Crown in these vast Domains to be the spreading of the Faith of Jesus Christ and the happiness of the wretched Heathens who having not the knowlelge of it groan in the tyrannous slavery of the enemy of mankind.

In order not to delay this most important news, the preceding account of it has been drawn up in short compass without awaiting the first despatches sent overland from Monterrey, until in time from the journals of the voyages by sea and land, and from other documents, a full account of both expeditions may be given.

Mexico City, August 16th, 1770.

By permission and order of the Most Excellent Lord Viceroy, at the Government Press.[10]


With the publication of this news, our Don Gaspar de Portolá had reached the headlines, and neither the Viceroy nor the Visitor-General withheld their praises.

It is here, at this moment in which Portolá is receiving his deserved reward of compliments and congratulations from superiors, companions in arms, and the people of Mexico, that I feel it necessary to underline the fact that in all the documents I have examined and read, noted down and referred to by place and date, archive and folio number, I have scarcely come across one word of self-praise for himself or for his deeds—well justified though it would have been—but only praise for the success of the expedition achieved by his men, for the missionaries, and for the higher authorities who planned it. This behavior is not surprising in a military man of noble rank, one following a vocation dedicated to the service of king and country, to loyalty to the person and the institution of the crown, and feeling for it the straightforward allegiance of the army man. Gaspar de Portolá never regarded the California project as a civil expedition, but as a military service, and therefore never expected any other reward than knowing himself to be worthy of greater respect from having understood and proved able to fulfill the instructions issued by his superiors. All through the march we never find him losing his temper, never failing in his honor or his professional military character, never questioning an order, never giving an order that was not well thought out and worth giving. His subordinates' respect was complete and sincere and the affection with which he treated Father Junípero and the other Franciscans was fully returned. Among all of the dif-

---

10.  Madrid, Museo Naval, Ms., *Virreinato de Méjico*, t. I, n.º 21.

ferent chroniclers, there might easily have been one to have let slip some complaint, happening or circumstance unfavorable to the Commander of the Expeditions. Quite to the contrary: there is nothing but regard and respect for Captain Portolá both as commander and as personage, so much so that one of Serra's biographers refers to him as "the magnificent Portolá."

It would be inhuman to suppose that the expeditionaries were not to be rewarded according to their undeniable deserts for their sacrifices and sufferings with some sort of bonus and promotion, in the normal way in which extraordinary services to the King were recognized. And it is not strange that Portolá, the Leridan far from his native land, a bachelor sparing in words, should have dreamed of returning homeward to the place where he had left all his relations. The Visitor-General and the Marquess de Croix themselves hasten to recommend Portolá and his fellows of the expedition for promotion in rank. A letter sent by the Viceroy to the Minister of the Indies, Don Julián de Arriaga, under date of August 25th, 1770, acknowledges the special deserts of Gaspar de Portolá, "who has so well and actively performed the discharge of the affairs committed to him." [11] On the 28th of the same month of August, Visitor-General Gálvez writes as follows to the King's minister, Arriaga:

Most Excellent Sir. — My dear and most respected sir: It is in every wise fitting that in fulfillment of the duty I owe Your Excellency I should report the successful progress achieved by the two expeditions by sea and land in the fortunate finding of Monterrey Harbor; since, however, the Marquess de Croix is doing the same, sending full and detailed accounts of the event accompanied by copies of the letters which we have so far received by the Packet *San Antonio*, as he has indicated to me, I shall avoid troubling you with repeating it, both of us being ready to begin drawing up the file (as befits its importance), and to send it to His Majesty, so soon as Don Gaspar de Portolá and Don Miguel Constansó reach this Capital as well as the Despatches which are to be brought by the post which they sent overland, and when the maps, bearings, and journal have been examined.

For the sake of our Religion and in the honorable discharge of the King's commissions, I have dedicated the entire impulse of

---

11. Archivo General de Indias, Guadalajara 417, n.º 11.

my activity and zeal to the achievement of his sovereign purposes, and it will be for me an overabundant reward, if His Majesty (I hope for no less from his August benevolence) should receive as a worshipful gift the countles hardships I have undergone in over two years' wanderings through wastes and deserts, the willing sacrifice of my rest for the good of the Nation, and the distraction of constant cares which have worn my spirit and ruined my health by the long sickness which I have suffered in such varying climates, lacking in all human aids.  In all this the Lord has shown His mercies, and has given me the comfort that, on my return here, I should witness the demonstrations of joy with which all good Patriots have welcomed the good news about this undertaking, in which, to my confusion, Heaven has ordained that I should be a weak instrument.

Those who have distinguished themselves in it by especial zeal and exactness are Don Gaspar de Portolá, Captain of the Dragoons of Spain regiment and Commander of the Land Expedition; Engineer Don Miguel Costansó; Lieutenant Don Pedro Fages, who has been left in command at Monterrey; Don Fernando de Rivera y Moncada, Captain of Loreto Presidio, who withdrew his application for retirement from that position because of the usefulness and importance of the charge I enjoined upon him; and the sailing-masters Don Vicente Vila, of the corps of pilots of the Royal Navy, and Don Juan Pérez, commander of the above-named *San Antonio* Packet: whose deserts I now set forth to Your Excellency, in addition to whatever I myself may have done, so that you may be pleased to obtain His Majesty's gracious consent to a promotion in rank for each, and to Frigate Lieutenants in the case of the sailing-masters, to serve each one for a reward and a furtherance of his career.

I offer Your Excellency my regards and respects, and pray Our Lord that He may keep your life many long years, as is my wish.

Mexico, August 28th, 1770.

Kissing Your Excellency's hand, your most humble servant, Joseph de Gálvez.

To the Most Excellent Lordship Knight-commander Don Julián de Arriaga.[12]

Here, following the same traditional tone and using almost the same words as José de Gálvez, is the petition which Gaspar

---

12.  Ibid., n.º 12.

de Portolá himself directed to the King on September 28th, 1770, based upon his services in California:

Don Gaspar de Portolá, Captain in the Regiment of Spain, At Your Majesty's Royal Feet, With highest respect: sets forth his deserts from over 36 years' service (as shown by the enclosed record), in which length of time he has taken part in all the campaigns of the Italian War, having been wounded in the Battle of the Olmo, and the late Portuguese war. Assigned to New Spain with the above-mentioned Regiment, he set out upon the Sonora Expedition, and at once was named Governor of Californias because of the Expatriation of the Jesuits, to take control of that Province; where he remained until being sent as Commander in Chief of the Expedition by Land for the Discovery of the Harbors of San Diego and Monterrey, which he achieved with the best effect, though at the expense of great cost, trouble, and toil, as may be supposed in having gone over 400 leagues in 16 months' marching through unknown Countries, pathless and full of hindrances from the lack of the most necessary things and the constant dread of the Heathen Indians; all of which your Petitioner's zeal and firmness overcame, for the Service of Your Majesty, as is known to his superiors.

He further represents to Your Majesty that he has had as his brother Don Pedro de la Cruz y Mayor, who died a Lieutenant-General. And wishing to possess some token that his services have been welcome to Your Majesty,

Humbly petition Your Majesty that in view of the above, and especially of his deserts recently contracted in the aforesaid Discoveries, which were so often attempted fruitlessly before, he may receive whatever favor Your Majesty is pleased to bestow, for which he looks to Your Majesty's kindness.

Gaspar de Portolà.[13]

Here, in Portolá's own words, we have his view of his accomplishment. Those who are unfamiliar with the style in which such petitions were composed at that period should not be surprised that Don Gaspar openly calls his Majesty the King's attention to his achievements in making discoveries which others before him had so often attempted without success, and dwells upon his efforts in overcoming the obstacles of an unknown country and insufficient supplies while marching for over a

13. Mexico, Archivo General de la Nación, Correspondencia de los Virreyes, Ser. II (Croix), t. 13 (1769-1770), fol. 46.

thousand miles through totally unexplored territory—not counting the ground gone over twice! Such a petition was necessary for any military promotion of this sort, and we may be sure that Portolá was expressly invited by his superiors to write it. And such formulas as "humbly petitions," "at Your Majesty's Royal Feet," strange as they now sound, will seem incorrect only to those unaware of the forms followed in the years when these expeditions took place.

We may doubt that Gaspar de Portolá wasted much time in worrying about the promotion or "favor" while his petition was pending, though he probably knew of the recommendation which had been forwarded by his superiors. Probably also, after the leave normally granted in such cases, he rejoined his regiment of dragoons unless he had been assigned some special mission under the direct orders of the Viceroy or Visitor-General. Certainly after a very short time, to be precise on January 5th, 1771, His Majesty granted the rank of Lieutenant Colonel to the leader of the Monterrey Expedition, and it would not be long before he received it at his assigned post in Mexico. The following message from the Palace to Minister Arriaga is clear:

I pass into Your Excellency's hands the attached two Royal Commissions, original and duplicate, issued in favor of Don Gaspar de Portolá, Captain in the Dragoons of Spain regiment, for the rank and pay of Lieutenant Colonel, which the King has seen fit to grant him, as Your Excellency advises me in a communication of the first of this month, in order for you to direct them as necessary. God keep Your Excellency many years. The Palace, January 5th, 1771. Juan Gregorio Muniain.

To his Most Excellent Lordship Julian de Arriaga.[14]

The royal commission granted by King Charles III at the Palace on that same day reads as follows:

Don Carlos by the Grace of God King of Castile, of Aragon, of the two Sicilies, (etc.)

Forasmuch as, considering the Services of you Don Gaspar de Portolá, Captain in the Regiment of Dragoons of Spain, and your especial deserts while in the command of the expedition to the Har-

---

14. See Note 12 above.

bor of Monterrey in Californias, I have determined to confer upon you the rank and pay of a Lieutenant Colonel...[15]

Now let us leave Portolá with his hard-won promotion to lieutenant colonel, which reached his hands in April, 1771, via the long sea route from Madrid to Mexico, and through complex administrative channels as well.

But before finally writing finish to his Californian adventure, I wish to put into print a letter which I regard as of interest both because of the juncture at which it was written and because of the ideas put forth by its authors.

These are Don Matías de Armona, a major in the expedition which had been sent to Sonora, and Don Joaquín Velázquez de León, professor of mathematics at the University of Mexico, both of them at the time occupying important official positions in Lower California, Armona serving as the Intendant or Governor, and Velázquez as the deputy of José de Gálvez.   The letter, addressed to Viceroy Croix and dated at Santa Ana Camp, June 30, 1770, I came across among documents in the library of the Museo Naval of Madrid.   It reads:

Most Excellent Sir

Sir: We learn through several letters from Loreto, a faithful abstract of which we enclose herewith, that the *Príncipe* packet reached San Diego Harbor the 23rd of March, and departed thence for the Harbor of San Francisco on the 16th of April, taking the Father President Fray Junípero Serra; and that Captain of Dragoons Don Gaspar de Portolá set out overland for the same place with seven Soldiers from this Presidio and Lieutenant of Catalonian Volunteers Fages with twelve of his men, and two Religious [friars]. That a party of one Sergeant and eight Soldiers remained behind at San Diego, for whom the *Príncipe* left 25 *fanegas* of corn to sustain them while waiting for the *San Joseph* to arrive shortly; and although this latter Ship touched at Cape San Lucas at the beginning of May and departed it a the end of the month, as Don Joaquín Velasquez writes Your Excellency, the people at San Diego will not yet, for all that, have been driven to abandon the Harbor.

Don Fernando Rivera y Moncada, Captain of the Presidio here, set out on the 14th of March from the new Mission of Villacata or San Fernando in order to bring the relief supplies sent from this

15.   Bancroft Library, University of California, Ms. M-M 1811.

Peninsula both overland and via San Luis Gonzaga Bay, pursuant to orders and measures issued to this effect by Governor Don Mathías de Armona while on the other shore [of the Gulf]. Since Rivera made the journey in 13 days upon his way back, even though this time, driving a great many jack mules and two hundred head of cattle, he were to delay an entire month upon the same way, he may still have reached San Diego by the middle of the present June, and we suppose that they will have had enough provisions there, with the 25 *fanegas* of corn left them by the *Príncipe*, to await Captain Rivera; but even should they have been forced to leave San Diego, they must necessarily encounter him on the way, and so turn back; and in the mean time the *San Joseph* will have reached there, it being the most favorable season for sailing to that destination—so that they can now be regarded as provided for.

This happy news, and that which Your Excellency must already have received concerning the discovery of the new Country and Harbor, provides us with the occasion of offering Your Excellency a number of reflections arising from our Zeal and loyalty toward our King and Nation, and from experience and acquaintance with these Lands; it is the importance of the subject which must excuse the lengthiness of these lines.

Those persons to whom this Expedition was committed set out in search of Monte-Rey because it was the best harbor of which there was any account to be found in the ill-preserved history of our former expeditions, or in the still less exact report of the Philippine Galleon sailing-masters; so that it is quite impossible, on these grounds, to build more than a very vague and inadequate notion of the location of this Harbor: a notion liable on the one hand to be totally in error and on the other hand to cause as many disagreements as there were minds which considered it. Astronomical observations should have been the surest guide; but those for Latitude were of very slight accuracy in former times, while the Longitude at sea is still very uncertain at the present day, and in order for an exact location to be determined thereby, both of them must needs intersect at a given point.

It is for this reason that our Pilgrims disagree: have they, or not, come across the Monte-Rey? Can it have been buried under the heights of sand along the shore? In many places they saw some, but nowhere saw all, of the landmarks they were seeking. Yet they agree upon having found a Harbor situated more or less where Monte-Rey ought to have been, one which if, the depth «which they have so far been unable to ascertain) corresponds to its other qualities, may well one of the best in the world; and this we believe must have been calculated to fulfill utterly the wishes of our royal Court, whether we name it Monte-Rey or San Francisco.

If we may be allowed, Most Excellent Sir, to inquire into the high motives for which this expedition was decided upon we shall set forth our own argument, adducing a number of principles which might appear extremely remote, were they not necessary to forming the system of our thinking.

Nearly the whole of America, whether in the continent or its islands, which has become known up to the present, is due to Spanish discoveries; yet, fatigued by continual war, our Monarchy its ambition had embraced.

Foreign nations have occupied many of our islands, and have penetrated the farthest north of this great continent, where, battening upon the fur trade with the barbarous Iroquois, they have succeeded in drawing such profit from lands in themselves less fertile than our own, that we have just seen a bloody war fought over the Newfoundland fishery and the boundaries of Acadia. With our enemies thus engaged in the northeast of America and the Gulf of Mexico, we have dwelt careless of the continent's western flank, relying upon the difficulties of sailing the South Sea; this despite the fact that on this side, the chain of mountains runs which we call the Sierra Madre—and mother it is, in both Americas, of our underground wealth; yet this it is that up until now we have protected less well, believing it less exposed to danger.

Certainly, so long as Europeans could find no other way into the South Sea than by Cape Horn or the Cape of Good Hope, we had nothing to fear beyond a fleeting raid by an occasional daring Freebooter. Yet let us inquire whether there may not be another direction by which Europe may be able to disturb the Pacific Ocean's quiet, and our own. Not, to be sure, through the long wished for connexion between the two oceans, and the St. Lawrence River and its lakes: we are agreed that since our former search, which has since been kept up by the English, has not found it out, it is very likely it does not exist. But can we say the same for the short passage between Eastern Tartary and our own coast, which Russia has now once and again achieved?

This vast empire, which is every day becoming more fearsome, cannot color its attempts upon America with the specious excuse of ascertaining and establishing its boundaries: for what has this to do with their searching out ours?—even less with mere curiosity of extending geographical knowledge: of what great importance can it be to Russia to correct the maps, that she must therefore send out, twice over, expeditions at once so costly and so ill-fated? One can only suspect a certain spirit of gaining discoveries, colonies and trade in America, and thus it is very likely that had Russia come across so fine a harbor as the one our men have described, her thoughts would already be bent upon occupying it and keeping it for herself.

These and other considerations which we do not pretend to the knowledge of will have been weighed by His Majesty in his decision to survey and occupy the farthest limits of our discoveries in this direction, they being deemed important as well to the interest of religion and of the crown as to the honor of the nation: Now is no longer the time to slumber upon an ill-examined notion of the safety of Spain's conquests, nor to rest satisfied at having once discovered many lands at great cost, leaving later centuries not even a full account of what was discovered. Now thought must be taken to following up discovery by genuine occupation, by a regular settlement able to realize the fruits of expense and toil, and to establish our lawful title of possession upon the surest foundations of natural law and the law of nations, by the sending of more missionaries and the placing of an adequate military garrison.

Your Excellency and the Most Honorable Don Joseph de Gálvez perfectly understood these considerations when you arranged this affair with so wise a foresight that the desired purpose has been brought off within a short space of time and at small expense indeed when compared with the former expeditions and the different purposes to which they were directed: *Those* were primarily directed to searching for the supposed connection between the two oceans in order to facilitate the much-coveted trade with the Spice Islands, and afterward to establishing a harbor for the Philippine sailors to touch at, a thing which time has shown to have been unneeded; but this expedition is designed to protect the most precious interests and honor of the Throne. If those former expeditions could well be abandoned, this one must not be let slip.

At all time California [i. e., Lower California] has been thought of as inescapably linked with discoveries to be made on the western coast of America, but this time the truth has been confirmed by very experience. The southern end of this peninsula is a necessary stepping stone in communication by sea between Mexico and the new Harbors of San Diego and Monte-Rey, whether the ships sail from Acapulco or San Blas, and its northern end is the limit of our spiritual conquests upon this coast, so that these new discoveries must always be understood as an extension of California, and would be but weakly supported were we to leave deserted the long interval between Villacata and San Diego, and between the latter and the Harbor of San Francisco. Thus the whole Peninsula is needed to support this undertaking, and where before it was necessary to sustain it for the maintenance of Catholic religion among its unhappy natives and to keep it from becoming a mere stepchild of the New Galicia, Sinaloa and Sonora coast, we must now add its necessity as an intermediate stop in order to reach the fortunate lands which have newly been learned of.

General view of the town of Balaguer, birthplace of Gaspar de Portolá.

A close description of this Peninsula is not to the purpose here: it will be enough to say that, being almost wholly uninhabited by Spaniards and the castes which we in America call *gente de razón* [rational folk, civilized people], it contains in its whole 300 leagues' length only about six thousand souls of its natives, who require to be provisioned from the mainland with both grain and clothing. There is some livestock, run wild, but very few horses and mules (also wild), since those that were needed for the Expedition to San Diego and Monte-Rey were all taken from here; so that at present it may be said to be nearly destitute of this necessary sort of stock, and thus though the discovery of those Harbors was made with men from California, with the soldiers of its garrison and beasts from its missions, so far is it from being able to repeat these efforts, it needs rather to have everything replaced which it has given, if it is to be able to subsist. So that this Peninsula must not be counted upon for fostering the new discoveries, but must be regarded merely as a necessary stage upon the way, one where everything required for this purpose may be replaced and sent onward to its destination, until the new countries, which are supposedly fertile, have had time to come to bearing and can send their products to the northernmost part of this Peninsula.

We have been amazed to read in our discoverers' letters that knives and other iron tools, blue wool cloth and other articles that could only have been got from Spaniards are to be seen among the inhabitants of the new countries; and since the Harbor of San Francisco is almost in the same latitude as New Mexico, one supposes they must have got them from there. But it is noteworthy that according to the maps the distance east and west between the city of Santa Fe and the new harbor is 400 to 500 leagues, a very great way for our little trade to have reached, much less the coastal Indians, who are said to report that they have seen people dressed in our fashion. We would sooner believe there to be some notable error in the maps, in view of the fact that they can only have been drawn up according to ancient, surreptitious, or mistaken accounts, there being no record of anyone's having travelled that way to measure the distance, nor of observations for longitude having been made at either place. If this is the case, it might not appear difficult to connect our possessions in this direction, ending them along a parallel of latitude; with which thought we ourselves shall also end a letter which must greatly have tried Your Excellency's patience. We pray that God may keep and bless your life during the many years

we hold needful.    Santa Ana Camp in the South of Californias, June
30th, 1770.

Most Excellent Sir,<br>
Kissing Your Excellency's Hand,<br>
Your most obedient, obliged and assured servants,<br>
Mathias de Armona        Joaquin Velasquez de Leon

To His Most Excellent Lordship Marquess de Croix.[16]


 There is very little that I have to remark upon that is not
covered by a careful reading of this letter sent to Viceroy Croix
by the governing officials left in the Lower California peninsula
by Gálvez in Portolá's place.   The writers are clear in their
views as to the necessity of holding the newly discovered harbors at all costs, as well as protecting the peninsula under their
rule from further drains of the sort caused by the manoeuv-
res for the expedition, first when soldiers were drawn from
Loreto Presidio, then when religious vessels and vestments were
taken from its missions, followed by horses, cattle, and the all-
necessary mules on which all economic activities depended.
The backwardness of Lower California could only be made worse
by such constant plundering—as we might as well call it—and
above all by the danger that the future supplying of the new
territories would be done at the cost of the peninsula alone,
without the losses being made good, as had already happened in
this case.   Matías de Armona and Joaquín Velázquez de León
were shortly relieved of their Lower California commands, and
pass out of our story, leaving Portolá's new settlement of Monterey and Junípero Serra at is mission there under the authority of
a new governor, and with Lieutenant Fages exercising the military
control on the scene.


 16.   Madrid, Museo Naval, Ms., California y Costa Noroeste de América, t. I,
fol. 137 ff. (also Bancroft Library, Transcript Z-E 2, Pt. II, Box 2:25).

# CHAPTER IV

Gaspar de Portolá returns to Spain, in-
gressing in the Dragones de Numancia Regiment. - Designation of Portolá as Governor of the City of la Puebla de los Angeles
in New Spain. - Promotion to Colonel and
return to Spain for the second time. - Designation as Lieutenant of the King of the
Place and Castles of the City of Lérida. -
Presence in Lérida of Colonel Portolá. -
Death of Gaspar de Portolá in the City of
Lérida and his burial in San Pedro's
Church. - Portolá's last will and donation
of all his possessions to the City of Lérida
to be used for works of charity. - Foundation of the Orphan and Poor House.

Sir:

Don Gaspar de Portolá, Captain in the Dragoons of Spain Regiment, brevetted Lieutenant Colonel, represents to Your Majesty with deepest respect: That he has served with the above-mentioned regiment in the realm of New Spain for the past seven years, for which duty he did not volunteer; and having had, at the time of his leaving Spain, a law-suit pending over property, he was forced to entrust the business to one of his relatives. He has since heard that not only the person so entrusted, but most of the rest of his family have died, and finds himself required to go in person to settle their affairs.

Humbly supplicates Your Majesty to be pleased to grant him two years' leave to proceed to Spain and settle the above-mentioned law-suit: And his pay being insufficient to meet the expense of ship passage, he likewise supplicates Your Majesty to be pleased to order it adjusted to Regulations: Which favor he hopes of Your Majesty's great bounty.

Mexico, May 26th, 1771.

GASPAR DE PORTOLÁ [1]

---

1. Mexico, Archivo General de la Nación, Correspondencia de los Virreyes (Croix), Libro 14 y 4.º, Via Reservada, 1770-1771, n.º 1093, fols. 473-471.

This short document may serve to introduce Lieutenant-Colonel Portolá's return to his native Spanish soil, after having been absent from it since 1762. The approval of this petition sees him not only given a long leave of absence to return home and settle a family law-suit, but also confirmed in his new rank, the "adjusting of pay to Regulations" being the way in which an advance from brevet to full grade was achieved. The Viceroy's recommendation, in the matter had been sent to Madrid by September, 1771, so that the final permission and promotion cannot have been in Portolá's hands before the middle of 1772 at the earliest, and the arrangements for finding someone to take his place in his regiment, and for arranging ship passage, must have taken a much longer time.

On September 30, 1774, His Majesty grants "to Lieutenant Colonel Gaspar de Portolá" a post attached to the military staff of the garrison of the city of Barcelona not far from his native province, with pay amounting to 540 *reales de vellón;* on November 1, 1774, the appointment is entered in the accounting office of the Army of the Principality at Barcelona.[2]

Four to six months later, we meet him again mentioned, in a document drawn up in his own Balaguer before the notary Francisco Sociats, by Doña María Francisca de Portolá y de Valls y de Rubalcava, widow of Don Antonio de Portolá y de Rubalcava, resident of Balaguer, in which she acknowledges that as the result of a loan made by her uncle, Don Gaspar de Portolá, "Lieutenant Colonel attached to the Military Staff of the City of Barcelona," she is indebted to him for the sum of 3,600 *libras barcelonesas,* and that not having this amount on hand, she sells to him upon a contract of redemption six parcels of land lying in the City of Balaguer and the bounds of Vilanova, for the said price of 3,600 pounds. The document refers to her uncle Don Gaspar as present in the City of Balaguer at the time the writing is enacted, April the twenty-second in the year of the Lord one thousand seven hundred and seventy five.[3]

That Don Gaspar remained most of the time at Barcelona we can suppose from the fact that he evidently turned the years which he spent attached to the staff there to good account in furthering the career which had gained so much from

---

2. Bancroft Library, University of California, U.S.A.
3. Archivo Notarial de Balaguer, Sociats, vol. 171, fol. 37.

the prestige of winning California.    Whether or not he petitioned
for advancement by the King to a colonel's pay is doubtful;
we have no record of such a request being granted.    What he
did receive was an appointment as governor of the city of Puebla de los Ángeles in central Mexico.    This position he must
already have sought and either obtained or have been sure of
obtaining by the 15th of April, 1776, on which date he assigned
powers of attorney before notary-public Sociats at Balaguer.

Be it known unto all who shall see this letter of power that
I Don Gaspar de Portolá y de Rovira, Lieutenant-Colonel attached to
the staff of the Barcelona garrison, being at present in the city of
Balaguer, do of my good will and disposing knowledge grant and
acknowledge that I give my complete and sufficient power as in law
ought and must most fully prevail, to Josep Balcells y Vidal, a familiar of the Holy Tribunal of the Inquisition, and to Doctor Antonio
Balcells y Pocurull, father and son, being residents of said City of
Balaguer...[4]

The same document grants the attorneys named the power to
substitute other representatives for the grantor in place of themselves, a privilege which as we shall see they availed themselves
of in 1782.    The broadness of this power of attorney leads me
to suppose that Portolá must have been reasonably certain, by
this time, of departing far from Balaguer and his home.

Certainly, on June 9, 1776, His Majesty King Charles IV was
to name Lieutenant-Colonel don Gaspar de Portolá governor of
Puebla de los Ángeles in a document which I shall reproduce
here, now in the Archivo General de Simancas.

DON GASPAR DE PORTOLÁ, *a copy.—Title of Governor, Puebla de los
Angeles.—G.G. June 9 '76.—D.T.L. 185 F 210 No. 24.*

DON CARLOS *IV*.    Forasmuch as, in consideration of the deserts
and services of you, Lieutenant-Colonel of Dragoons Don Gaspar de
Portolá, and in special view of your actions in the Governing of the Californias and the first Expeditions within that Peninsula as far as the
Harbor of Monterrey, I have seen fit by my Royal Decree of May
twenty-third last past to confer upon you (as by this my Royal Title I
do so confer) the Government of Puebla de los Ángeles in the provinces of New Spain:

---

4. Ibid., vol. 172, fols. 49-50.

THEREFORE,

I command the Grand Chancellor and those of my realm of the Indies to take and to receive from you the above-named Don Gaspar de Portolá the accustomed Oath, with the ceremony enjoined for such occasions, that you will well and faithfully serve the aforesaid Governorship of Puebla de los Ángeles; and they having done so, it is my will that both they and my Viceroy, Chairman and Members of my Royal Audiencia of the City of Mexico shall have and hold you for Governor Political and Military over the aforesaid city of Puebla de los Ángeles, giving to you the same Offices and instructions as to your predecessor Don José Merino Ceballos, to the end that with what is bestowed on you by the present Title, signed by my own hand and countersigned below by my Secretary, you may at once enter into the position and shall be enabled to serve in and perform it for the period of five years more or less as my will shall be, complying therewith in everything, just as your above-named predecessor was required to do and as is commanded or I shall command you to do by the Orders which you are given or may be given you by the Secretariat of Office of my Realms of the Indies, observing the Laws in all matters respecting Civil Government and Justice, and with respect to the Courts in all other matters obeying them in everything without exception, unless you have my Orders to the contrary. And I command my Viceroy aforementioned, and the Courts of those Provinces, and all other of their Ministers, Judges, and Justices, to keep and to cause to be kept toward you as Governor Political and Military of Puebla de los Ángeles all such respects, honors, favors, freedoms and liberties, exemptions, precedences, immunities and prerogatives as are due to you, without any restriction. And I command the Council, Tribunal and Administration of the aforesaid City of Puebla de los Ángeles that at once upon intimation of this my Royal Title they and all other persons being or dwelling in the same City shall have and hold you as Governor Political and Military during the period of my pleasure, and shall maintain you in that position, the same being done by the Captains and other Officers and Military Men who may be in the same City of Puebla, obeying the orders which you shall give them by word or by writing in my royal service. And I likewise command the Officials of my Royal Exchequer of the City of Mexico that from that day forward when they are advised by public record of your having taken possession of that Government they are to give and to pay you during the time that you shall serve therein the salary of four thousand pesos a year, the same amount enjoyed by your above-named predecessor Don José Merino y Ceballos, by virtue of the present Title and of your letters of pay; and that they are to receive them and enter an account of what they thus render you, but with the further condition that in accord with the provisions of my Royal Writ of May twenty-sixth, seventeen hundred seventy-four, you are to enter the Royal Treasury office under your charge and there

DON CARLOS, POR LA GRACIA DE DIOS, REY DE CASTILLA, 150.
de Leon, de Aragon, de las dos Sicilias, de Jerusalén, de Navarra, de Granada, de
Toledo, de Valencia, de Galicia, de Mallorca, de Sevilla, de Cerdeña, de Cordoba, de
Corcega, de Murcia, de Jaén, de los Algarves, de Algecira, de Gibraltar, de las Islas de
Canaria, de las Indias Orientales, y Occidentales, Islas, y Tierra firme del Mar Occeano,
Archiduque de Austria, Duque de Borgoña, de Brabante, y Milán, Conde de Abspurg, de
Flandes, Tiról, y Barcelona, Señor de Vizcaya, y de Molina, &c. Por quanto aten-
diendo al merito y servicios de vos Dn Gaspar de Por-
tola, Coronel agregado al Regimiento de Dragones de
Numancia; hè venido en conferiros el Empleo
de Teniente de Rey de la Plaza de Lerida, vacante
por muerte del Conde de Lannoy. — — — — — —

Por tanto mando al Capitan General, ò Comandante General del Principado de Cataluña — — — dé la orden conveniente para que se os ponga en possesión del expressado
Empleo de Teniente de Rey; y à los Oficiales, y Soldados del Estado Mayor de aquella Plaza, y su
Guarnicion, que os reconozcan por tal, y obedezcan las ordenes, que les diereis de mi servicio,
por escrito, y de palabra, sin escusa, ni dilacion alguna; y tambien mando al referido Capitan General, Oficiales del Estado Mayor, y Guarnicion, y à los demás à quienes tocáre, os guarden, y
hagan guardar las honras, gracias, y preeminencias, que os tocan, y deben ser guardadas, sin que
os falte cosa alguna, que assi es mi voluntad, y que el Intendente de Cataluña — — — —
prevenga lo conveniente para que se tome razon de este Despacho en la Contaduria principal,
donde se os formará asiento, con el sueldo de Ciento sesenta y cinco — escudos de
vellon al mes, que es el que está señalado à este Empleo, y el goce de él, desde el dia que prece-
diendo estos requisitos, tomáreis possesion de él, segun constáre de la primera Revista. Para todo lo qual mandé despachar el presente Titulo, firmado de mi Real mano, sellado con el Sello
secreto, y refrendado del infrascripto mi Secretario de Estado, y del Despacho de la Guerra, de
que se ha de tomar tambien razon en la Contaduria General de la Distribucion de mi Real Hacienda, dentro de dos meses, contados desde el dia de su fecha; con advertencia, de que no exe-
cutandose assi, quedará nulo. Dado en el Pardo — — — à siete — — de
Febrero — — — — de mil setecientos y ochenta y seis.

Yo El Rey.

Geron Valdecarzana

confiere el Empleo de teniente de Rey de la Plaza de
rida al Coronel Dn Gaspar de Portola.
Pastor

Reproduction of the Commission of Portolá as King's Lieutenant of the city of Lérida. (Arch. Hist. Nacional. Madrid).

in the presence of the Commissioner and accountant of the Half-Annate pay what is due from you for this tax, in addition to the amount corresponding to the third part of emoluments and the eighteen per cent for transmitting the whole sum to this country, as provided in the regulation of rates of the said tax and in the provisions of later dispatches addressed to this purpose. And an entry shall be made of this Title in the General Auditorship of Revenues—Outgo— of my Royal Exchequer belonging to my Indies Council within two months from the date of giving, without which entry this bestowal shall be null and void, and an account shall also be taken by the aforementioned royal officials of Mexico, who shall do the same with the instruction which is conveyed to them along with it.

Given at Aranjuez June ninth one thousand seven hundred seventy six.

I THE KING.

I Don Pedro Mayoral, Secretary of Our Lord King have caused this to be written by his command.—Don Phelipe del Arco.—Don Domingo de Trespalacios y Escandon.—Don Phelipe Santos Domínguez.[5]

With this appointment, Gaspar de Portolá received a resounding recognition for his services from the king, and, with the title of Governor and four thousand pesos of yearly salary, was on the way back to the New World. He must have taken possession of his new office immediately on reaching its shores.

The term of "five years more or less ... during the period of my pleasure" which the King had promised him in the governorship was fulfilled and extended of another five. At last, it must have been in response to this news that Portolá's Balaguer attorneys, on July 4th, 1782, record that Don José Balcells y Vidal, familiar of the Holy Office, merchant and resident of Balaguer, by virtue of the powers possessed by him since the 15th of April, 1776, "legitimately ordered and constituted as such by Don Gaspar de Portolá y de Rovira, formerly Lieutenant-Colonel attached to the Staff of the Barcelona Garrison and at present Colonel and Governor of Puebla de los Ángeles in the Realms of New Spain," in turn names as attorney for himself in the matter, and thus for Gaspar de Portolá, one Don Juan Bautista Mirada y Barri, advocate of the City of Balaguer.

---

5. Archivo General de Simancas, *Títulos de Indias*, Inv. 24, Legajo 185.

Portolá's promotion to colonel was dispatched to him on November 5th, 1777, as the result of a royal commission signed at
San Ildefonso palace in the same year.

In consideration of your deserts and services, which the Viceroy of New Spain has seen fit to commend in a communication
of March 27th of this year, the King has been pleased to condescend
to your petition dated the 28th of that month, and has granted you
the rank of Colonel of Dragoons in the Army, which commission is
being remitted to the Viceroy, who will address it into your hands;
all of which I am conveying to you upon his Majesty's orders, for
your own satisfaction and in order that you may possess this further
indication of his royal benevolence.[6]

By this document it appears that our Don Gaspar was, in the
year 1777, firmly installed as a Colonel and as Governor of the
City of Puebla de los Angeles, now known simply as Puebla, in
the position he was to fill for nearly ten years, from beginning to
end.  I have found little pubished on this period of Portolá's life,
and have so far sought in vain to complete this part of his history.
Attempts to contact the Puebla city government by letter and
through an esteemed Pueblan friend have yielded no result: but
perhaps possibly in years to come I may become acquainted with
the archive of that city, which must surely preserve fascinating
information about the years of Spanish rule in Mexico.

Here, then, I will end this period in the life of the Conquistador of California, not before pointing out the two main phases
of his New World career: the first one beginning upon his
arrival as Captain of Dragoons in the Regimiento de España and
including his participation in the expedition to Sinaloa and Sonora, his appointment as governor of the Lower California peninsula
and his command of the expedition to Monterey; the second
phase beginning after his return to Spain with the rank of Lieutenant-Colonel, when he proceeded to Pueblo de los Ángeles with
the title of Governor and there gained the rank of Colonel, offices which he filled until he appears once more in Spain, having
remained away from his homeland, with no more known journeys back and forth, until the year 1785.

A royal decree of August 20, 1785, grants to Don Gaspar de
Portolá a post as colonel attached to the Numancia Regiment,

---

6. Bancroft Library, University of California, Ms. M-M 1811.

and a corresponding entry is made in the regimental records at Barcelona on September 7 the same year, thus showing that Portolá's return to Spain was accomplished via a transfer of regimental duties, and not by a retirement directly to Lérida.[7] Historians who have studied the figure of Gaspar de Portolá, and first among them Father Sanahuja, have recognized 1786 as the date when Don Gaspar reappeared in Spain, since there is a soldier with the same given and family names who is found acting as Royal Deputy of Lérida City and Castles between May and October of that year, and it seemed unlikely to them that anyone other than *our* Don Gaspar de Portolá of Balaguer could have been meant. With further documentation from this period at hand, I will first quote his commission of appointment to the position, published here for the first time, from the Archivo Histórico Nacional at Madrid, and will then add some conclusions drawn from it.

Don Carlos, by the grace of God, King of Castile, Leon, Aragon, the two Sicilies, Jerusalem, Navarre, Granada, Toledo, Valencia, Galicia, Majorca, Seville, Sardinia, Cordoba, Corsica, Murcia, Jaén, the Algarves, Algeciras, Gibraltar, the Canary Islands, the East and West Indies, Isles and Mainland of the Ocean Sea, Archduke of Austria, Duque of Burgundy, Brabant and Milan, Count of Hapsburg, Flanders, Tyrol and Barcelona, Lord of Biscay and Molina, etc.

Forasmuch as, in consideration of the deserts and services of you Don Gaspar de Portolá, Colonel attached to the Numancia Reiment of Dragoons, I have seen fit to confer upon you the office of Royal Deputy of the City of Lérida, which has been left vacant by the death of the Count of Lannoy, ...therefore I command the Captain-General or Commandant General of the Principality of Catalonia ... to issue the corresponding order for you to be placed in possession of the aforesaid office of Royal Deputy and I command the Officers and Soldiers of the Military Staff of that City and its Garrison to acknowledge you as such and to obey the orders which you shall give them in my service by word or by writing, without excuse or delay. And I likewise command the aforesaid Captain-General, officers of the military staff, and garrison, and all others whom it shall concern, to keep and to cause to be kept toward you all such respects, honors, favors and precedences as are due you and are to be held without any diminution, for such is my will. And I command that the In-

---

7. Ibid.

tendant of Catalonia ... make proper disposition for this Commission
to be entered in the central accounting office, where an account is to
be established for you, with the salary of one hundred sixty five...
*escudos de vellón* per month, the amount assigned to this office, and
the enjoyment thereof, commencing on the day when, these prere-
quisites having been completed, you shall take possession thereof, as
shall appear by the next official Review.   To all of which ends I have
commanded the present title to be issued, signed by my royal hand,
sealed with the secret seal and countersigned below by my Secretary
of State and of the War Office, by whom it is also to be entered
at the General Accounting Office—Outgo of my Royal Exchequer,
within two months from the date of issuing, and if not so entered,
to remain null and void.

Given at El Pardo... the seventh... of February... one thousand
seven hundred eighty six.

I the King

His Majesty confers the Office of Royal Deputy of the City of
Lérida upon Colonel Don Gaspar de Portolá.

Entered at the General Accounting Office of Outgo of the
Royal Exchequer, Madrid, February 9th, seventeen hundred eighty
six.   Antonio Bultillo y Pamble.—Barcelona, March 20, 1786.   Let the
command of the King be fulfilled.   The Count of Asalto.

Barcelona, March 20, 1786.   Let it be recorded in the Army Accounting Office of this Principality.   Baron de la Linde.

So entered.   Bernabé González.[8]

Here then is the original document which removes the un-
knowns over which previous historians, lacking the good luck
to have found it, have had to stumble.   We see here that Don
Gaspar de Portolá was, at the moment of his new appointment,
a colonel attached to the Numancia dragoon regiment, in which
he had long before been an ensign and lieutenant, in the years
from 1734 to 1743.   Therefore it seems that he must have come
directly from his governorship of Puebla in Mexico to the staff
position in Barcelona, and there waited until the death of his
predecessor in the deputyship of Lérida, Count of Lannoy.

I have also come across a notarial document issued at the
city of Balaguer on May 1, 1786, showing Don Gaspar already
serving in his new position at that date, three months earlier

8.   Madrid, Archivo Histórico Nacional, *Carlos III*, Exped. 1546.

than the first document found by Father Sanahuja in the Lérida
city archives. The record of which I am speaking commences:
"Be it known by this public writing, that I Don Gaspar de Portolá, Royal Deputy of the City and Castles of Lerida, being at
present in the City of Balaguer...," and goes on to the purpose
of the document, which is to grant a letter of payment to his
attorney, Don José Balcells y Vidal, "familiar of the Holy Tribunal of the Inquisition, resident of said City of Balaguer, here
present, the amount of one thousand seven hundred seventy
nine pounds, sixteen sueldos, eleven dineros in Barcelona money, being the amount collected and paid up to the present day
by said José Balcells, as my empowered attorney, from several
persons for the lease of lands owned by me." It ends, "Done
in the said city of Balaguer upon the first of the month of May,
in the Year of the Lord seventeen hundred eighty six", and is
signed by Don Gaspar de Portolá in person.[9]

But the honored soldier's health cannot have been very
good at this time, for the next reference we have to him is his
own will, drawn up before the notary Ignacio Madriguera in
the City of Lérida on the 29th of May, 1786. Despite a good
deal of searching, it has been impossible to locate this document
in the Lérida notarial registrar's archive, which is and has been
for some years in total disorder because of the repairs being
made on the edifice called El Roser where it is housed; and I
doubt that it will ever turn up there, since the registries of this
notary were almost entirely destroyed during the Spanish Civil
War. Nor have we been able to find the will among the records
of the episcopal archive of the Diocese of Lérida, for the simple
reason that this archive, though perfectly well maintained, has
never been put into proper order and looks today just as it did in
1945, piled up on shelves in the Bishop's Palace. The Catedral
Archive has also been searched, with the same negative results.
Perhaps some day we will be able to revisit the above mentioned
archives, and just possibly turn up the will itself.

What we do know is that Don Gaspar's will, drawn up May
29th at Lérida, is referred to in the book by Agustín Prim y Tarragó, in the record of the City Council, and in the Balaguer registrar's Notarial Archive.[10] We shall return to these sources later.

---

9. Archivo Notarial de Balaguer, Sociats (1786), fol. 102.
10. Prim y Tarragó, *Cosas viejas de Lérida.*

The duties of the Royal Deputy of Lérida included presiding in person over the municipal council sessions whenever the city's Political and Military Governor was absent. The Governor of Lérida at that time was Don Luis Blondel y Drouhot, Field Marshall. The municipal council record books show him presiding at all of the sessions until August 8, 1786, when he ceases to do so. In this circumstance, the Royal Deputy should have taken over the chair, but does not, by reason of sickness. Therefore, says the record under date of August 21, 1786, due to "the absence of the Governor and illness of the Royal Deputy," the sessions are being presided over by the mayor of the city, Don Antonio Mesía. Matters continue on this basis, with the record repeating that the Govenor is absent and the Royal Deputy ill, until October 11, 1786, when the latter's death is recorded.

Nonetheless, though his illness kept him from attending the council sessions, he was not prevented from discharging other duties of his position, as is shown by a reply of August 31, 1786, from the Royal Deputy to a request by the council for the punishment of a Leridan who had cut down trees in the Royal Plantation:

I have received your communication of the 26th of the present month ending, concerning the information of the cutting down of trees laid against Francisco Amorós, a landowner of Rufea district in this city's limits, and the usurpation of lands expressed therein; which I have duly weighed together with the affidavits enclosed by the knight mayor, to resolve upon what measures are to be taken in punishment.

May God keep you many years.

Lérida, August 31, 1786.

GASPAR DE PORTOLÁ.

To the Municipal Council of Lérida City.[11]

There follow other letters dated September 5th, September 16th, September 17th and 18th, the last of which I shall give in full, since it seems, at least as far as is known, to be the last document bearing the signature of Gaspar de Portolá, and probably the last which left his hands:

I send you herewith the attached copy containing the Royal Writ of February 3rd, of the year last past, in order that the Charity Coun-

---

11.  Archivo Municipal, Lérida, Reg. 508, *Actas del Ayuntamiento* (1786), f. 290

cil therein provided for may be set up, in accordance with the command. And in order that in the future the Writs which are sent to me, or other imprints, shall not be lost, I shall send them to your Honorable Body to be assembled and observed in your office.

God keep you many years.

Lérida, September 18th, 1786.

GASPAR DE PORTOLÁ.

To the Honorable Municipal Council of Lérida City.[12]

Father Sanahuja's efforts to show that the Royal Deputy of Lérida was Don Gaspar de Portolá, and that it was in that capacity that he signed these records, are unnecessary for us, since we have been able to provide the original document, unknown to Sanahuja, which bestowed that position on him.

At the end of the long sickness which as we have seen kept him prostrated though not incapable of keeping up the duties of his office, we have no news of him or references that have been found anywhere, up until the 10th of October, 1786, on which date the death of Don Gaspar de Portolá in his residence at Lerida is announced.

The city council, informed of the news, immediately proceeded to communicate it to Baron de Linde and Marshal Blondel, who was still at Barcelona city. The Baron de Linde's answer to the city council, dated October 11th, is in the following terms:

By your letter of the 11th of the current month, I am informed that the Deputy of your City, Don Gaspar de Portolá, died at five o'clock in the afternoon of the 10th.

Good keep you many years, as... [sic].

From Barcelona, October 14th, 1786.

THE BARON DE LINDE.

To the Municipal Council of Lérida City.[13]

Governor Blondel, a little less curt in his reply to the council's news, speaks of Portolá's decease in a letter which also deals with other affairs:

Gentlemen: I have received the advice which you have been pleased to give me on the 11th instant of the Royal Deputy's having

---

12.  Ibid., fol. 297.
13.  Ibid., fol. 314.

died. I have been sorry for his loss because of the fine qualities
which distinguished him, and have been grateful for the way in which
you bore yourselves toward that gentleman...[14]

The letter is signed at Barcelona on October 14th, 1786, by
General Luis Blondel personally.

The minutes of the city council of Lérida contain, following
the entry for October 11, a document which I will copy in full,
relating to the funeral and military honors granted to the Royal
Deputy Don Gaspar de Portolá.

Lérida, October eleventh, seventeen hundred eighty six.

I CERTIFY that the Honorable Municipal Council of this city,
having assembled at a half before ten o'clock in the morning of this
day at the house inhabited by Don Gaspar de Portolá, late Royal
Deputy of Lerida, there being present the aldermen Don Juan de
Tapies, senior member and as such (the Mayor Don Antonio Mesía
being busied elsewhere) chairman, Don Vicente Gallart, Don Jaime
Gomar, Don Anastasio de Ager, Don Tomas Segura; and Don Francisco Casanovas, Juan Mensa, Antonio Serret, and Francisco Ribé,
delegates; Dr. Pelegrín Turull, syndic-general; Dr. Carlos Soldevila,
representative; and I, the undersigned secretary of the council, assis-
ted also by Ignacio Soldevila, auditor of municipal properties, Policar-
po Bayona, city steward, and syndic-ordinary Dr. Pablo Pocurull, for
the purpose of accompanying the corpse of the said Royal Deputy
and attending his last funeral honors, proceeded to and in fact did,
as a body and in due form, accompany the corpse from the said
house to the Church of St. Francis of Assisi, the regular parish for
the military officers, with six of the officers who were present
in the city surrounding the body and carrying the belt, then, immediately after them, the Major of the garrison Don Juan Chartrón,
with Captain of the Keys Don Juan Martus and Don Mariano Temple,
Ensign of the Catalonia Regiment, at his side; following them, the
city, led by the funeral guests and mace-bearers dressed in mourning,
and then, immediately behind the chairman, the Adjutant of the
garrison, Don Antonio Ferrari, bearing sword in hand, and a small
detachment of the Walloon Guards garrisoned in this city, marching
with muffled drums. In this fashion the procession proceeded to the
said church, where, the Council and guests having taking their proper
seats, the funeral Mass was begun; and immediately it was noted that
the said Major and other officers went out of the church, and shortly
afterward a volley of shots was heard, as is the practice in such
funerals. This having been carried out, I was called forward

---

14.  Ibid., fol. 317v.

by the Senior Alderman, as chairman, and at his orders went out of the church into the aforesaid little square outside where the troops are to remain until the military honors are concluded, in order to see whether they were there, and having examined it carefully, I found no officer or soldier remaining in it, being still at the beginning of the Mass.

And for such purpose as it may serve, I have drawn up this statement.

ANTONIO SANMARTÍ.[15]

It seems certain that the body of Don Gaspar was buried in the Church of St. Francis of Assisi, which is known today as the parish church of San Pedro. My reasons for believing so include the fact that this church, "the regular parish for the military officers," provided the burial ground for years for those who died at Lérida. Actually, despite the title given to it in this document, it was not really a parish until even later, very late in the eighteenth century. At the time of the burial, it belonged to the Franciscan Order, and was much favored and frequented by highly placed persons from the local upper classes. The regular cemetery was located where the Plaza de San Francisco and the building of the Delegación de Hacienda now are, as was shown during their construction when a great many burials were found, which had to be exhumed and transferred to the City Cemetery. Important personages, however, were buried inside the Church, as was the case of Don Gaspar de Portolá, who combined the qualifications of a military nobleman and benefactor of the city.

We are told in a work published by don Eduardo Rodeja, a historian of Figueras and connected with the last of the Portolás bearing that name, don Buenaventura Portolá y Rodeja, known to us as the possessor of the Portolá family papers up until the time of their loss, that he had often heard from his uncle and seen in the family archive that his ancestor Don Gaspar was buried in the Church of St. Francis.[16]

There must have been little to relate about the life which Don Gaspar spent during the last six months which remained to him, between his return to Lérida and his death, especially since

15. Ibid., fol. 56r-v.
16. RODEJA, E., "Gaspar de Portolá en el descubrimiento y colonización de California", *Gerona*, VI, n.º 10 (1960).

he spent most of that time in his sickbed. This is why we have no information but that furnished by the purely official record. We know nothing of whether his relations with his family in Balaguer were renewed and kept up during this last period in Lérida, only that he re-deeded to his niece Doña María Francisca the property which he had received from her in satisfaction of a debt, when she had been unable to repay her uncle the 3,600 pounds he had lent her. And it does not appear that his executors received any payment for the return of this property.

Our knowledge of Don Gaspar's will comes not from the document itself, which as has been seen I have been unable to find, but from references to it such as those I have already mentioned. To these we can add the following which I find in the Balaguer registrar's archive, dated February 2, 1787. In this Doña María Francisca de Portolá, de Valls, y de Rubalcava, widow of Don Antonio de Portolá y de Rubalcava, acknowledges that on April 22, 1775, she had sold, upon contract of redemption, six parcels of land to "Don Gaspar de Portolá, then Lieutenant-Colonel attached to the Military Staff of Barcelona"; and that "by a will drawn up at Lérida on May 28th, 1786, before the Notary Don Ignacio Madriguera y Miret," she has received, according to the instructions left to his executors by her uncle, Don Gaspar de Portolá, the six parcels which he had owned. The executors named by this will are the Bishop of Lérida, Don Gregorio de Torres; Field Marshall and Governor of Lérida Don Luis Blondel de Drouhot; and Deputy Staff Advocate Dr. Don Francisco Pinós.[17]

Another clause in the same will, we know, referred to his brother José de Portolá y de Rovira (at whose confirmation he had once stood sponsor), leaving him a pension of 60 pounds until he should reach the rank of captain; at the date of the will, he was a first lieutenant in the Guadalajara Regiment of infantry.

The greater part of his fortune was left in the hands of the executors with full authority to dispose of it, though always in accordance with the deceased's express desire that it should be applied to works of charity, "as they shall see fit, by turning it to charitable purposes, or those befitting such public uses as they may choose." This legacy to charity has proved of such

---

17. Archivo Notarial de Balaguer, Sociats, vol. 184, fol. 7.

importance for the city of Lérida that we shall spend some time discussing it, using material given by Agustín Prim y Tarragó and by Father Sanahuja which we have also studied in the same archives where they found it.

Those entrusted with the executorship were the prominent citizens Dr. Pinós, General Blondel, and Gregorio de Torres, who were thus given a considerable sum of money and a broad field in which to apply it, for in those years the city and province of Lérida was short of funds to support even those charities already established. The so-called Pía Almoina had been passing through a serious economic crisis due to insufficient and badly invested income, with which it supported, besides a number of unauthorized projects and persons, the poor and certain institutions of welfare. The orphan asylum, Infans Orfens, was supposedly protected by the municipal council, by the Pía Almoina and by the contributions of the residents, but it led a precarious existence with room for a very limited number of orphans. The Hospital of Santa María, which before the arrival of the Daughters of Charity in 1792 lacked a staff capable of caring for the sick, harbored a good-sized group of abandoned children at the charge of Bishop Torres.

The full terms of Don Gaspar de Portolá's will were as follows:

I commit and give all necessary powers to the Most Honorable Lord Bishop of this City, to Don Luis Blondel y Drouthot, Governor of this Town, and to Don Francisco Pinós, Deputy Staff Advocate of the same, the three of them together or the greater part of them, or to each one individually in the absence or refusal of the others, to dispose of all of my goods as they shall see fit, by turning them to charitable purposes or those befitting such public use as they shall choose.[18]

The executors had not yet chosen a course of action when, in a letter from Prime Minister Floridablanca dated December 24, 1788, they were reminded, in the name of the Supreme Council of Castile, that some immediate action must be taken to decide what use was to be made of the estate of Don Gaspar de Portolá. The decision was reached at a formal meeting of the executors on January 21 st, 1789, after suggestions and discussions stretching throughout the previous month. It was agreed to

18. PRIM Y TARRAGÓ, *Cosas viejas de Lérida*, p. 31.

erect a Home for Abandoned Children, thus solving a problem
posed by the growing number of orphans and homeless, and at
the same time affording work for the large number of our local
laborers who were suffering extreme want and hunger, "there
being no work available at this season, and the price of bread
having risen to an unheard of level." The land known at the
time as Era del Moro was first chosen for the purpose, but it
was abandoned after encountering opposition on some high
levels.

At this juncture it came to the attention of the executors
that two other estates existed which had been willed for purposes
similar to that of Portolá. One of these had been left by the
farmer José Grau in the year 1767, who expressly willed that
his fortune should be given to a house of mercy, should one
be constructed within the period of twenty years from the making of his will; it was to be a house for the "gathering and training in good morals of orphans, invalids, the aged, profligates,
and other unemployed persons." Similarly, in the testament of
an earlier Royal Deputy of Lérida, Don Enrique de Wiels, drawn
up on November 18, 1779, was found the clause:

But forasmuch as I wish most of all to favor the charitable
work of erecting a House of Mercy to serve as a shelter, refuge and
guard for poor girls of this City, and to second the good intentions of
other devout persons favoring the same, I will that the buildings of my
dwelling, with adjacent property owned and possessed by me in this
city, in the parish of Santa María Magdalena, on the Plazuela del
Crusifixi, be employed for the establishment of said House of Mercy,
with the parcel of land which I possess in the *huerta* of this same
city, in the section called Guindavols, to be applied to the same
purpose.[19]

The executors found the location of the former Enrique de
Wiels property to be highly acceptable, since it turned out to
be contiguous to the lands of the estate of José Grau, mentioned above. At a meeting of all of the executors on August 3rd,
1790, it was agreed all three estates should be thrown together
in one project, the Grau and Wiels properties upon the Plazuela
del Crusifixi should be filled out as needed by purchases with
part of the funds of the Portolá estate, and construction should

---

19. Ibid., pp. 34-40.

be begun upon a hospice for abandoned infants, orphans, invalids, poor girls, and so forth as provided in the three wills.

Available from the Wiels estate were:

one building with appurtenances on the Plazuela del Crusifixi or Crucifijo; one parcel of two and a half *jornales* of land in the Guindavol section.

The José Grau estate provided:

a building located on the Plazuela del Crucifijo, contiguous to the aforementioned Wiels house; a quit-rent in the amount of 1,333 pounds; other quit-rents for 2,733 pounds; a credit of one hundred pounds.

From the Portolá estate was to come the money "to complete the area which would be needed by" the future Hospice. It paid for the purchase of:

Four buildings belonging to Vicente Cau and José Sirach.

Two pieces of land belonging to Pedro and María Nicolau and to the Tanners' Guild, contiguous to the preceding.   (All of these purchases were carried out between 1787 and 1791).

One house with cellar in Calle San Antonio.

One house purchased by the executors and later sold to the Carmelite Order for a quit-rent of 2,000 pounds, returning 60 per year, the amount left by Don Gaspar de Portolá to his younger brother, so that as the trustees put it, "this pension cannot be touched at the moment, having been assigned to Don José de Portolá, First Lieutenant in the Guadalajara Infantry Regiment, until such time as he reaches the rank and pay of captain." [20]

And finally, the amount of capital left over after the above purchases of houses and lands, which was sufficient to permit the building of the Hospice of Mercy.

In addition, this Hospice having been built with the funds of this estate to the amount of *over three hundred thousand reales*, the building must belong to it, in joint ownership with the estates of Don Enrique de Viels [sic] and Joseph Grau in proportion of the

---

20. SANAHUJA, «Ilerda», n.º III, 1945, p. 106.

value of the building to that of the houses owned by these charitable testators.

The following expenses were also chargeable against the Portolá estate.

One passive quit-rent of 1,000 Barcelona pounds principal, paying 30 pounds annuity, payable to the Chapter of the Parish of La Magdalena.

Another quit-rent, 200 pounds principal, annuity of six pounds, to the same Chapter.

Another property of 315 pounds, annuity 9 pounds, 9 sueldos, to the Dominican Convent of Lérida.

Another property of 100 pounds, annuity 3 pounds, to the executors of Gerónimo Salon.

One pension of four sueldos to the Monastery of Poblet, for the court or piece of property which the Tanners' Guild sold to this estate;

but all of the income and returns of this estate are to be applied to the charitable purposes of the House of Mercy, to which is added the other intention concerning abandoned children. [Note: ] The preceding estates of Portolá, E. Viels and José Grau are adjudged with all of their goods to the purposes of the Hospice, by the approval of the Supreme Council of Castile as given in a Royal Provision of the 18th of December, 1794:

In all matters, the purposes of the said three estates, united into one by a writing drawn up by all the respective executors on February 9, 1791, before the notary-public Ignacio Madriguera, and found inserted in the Royal Provision above referred to, are to be observed by the trustees, as set forth in detail in the same writing.

Further, the annuities being paid to the Dominican Fathers, to the Mercedarians, and to the Chapter of Prebends of La Magdalena Parish in Lerida by this House of Mercy have been paid off from the funds in the treasury of this Holy Hospital deriving from the establishment of the endowment made by Dr. Francisco Pinos as executor of José Basea, as shown in the attached agreement.[21]

With the whole of Portolá's estate, along with the other two, converted and dedicated to one purpose by these arrangements,

---

21. Archivo Municipal, Lérida. *Fondos del Hospital.* Libro pergamino sin foliar.

work on the hospice was begun, persons being appointed to draw the plans, others to account for expenses, and still others to advertise the auction of disposable property, and so forth. In view of the great variety of needy cases who would be received in the institution, it was agreed that work should be commenced toward drawing up a suitable code of regulations to govern its inmates and interior relations.

Upon receiving the authorization of the Captain-General of Catalonia, Count Lacy, dated June 20, 1789, the work of construction began, and was already far advanced when, in 1792, the executors of the three estates came to an agreement with the administrators of the Hospital that, in view of the latter's lack of resources, the income of both institutions should be combined into that for a single House of Mercy-Hospital, under a board consisting of the Governor, the Bishop of the Diocese of Lérida, the Senior Alderman of the city, two prebends of the Cathedral, two magistrates, and two residents, one from the nobility and one from the lower class. In the meantime, those who would later be admitted to the building under construction were to be sheltered in the Hospital.

When the building was completed at the beginning of 1795, it was first occupied as a barracks and as a warehouse for the Royal Exchequer, so that not until 1819 were the inmates and the Nuns of Charity it was designed for allowed to enter it. Yet soon twice again, in the years 1822 and 1825, it was taken over by soldiers, its inmates forced to leave, until finally in 1826 the charities obtained permanent possession of the building. There they remained until transferred in mass to the present great building on Rambla de Aragón.

The original building, erected on the Plaza del Crucifijo by the estate of Don Gaspar de Portolá and the gifts of the lands and buildings of Wiels and Grau, is now the Palace of the Most Excellent Chamber of Deputies of the Province of Lérida.

Church of San Pedro in Lérida where Don Gaspar de Portolá was
buried on 11th of October, 1786.

# APPENDIX A

## Gaspar de Portolá's expedition journal[1]

1. Translated from a copy in Madrid, Biblioteca Nacional Ms. 19, 266, as printed by José Porrúa, *Noticias y Documentos acerca de las Californias 1764-1795* (Madrid, 1959), pp. 49-76, and in the original edition of the present book. Material added in brackets is translated from another early text (in the Bancroft Library) as printed by Donald Eugene Smith and Frederick J. Teggart, *Publications of the Academy of Pacific Coast History* I:3 (Berkeley, 1909), pp. 30-81.

*A Journal of the Voyage being made by land by Don Gaspar de Portolá Captain of Dragoons in the España Regiment, Governor of Californias, to the Harbors of San Diego and Monterrey* [2] [*situated in 33 and 37 Degrees Latitude, he having been named Commander in Chief of this Expedition by the Most Honorable Don Joseph de Gálvez by virtue of the viceregal faculties conferred by His Excellency. This Expedition consisted of 37 buffcoat soldiers with their Captain Don Fernando de Rivera, who was to proceed in advance with twenty-seven soldiers; and the Governor with ten soldiers and a sergeant.*]

May 11th. I set out from Santa María, the last mission to the north, escorted by four soldiers, in company with Father Junípero Cerra, the President of the Misisons, and Rev. Father Fray Miguel Campa. Went this day about four hours, with extremely little water for the animals and no grass, and so forced to march in the evening to get to some, though no water. [6 hours.]

12th. Travelled five hours by a good road. Stopped at the place they call the Sweetwater pool. No grass.

---

2. The Madrid version reads only «to the Harbors of San Diego and Monterrey in the Californias.»

13th.  Went about four leagues,[3] no water or grass.  This day I went ahead to Belicatá with the Reverend Fathers; we travelled about four hours.  Lay by on the following day in order to see Father Campa settled at Belicatá as minister of the new mission there and see to the removal of Santa María Mission as ordered by the Most Honorable Don José [de] Gálvez.  [9 hours.]

15th.  Set out from this mission with Rev. Father Junípero Cerra.  Went five hours by a good road.  A great deal of grass, no water.

16th.  Went about five hours, not a very good road; stopped at San Juan de Dios, a stream with a good deal of grass and water.  Here we stayed four days in order to arrange our march, having overtaken the Sergeant with another six men, making ten men in all.

21st.  Went [about] three hours and a half, always along the slope of a large range, with a stream with grass and water to our right.

22nd.  Went three hours, stopping at a pool in the same stream.

23rd.  Went about five hours, four of them all mountain and the remainder a level tableland; lay by here.

24th.  Went about four hours, half of the way along a stream with a great deal of sand and the remainder mountainous, very hard going.  No grass for the mounts nor water, but some for the people at a league and a half from the stopping place.

25th.  Went four hours, most of the way a long climb, and the remainder along a mountain slope.  Stopped at a stream with lush cottonwood and mesquite trees; a great deal of water and grass.  Lay by here.  Saw three heathens, and sent three[4] of our friendly Indians after them; they caught one; we treated him as well as we might, and understood from his sign language that his chief had sent him to spy us out, so that by gathering other villages they would lie in wait to kill the Father and his company.

---

3.  The Bancroft text has a copyist's correction: «four hours (I mean) leagues.»
4.  The printing of the Brancoft copy does not have the word «three» here.

27th.   Went about five hours, a good road, and stopped at the Cieneguilla, a name given by the Jesuit Father Linc; we took a different direction from his here.   Halted at a little stream where, though dry, it was easy to dig a water-hole.

28th.   Went four hours and a half.   Near camp saw heathens and sent out our friendly Indians, who brought back ten of them with their chief; treated them as well as we could, and took leave.   When ready to march, thirty-two heathens with their chiefs appeared, with a great deal of gesturing and shouting. Ordered the Sergeant to go out to them with the interpreter, find what they wanted, and tell them we were going ahead.   Managed to persuade them we were friendly, but they held their position saying they would fight us if we went ahead.   Tired of arguing to no point, I ordered the Sergeant and two soldiers to fire two shots into the air, not so as to endanger them, which was enough to send them away.   On this day's march came across a village group of twelve men with their chief, who offered to come with us as friends and show us the wateringplace.   Gave them such presents as we could, and they responded with mescalheads; also offered to accompany us on the next day, and did so.

29th.   Went about four hours through very high steep hills, stopping at a stream with a great deal of water and grass and a large grove of cottonwoods.   Spent a bad night, the animals repeatedly being stampeded all night long, and so lay by on the following day.   A fine place to found a mission at: it was named San Fernando, this being St. Ferdinand's day; a village group of heathens joined us here, as many as twenty-five or so.

31st.   Went four hours; three hours over hills and slopes, the rest along streams [a stream] with very little water and a great many trees, where a village group of twenty-five heathens joined us.   [4 hours.]

June 1st.   Went three hours and a half along a stream where there was a great deal of water, backwaters, rocks and a great deal of trees.

2nd.   Went three and a half hours over very steep hills; the Captain had opened a trail over one.   Stopped at a stream with a good deal of water and grass, and lay by here.

4th.   Went four hours, very steep grades the whole way, and stopped with no grass or water.

5th. Went [two] [5] hours and a half. Dug a water-hole here; almost no grass.

6th. Went six hours and a half. A great many mescal-plants along the way. Stopped at a very large pool of water. A fine spot for a summer-pasture for large herds of horses, even for the year round; a great deal of good soil for planting. Saw many traces of heathens, and a few showed themselves. Lay by for two days, and saw countless antelopes, hares, and rabbits.

9th. Went about three hours and a half, a good road; stopped at a stream with a great deal of [grass,] water and trees, and soil for planting.

10th. Went five hours and a half, the whole way very steep hills, stopping at a very large stream with a great deal of grass and some water for our mounts.

11th. Went [about] four hours and a half, a good level stoneless road all the way. Stopped at a large stream with grass but not much water; some cottonwoods are to be seen on it; plenty of good soil.

12th. Went about four hours and a half uphill and down; there was no water here for men nor animals.

13th. Went about three hours and a half, a rough road with precipitous grades uphill and down. Dug water-holes, but got enough only for the men.

14th. Went about three hours and a half; had good ground part of the way, and partway over slopes. Stopped at a broad stream with several springs at it; I regard this as the best of the places we have seen, well suited for a mission, easily cultivated and irrigated. It was named San Antonio. Lay by here for a day, in order to recover our animals from their two bad days before.

17th. Went a little over three hours, most of the way a good road. Plenty of water, except that it was hot; but allowed to cool for a short while we found it very good.

18th. Went four hours of extremely bad road; camped with no water and no means of getting any.

---

5. Madrid text «five»; «two» from Bancroft text which repeats the figure «2-½» in the margin.

19th. Went about three hours and a half, a fairly good road. Stopped with no water, and after scouting about could only get some by having to dig a water-hole. Middling good grass.

20th. Went six hours, stopping at two leagues' distance from the seashore, with water for neither men nor mounts. Half the way was uphill and down, the rest a bushy [6] plain.

21st. Went four hours of good road in sight of the sea, stopping at a stream with a great deal of water and grass. The Expedition lay by for a day here, during which time some heathens came by, and one of them made signs that other people had gone past ahead of us, signalling also that we would come in twelve days' march to where they had halted and were living in houses; all of which was a considerable comfort, as we took it to refer to the Captain being before us, and that the ships would be there as well. We noted that there were two islands here: it is a large bight with all the marks given by Cabrera for the Ensenada de Todos Santos.

23rd. Travelled four hours with a good road. Had a good deal of water and grass, by stopping opposite a very large heathen village. They immediately came over to the camp and made us a present of fish; we responded.

24th. Travelled about five hours; on setting out, we had to climb up a very long steep grade, and the rest of the way was a good road. One village came to meet us and go with us to the watering-place, around about twenty-five heathens; we stopped at a good-sized stream with a great deal of grass and water.

25th. Went five hours, a good road save for a very bad descent to the stream where we stopped, with a great deal of grass, water and trees, and a large inlet of fresh water.

26th. Went five hours, up a very high grade and the rest of the way a good one save for the way down onto the stream, which had a good deal of water, grass and trees. Here two villages of heathens visited us, around fifty of them there must have been.

27th. Went seven hours, almost always along the shore. Having come across seven villages during the march, we stopped

6. *Montuoso*. Here and elsewhere, Portolá seems to use the word *monte* and its relatives in the strictly Castilian sense of «woods, brush, bushes.»

at a stream with a great deal of grass, water and trees.  Upon the instant, two villages came to visit us.  It is remarkable that these heathens are so extremely mercenary that they solicited for the women whom they brought, in order to be given pieces of clothing; food they would have none of.  Lay by here for a day.

29th.  Went about three hours along the edge of the sea. Dug a water-hole here for the men; several heathens visited the camp.

30th.  Went about four hours along the edge of the sea, stopping at the point of the shoreline of San Diego Harbor.

July 1st.  Travelled five hours in view of the Harbor.  This day we reached the San Diego Camp, where we found Captain Don Fernando de Rivera [Ribera] with his men, and the *San Carlos* and the *Príncipe* packet at anchor in the harbor; the Volunteer Troop ashore, most of them sick abed; only one or two sailors left out of the sea crews, the *San Carlo's* men in particular having almost all died, for lack of whom they were helpless.  We remained here until the 14th of the month, both in order to unload the goods for the missions, and to see to other measures for putting our departure into effect.  Seeing some of our own men beginning to fall ill, I sought to leave as soon as possible.  Because of Don Pedro Prat's advising so much[7] that the best treatment was a change of climate, I took six Volunteers along with me, with their lieutenant Don Pedro Fages, and Engineer Don Miguel Costansó, both of whom were also ill.

[July 14th.]  Went three hours; a great deal of grass, but no water for people or mounts.

15th.  Went five hours, a good road; stopped at a stream with a good deal of grass and water.

16th.  Went fou hours, a good road.  On this day's march came across two villages of heathens, there must have been about forty of them.  Stopped at a hollow with a great deal of grass, but had to dig a water-hole.

17th.  Went three hours, a good road; came across a village with no one in it; stopped at a creek with a good deal of water and grass.

---

7.  The printing of the Bancroft text gives *tam.*, no doubt misread for *tanto*.

18th.   Went three hours, most of the way soft going stopped in a very pleasant valley with a vast amount of grass and water. Lay by here for a day;  over two hundred heathens came by.

20th.   Went three hours, the whole way over knolls and soft going. Stopped at a hollow with a great deal of grass and water; here were visited by a village of heathens with their women and children and gave presents to all of them [made all of the women and children a present of beads].[8]

21st.   Travelled two hours over low sloping knolls and stopped at a hollow with a great deal of grass and water, where three heathen men and five women visited us.

22nd.   Went three hours and a half, all soft soil with low sloping knolls.   Stopped at a stream with a great deal of grass where there was a pool of water; here was a village of about twenty heathens where Father Crespí and Father Gómez baptized two dying children.   [3 hours.]

23rd.   Went four hours;  a great deal of grass, water and trees.

24th.   Went about three hours and a half, stopping at a stream with a great deal of water, grass, and trees, where a heathen village of about fifty people was encountered; they made us a present of a great deal of seed, and were given presents in return.   Lay by for a day here.

26th.   Went three hours, a good road.   Not much grass for the mounts and no water for them, but the men had enough.

27th.   Went three hours, a good road.   A great deal of grass and water.

28th.   Went two hours, a good road, and stopped at a stream about eight yards wide and two hands deep, very swift-flowing. [At midday] here we had an extremely powerful earth-shock lasting about half as long as an Ave Maria when praying to the

8.  Here, as elsewhere, a slight difference of wording between the two printings occurs in the vicinity of other words lost in the Bancroft text through trimming.

Virgin.   After half a quarter-hour it came again though not as
strongly.   A great deal of grass and water here, with a very large
village of heathens, [about seventy of them,] seeming very
tractable.

29th.   Went three hours, a good road.   A great deal of grass
but water only for the people; here there was a heathen village
of about fifty people.

30th.   Went about[9] four hours, a good road save for two
very high steep grades: stopped in a very large valley with a
great deal of grass and water.   A bridge had to be built here
in order to cross the stream; I think this a good spot for a
mission.

31st.   Went four hours.   Close to camp came across a great
deal of water with a great deal of grass, so tall that our mounts
had to jump through it.   Lay by here; we have had six or seven
big earthquakes; on the south side of this same valley between
two woods[10] a spring of water like a sort of river has been discovered, so planly there is a great deal of soil around.

[August] 2nd.   Went three hours by a good road and stopped close by a river about fourteen paces wide.   Four or five
earthquakes were noted today.

3rd.   Went three hours, a good road, to the right of which
lie a great many swamps of pitch which they call *chapopote* [as-
phalt]; we have supposed[11] it may be this stuff flowing up
molten from underground that has caused so many earthquakes.
A great deal of grass and water here, and a plenty of antelopes
and deer.   A village of about thirty heathens met us and gave
and were given presents in return.

4th.   Went about[12] two hours and a half, a good road.   A
good deal of water and grass, by which dwelled a village of
thirty heathens; they presented us nuts and acorns, and were
given presents in return.

---

9.   «About» is missing from the Bancroft text printing.
10.   *Montes,* just possibly meaning «heights», not «woods.»   The site had both.
11.   Bancroft text «wondered whether» *(que si).*
12.   «About» not in the Bancroft printing.

5th. Went four hours through mountains, the range having blocked our way along the shore. Here there was a heathen village of about sixty people who made us a present of a great deal of seeds. Lay by here and were visited by over two hundred heathens bringing a great deal of seeds; they are very tractable and unselfish people, and were given presents in return.

7th. Went for three hours across a hollow stopping [13] at the foot of some hills, with a good deal of water and grass.

8th. Went six hours, through one of the highest and steepest of mountain ranges, and stopped at a stream with a great deal of water and grass, where we were met by some heathens begging us to come to their village close by; there we found eight village groups gathered with a great deal of seeds prepared for us, a number which must have included over three hundred heathens. Lay by here, where there is a village of about fifty heathens.

10th. Convinced at last of its being impossible to continue further northwestward, because of countless high steep mountain ranges with no way to be found through them, we determined to go down to the seacoast, which lies to the westward, and try to get around the obstacle presented by all these mountains running down to the shore. We have made three leagues along a stream with a good deal of grass and water.

11th. Went three hours along the same stream, on its way out to the sea. A great deal of grass and water; here around about five hundred heathens visited us, presenting a great deal of seeds.

12th. Went three hours through a hollow where there was a large stream of water and a great deal of grass and a village of forty people.

13th. Went three hours through the same hollow still looking for the sea, and stopped at a stream with a good deal of water and a great deal of grass. Met with a village of forty people here.

---

13. Madrid *que paró*, Bancroft *se para;* sense not in doubt.

14th.  Went three hours and at last came out upon the
Santa Barbara Channel, where we have found a town of thirty-
some houses and about three hundred heathens.  The moment
they saw us they sent three canoes out to fish, and presented us
with a great many fishes.  Though narrow, their canoes are eight
yards long, well made, built of boards.

15t.  Went two hours along the shore, stopping close to a
town of eight houses; no water or grass.

16th.  Went three hours, always along the edge of the sea,
and have stopped at a place with not much grass.  Here there is
a town which has thirty-some houses made of tule-rushes; there
are beyond three hundred [14] persons in the town.  We have been
visited by several heathens belonging to the islands we have opposite us here.  Here at this town there are seven well built
canoes eight yards in length, one in width, and the boards are
lashed with cords and well tarred, instead of beig nailed together.
They presented us with a great deal of fish.

17th.  Went two hours, a good road, stopping at the edge
of the sea.  There is a town here that had 38 houses and about
300 people in it, with seven of their very good-sized canoes.  A
great deal of grass and water.

August 18th.  Went five hours along the shore, stopping at
a town with forty-some houses in it, inhabited by more than
500 heathens.  They gave us a great deal of fish and got presents in return.  This town had ten canoes.  Beside all this, there
were in its neighborhood two ruined abandoned towns, destroyed
by wars between these people.

August 19th.  Went one hour.  Grass and water here.  Some
twenty-odd heathens came up and were made a present of beads.
[1-½ hours.]

August 20th.  Went four hours.  In the course of this march
we have come across seven towns, the smallest with twenty
houses, the largest with over eighty houses, having seen about
800 heathens.  A great deal of grass, water and trees here.  They
presented us with a great deal of food, and treated us to much
music and dancing.

--------

14.  Madrid «thirty» (wrongly); Bancroft «300.»

August 21st. Went three hours, always along the sea, and stopped opposite two towns of about sixty houses apiece populated by about 800 heathens. They visited the camp with their chiefs, presenting us with a great deal of fish. Grass and water here, with a vast amount of trees; and there are a very great many canoes at these two places. It seems plain that these towns are not getting along very well, peaceable though the people appear; which we suppose to be because they grudge our passing through these towns, so as not to have beads given to them.[15] The heathens here live in a more civilized way than others, as many of them even sleep on raised beds. All of these towns have their cemeteries, with the headmen's graves marked by a taller pole; for a woman, they put baskets or bowls on the pole, and for a man his long hair. All of these towns are commanded by three or four chiefs of whom one rules the others; these bosses all have two wives, the rest only have one. [Lay by here.]

August 23rd. Went four hours and a half, partly along the edge of the sea. Stopped at a town of 80 houses; the number of heathens we saw must have been about 400. A great deal of running water and grass. They presented us with a vast amount of fish; all along the Channel here, the first thing that they have been asking is to be allowed to dance, a permission we grant in return for keeping them happy.

August 24th. Went three hours and a half; the way, while fairly level, had a great many ravines caused by waters flowing down off the mountains. We have stopped at a town composed of fifty houses and inhabited by over 300 heathens; they presented us with a great deal of fish. We had a great deal of grass and water here.

25th. Marched three hours. Had to dig a trail by a very high hill, and all along the way in order to gent across the very deep dry streams we had. Stopped at a town where there were 25 houses, inhabited by 130 heathens. A great deal of water but not much grass. The town here had some canoes. The people we meet here become more tractable every day.

---

15. This syntax seems very obscure. It may mean that the two towns each grudged the beads given to the other one, or to other towns; or, less likely, that they were not getting along with the Spaniards because of too scanty presents.

August 26th. Went three hours along the edge of the sea. Pick and crowbar were kept at work during the whole march. Stopped at a town of fifty houses, inhabited by about 150 heathens, where there was a good deal of grass and water.

August 27th. Went three hours, a pretty good road save for some ravines which had to be worked upon. Stopped at a town of 30 houses inhabited by two hundred heathens; there was a [very] large stream with a great deal of grass and water. According to the marks given by Cabrera, this place was Point la Concepción, in 35-½ degrees latitude.

28th. Marched three hours, a good road save for some streams requiring to be worked on. Stopped at a town close to the sea, inhabited by 60 heathens, with a great deal of grass and water.

August 29th. Went about three hours and a half, part of the way good road, but the rest of it very large sand dunes. Stopped in a hollow somewhat out of our way in order to find water, but scarcely got enough for the people.

30th. Went an hour and a half, part of the way along the shore; this was a short day's march, in order to let the mounts recover from their having had to go thirsty. We were visited here by a village of about fifty people.

September 1st. Went about [16] four hours and a half, the whole time through brushwood with a great number of sand dunes; stopped at an extremely large pool of water next to which were two villages, amounting to about a hundred heathens.

[September] 2nd. Went five hours through very sandy woods, stopping at a very large pool, from whose immediate vicinity we were visited by two villages consisting of about sixty heathens. Lay by here.

4th. Went four hours, a good road the greater part of the way, the rest next to the shore, with larger [17] sand dunes; we were forced to circle around a great many lakes and inlets which have given us [a great deal of] trouble. A great deal of water and grass here, where we were visited by a village group having about forty heathens, not counting others found in its immediate vicinity. Here we are at the foot of the Santa Lucia [Mountains].

---

16. «About» not in Bancroft printing.
17. So Madrid (mas grandes); Bancroft «some large» (unos grandes).

It is to be remarked that the villages here are less populous and they do not live in regular houses as on the Channel, yet they seem more tractable.

5th. Went four hours, the whole way over hills, stopping at a stream with a great deal of water and grass, surrounded by extremely high hills. Lay by on the 6th.

7th. Went five hours, partway over hills and the remainder through a hollow, in which we saw fourteen to sixteen bears in a group and shot a few of them. Stopped at a stream with a good deal of water and grass.

8th. Travelled two hours, stopping at a hollow close to the shore with a great deal of grass and water, where there was a village of about sixty people.

9th. Went four hours along the shore, and stopped at an inlet where a stream came down from the hills, having come across six other running streams in this day's march.

10th. Went [two hours] through a hollow and have stopped at a stream well lined with trees and all surrounded by pine woods.

11. Went three hours: hills the whole way. A vast deal of grass and water.

12th. Went three hours and a half, stopping at a running stream where we were visited by a village of about thirty heathens.

13th. Went three hours over hills and stopped at the foot of a very high mountain range, remaining here two days in order to scout out a way into it, with no other way in further on. We supposed it to be the Santa Lucia Mountains. Lay by for two days.

16th. Went two hours into the mountains, keeping constantly along a stream formed by mountains on either side it having been necessary to send soldiers and Indians ahead to prepare the crossings, which took a great deal of toil. We stopped upon a small height at the place where we could get no farther up the creek, and had to delay here in order to open a trail over an extremely high mountain.

September 17th. Got past part of the mountains, the trail having been opened, and at two hours' march stopped in order

to open another trail over another and loftier range. There was
a village here consisting of 80 extremely tractable heathens.
There is a great deal of water and grass all throughout these
mountains. Lay by here on the 18th and 19th in order to break
another trail.

20th. Marched for four hours through mountains, extremely
lofty ones as I have said, over a trail which had to be opened
the whole way, the hardest toil having been in clearing away
so much rough brushwood. The History of Cabrera [Bueno]
was right to set down the Santa Lucia Mountains as being so
high, steep and big; none greater, it was supposed, might be
found, both because of its length, which must be twenty leagues,
and its width, sixteen. Stopped at a ravine with not much water
and grass; about 400 heathens visited us here.

21st. Went two hours. Had to alter our course, the mountains being impassable, and had to open a trail; stopped at a
stream. Lay by here on the 22nd, and spent the 23rd in scouting ahead.

24th. Travelled two hours northeastward going downward
in order to escape the difficult break lands along the skirts of the
impenetrable mountain range. Stopped at a stream with a good
deal of water and grass, where there was a village of about sixty
heathens.

25th. Went an hour and a half, always alongside the same
range, stopping where there was neither water nor grass.

26th. Went four hours alongside the same mountains, and
stopped at a river where we were visited by a village of 220
heathens, not counting another one, met along the way, of two
hundred.

27th. Went five hours, always along the same river.

28th. Went five hours along the same river.

29th. Went [four] [18] hours along the same river; here there
was a village but they ran away.

30th. Went five hours along the same river, which we were
supposing might prove to be the Carmelo.

---

18. Madrid «five»; Bancroft repeats «4» in its margin.

Diario del Viage que haze por tierra D.n Cas-
par de Serrolá Capitan de Dragones del Regim.to
de España Governador de Californias à los Puertos de San Diego y Monterre y situados en 33 y 37
grados haviendo sido nombrado Comandante en Gefe de esta expedicion por el Ill.mo Señor D.n Joseph de
Galbez, n virtud de las facultades Vice-Regias que le
ha concedido su Excel.a Dicha expedicion se componia
de 51 Soldados de Cuera con su Capitan D.n
Fernando de Rivera deviendo este adelan-
-tarse con Veinte y siete Soldados, y el
Governador con diez, y un
Sargento

Sali del Real de Sant.a Maria ... Mars ... a las ... miñia
de los ... ... ... ... ... el Luss
... por ... de los Alamos y el ... ...
A ... ... su se hananos como quatro ...
... agua para las ... nada de ... por ...
... á marchas por la ... para luego lo ... ...
... En ... ... por buen camino ... horas
... ... ... que llaman la Sauda ... ...
... ...

First page of Portolá's diary of his expedition to Monterey.
(University of California. Bancroft Lib.).

October 1st. Went one hour, to a spot close to the mouth of the said river. Here the Expedition made a halt for five days, in order to explore the détour which had been caused by these mountains: we had all been agreed that we would surely find Monterrey Harbor.

7th. Went two hours and a half by swamps and lakes. Here a meeting was held, requested by the [Expedition's] commander; I enclose the record.

8th. Went four hours, constantly escaping from swamps and lakes. Here, so the scouts said, a heathen village had been found, but when the whole camp arrived they had run away. On the 9th, lay by.

10th. Travelled about an hour and a half; the sick men having become very ill and requiring to be given the Sacraments, we stopped here for four days.

15th. Went an hour and a half, because of the sick men, stopping at a lake with a great deal of water and grass.

16th. Went two hours and stopped at the edge of a river, with very little grass.

17th. Travelled two hours and a half, partway through a hollow between ranges,[19] and the rest by a good road, coming across a great many watering-places and two rivers; stopped close to one of the rivers, next to the sea, where the scouts said small craft might come to land with shelter from the north.

18th. Went four hours alongside the sea; several water-courses were crossed on this march. Stopped at the edge of a stream that made an inlet on the sea and delayed us by its size, the way around farther up being a ravine with a great deal of woods. At this place there was a cove sheltered from the north for small craft.

19th. Travelled four and a half hours close to the sea; work was needed upon several ravines caused by the rains. Stopped at a little river emptying into the sea; there was a village here which we found abandoned on our arrival.

20th. Travelled three and a half hours close to the sea-shore, stopping at a stream with a great deal of water and grass. Lay by here for two days, as it had been raining.

---

19. There are hills only on one side of the route; this must be an error.

23rd.   Travelled two hours and a half, stopping at a stream with a great deal of water and grass, where there was a village of two hundred heathens.

24th.   Travelled seven hours, a bad road; stopped at a stream with a good deal of water where there was a village of eighty heathens.   Stopped here for two days.

27th.   Travelled two hours and a half, a bad road, stopping at a stream with plenty of water and grass.

28th.   Travelled two hours close to the sea, stopping at a stream with a good deal of water and grass.   Lay by here for a day because of rain.

30th.   Travelled two hours and a half, where some streams had to be worked upon, and two bridges made.   Stopped upon the seashore, with a good deal of water but no wood.

31st.   Travelled two hours of very poor road uphill over a very high mountain, stopping on the height.[20]   Here twenty five heathens visited us; and the Sergeant and eight soldiers were despatched to explore, inasmuch as some *farallones*, a point of land, and a bight had been seen and according to the History of Cabrera we were close to San Francisco Harbor.   We stayed four days here.

November 4th.   Travelled [three] [21] hours, a poor road all the way; stopped with no water.

5th.   Travelled four hours, a poor road, and the remainder through a level hollow where a large sea-arm sixteen to twenty leagues long runs; the scouts say it makes a sheltered harbor with two islands in the midst.   Stopped with no water.

6th.   Travelled skirting this sea-arm or harbor and stopped at a plain grown over with a great many live-oaks, with many inlets and lakes, and surrounded with many villages, where we were met by a hundred and twenty heathens.   Here we had a great deal of water and grass.   [3 hours.]

7th.   [Captain] [22] Don Fernando de Rivera ordered the Sergeant and eight soldiers out to explore, keeping along the same

---

20.  Some error is involved here, as the other journals show camp was in a valley north of the mountain; perhaps this phrase originally referred to stopping to survey the country from the summit.
21.  Madrid «four»; Bancroft repeats «3» in its margin.
22.  Madrid «Commandant» (wrongly).

sea-arm or harbor. Four days later, having returned, they said they had found nothing, and were doubtful whether anything might be found further on. Wherefore, being now at such an extreme of latitude, with none of Cabrera's marks for Monterrey Harbor, I called a halt; and upon our meeting in council, the decision was for the Expedition to turn back, and to look for the harbor at greater length; which was carried out, and I enclose the record of the meeting.

On November 11th the Expedition turned back, returning partly by way of the same stages, but looking to find other routes which might prove shorter. This day went five hours by the same road.

12th. Went five hours by the same road; same stage.

13th. Went two and a half hours by the same road.

14th. Went two hours and a half by the same road, same stage.

15th. Went three hours by the same road, same stage.

16th. Went three hours and a half, making a stage and a half.

17th. Went a stage and half in four hours by the same road.

18th. Went a stage and a half in what must have been four hours by the same road.

19th. Same stage and road as before, it must have been three hours.

20th. Went four hours and a half, making two stages, by the same road.

21st. Went two stages, which must have been three hours and a half.

22nd. Went a stage and a half, which must have been 3-½ hours. Lay by on the 23rd.

24th. Went two stages, four hours, by the same road.

25th. Went to the Point of Pines, four hours.

26th. Went two hours and a half, to the foot of the Santa Lucia Mountains, and camped as had been decided at the meeting. From here Captain Don Fernando de Rivera set out to explore these mountains once more, goig as deep into them as he could; and he reported back that he had not found Monterrey Harbor. On the return from the vicinity of San Francisco Harbor, we made in 18 days the distance which took forty three days on the way up because of the number of sick men.

December 10th, 1769.   The Expedition's return to San Diego having been decided upon, as will appear by the record of the third council which I enclose, we travelled for what must have been two hours and a half along the same path and making the same stage as upon coming here, stopped at a lake close to the Point of Pines and a bight where it appears that Monterrey Harbor may once have been.

11th.   Travelled the same day's march, by the same road, for what must have been six hours.

12th.   Travelled five hours by the same road, stopping at the same spot, where there was a village of forty heathens.

13th.   Travelled six hours by the same road, same stage.

14th.   Travelled five hours, same road and stage.

15th.   Travelled five hours, same spot and stage as before. Here a village of about fifty people showed themselves.

16th.   Travelled five and a half hours by the same road and stage.

17th.   Went two of the same stages we had made on the way up, four and a half hours.

18th.   Went two hours and a half, same stage and road, going up into the mountains.

19th.   Went three hours, crossing the steepest part of the mountains, where there was a good deal of snow; made the same stage as before.   Lay dy here for a day.

21st.   Made two stages of the marches we had made before, and got out of these mountains.   Here one of the two muleteers who had left us at the Point of Pines presented himself, reporting that he had left the other one back in the mountains with three of our Indians who had been with him, and further stating that these were the steepest mountains he had ever seen in his life, he had got past them along the edge of the sea only by a vast deal of toil, and that not only were there no signs of a harbor anywhere along the shore, but not even any coves; all of which did away with our last doubt [which no-one had any more] that the harbor might still lie there somewhere. Went five hours today, and lay by on the 22nd.

23rd. Went a stage and a half of the marches made upon the way up, four and a half hours it must have been. Here a village of fifty heathens appeared, and we had seen another with forty of them on the same march.

24th. Went five hours, making a stage and a half of our previous marches. Here a village of sixty people which we had not seen upon the way up appeared.

25th. Went four hours and a half by the same road; here saw 30 heathens not seen upon the way up.

26th. Travelled six hours, making two of the marches upon the way up. Here sixty heathens not seen earlier appeared.

27th. Went four hours, same stage as before; stopped at a hollow named Cañada de los Osos [23] for the great many bears there. Had a rain here, and therefore lay by on the 28th.

29th. Travelled three hours by a different course than we had taken upon the way up, stopping at the flat we named Plan de los Berros.[24] Here there appeared a heathen man, very serviceable to us, who is much feared among all of these tribes; he made us a present of a fabric interwoven with handsome featherwork, like plush in a way, as well as a great deal of seeds.

30th. Travelled four hours, the same stage and road as before.

31st. Went five hours, the same stage and road.

January 1st, 1770. Went four hours, by the same road and stage.

2nd. Went four hours by the same road and stage.

3rd. Went four hours, same road and stage.

4th. Went six hours, making two of the same stages we had marched before.

23. Misspelled *Ojos*, *oxos* in the two copies (similarly *ojos* under Sept. 7 in Bancroft).
24. «Watercress Flat.»

5th. Went four hours along the edge of the sea, now the Santa Barbara Channel; same road and stage.

6th. Went about four hours, same road and stage. Had fish in camp tonight.

7th. Travelled about four hours, same stage and road; here got some provision of fish and seeds.

8th. Went about four hours, same road and stage; again found a little fish.

9th. Went about three hours and a half, same road and stage.

10th. Went a little more than three marches of the stages done before, about six hours' travel. Stopped at the town of [la] Carpinteria, where we had been hoping for a good supply of fish, but there was almost none.

11th. Went about six hours, a bit more than two of our earlier marches, stopping at the last town, where we take leave of the Channel. All the while going along this Channel we have experienced very mild weather, almost hot; this in January, and with a very clear sky, which we did not have on the way up in the month of August, when there was nothing but fog and wind.

12th. Travelled over seven hours, taking a different course from the one taken before, across a mountain range that makes a point upon the sea close to where we left the Channel. After goig over a most handsome plain belonging to the river we had previously gone along, we stopped at a village that must have comprised forty heathens.

13th. Travelled about five hours, still following the cut-off toward the Valle del Encino; not a very good road here; stopped at a village of about 50 heathens.

14th. Went about five hours by a different way, and stopped at a village where there must have been about thirty heathens.

15th. Went about seven hours, a poor road, and hit upon the wished-for Encino plain.

16th. Went four hours, taking another route than the one we had followed earlier, and stopping at a small-sized watering place; along the way met a village of about sixty people.

17th.   Went about five hours, makin good two of our earlier marches, came out upon the Llano de la Puente opposite the big snow-covered mountains and crossed the river named la Porciuncula.[25]

18th.   Went about six hours by a different course, since it was a shorter one making good three stages.

19th.   Went five hours, two stages of the march on the way up.   Had a great deal of rain today.

20th.   Went five hours, making good two stages; same road.

21st.   Went about five hours by the same road, as was necessary since water was scarcer than on the way up.

22nd.   Made five hours, 2-½ stages of the earlier march.

23rd.   Went about six hours, three of our former marches.

24th.   Went about five hours, two stages of our earlier march.   Today reached San Diego.   Thank God, not a man has perished in all of the toil, trouble and want we have been through; for we have been depending solely, during our return, upon God's great providence, without any recourse in the human sphere save that of slaying mules for food in our utmost extremity

We found San Diego with exactly the same garrison of eight buff-coat soldiers who had been left there; the three Fathers were there; but eight of the fourteen Volunteers who remained beind had died.   The *San Carlos* was still anchored in the same spot we had left her, neither the *San José* nor the *Príncipe* having yet appeared in all this time: it must be eight months since the first was to have set sail from Guaymas, and the second had been away from this Harbor for seven months.   For this reason and because of the lack of supplies, a meeting was held, and it was decided, in order to hold this Harbor longer, that the Captain of the Presidio Don Fernando de Rivera should set out with a strong party, for the pupose of returning to Californias and of driving back the livestock that has been designed for the mission here; while the rest of the Expedition is to hold this Harbor, with the important hope and comfort that God may let us sight a ship.[26]

---

25. Misspelled *Porcincula, Porcinucula* in the copies as printed (as upon the copy of a map by Miguel Costansó).

26. So in Madrid as printed. The Bancroft printing reads, perhaps more plausibly, «to hold this most important Harbor, while awaiting the comfort that God,» etc.

# APPENDIX B

Portolá's Expedition Letters: from San Diego, July 4th, 1769, and April 17th, 1770; from Monterey, June 15th, 1770.*

* The important letter of February 11th, 1770, on the northern exploration is translated above in the text. All of the material is found in Mexico, Archivo General de la Nación, ramo Californias, t. 76, fols. 63 to 73 (consulted by Bancroft Library microfilm). The June 15, 1770, letter is entirely in Portolá's hand, as are the complimentary closes of the others. There is a copy of the April 17, 1770 letter in the Houghton Library, Jared Sparks Ms. 98, Papeles varios de América, portfolio 3, no. 7, encl. 2. Beneath inch-high headlines, translations of these letters by the late H. E. Bolton were printed in the San Francisco *Call*, October 17, 1909; that of April 17, 1770, has also been translated by Maynard Geiger, O. F. M., *Southern California Quarterly* XLVII (1965), 398-400, in an article also containing translations of the official act of possession and a letter from Portolá to Gálvez from San Blas, August 1, 1770, similar in contents to the last letter given here. There is a third similar letter of Portolá to the Viceroy, from Guadalajara, August 28, 1770, shorter than either of the other two, which was also translated by Bolton.

Most Excellent Sir

Sir: I set out on May 21st from the place called San Juan de Dios, twenty-four leagues away from Mission Santa María, the last mission in the north of the peninsula, with ten soldiers belonging to my Presidio and one hundred seventy mules, with a sufficient lading of provisions for my journey.    I pursued my march along the same track and by the same stages as Captain Don Fernando Rivera, who had gone ahead of me, and after thirty-nine days I arrived happily at the Harbor of San Diego here, on July 28th.

At this camp I encountered my men from the first section just as full of strength and health as the ones I had brought with me; I found the sea expedition, however, as good as immobilized and in so unhappy and deplorable a state as moved my deepest pity: all of them without exception, soldiers, sailors and officers, are tainted with the scurvy, some of them brought low completely, others half crippled, others upon their feet but strengthless; and this terrible malady has now taken off thirty-one men.

They had decided to send the packet *el Príncipe* to San Blas with this gloomy news, with despatches for Your Excellency and for the Most Honorable Visitor-General, a resolution which I have approved, in view of how important it is; and considering also that all of the seamen aboard that packet are willing to go to San Blas, hoping for their cure, and I regard them as rendered incapable and useless for continuing on to Monterrey.

On the same day of my arrival, I proposed going on to Monterrey to the Commander by Sea, Don Vicente Vila, offering him for the purpose every means to hand, including all of sixteen men from among my soldiers, mule-drivers and Indian allies.

My offert to Vila was no more than what he had been wishing for; but since he had been stripped of seamen, his answer was that if only half of the sixteen men I was offering had been sailors, he would have accepted the proposal and have done everything on his part to continue his voyage to the goal of all of us.

Having, however, no sailors in my company, I could not fulfill his request; and in view of his reply, I have come to a decision which seems to me the most conducive to the wished for purpose (with Your Excellency's approval), and that is, to continue my journey by land, taking Lieutenant of Volunteers Don Pedro Fages with me, with eight of his troops, and Engineer Don Miguel Costansó, all of whom the surgeon says will recover their strength and health in the course of the march by a change of climate.

I am leaving Surgeon Don Pedro Prat here with the sick men, in the shelter and protection of the new mission to be founded in accord with the Reverend Father President here at this harbor; I have ordered a guard of eight men belonging to my Presidio for the purpose.

Also, I shall take all the amount I can of provisions, letting God's Provindence care for our relief by sea, with the arrival of the packet San Joseph, and Commander by Sea Don Vicente Vila care for sending her on to Monterrey once she reaches this harbor.

I am well aware, Most Excellent Sir, that it is a rather bold decision, but I can see that need brooks no delay: the present season is the only one of the year for travelling in these lands, and even during it one suffers chilly and uncomfortable nights from the climate. Were I to delay my march until the coming of the San Joseph and the ship were to be slow, I would invite having the cold, snow, rains and bad roads close off our way; and further, having my men fall ill, a worse plight than being reduced to half rations at Monterrey should that prove to be necessary. However, I count upon finding a sufficiency in that country (for which I have the comfort that the old accounts call it a good and a fertile one), what with the sea and with our own measures, to allow of our sustaining ourselves there.

In fine, I am both ready and eager, wishing to contribute toward an undertaking with so praiseworthy a purpose as this is; and to make me sacrifice myself in it, it will be enough for me to know that Your Excellency and the Visitor-General have such a true interest in its outcome.  Just as truly, I pray Heaven to guide the important life of Your Excellency many years.

Harbor of San Diego, July the 4th, 1769.

Most Excellent Sir,


Your most grateful servant and subject,
Kissing Your Excellency's Hand,
Gaspar de Portolá
[rubric]

His Excellency the Marquis de Croix

Most Excellent Sir

Sir: I am leaving this as written at the San Diego Camp here, in order to be mailed whenever a chance presents itself, and I am heartily sorry that I am unable to despatch a post so as not to delay informing you of the news that the packet named *el Príncipe* is at this harbor. His reason for it, I am told by her Captain, Don Juan Pérez, who has handed me Your Excellency's favor of August 18th last past, is his having lost an anchor while taking on water at 35 degrees latitude and having learned at the same time from the heathens of the land expeditions's return here to San Diego harbor; not to omit to mention that she was sighted in the vicinity of this harbor on St. Joseph's Day (the patron saint of our expedition), entering the harbor two days afterward, and I firmly believe the saint had a hand in her not completing her voyage to Monterrey harbor, in order that the Expedition might the sooner achieve its purposes, which I so earnestly desire.

At the same time, Sir, while the Expedition has had the great comfort of seeing this ship bringing an extreme plenty of provisions and no less seamen with fortunately no sickness among them, I have been greatly regretting not having sufficient troops to undertake a return journey to Monterrey with. But it being borne in upon me that should I lose so precious an occasion the undertaking could scarcely be achieved otherwise, and that not a moment was to be wasted, confident that the work is of God and that He must support me, I have taken the decision to march out at the same time the *Príncipe* sets sail, with only seven buff-coat soldiers, all that I can take away from the garrison here, while adding to their number the twelve Volunteers who are left, with their Lieutenant, Don Pedro Fages, or whoever I can. I am encouraged in this decision by the profit I have gained in having explored the country and the intentions of the heathens, and am convinced that should I fail to do so I should be wanting toward God, toward the King, toward my own honor, and toward the gratitude I owe in having earned Your Excellency's confidence. To make plain the manner in which we have agreed with Captain Don Juan Pérez for both expeditions to set out, it is as follows:

First, he is to follow out the instructions given him by the Most Honorable [José de Gálvez] as to the latitude he is to reach, and is to survey the harbor of San Francisco in passing; having taken soundings there, he is to drop a little lower down the coast, where he will find a sizeable inlet shooting twelve or sixteen leagues inland, which we all thought might be a good harbor and at the same time a very suitable spot for a mission; Don Miguel Costansó, who is to go on the ship, knows it well. Once this is surveyed, she is to search for Monterrey harbor, which I have hopes that the seamen will be able to find though the land expedition could not encounter it; or failing that, the Point of Pines, which place has been chosen for her to await us at if she comes there before the land expedition, and if the land expedition arrives before her, she will do the same; should the weather be such as to prevent her from remaining there, signals of her having been there and of what she intends to do are to be left set up for us. Don Miguel Costansó is well informed of all of this. Should Monterrey harbor exist in the place mentioned by the *History*, both expeditions will then have the good fortune of having achieved their destination; however, should it not exist, or should it be at the harbor of San Francisco, or at the other spot mentioned above, then the mission and presidio will be established there, for I think that Your Excellency will not mind its being done in this way, since the further northward we reach the greater the domains will be which the King possesses, with better lands and many more heathen folk; I shall in all cases, however, always give preference to Monterrey Harbor, in order not to depart an inch from blind strict obedience to my orders.

I only regret, Sir, that distance and circumstances do not allow me to report events to Your Excellency in order to receive Your Excellency's orders, which doubtless would be the surest means; but recognizing that Your Excellency intends for this great work to succeed, I shall stop at no hindrance, obstacle or risk.   Since I first set out from Californias, my resolve has been either to die or to fulfill my mission.

At the Father President's request, the mission here has been moved, with a guard of nine men including the sergeant, and not counting three or four other persons, well fortified in a very advantageous spot, so that I have no fears of not leaving it in safety, though I intend that when the troops who are to drive livestock here shall return from California, the guard here shall be reinforced, and the one at Monterrey, and at the same time if not sooner the mission of San Buenaventura founded: I shall do all that I can to finish this work, to keep up the number of the guard for that mission, and to bring up the livestock for both new missions.

As this is written, it being now the 16th, the *Príncipe* is getting under way, and I shall do likewise tomorrow; which is all that I have worth informing Your Excellency of.

I desire God our Lord to keep Your Excellency's person the many years that He may and I wish for.   Mission and Camp of San Diego, April 17th, 1770.

Your most humble subject and affectionate servant, Most Excellent Sir

Sir:

Kissing the hand of Your Excellency, GASPAR DE PORTOLÁ [rubric]

Picture of the Mercadal Square of Balaguer before the Portolá's house was demolished. The house is the second from the left.

Most Excellent Sir

Sir: On the eve of my departure from San Diego on April 17th last past, I despatched two Indians as couriers with a post notifying Your Excellency of the *Príncipe's* having arrived two days after St. Joseph's Day, and that she was getting under way upon the 17th of May [*sic*] last past and I was about to perform the same with only seven buff-coat soldiers and the party of Volunteers, by land. Today, the 15th of June now, I have the great satisfaction of despatching a post to give Your Excellency the gratifying news of both expeditions being now at their Monterrey destination, Cabrera Bueno not having been mistaken in one tittle of the marks mentioned in his History, as will appear by the record of the act of possession which I enclose for Your Excellency. My journey, thanks to God, was attended with all good fortune, without one man ill, and it seems the holy patron of this expedition must have smiled upon it, for I reached the place where I now am in thirty-seven days, and the sea expedition in forty-five, and also with almost none sick. At the moment, work is going forward with great haste to put up roomy cabins, a church, and whatever else is needed, and the *Príncipe* is to sail immediately for San Blas; I shall go upon her, landing upon the way at San Diego, to have the Captain [Rivera], in case he should be there with the livestock he was to drive up from California, continue onward to Monterrey, and if he has not arrived, I shall leave him an order to do so upon his arrival, or if not he then the sergeant on duty at San Diego, unless I receive superior orders which take account of my second journey; and I shall pursue my way by ship to San Blas and landing there thence onward to Mexico, having as I do Your Excellency's permission (or so the Most Honorable Visitor Don Joseph de Galbes has written me) to report in detail to Your Excellency of what I thought most fit to do and my slight talents could attain.   We found the heathens tractable in my first journey; they were the same this time and even more pleasant, with no fear of us, freely bestowing whatever their misfortune allowed.   Here where we are now the villages are coming in with deer-meat and seeds, and I am finding these heathens much better than those on the Channel.   May God touch their hearts, to achieve the purpose for which this expedition was made, as I am sure He will.

I desire God our Lord to keep Your Excellency's person many happy years.   San Carlos de Monterrey, June 15th, 1770.

Your most humble servant and subject,<br>
Most Excellent Sir,<br>
Kissing Your Excellency's Hand,<br>
GASPAR DE PORTOLÁ<br>
[rubric]

The Most Excellent Marquis de Croix.

# Contents